Fear

Also from Fearless Critic

The Wine Trials: 100 wines under $15 that beat $50
to $150 bottles in brown-bag blind tastings
by Robin Goldstein

Fearless Critic Austin Restaurant Guide, 2nd Edition

Fearless Critic Houston Restaurant Guide

Fearless Critic Washington DC Restaurant Guide

Fearless Critic

New Haven
Restaurant
Guide 3rd
Edition

Third edition, 2009/2010

Printed in the United States of America

10 9 8 7 6 5 4 3 2 1

ISBN 978-09740143-7-1

For Isabelle Sylvia Lazarus Levin
and Cian Bergan Miller

Fearless Critics

Robin Goldstein, Editor-in-Chief
Alexis Herschkowitsch, Associate Publisher
Erin McReynolds, Managing Editor
Kent Wang, Chief Technology Officer
Justin Yu, Executive Chef
Nat Davis, Wine Director

Clare Murumba, Fearless Critic
Laura Tatum, Fearless Critic
Nicholas Day, Fearless Critic
Jake Conway, Fearless Critic
Austin Shiner, Fearless Critic
Coco Krumme, Fearless Critic
Carolyn Kriss, Fearless Critic

Contributing editors

Andrea Armeni, Mytili Bala, Paul Beaton, Brookes Brown, Stephanie
Cha, Amos Friedland, Daniel Frommer, Barry Goldstein, Jessica Gordon,
Reiko Hillyer, Christine Kim, Sarah Kozlowski, Benjamin Lima, Daniel
Linik, Brad Lipton, Daniel Luskin, David Menschel, Laurie Santos, Lea
Shaver, Susan Stubbs, Hal Stubbs, Lu Stubbs, Kate Unterman

Special thanks

Daisy Abreu, Michael Agger, Ali Ahsan, Bruce Alexander, Sonia
Baghdady, Andrew Bonia, Richard Carlson, Colleen Carroll, Ed Cavazos,
Kathleen Cei, Charlie Collins, Anne Coyle, Jonathan Cooper, Bruce
DelMonico, Jan Deutsch, Nancy Erickson, Julian Faulkner, Henry
Fernandez, Andrew Gajkowski, Tom Gogola, Harvey Goldblatt, Rosie
Goldstein, Charu Gupta, Steve Hill, Jamie Kaiser, Jeff Kaplan, Greg
Khalil, Jaehee Ju, Jacob Katz, Sidney Kwiram, Chris LaConte, Barbara
Lamb, Shoshana Lash, Samantha Lazarus, John Leibovitz, Duncan Levin,
Josh Mamis, Jenny Mandel, Frank Marco, Rebecca Markovits, Michael
Morand, Mark Oppenheimer, Steven Pace, Justin Preftakes, Jedediah
Purdy, John Rogers, Cornelia Rogers, Benjamin Rosenblum, Jane
Rushmore, Maura Sichol-Sprague, Olaf Schneider, Shana Schneider,
Marci Saunders, Walter Schmamp, Nick Shalek, Rebecca Sherman, Ian
Solomon, Claire Stanford, Jane & Michael Stern, Giuliano Stiglitz, Frank
Tasty, Heather Tietgens, Cari Tuna, Walter Weintz, Annick Winokur,
Peter Workman, Christie Yang, the Yale Entrepreneurial Society, the
Yale Law School, the Yale School of Management, Tim Zagat

Contents

Fearless Critics

Robin Goldstein is founder of the Fearless Critic series and author of *The Wine Trials*. He has been food critic for the *New Haven Advocate* and written for 35 *Fodor's* travel guides, from Italy to Mexico to Hong Kong. Robin is a graduate of Harvard University and the Yale Law School. He has a certificate in cooking from the French Culinary Institute and a WSET advanced wine and spirits certificate.

Clare Murumba is a graduate of Harvard College and the Yale Law School. Clare has been food critic for the *New Haven Advocate*, and has a certificate in cooking from the French Culinary Institute. She grew up in Kampala, Uganda, and Melbourne, Australia.

Laura Tatum is the Architectural Records Archivist at the Yale University Library and creator of the blog "Mrs. Delicious." Her education has taken her from Tom's Diner (Columbia) to Blimpy Burger (Michigan) to grass-fed, hormone-free beef (Berkeley) and finally back to New Haven in time for several Dandy Double Doodles before Yankee Doodle shuttered. Laura lives in Guilford with her husband Andrew.

Nicholas Day is a graduate of the University of Chicago and has reviewed restaurants for the *New Haven Advocate*, *Chicago Reader*, and *Time Out Chicago*. He has worked in the wine industry and written on food and wine for *Slate* and *Saveur*. He lives in New Haven.

Alexis Herschkowitsch has written for *The Wine Trials,* five *Fearless Critic* guides, and five *Fodor's* travel guides, from El Salvador to Thailand. Alexis is a graduate of the University of Texas at Austin and has a WSET advanced wine and spirits certificate.

Erin McReynolds worked in the restaurant industry for 10 years. She has an M.F.A. in Creative Writing from Queens University and is a graduate of California State University, Fullerton.

Jake Conway is an amateur chef who lives in New Haven and believes in eating sustainably. He was runner-up at a college-level Iron Chef competition on the strength of his butternut squash gnocchi.

Austin Shiner fell in love with sea urchin and broiled monkfish liver at age four. As a professional chef, he has cooked at the restaurants Noble Rot and Hurley's in Portland, Oregon. His journalism seeks to link dining with social responsibility. Austin lives in New Haven.

Fearless Critics are not allowed to participate in the evaluations of any restaurants with which they are or ever have been associated.

Preface

300 places to eat in and around New Haven?

You'd better believe it. The Elm City's renaissance has hit full swing, and its world-class culinary engine—oiled by New Haven's remarkable ethnic diversity—is firing on all cylinders. Thankfully, the city has seemed relatively impermeable to the economic roller-coaster ride of the late noughties, and its restaurant scene remains supremely healthy.

In fact, we've added more than 75 new establishments to this new Third Edition—including all the big openings in town, plus a lot of lesser-known places in the city and suburbs that we missed the last time around.

By now, you've surely caught the news: *The Menu* (the title of past editions of this book) is now *Fearless Critic*. In terms of style and format, it's just a name change—we think our new name better reflects our brutally honest, independent perspective on food writing. What's quite different, though, is the length: with 300 reviews, this book is much more comprehensive than any before it.

Within these 384 pages, we're delighted to have the opportunity to talk about some truly groundbreaking restaurants, and none is more paradigm-shifting than Caseus, a humble cheese shop and informal restaurant on the corner of Orange and Trumbull—the old Haya's space—whose deceptively simple menu is powered by a regionally focused, market-driven kitchen that's capable of remarkable power and complexity. Caseus's haute-nostalgic menu is a tasting flight through the next generation of American food, right down to the obsession with offal and the carefully selected craft beers and wines. This is the most exciting restaurant to open in New Haven in a decade.

Right on its heels, though, is 116 Crown, opened by Bar alumni; the food is great here too, and again unpretentious (pizza margherita, burgers, truffle fries, cheese plates), but the real main event is a cocktail list that—hallelujah—is a real cocktail list. If Firehouse 12 in Ninth Square introduced the city to the notion of well-constructed, nostalgic cocktails, 116 Crown took it to a completely different place: artisanal, beautifully conceived drinks for which those nostalgic recipes as mere starting points.

The other node of new downtown-ish excitement is a pair of Indian restaurants, Thali (an upmarket showpiece in Ninth Square) and Thali Too (a more casual Southern Indian vegetarian restaurant off Broadway, in the old La Piazza space) that have, in many ways redefined the upper ends of both the ethnic and vegetarian dining scenes here. Heirloom (the New American restaurant at the suave new Study boutique hotel) and Prime 16 (a burger-and-beer joint par excellence) have been important arrivals in the upmarket and casual categories, respectively.

To some outsiders—people who still stereotype New Haven as a gritty postindustrial city—to hear us talking about New Haven restaurants this way might seem surprising. But that tired old image of New Haven no longer reflects reality. The Elm City has now cemented its status as a haven for young professionals, alternative artists, and people who are fed up with the high rents of New York—or just seeking a utopolis at the nerve center of New England.

At the same time, the city has also become a magnet for suburban residents looking for a night on the town. New Haven's renewed appeal—as a place to visit and as a place in which to live—both reflects and stimulates the further growth of its cultural offerings and the revitalization of its urban spaces. Downtown New Haven's vibrancy had created a vast new market space for cultural and culinary intermingling among the city's diverse populations, which is finally starting to be realized—but there is also much more to come.

Witness the restoration of Ninth Square, the old business district that largely had been deserted, and the dramatic refashioning of Broadway into the main Yale student shopping and eating district. Savor the lively International Festival of Arts and Ideas in June, and the eclectic artisans displaying their wares at a market along Chapel Street on autumn weekends.

Appreciate the transformation of the old Chapel Square Mall into a locus of commerce and residential space, or the conversion of an abandoned back alley behind the Taft into an urban arcade—an alley that now links College Street and the Shubert Theater to a whole new group of restaurants, bars, and shops along a once-deserted stretch of Temple Street, expanding even further the reach of downtown's economic boom.

Take in the grandeur of the apartments springing up on every corner of the Town Green and its surrounding blocks. And marvel at the proliferation of nightclubs along Crown Street, the new thoroughfare where twentysomethings throughout Connecticut flock to find love—at least for a night.

In short, aside from Boston, New Haven is now the most cosmopolitan and culturally vibrant city on the eastern seaboard north of New York City.

As you've probably noticed from our descriptions thus far of the city's new culinary guard, what constitutes "groundbreaking" has changed quite a bit since the first edition of The Menu came out in 2003. Back then, we wrote that New Haven's culinary cutting edge was represented by the "Nuevo Latino of Roomba; the haute Malaysian of Bentara; the Asian-inflected New American of Zinc; the gleaming postmodern microbrewery-pizzeria aesthetic of Bar; the Eritrean-Mediterranean fusion of Caffè Adulis."

Only one of these five restaurants still remains on New Haven's cutting edge, really, and it's the simplest: Bar, which is still wood-firing thin-crust pizzas about as good as any in the city. But that's an edge that's been cutting in town for more than 70 years, And two of these formerly cutting-edge five—Roomba and Caffè Adulis, both real downtown icons—have closed.

But, as is etched on the gate to the Grove Street Cemetery, the dead shall be raised: from Roomba's ashes has risen the sleek, sexy Bespoke and Sabor Latino, and from the ex-Adulis owner comes Gerónimo, an exuberant Southwestern/Mexican hotspot that has finally brought proper margaritas to the city of New Haven—and not a moment too soon.

A couple of proper obituaries are in order, though. First and foremost, we are deeply saddened over the shuttering of the great Yankee Doodle, the classic greasy spoon whose bacon, egg, and cheese sandwiches and addictive little burgers we were sure we would still be eating at our 50th reunions.

We're also distraught by the departure of Mory's. This historic not-so-private club that felt like an ancient tavern and served Welsh rarebits and giant cocktail cups to generations of Yale students, alumni, and, of course, Whiffenpoofs, was done in by investment losses and will be sorely missed. Perhaps Mory's, too, will rise again someday.

Saddest of all, perhaps, was the failure of both branches of Sandra's, the soul-food restaurant that brought together the city's most racially diverse restaurant crowd and served down-home Carolina BBQ, hush puppies, and delicious fried chicken that pleased the nine-year-olds and 90-year-olds equally. In the end, in spite of the admirable ambition of opening downtown, perhaps the ownership and management were spread too thin. It's a great loss for the city's cuisine and culture.

But there has never been a better time than this to eat in the area. We are especially happy to report that the two top tables in the book—Le Petit Café in Branford (#1 for the third edition in a row) and Ibiza in New Haven—have maintained consistency, explored new territory, and defended their positions against a very crowded field. The grande dame, Union League Café, has also remained impressively consistent even as it's getting on in restaurant years; and the top pizzeria, Frank Pepe's, has staged a comeback even as it expands to other cities.

The other thing that has remained so magical about this city is the way it has not just maintained but really *grown* its cadre of out-of-the-way ethnic finds that sell unbelievably authentic dishes at equally unbelievable prices. Every time we drive down Campbell Avenue in West Haven—currently the central nervous system of this culinary phenomenon—we seem to discover something totally new: an authentic Taiwanese hole-in-the-wall, two totally legit Turkish grilled-meat houses, Salvadoran lunch stops with pupusas patted out by hand in the back room. As ever, these additions to New Haven's culinary mix complement the older-school-ethnic Italian strips along Wooster Street and Grand Avenue in Fair Haven, whose odes to the cooking of immigrants from the area around Naples still thrive even as they serve as a testament to the settlement trends of an earlier era.

We'll leave you with some parting advice from Clare Murumba, co-author of this book's first two editions, who writes from her current home base of Uganda: "Please, eat well. Even if it takes some extra effort and planning. Living is too delicious to waste it on mediocre meals. If you suddenly find yourself hungry and the available options aren't stellar, just have a banana and hold out for real food, okay? Then, reach for this book and make a considered decision."

In other words, you should strive to make every single meal in your life great. Don't count calories, but do make every calorie count. It's a surprisingly simple piece of advice, yet imagine how different the world would look if we all followed it.

Luckily, it's easy to do so in New Haven. So enjoy the book, give us your feedback at **fearless@fearlesscritic.com,** and come visit us at **newhaven.fearlesscritic.com**. Bon appétit!

–Robin Goldstein, David Menschel, and Reiko Hillyer

The Fearless Critic system

If you're familiar with *The Menu*, the Fearless Critic style and philosophy won't come as a surprise. Otherwise, welcome to a new kind of restaurant guide. The Fearless Critics have written, edited, and fact-checked 300 full-page reviews of places to eat in the greater New Haven area, including Milford, Orange, West Haven, North Haven, Hamden, Branford, Guilford, Derby, and more.

The Fearless Critic's "brutally honest" philosophy can be summed up in one sentence: our duty is to the readers, not the restaurants. We do not accept advertising from dining establishments, chefs, or restaurateurs. We visit all restaurants incognito and pay for our own meals. We visit most establishments several times, and most of our reviews are informed by years of repeat visits by our Fearless Critic Council, a team of local food nerds who visit and evaluate each other's restaurants without identifying themselves.

In order to qualify for inclusion in this book, an establishment must serve food. Of course, we haven't included every single restaurant in the New Haven area. We've focused on the restaurants that we thought it most important to review, whether for positive or negative reasons. This meant omitting many restaurants, including many restaurants that, for people who live in the immediate neighborhood, might be relevant. We've visited many more restaurants than we wrote up, and we've chosen to include only the places that we thought would be most relevant for readers given our space constraints. As a general rule, in order to be included, a restaurant must be relevant: either good, famous, or centrally located, but not necessarily all of the above.

We're also sure, however, that we have also unwittingly omitted many true out-of-the-way gems, and for that we apologize in advance (and encourage you to let us know about them at **fearless@fearlesscritic.com**, so that they might be included in the next edition). But we hope that we'll also turn you on to a lot of little places with which you might not be familiar, and we hope we've done a generally good job covering many of the eateries worth knowing about in and around the city of New Haven. We have also included many restaurants in the suburbs that, by our judgment, are notable enough to be included.

If you're not already familiar with our philosophy, as you'll see once you start reading, the Fearless Critic style is relentlessly opinionated—something you might not be used to when you read a restaurant review. We're happy to wax poetic if we love a place, but as First Amendment fans, we're also not afraid to tell you if a place is overpriced, rude, or just plain bad. (That said, whenever possible, we try to be entertaining while doing it.) Our goal is to evaluate the restaurants—good or bad—so you don't have to; we hope to help you decide where to eat, and also where *not* to eat.

Our book is ultimately a reference guide, so we focus more on evaluation of food and feel than we do on chefs' names and pedigrees. We're more restaurant inspectors than restaurant promoters, and we aim for a punchy evaluation of a restaurant's strengths and weaknesses that ends with a clear judgment and recommendation.

Your hard-earned dollars matter a lot to us, and we hope that the money you've spent on this book will save you untold sums in the future by preventing you from wasting hundreds of dollars on potentially bad, boring meals. Therein, we believe, lies much of the usefulness of food criticism.

So, if you're a longtime *Menu* reader, welcome back. If you're a newbie, then we thank you for giving us a shot to help out with your dining decisions. We hope you'll be a convert.

The rating scale

After the Fearless Critics evaluate each establishment incognito, we all get together and assign two numerical ratings to each establishment.

Food rating (1 to 10): This is strictly a measure of whether the food on offer is appetizing or objectionable, insipid or delicious. We close our eyes to reputation, price, and puffery when we taste, so don't be surprised to find a greasy spoon outscoring a historic, upscale, sit-down establishment, for one simple reason: the food just tastes better. Markets, bakeries, sweets shops, and ice cream shops, since they're not primarily in the business of serving meals, are ineligible for this rating. Be forewarned that we use the whole 10-point scale, and this is the area where we're most severely critical, so if you're in the if-you-don't-have-something-nice-to-say-then-don't-say-anything school of thought, please take the ratings with a grain of salt. We hope that fanatical foodies will appreciate our rigor and honesty. A food score above 8 constitutes a recommendation; a 9 or above is a high recommendation.

Feel rating (1 to 10): Many guides rate the service and décor at a restaurant, but rather than counting the number of pieces of silverware on the table or the number of minutes and seconds before the food arrives, we ask ourselves a simple question: does being here make us happy? The most emphatic "yes" inspires the highest rating. We don't give out points for tablecloths or tuxedos. We reward warm lighting, comfortable accomodations, a finely realized theme, and a strong sense of place. If it's a place steeped in history, or just an eminently classic New Haven joint (think Louis' Lunch), we give bonus points for that, because it's certainly part of the "feel." The dim glow of candles, dark wood, and old New Haven paraphernalia at your local dive might just garner more accolades than the proliferation of accoutrements at a stuffy so-called "fine dining" restaurant.

Also figured into the "feel" rating is the question of whether you'll love or loathe the prospect of interacting with the people who stand between you and your meal. We don't expect the burger flipper at a greasy spoon to start spouting off elaborate wine adjectives, but if a restaurant's staff is unusually helpful and caring, or extraordinarily enthusiastic and knowledgeable about what's coming out of the kitchen, then the "feel" rating will reflect that. On the flip side, if the staff is consistently indifferent or condescending—or seems to have gone on strike—then points will be deducted from the experience rating of the restaurant, which happens as often at high-priced places as it does at corner take-out joints. Consider this a nonviolent revolution in the food-review world. Viva.

The math: There's no grade inflation here. For the city as a whole, the average food rating in the book is approximately 6.6, and the average feel rating is approximately 6.7. Let yourself get used to our system, and don't be scared off by a restaurant with a grade in the 6's. Only 53 (21%) of the 249 rated restaurants in the book (the other 51 were in unrated categories) scored an 8 or above, and only 14 (5.6%) scored a 9 or above. Only one restaurant in the book was awarded a food score above 9.5 or above: Le Petit Café, which received a 9.6.

Geography 101

Back in the day, New Haven was laid out neatly in nine squares. These days, things are a little more haphazard, although if you look carefully at a map of the city you can see the original shape of the nine-square layout; the Ninth Square neighborhood still pays homage to this nomenclature. To make things easier for everybody, we have established our own subdivisions of the city. They are sections based on compass orientations and well-known neighborhood names. For locals, some of these will be familiar. Others are somewhat arbitrary, but, we hope, inherently intuitive.

In *Fearless Critic*, we have provided exact street addresses for each establishment that we list. For specific directions, since we don't know where you're coming from, we advise that you consult Google Maps (linked from fearlesscritic.com entries), Mapquest, or one of the other Web-based mapping systems, all of which which tend to work quite well in the New Haven area. We have included a map of the most central neighborhoods in downtown New Haven, which is on pages 10–11, following these descriptions. Our New Haven neighborhood subdivisions are as follows (each is listed with its northern, southern, eastern, and western bounding streets in parentheses):

Chapel District (borders: Chapel St., George St., Church St., York St.): In downtown New Haven there are two major intersecting thoroughfares: Chapel Street, which runs roughly east-west, and Church Street, which runs roughly north-south. In this book, the part of town south of Chapel and west of Church is referred to as the Chapel District, also known as the "Chapel Historic District." (In previous editions of the book, this was called the Theater District, named for the landmark Shubert Theater and the old Palace Theater on College between Chapel and Crown.) Still the cultural and entertainment center of New Haven, this area also includes the Taft apartment complex; the Yale Art Gallery and Center for British Art; a raft of eating establishments, stores, and coffee shops, especially near the intersection of College and Crown; and the new proliferation of restaurants and bars on Temple. Some of the best-known restaurants and bars in town can be found here, and the entertainment venues on Crown Street are the center of New Haven's lively night scene.

Upper Chapel Area (borders: Edgewood St., North Frontage St., York St., Howe St.): This part of town was once beyond the purvey of the college area, but has lately become truly a part of the Yale-New Haven mix. The southern part of this area, toward George Street and Route 34, is more representative of the old neighborhood than the new. The eastern border of the Upper Chapel Area is York Street, which runs north-south through the middle of the downtown area. West of York, the center of this neighborhood is the completely revitalized Howe Street, which is home to a bevy of affordable restaurants, including almost all of the Thai and Indian restaurants in town. To the north, the Upper Chapel Area gives way to the Broadway area.

Broadway District (borders: Tower Pkwy., Edgewood St., York St., Dwight St.): In some cities, Broadway goes on for miles. In New Haven, if you blink you might miss it. This brief thoroughfare begins at the intersection of York and Elm, and ends where Whalley and Dixwell Avenues begin. For such a small tract of town, the Broadway District has more than its share of stores and places to eat, in part due to revitalization efforts led by Yale University over the past decade. As a result, many of the establishments in the Broadway area cater specifically to students, whether they're bustling cafés, cheap lunch joints, all-night pizza places, or dive bars. For this guide, the Broadway District extends north beyond Broadway proper to include York Street between Elm and Grove.

South Town Green (borders: Grove St., Chapel St., State St., College St.): Northeast of Ninth Square, and southeast of the Green, this is New Haven's downtown business, government, financial, and academic center. This is no concrete jungle; while a few blocks of civic buildings, courthouses and office complexes mark the center of administration for the city, the Yale College campus sits just to the west and north (the campus itself has few commercial eating establishments). The neighborhood is characterized by a lot of good, quick, cheap lunchtime delis. This neighborhood was known as the Financial District in previous editions of the book.

Audubon Arts District (borders: Trumbull St., Grove St., State St., Whitney Ave.): The Audubon Arts District (so named by the City of New Haven) centers around Audubon Street, but its nerve center is really along Whitney Ave., which is Church St.'s continuation north of Grove St. Along with Broadway and Ninth Square, this area represents one of the city's most proactive development efforts. We're thankful for their work; while the name of the neighborhood might still be a bit premature, Audubon is indeed host to the Neighborhood Music School and a few art galleries, and the area has a pleasant feel. The neighborhood has its northern end at Trumbull Street, where the East Rock area begins.

East Rock (borders: East Rock Park, Trumbull St., State St., Whitney Ave.): Immensely popular with young professionals, Yale grad students, and—these days—just about everyone else, this wonderfully laid-back part of town stretches north of Trumbull Street toward East Rock Park, where the bustle of downtown offices and shops gives way to wide streets, gracious multi-family houses, and expansive green lawns. Although the uninitiated may find this area to be a confusing maze of quiet, tree-lined streets that end abruptly or make unexpected turns, most of the relevant locations are on or just off the broad main streets like Orange and State. This subdivision also includes the area known as Science Hill.

Ninth Square (borders: Chapel St., George St., State St., Church St.): East of the Theater District and south of the Financial District is Ninth Square, the southeastern-most of the old nine squares of New Haven. Once a desolate part of town, Ninth Square is now a cultural mecca, including a prominent art gallery, a great live music space, and some of the city's hippest and most creative restaurants. Ninth Square ends at the railroad tracks just east of State Street; a couple of blocks away, on the other side of the tracks, is Wooster Square. For *Fearless Critic*, the northern border of this district is Chapel Street, although local parlance defines the area a little less precisely.

Wooster Square Area (borders: St. John St., Water St., Chestnut St., Olive St.): This is a quiet, residential quadrant due east beyond State Street and across the train tracks; it's characterized by gracious old brownstones and plenty of greenery. Historically an Italian neighborhood, this part of town—especially Wooster Street—is home to many of New Haven's favorite pizza places and Italian restaurants, even though a lot of the old residents, many of whom came over from the Naples area at the beginning of the 20th century as a result of a grand recruitment effort by the Winchester Rifle company, have long since moved to the suburbs. The City-designated Historic Wooster Square district begins at Olive Street and centers around Wooster Street, but continues down to Water Street.

Fair Haven (borders: Middletown Ave., Chapel St., Quinnipiac Ave., State St.): A lively part of New Haven more modest and old-school than the downtown neighborhoods, Fair Haven, which is reached by continuing on Grand Avenue east of the train tracks and under the I-91 overpass, is little known to many downtown residents, who will need a car to reach it. Fair Haven is home to many of New Haven's more recent immigrant communities, particularly the Hispanic community, and thus also home to some of the best and most authentic Mexican and Latin American food in town. The western edge of Fair Haven, north of Wooster Square, also has some old Italian-American immigrant culture. To the east, the neighborhood continues to the Quinnipiac River, which is home to a couple of picturesque riverbank restaurants.

Long Wharf (borders: Water St., Church St. South, I-95, Union Ave.): The arrival of IKEA has jolted this long-underdeveloped area down toward New Haven Harbor, an area south of Wooster Square that is also home to the Long Wharf Theater and the Connecticut Limo terminal. You'll need wheels to get there from downtown.

Medical Area/The Hill (borders: South Frontage Rd., New Haven Harbor, Church Street South, the Boulevard): While there still aren't many restaurants in this redeveloping area of New Haven, it's home to some good, local food. The district also extends south to Bayview Park by the New Haven Harbor, where you can dine with beautiful waterfront views.

Whalley (borders: Fitch St., Dwight St., Whalley Ave.): This no-man's-land section of Whalley Ave. between the Broadway Area and Westville is not really connected to any other specific 'hood, and it's home to a vibrant mix of inexpensive ethnic restaurants, from Jamaican to kosher to soul food, including some of New Haven's best-kept secrets. Don't let yourself be guilty of tunnel vision when shuttling between downtown and Westville.

Westville (borders: Woodbridge town line, Fitch St., Fountain St., West Rock Park): Home to Southern Connecticut State University and a cute little assortment of shops and restaurants along a particular stretch of Whalley Avenue that lies about 2 miles northwest of the Broadway area and downtown, this is one of New Haven's most atmospheric little neighborhoods, and it's up-and-coming as a food destination, too. Continuing along Whalley past the Wilbur Cross Parkway, you'll reach Amity Road and the town of Woodbridge, which we also cover.

Other cities: Other cities' neighborhood designations are simply the cities themselves, and are more straightforward. The book covers the following cities:

North: To the north, Hamden and North Haven can be reached either by taking I-91 North (exits 9-12), or by heading north from downtown New Haven on Whitney Avenue or State Street. To reach Derby, head west from downtown New Haven on Derby Avenue (Route 34).

East: To the east of New Haven along the shoreline, reachable on I-95 North, are East Haven (exits 50-52), Branford (exits 53-56), and Guilford (exits 57-59).

West: To the west of New Haven on I-95 South lie West Haven (exits 43-44), Orange (exits 41-42), and Milford (exits 39-40). West Haven and Orange are also easily accessible from downtown New Haven by following Congress Avenue southwest through the Hill neighborhood, where it runs into Route 1 and heads into West Haven and then Orange.

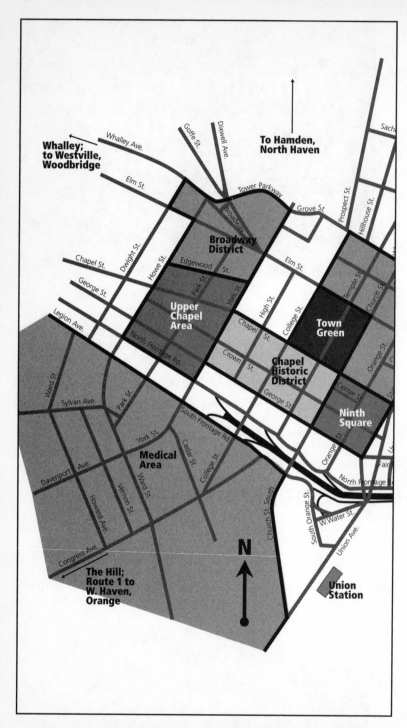

Central New Haven Neighborhoods: West

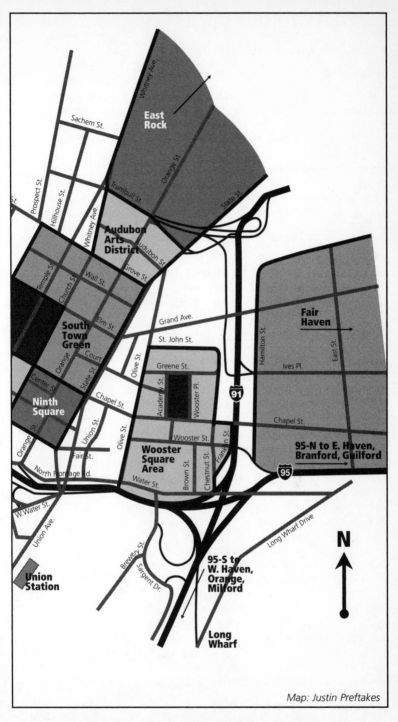

Central New Haven Neighborhoods: East

Map: Justin Preftakes

The other stuff on the page

Average dinner price: This dollar value is a guide to how much, on average, you should expect to spend per person on a full dinner at the restaurant, including one alcoholic beverage, tax, and a 20% tip (for table-service establishments; we encourage you to tip at coffeeshops and take-out joints too, but we don't figure it into the meal price). This is an imperfect science, but we go by what the average person tends to order at each place. At simple take-out places, this might be just a sandwich and a soda; at more elaborate sit-down restaurants, we usually figure in the cost of an appetizer (one for every person) and dessert (one for every two people). If the restaurant pushes bottled water or side dishes on you, we figure that in, too. For alcoholic drinks, too, we are guided by what people generally tend to order. At Archie Moore's, it's a beer. At Gerónimo, it's a margarita. At Union League, it's a third of a bottle of a low-to-mid-priced wine. Keep in mind that at the higher-end restaurants, you will generally spend considerably less than the quoted price if you go for lunch, or if you order non-alcoholic drinks instead. Only restaurants that serve meals are eligible for price estimates; this excludes dessert-and-coffee places, markets, and so on.

Genre: Every establishment in *The Fearless Critic* is associated with one or more culinary genres. Our "Lists" section includes a cross-referenced guide to all restaurants by genre. Most genres—e.g. Indian or pizza—are self-explanatory, but some require clarifiation: **American** covers traditional meat-and-potatoes fare, bar food, burgers, greasy spoons, and such, but **steakhouses** have their own category, as does **Southern** cuisine, which includes soul food, fried chicken, Cajun, and Louisiana Creole cooking. **New American** is fast becoming an over-broad catch-all, but we haven't come up with a better term to describe the upmarket American culinary category that draws upon diverse world ingredients and techniques. New American also encompasses the market-to-table and haute nostalgic restaurants that have become fashionable lately. The **Latin American** category includes Central American, South American, Dominican, and Puerto Rican, but not Mexican or Cuban, which have their own categories. **Caribbean** is focused on the islands of the West Indies (e.g. Jamaica, Trinidad). **Baked goods** can be sweet or savory. **Groceries** can include unprepared foods of any type.

Establishment type: We have divided eating establishments into several categories. The largest category is **casual restaurant,** which means a place with waiter service at tables but a generally laid-back atmosphere without much fuss. An **upmarket restaurant** is a place with more elegant, trendy, or special-occasion ambitions. The **counter service** category includes cafeterias, self-service places, and also establishments where you place an order at a counter but it is then brought out to your table. We see a **bar** as an establishment that's fundamentally about serving drinks at heart, but it must serve food to be included (although the kitchen often closes before the doors). **Café** means a place whose primary business is the provision of coffee or tea, but it must serve food of some sort to be included in the book. We've also included several notable **markets** in the New Haven area, most of (but not all of) which also serve certain varieties of prepared foods that can be eaten straightaway.

Address: We have included addresses and neighborhood designations for up to three locations, although, where feasible, we have indexed additional locations in the Lists section of the book. See pages 5–8 for the delineations of New Haven neighborhoods, and see pages 10–11 a map of most of the neighborhoods. For chains with more than three locations, you should consult our web site, **fearlesscritic.com**, for a listing of all New Haven-area locations.

Special features: These appear in the middle column of information. **Breakfast** and **brunch** generally mean that a restaurant has a special menu, or separate portion of the menu, geared toward those meals, not just that the place is open in the morning. By **date-friendly,** we mean establishments that we find particularly romantic in some way— and that doesn't necessarily mean tuxedoed waiters or high prices. We look for warm lighting, good vibes, and a sense of easy fun. **Delivery** can be limited to a certain geographical range or minimum order. **Good wines** needn't mean a long list, but it must be well chosen and well priced—you'd be surprised how rare that is. **Kid-friendly** doesn't just mean a couple of high chairs in the corner; it means a place where the little ones will actually be happy, whether for culinary reasons or for the availability of special activities or play areas. The **live music** designation includes establishments that have it only on certain days or nights, so call ahead if it's atmospherically important to you. **Outdoor dining** can mean anything from a couple of sidewalk tables to a sprawling beer garden. **Wi-Fi** has to be free to qualify—this is the 21st century, after all. We are particularly careful when choosing which establishments to flag as **veg-friendly.** The designation is not limited to vegetarian-only places, but we look for menus where vegetarians will not just be accommodated—they'll actually have an ample selection.

Brutally honest

As you might guess from the name of the book, *The Fearless Critic* is brutally honest. One of our Contributing Editors calls it "in-your-face" restaurant reviewing. One newspaper called it "scathing." Some people have suggested that our style is rude to restaurants. But we consider it rude for some restaurants to serve tasteless food at high prices, or to subject patrons to a disaffected attitude. And we're here to help you.

How is one to choose between two places if both are portrayed in dizzying, worshipful prose? And how frustrating is it to find out that at least one of them was a waste of your time and money? If you're celebrating a special occasion, as one often does by dining out, the sting of disappointment after a bad meal is that much more acute. What's *definitely* rude—and costly—is for an unsuspecting patron to dine on the strength of a sugar-coated review, only to discover the truth the hard way, with friends or date in tow. In short, our duty is to our readers, not to the restaurants.

Our goal is to save you the cost, disappointment, and possible discomfort of a bland, overpriced meal—and to point you preemptively in the direction of something better. Helping you choose, every time you eat out, is what makes this endeavor worthwhile for us. And so, within these pages, we tell you exactly what we'd tell a good friend if she called us up and asked what we *really* thought of a place.

This unapologetic approach may take a moment to get used to. But in the end, we believe opinionated commentary to be the highest possible compliment to the local dining scene. That is to say, the food here is definitely worth talking about.

We don't expect you to agree with everything we say—sometimes, we don't even agree with each other—but we do hope you can appreciate our conviction that, in food writing, opinion is better expressed openly than buried between the lines. We believe that, over the course of a book of 300 reviews, we will earn your trust. And whether you concur or dissent, we would love to hear from you; we'd like nothing better than to inspire more relentlessly opinionated diners in and around New Haven. Visit us at **fearlesscritic.com** to post your own opinions, or your thoughts on ours.

Fearless Critic quirks

Cooking times: as you might notice within these pages, we prefer most cuts of meat rare or medium-rare, and we prefer our fish and fowl moist and juicy rather than dry and more fully cooked. Specifically, our reviews often comment on whether or not establishments are willing to serve a dish as rare as requested. Although we understand that there are many people who like their meat more cooked than we do, our complaint isn't with restaurants that serve meat medium or medium-well by default; it's with restaurants that refuse to serve meat rare *even upon request*. Still, people who like their meat cooked medium or more should take our comments with a grain of salt.

Seasoning: speaking of a grain of salt, we complain from time to time about undersalted dishes. Our position is that there is no such thing as salting "to taste" in the professional kitchen. As a matter of chemistry, a certain amount of salt is necessary to bring out the complexity in most savory flavors: meats, fishes, soups, sauces, and so on. If you don't believe us, try this experiment, suggested by Italian food guru Marcella Hazan: pour two half-glasses of red wine, dump some salt into one of them, swirl them both around, and smell both glasses. The salt really brings out the bouquet (you won't want to drink it, though...).

Undersalting is one of the most common ways that an otherwise well-executed dish can fall completely flat. This problem can usually be corrected with the salt shaker (unless the food is deep-fried, in which case it's too late). But we think a dish should come to the table properly seasoned and ready to eat, not left in the final stages of preparation. (This is why we're so baffled by the peppermill service—

how are you supposed to know if a dish needs pepper before you've tasted it? And if it does, why didn't the chef already add the proper amount?) If you want your meal with less salt than normal, you can ask for it, and the restaurant should honor the request. Otherwise, forcing the customer to finish that process is as absurd as plopping a salad down in front of a customer with a whole carrot and a peeler.

Most top chefs around the world would agree that proper seasoning is a matter of necessity, not opinion. At a seminar given by famed chef Jacques Pépin, an audience member asked him whether or not the classic French recipe that he was preparing would "work" with less salt. Responded Pépin: "If you have dietary restrictions, then let me know, and I will underseason your food—at your own risk. But I'm your chef, not your doctor." Amen.

"Mains": you won't find the word "entrée" in *The Fearless Critic*. The word is inherently ambiguous, and particularly confusing to foreigners, as the French word "entrée" means "starter" or "appetizer." We're not sure how "entrée" came to mean a main course in the United States, but here we say "main course," or "main," if that's what we mean.

The *Fearless Critic* style guide: we don't italicize foreign words in this book, nor do we capitalize dish names unless they're invented by the restaurant. We're minimalists.

Fearless feedback

The heart and soul of this endeavor is our firm belief that the world of restaurant reviewing can only be improved by opening outspoken channels of communication between restaurants and their customers. We hope that the honest articulation of our opinions and dining experiences will encourage you to do the same—if you have a bad meal, or a great one, *tell the restaurant*. Tell them what was right and what was wrong. It can only help. And tell us; we've set up an interactive space at **fearlesscritic.com**, where readers can express agreement or dissent of any sort. The commentary found on the site is moderated only to keep out spammers, not to edit readers' opinions. It doesn't require registration, and you can even post anonymously. Please, read some reviews, go try some restaurants, and then log on and let us know what you think. Our critics will do their best to respond to posts from time to time. We look forward to hearing from you.

The fine print

This entire book is a work of opinion, and should be understood as such. Any and all judgments rendered upon restaurants within these pages, regardless of tense, are intended as statements of pure opinion. Facts have been thoroughly checked with the restaurants in person, via telephone, and on the restaurants' web sites; we have gone to the utmost lengths to ensure that every fact is correct, and that every ingredient in every dish is properly referenced. Any factual errors that nonetheless remain are purely unintentional. That said, menus and plates (not to mention hours of operation) change so frequently at restaurants that any printed book, however new, cannot help but be a bit behind the times. Check in at **fearlesscritic.com** for new reviews, updates, discussion boards, and more.

About Fearless Critic Media

Fearless Critic Media is a lean, fiercely independent publishing house founded by Robin Goldstein in 2006 and dedicated to providing useful information in an engaging format. In conjunction with its partner, Workman Publishing Company, Fearless Critic Media publishes relentlessly opinionated, irreverent food and wine books. Look for *The Wine Trials*, our blind-tasting guide to wine under $15, in bookstores and food and wine shops nationwide.

Other Fearless Critic books include the *Fearless Critic Washington DC Restaurant Guide*, the *Fearless Critic Austin Restaurant Guide, 2nd Edition*, and the *Fearless Critic Houston Restaurant Guide*, all of which can be bought at barnesandnoble.com, amazon.com, bookstores, and retail stores.

For all the latest book and distribution information, see **fearlesscritic.com**. Fearless Critic books are distributed by **Workman Publishing Company (workman.com)**.

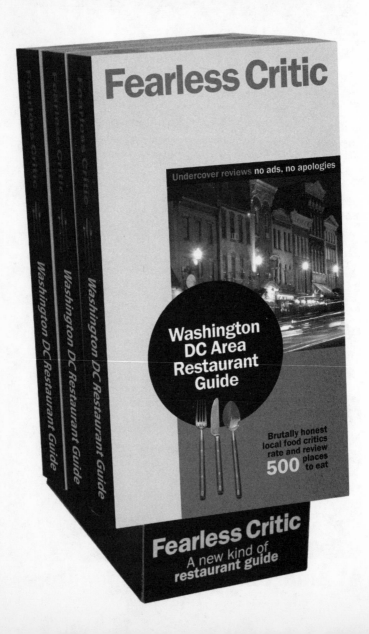

Fearless Critic

Lists

Most delicious

These are New Haven's **top 100 kitchens** judged from a **pure food** perspective. Ties are ordered by feel rating.

Rank		Food	Cuisine	Location	Type	Price
1	Le Petit Café	9.6	French	Branford	Upmarket	$65
2	Caseus	9.4	New American	East Rock	Casual	$40
3	Ibiza	9.3	Spanish	Chapel District	Upmarket	$80
4	Union League Café	9.1	French	Chapel District	Upmarket	$75
5	116 Crown	9.1	New American	Ninth Square	Upmarket	$35
6	Bar (Brü Room)	9.1	Pizza	Chapel District	Bar	$25
7	Frank Pepe's	9.1	Pizza	Multiple locations	Casual	$20
8	East Japanese Restaurant	9.1	Japanese	Milford	Upmarket	$45
9	Sally's Apizza	9.1	Pizza	Wooster Square	Casual	$20
10	Heirloom	9.0	New American	Upper Chapel Area	Upmarket	$85
11	Modern Apizza	9.0	Pizza	East Rock	Casual	$20
12	Swagat	9.0	Indian	West Haven	Casual	$15
13	Thali Too	9.0	Indian	Broadway District	Casual	$35
14	Szechuan Delight	9.0	Chinese	Hamden	Casual	$25
15	Barcelona	8.9	Spanish	Chapel District	Upmarket	$65
16	Saray	8.8	Turkish	West Haven	Casual	$30
17	Prime 16	8.7	American	Chapel District	Casual	$25
18	Turkish Kabab House	8.7	Turkish	West Haven	Casual	$30
19	China Great Wall	8.7	Chinese	Audubon District	Casual	$15
20	Mezcal	8.7	Mexican	East Rock	Casual	$25
21	Iron Chef	8.7	Taiwanese	West Haven	Counter	$15
22	Glen's Bar-B-Q	8.6	Caribbean	The Hill	Take-out	$10
23	Mother's	8.6	Caribbean	Medical Area	Take-out	$15
24	The Terrace	8.6	Thai	Hamden	Casual	$35
25	Rice Pot	8.6	Thai	East Rock	Casual	$30
26	Carmen Anthony	8.5	Steakhouse	Audubon District	Upmarket	$75
27	Sono Bana	8.5	Japanese	Hamden	Casual	$30
28	Gastronomique	8.5	French	Chapel District	Take-out	$25
29	Sabor Latino	8.5	Salvadoran	West Haven	Counter	$10
30	The Place	8.4	Seafood	Guilford	Casual	$25
31	Thali	8.4	Indian	Ninth Square	Upmarket	$50
32	Juna's Northern Style BBQ	8.4	Barbecue	North Haven	Take-out	$10
33	Zuppardi's	8.4	Pizza	West Haven	Casual	$25
34	Atticus	8.3	Sandwiches	Upper Chapel Area	Café	$10
35	The Beach House	8.3	Seafood	Milford	Upmarket	$60
36	Machu Picchu	8.3	Peruvian	Fair Haven	Casual	$25
37	Caribbean Connection	8.3	Caribbean	Whalley	Take-out	$10
38	La Cocinita	8.3	Mexican	Upper Chapel Area	Counter	$15
39	Lena's	8.2	Sandwiches	Westville	Casual	$15
40	L'Orcio	8.2	Italian	East Rock	Upmarket	$45
41	The Blue Cottage	8.2	Seafood	Branford	Casual	$30
42	Star of India	8.2	Indian	Orange	Casual	$10
43	Book Trader Café	8.1	Sandwiches	Upper Chapel Area	Counter	$10
44	Bella's Café	8.1	American	Westville	Casual	$25
45	Roseland Apizza	8.1	Pizza	Derby	Casual	$35
46	The Stone House	8.1	Seafood	Guilford	Upmarket	$50
47	Dayton Street Apizza	8.1	Pizza	Westville	Counter	$15
48	Guadalupe La Poblanita	8.1	Mexican	Fair Haven	Casual	$15
49	Lenny's Indian Head Inn	8.0	Seafood	Branford	Casual	$30
50	Louis' Lunch	8.0	Burgers	Chapel District	Counter	$10
51	Soho New Haven	8.0	Korean	South Town Green	Casual	$30
52	Restaurante Salvadoreño	8.0	Salvadoran	West Haven	Casual	$10
53	Zaroka	8.0	Indian	Upper Chapel Area	Upmarket	$40
54	Coromandel	7.9	Indian	Orange	Upmarket	$40

55	Five Guys	7.9	Burgers	Whalley	Counter	$15
56	Bistro Basque	7.8	Spanish	Milford	Upmarket	$60
57	Daiko (Jerry-san's)	7.8	Japanese	Multiple locations	Upmarket	$40
58	Sahara	7.8	Middle Eastern	Chapel District	Counter	$10
59	Tropical Delights	7.8	Caribbean	Westville	Take-out	$10
60	El Charro	7.8	Mexican	Fair Haven	Casual	$15
61	Royal Palace	7.8	Chinese	Ninth Square	Upmarket	$30
62	Stony Creek Market	7.7	Pizza	Branford	Counter	$15
63	Gerónimo	7.7	Southwestern	Chapel District	Upmarket	$50
64	Istanbul Café	7.7	Turkish	Chapel District	Upmarket	$45
65	Lalibela	7.7	Ethiopian	Chapel District	Casual	$25
66	Glenwood Drive-In	7.7	American	Hamden	Counter	$10
67	Thai Awesome	7.7	Thai	Hamden	Casual	$25
68	Darbar India	7.7	Indian	Branford	Upmarket	$35
69	Sushi Palace	7.7	Japanese	Hamden	Casual	$35
70	Adriana's	7.7	Italian	Fair Haven	Upmarket	$35
71	Christopher Martin's	7.6	American	East Rock	Casual	$25
72	Tandoor	7.6	Indian	Upper Chapel Area	Casual	$25
73	Sushi on Chapel	7.6	Korean	Chapel District	Upmarket	$40
74	Warong Selera	7.6	Malaysian	West Haven	Counter	$20
75	Taquería Mexicana #2	7.6	Mexican	West Haven	Counter	$10
76	The Pantry	7.5	American	East Rock	Casual	$15
77	Zinc	7.5	New American	Chapel District	Upmarket	$70
78	Café George by Paula	7.5	Sandwiches	Chapel District	Counter	$10
79	Bespoke/Sabor Latino	7.4	Nuevo Latino	Chapel District	Upmarket	$80
80	Billy's Pasta Così	7.4	Italian	Branford	Upmarket	$45
81	Taste	7.4	New American	North Haven	Upmarket	$45
82	Tijuana Taco Company	7.4	Mexican	Multiple locations	Take-out	$5
83	Jeffrey's	7.4	New American	Milford	Upmarket	$45
84	Whitfield's	7.4	New American	Guilford	Upmarket	$55
85	Judies European Bakery	7.4	Baked goods	Audubon District	Counter	$10
86	Miya's	7.3	Japanese	Upper Chapel Area	Upmarket	$45
87	Temple Grill	7.3	American	Chapel District	Casual	$40
88	Zoi's on Orange	7.3	Sandwiches	Audubon District	Counter	$10
89	Portofino	7.3	Italian	East Rock	Upmarket	$40
90	Citrus	7.3	New American	Milford	Upmarket	$55
91	Som Siam	7.3	Thai	Guilford	Casual	$30
92	Seoul Yokocho	7.3	Korean	Upper Chapel Area	Upmarket	$40
93	Luce	7.2	Italian	Hamden	Upmarket	$55
94	Anastasio's	7.2	Italian	Wooster Square	Casual	$45
95	Campania	7.2	Italian	Branford	Upmarket	$45
96	El Coquí	7.2	Latin American	Fair Haven	Counter	$10
97	Elaine's Healthy Choice	7.2	American	Whalley	Counter	$10
98	Vito's Deli	7.2	American	Ninth Square	Counter	$10
99	Soul de Cuba	7.1	Cuban	Chapel District	Upmarket	$30
100	Il' Forno	7.1	Italian	Milford	Upmarket	$50

Good vibes

Fearless Critic's feel rating measures the enjoyment we get from the atmosphere and people. Here are the **top 50.** Ties are ordered by food rating.

Rank		Feel	Cuisine	Location	Type	Price
1	Le Petit Café	10	French	Branford	Upmarket	$65
2	The Place	10	Seafood	Guilford	Casual	$25
3	The Owl Shop	10	Sandwiches	Chapel District	Bar	$10
4	Caseus	9.5	New American	East Rock	Casual	$40
5	Union League Café	9.5	French	Chapel District	Upmarket	$75
6	Atticus	9.5	Sandwiches	Upper Chapel Area	Café	$10
7	Stony Creek Market	9.5	Pizza	Branford	Counter	$15
8	Bespoke/Sabor Latino	9.5	Nuevo Latino	Chapel District	Upmarket	$80
9	116 Crown	9.0	New American	Ninth Square	Upmarket	$35
10	Barcelona	9.0	Spanish	Chapel District	Upmarket	$65
11	The Beach House	9.0	Seafood	Milford	Upmarket	$60
12	Book Trader Café	9.0	Sandwiches	Upper Chapel Area	Counter	$10
13	Lenny's Indian Head Inn	9.0	Seafood	Branford	Casual	$30
14	Louis' Lunch	9.0	Burgers	Chapel District	Counter	$10
15	Gerónimo	9.0	Southwestern	Chapel District	Upmarket	$50
16	Miya's	9.0	Japanese	Upper Chapel Area	Upmarket	$45
17	Soul de Cuba	9.0	Cuban	Chapel District	Upmarket	$30
18	Bentara	9.0	Malaysian	Ninth Square	Upmarket	$50
19	Contois Tavern	9.0	American	East Rock	Bar	$10
20	Martin's	9.0	Seafood	Fair Haven	Upmarket	$50
21	Café Nine	9.0	American	Ninth Square	Bar	$15
22	Scoozzi	9.0	Italian	Upper Chapel Area	Upmarket	$60
23	Anna Liffey's	9.0	Irish, American	Audubon District	Bar	$25
24	Skappo	9.0	Italian	Ninth Square	Upmarket	$40
25	Tony & Lucille's	9.0	Italian	Wooster Square	Casual	$35
26	Heirloom	8.5	New American	Upper Chapel Area	Upmarket	$85
27	Saray	8.5	Turkish	West Haven	Casual	$30
28	Prime 16	8.5	American	Chapel District	Casual	$25
29	Carmen Anthony	8.5	Steakhouse	Audubon District	Upmarket	$75
30	Thali	8.5	Indian	Ninth Square	Upmarket	$50
31	Lena's	8.5	Sandwiches	Westville	Casual	$15
32	L'Orcio	8.5	Italian	East Rock	Upmarket	$45
33	Bella's Café	8.5	American	Westville	Casual	$25
34	Roseland Apizza	8.5	Pizza	Derby	Casual	$35
35	Bistro Basque	8.5	Spanish	Milford	Upmarket	$60
36	Christopher Martin's	8.5	American	East Rock	Casual	$25
37	Sage American Bar & Grill	8.5	American	The Hill	Upmarket	$55
38	Thai Taste	8.5	Thai	Upper Chapel Area	Casual	$35
39	Leon's	8.5	Italian	Long Wharf	Upmarket	$45
40	Anchor	8.5	American	Chapel District	Bar	$15
41	Rainbow Gardens Inn	8.5	New American	Milford	Upmarket	$45
42	Pacífico	8.5	Nuevo Latino	Chapel District	Upmarket	$50
43	Delaney's Grille	8.5	American	Westville	Casual	$25
44	Nini's Bistro	8.5	New American	Ninth Square	Upmarket	$45
45	Claire's Corner Copia	8.5	American	Chapel District	Casual	$20
46	Turkish Kabab House	8.0	Turkish	West Haven	Casual	$30
47	Glen's Bar-B-Q	8.0	Caribbean	The Hill	Take-out	$10
48	The Stone House	8.0	Seafood	Guilford	Upmarket	$50
49	Coromandel	8.0	Indian	Orange	Upmarket	$40
50	Istanbul Café	8.0	Turkish	Chapel District	Upmarket	$45

By genre

Places to eat **listed by culinary concept, ranked by food rating**. Establishments that don't serve full meals (e.g. cafés, bakeries, grocery stores) appear as "NR" at the bottom of the list.

American *includes traditional American food, bar food, burgers, and greasy-spoon fare. For creative American, California-influenced or Asian-influenced American, or market-to-table cuisine, see "New American." For steakhouses, Southern cuisine, sandwiches, or baked goods, see those genres.*

8.7	Prime 16	Chapel District	Casual	$25
8.2	Lena's	Westville	Casual	$15
8.1	Bella's Café	Westville	Casual	$25
8.1	The Stone House	Guilford	Upmarket	$50
8.0	Lenny's Indian Head Inn	Branford	Casual	$30
7.7	Glenwood Drive-In	Hamden	Counter	$10
7.6	Christopher Martin's	East Rock	Casual	$25
7.5	The Pantry	East Rock	Casual	$15
7.3	Temple Grill	Chapel District	Casual	$40
7.2	Elaine's Healthy Choice	Whalley	Counter	$10
7.2	Vito's Deli	Ninth Square	Counter	$10
7.0	Sage American Bar & Grill	The Hill	Upmarket	$55
7.0	Eli's	Multiple locations	Casual	$45
6.9	Richter's	Chapel District	Bar	$15
6.9	Scribner's	Milford	Upmarket	$45
6.8	Contois Tavern	East Rock	Bar	$10
6.8	Anchor	Chapel District	Bar	$15
6.8	Rudy's Restaurant	Broadway District	Bar	$10
6.7	Martin's	Fair Haven	Upmarket	$50
6.7	Archie Moore's	Multiple locations	Bar	$20
6.7	Wall Street Pizza	South Town Green	Counter	$10
6.6	Copper Kitchen	Chapel District	Casual	$15
6.5	Café Nine	Ninth Square	Bar	$15
6.5	J.P. Dempsey's	East Rock	Bar	$30
6.4	The Playwright	Multiple locations	Bar	$30
6.4	Orangeside Luncheonette	South Town Green	Counter	$10
6.4	S'Wings	Chapel District	Casual	$15
6.3	Katz's Restaurant	Multiple locations	Casual	$20
6.1	Humphrey's East	East Rock	Bar	$20
6.1	Buffalo Wild Wings	Multiple locations	Casual	$25
6.1	Donovan's Reef	Branford	Casual	$35
6.0	Delaney's Grille	Westville	Casual	$25
6.0	Edge of the Woods	Whalley	Take-out	$15
6.0	Jimmies of Savin Rock	West Haven	Upmarket	$40
6.0	The Tymes	Hamden	Upmarket	$50
6.0	168 York St. Café	Upper Chapel Area	Casual	$20
5.8	Anna Liffey's	Audubon District	Bar	$25
5.8	Athenian Diner	Multiple locations	Casual	$25
5.7	Clark's Dairy	Audubon District	Casual	$15
5.6	Black Bear Saloon	Multiple locations	Bar	$30
5.6	SBC	Multiple locations	Casual	$30
5.6	The Educated Burgher	Broadway District	Counter	$15
5.6	McDonald's	Multiple locations	Counter	$10
5.5	Yorkside Pizza	Broadway District	Casual	$20
5.4	Chili's	Hamden	Casual	$25
5.3	Alpine Restaurant	South Town Green	Counter	$10
5.2	John Davenport's	Chapel District	Upmarket	$65
5.1	Chip's II	Guilford	Bar	$20

American *continued*

5.1	Brown Stone House	Hamden	Casual	$15
5.0	Parthenon Diner	Branford	Casual	$25
5.0	Chap's Grille	Upper Chapel Area	Counter	$15
4.7	Moe's Southwest Grill	Multiple locations	Counter	$10
4.7	Gourmet Heaven	Multiple locations	Take-out	$10
4.6	A One Pizza Restaurant	Broadway District	Counter	$10
4.4	Cody's Diner	Wooster Square	Casual	$15
4.2	Landsdowne Bar & Grille	Chapel District	Bar	$30
4.1	Claire's Corner Copia	Chapel District	Casual	$20
3.9	Burger King	Multiple locations	Counter	$10
3.5	Sullivan's	Upper Chapel Area	Casual	$20
3.2	Town Pizza	Audubon District	Casual	$10
2.9	Patricia's Restaurant	Broadway District	Casual	$10
2.8	Applebee's	Multiple locations	Casual	$25
2.6	Marius	Chapel District	Upmarket	$55
2.1	Dunkin' Donuts	Multiple locations	Counter	$10
2.0	TGI Friday's	Multiple locations	Casual	$30

Baked goods

8.3	Atticus	Upper Chapel Area	Café	$10
8.2	Lena's	Westville	Casual	$15
8.1	Book Trader Café	Upper Chapel Area	Counter	$10
7.5	Café George by Paula	Chapel District	Counter	$10
7.4	Judies European Bakery	Audubon District	Counter	$10
7.3	Zoi's on Orange	Audubon District	Counter	$10
7.1	La Cuisine	Branford	Counter	$15
6.0	Edge of the Woods	Whalley	Take-out	$15
5.3	Celtica	Chapel District	Counter	$15
4.9	Café Java	South Town Green	Counter	$10
4.0	Bruegger's Bagel Bakery	Multiple locations	Counter	$10
2.5	Au Bon Pain	Broadway District	Counter	$10
2.1	Dunkin' Donuts	Multiple locations	Counter	$10
NR	Bishop's Orchards	Guilford	Market	
NR	Blue State Coffee	South Town Green	Café	
NR	Bon Appétit	Hamden	Market	
NR	Bru Café	South Town Green	Café	
NR	Chestnut Fine Foods	East Rock	Market	
NR	The Cupcake Truck	Multiple locations	Take-out	
NR	Farmer's Market	Multiple locations	Market	
NR	Four and Twenty Blackbirds	Guilford	Counter	
NR	JoJo's	Upper Chapel Area	Café	
NR	Koffee on Audubon	Audubon District	Café	
NR	Libby's Italian Pastry Shop	Multiple locations	Counter	
NR	Lucibello's Pastry	Fair Haven	Take-out	
NR	Lulu's	East Rock	Café	
NR	Marjolaine	East Rock	Counter	
NR	The Publick Cup	Broadway District	Café	
NR	Starbucks	Multiple locations	Café	
NR	Take the Cake	Guilford	Take-out	
NR	Willoughby's	Multiple locations	Café	
NR	Woodland Coffee & Tea	Ninth Square	Café	

Barbecue

8.4	Juna's Northern Style BBQ	North Haven	Take-out	$10
7.0	Uncle Willie's BBQ	West Haven	Casual	$20
6.8	Southern Hospitality	Whalley	Counter	$15
6.4	The Rib House	East Haven	Casual	$30

Burgers

9.1	116 Crown	Ninth Square	Upmarket	$35
8.7	Prime 16	Chapel District	Casual	$25

Burgers *continued*

8.5	Gastronomique	Chapel District	Take-out	$25
8.0	Louis' Lunch	Chapel District	Counter	$10
7.9	Five Guys	Whalley	Counter	$15
7.7	Glenwood Drive-In	Hamden	Counter	$10
7.6	Christopher Martin's	East Rock	Casual	$25
6.8	Contois Tavern	East Rock	Bar	$10
6.7	Archie Moore's	Multiple locations	Bar	$20
6.5	J.P. Dempsey's	East Rock	Bar	$30
6.1	Humphrey's East	East Rock	Bar	$20
5.6	The Educated Burgher	Broadway District	Counter	$15
5.6	McDonald's	Multiple locations	Counter	$10
5.1	Chip's II	Guilford	Bar	$20
3.9	Burger King	Multiple locations	Counter	$10

Cafés

8.3	Atticus	Upper Chapel Area	Café	$10
NR	Blue State Coffee	South Town Green	Café	
NR	Bru Café	South Town Green	Café	
NR	JoJo's	Upper Chapel Area	Café	
NR	Koffee on Audubon	Audubon District	Café	
NR	Lulu's	East Rock	Café	
NR	The Publick Cup	Broadway District	Café	
NR	Starbucks	Multiple locations	Café	
NR	Willoughby's	Multiple locations	Café	
NR	Woodland Coffee & Tea	Ninth Square	Café	

Caribbean

8.6	Glen's Bar-B-Q	The Hill	Take-out	$10
8.6	Mother's	Medical Area	Take-out	$15
8.3	Caribbean Connection	Whalley	Take-out	$10
7.8	Tropical Delights	Westville	Take-out	$10

Chinese

9.0	Szechuan Delight	Hamden	Casual	$25
8.7	China Great Wall	Audubon District	Casual	$15
8.7	Iron Chef	West Haven	Counter	$15
7.8	Royal Palace	Ninth Square	Upmarket	$30
6.1	China Pavilion	Orange	Upmarket	$30
5.6	House of Chao	Westville	Casual	$15
4.7	York Street Noodle House	Upper Chapel Area	Casual	$10
4.7	Gourmet Heaven	Multiple locations	Take-out	$10
4.1	Hunan Café	Upper Chapel Area	Counter	$10
4.0	Corner Deli	South Town Green	Counter	$10
3.5	Ivy Noodle	Broadway District	Casual	$10
3.4	Main Garden	Broadway District	Counter	$10
3.4	China King	Chapel District	Take-out	$10
NR	Hong Kong Grocery	East Rock	Market	
NR	J Mart	Ninth Square	Market	
NR	State Fish Farm Market	East Rock	Market	

Cuban

7.1	Soul de Cuba	Chapel District	Upmarket	$30

Ethiopian

7.7	Lalibela	Chapel District	Casual	$25

French

9.6	Le Petit Café	Branford	Upmarket	$65
9.1	Union League Café	Chapel District	Upmarket	$75

French *continued*

8.5	Gastronomique	Chapel District	Take-out	$25
7.8	Bistro Basque	Milford	Upmarket	$60

Greek

6.7	Alpha Delta Pizza	Broadway District	Take-out	$10
5.8	Athenian Diner	Multiple locations	Casual	$25
5.5	Yorkside Pizza	Broadway District	Casual	$20
5.0	Parthenon Diner	Branford	Casual	$25
5.0	Chap's Grille	Upper Chapel Area	Counter	$15

Groceries

NR	Bishop's Orchards	Guilford	Market
NR	Bon Appétit	Hamden	Market
NR	Bud's Fish Market	Branford	Market
NR	Chestnut Fine Foods	East Rock	Market
NR	Farmer's Market	Multiple locations	Market
NR	Ferraro's Foods	Fair Haven	Market
NR	Forte's Gourmet Market	Guilford	Market
NR	Hong Kong Grocery	East Rock	Market
NR	J Mart	Ninth Square	Market
NR	Liuzzi's Cheese Shop	North Haven	Market
NR	Nica's Market	East Rock	Market
NR	#1 Fish Market	Hamden	Market
NR	Romeo & Cesare's	East Rock	Market
NR	Star Fish Market	Guilford	Market
NR	State Fish Farm Market	East Rock	Market
NR	Trader Joe's	Orange	Market
NR	Westville Kosher Market	Westville	Market

Ice cream

NR	Ashley's Ice Cream	Multiple locations	Counter
NR	Cold Stone Creamery	Multiple locations	Take-out
NR	Liberry	Chapel District	Counter
NR	Wentworth's Ice Cream	Hamden	Counter

Indian

9.0	Swagat	West Haven	Casual	$15
9.0	Thali Too	Broadway District	Casual	$35
8.4	Thali	Ninth Square	Upmarket	$50
8.2	Star of India	Orange	Casual	$10
8.0	Zaroka	Upper Chapel Area	Upmarket	$40
7.9	Coromandel	Orange	Upmarket	$40
7.7	Darbar India	Branford	Upmarket	$35
7.6	Tandoor	Upper Chapel Area	Casual	$25
7.1	India Palace	Upper Chapel Area	Casual	$25
7.0	Royal India	Broadway District	Casual	$25
5.9	Sitar	Audubon District	Casual	$35

Irish

6.4	The Playwright	Multiple locations	Bar	$30
5.8	Anna Liffey's	Audubon District	Bar	$25
5.3	Celtica	Chapel District	Counter	$15

Italian

8.2	L'Orcio	East Rock	Upmarket	$45
7.7	Adriana's	Fair Haven	Upmarket	$35
7.4	Billy's Pasta Così	Branford	Upmarket	$45
7.3	Portofino	East Rock	Upmarket	$40
7.2	Luce	Hamden	Upmarket	$55

Italian *continued*

7.2	Anastasio's	Wooster Square	Casual	$45
7.2	Campania	Branford	Upmarket	$45
7.2	Vito's Deli	Ninth Square	Counter	$10
7.1	Il' Forno	Milford	Upmarket	$50
7.1	Tre Scalini	Wooster Square	Upmarket	$45
7.0	Eli's	Multiple locations	Casual	$45
7.0	Gabriele's	Orange	Casual	$35
6.9	Leon's	Long Wharf	Upmarket	$45
6.9	Caffé Bravo	East Rock	Casual	$35
6.9	Quattro's	Guilford	Upmarket	$50
6.8	Consiglio's	Wooster Square	Upmarket	$50
6.6	Basta Trattoria	Chapel District	Upmarket	$60
6.5	Café Goodfellas	East Rock	Upmarket	$55
6.4	Est Est Est	Upper Chapel Area	Counter	$10
6.1	Amato's	East Rock	Casual	$25
5.9	Scoozzi	Upper Chapel Area	Upmarket	$60
5.9	Bella Haven Pizza	Chapel District	Casual	$15
5.8	Skappo	Ninth Square	Upmarket	$40
5.8	Tony & Lucille's	Wooster Square	Casual	$35
5.7	Bertucci's	Orange	Casual	$35
4.9	Olive Garden	Multiple locations	Casual	$25
4.7	Abate Apizza & Seafood	Wooster Square	Casual	$30
4.1	Marco Polo Pizza	Ninth Square	Counter	$20
3.8	Brazi's Italian Restaurant	Long Wharf	Casual	$30
3.2	Town Pizza	Audubon District	Casual	$10
NR	Ferraro's Foods	Fair Haven	Market	
NR	Liuzzi's Cheese Shop	North Haven	Market	
NR	Nica's Market	East Rock	Market	
NR	Romeo & Cesare's	East Rock	Market	

Japanese

9.1	East Japanese Restaurant	Milford	Upmarket	$45
8.5	Sono Bana	Hamden	Casual	$30
7.8	Daiko (Jerry-san's)	Multiple locations	Upmarket	$40
7.7	Sushi Palace	Hamden	Casual	$35
7.6	Sushi on Chapel	Chapel District	Upmarket	$40
7.3	Miya's	Upper Chapel Area	Upmarket	$45
7.1	Miso	Ninth Square	Upmarket	$40
6.9	Akasaka	Westville	Upmarket	$35
6.8	Wild Ginger	Orange	Upmarket	$45
6.8	Kumo	Multiple locations	Upmarket	$40
6.7	Kampai	Branford	Upmarket	$40
3.6	Samurai	Chapel District	Upmarket	$45

Jewish deli

NR	Westville Kosher Market	Westville	Market	

Korean

8.0	Soho New Haven	South Town Green	Casual	$30
7.6	Sushi on Chapel	Chapel District	Upmarket	$40
7.3	Seoul Yokocho	Upper Chapel Area	Upmarket	$40

Latin American

8.5	Sabor Latino	West Haven	Counter	$10
8.3	Machu Picchu	Fair Haven	Casual	$25
8.0	Restaurante Salvadoreño	West Haven	Casual	$10
7.2	El Coquí	Fair Haven	Counter	$10
7.1	Soul de Cuba	Chapel District	Upmarket	$30

Malaysian

7.6	Warong Selera	West Haven	Counter	$20
7.0	Kari	Westville	Casual	$30
6.8	Bentara	Ninth Square	Upmarket	$50

Markets

NR	BevMax	Multiple locations	Market
NR	Bishop's Orchards	Guilford	Market
NR	Bon Appétit	Hamden	Market
NR	Bud's Fish Market	Branford	Market
NR	Chestnut Fine Foods	East Rock	Market
NR	Farmer's Market	Multiple locations	Market
NR	Ferraro's Foods	Fair Haven	Market
NR	Forte's Gourmet Market	Guilford	Market
NR	Hong Kong Grocery	East Rock	Market
NR	J Mart	Ninth Square	Market
NR	Liuzzi's Cheese Shop	North Haven	Market
NR	Mt. Carmel Wines & Spirits	Hamden	Market
NR	Nica's Market	East Rock	Market
NR	#1 Fish Market	Hamden	Market
NR	Romeo & Cesare's	East Rock	Market
NR	Star Fish Market	Guilford	Market
NR	State Fish Farm Market	East Rock	Market
NR	Trader Joe's	Orange	Market
NR	Westville Kosher Market	Westville	Market
NR	The Wine Thief	Multiple locations	Market

Mexican

8.7	Mezcal	East Rock	Casual	$25
8.3	La Cocinita	Upper Chapel Area	Counter	$15
8.1	Guadalupe La Poblanita	Fair Haven	Casual	$15
7.8	El Charro	Fair Haven	Casual	$15
7.7	Gerónimo	Chapel District	Upmarket	$50
7.6	Taquería Mexicana #2	West Haven	Counter	$10
7.4	Tijuana Taco Company	Multiple locations	Take-out	$5
6.9	La Carreta	East Rock	Counter	$10
6.8	Su Casa	Branford	Casual	$30
6.6	Jalapeño Heaven	Branford	Casual	$30
6.5	Baja's	Orange	Casual	$25
6.4	Ixtapa Grille	Hamden	Casual	$25
6.0	Fresh Taco	South Town Green	Counter	$10
5.5	Aunt Chilada's	Hamden	Casual	$30
5.4	Chili's	Hamden	Casual	$25
5.0	Bulldog Burrito	Broadway District	Counter	$5
4.7	C.O. Jones	East Rock	Bar	$20
4.7	Moe's Southwest Grill	Multiple locations	Counter	$10
4.4	El Amigo Felix	Broadway District	Bar	$25
4.3	The Whole Enchilada	Audubon District	Counter	$10
2.0	Viva Zapata	Upper Chapel Area	Bar	$25

Middle Eastern

7.8	Sahara	Chapel District	Counter	$10
6.7	Mamoun's	Upper Chapel Area	Casual	$10
6.7	Mediterranea	South Town Green	Counter	$10
5.0	Chap's Grille	Upper Chapel Area	Counter	$15
4.8	Aladdin Crown Pizza	Chapel District	Take-out	$15

New American

9.4	Caseus	East Rock	Casual	$40
9.1	116 Crown	Ninth Square	Upmarket	$35
9.0	Heirloom	Upper Chapel Area	Upmarket	$85

New American *continued*

7.5	Zinc	Chapel District	Upmarket	$70
7.4	Taste	North Haven	Upmarket	$45
7.4	Jeffrey's	Milford	Upmarket	$45
7.4	Whitfield's	Guilford	Upmarket	$55
7.3	Citrus	Milford	Upmarket	$55
7.1	Foe	Branford	Upmarket	$50
6.8	Rainbow Gardens Inn	Milford	Upmarket	$45
6.7	Dolci	East Rock	Upmarket	$45
6.5	Nikkita	Audubon District	Upmarket	$45
6.2	Assaggio	Branford	Upmarket	$45
5.9	The Blue Pearl	South Town Green	Upmarket	$45
5.7	Nini's Bistro	Ninth Square	Upmarket	$45
5.7	Ahimsa	Upper Chapel Area	Upmarket	$55
3.8	Downtown @ the Taft	Chapel District	Upmarket	$50
1.8	Foster's	Ninth Square	Upmarket	$50

Nuevo Latino

7.4	Bespoke/Sabor Latino	Chapel District	Upmarket	$80
6.1	Pacífico	Chapel District	Upmarket	$50

Pan-Asian

4.7	Kudeta	Chapel District	Upmarket	$50
4.7	York Street Noodle House	Upper Chapel Area	Casual	$10
2.2	Thai Pan Asian	Upper Chapel Area	Casual	$25
NR	Chow Wine Bar	Chapel District	Upmarket	

Peruvian

8.3	Machu Picchu	Fair Haven	Casual	$25

Pizza

9.1	Bar (Brü Room)	Chapel District	Bar	$25
9.1	Frank Pepe's	Multiple locations	Casual	$20
9.1	Sally's Apizza	Wooster Square	Casual	$20
9.0	Modern Apizza	East Rock	Casual	$20
8.4	Zuppardi's	West Haven	Casual	$25
8.1	Roseland Apizza	Derby	Casual	$35
8.1	Dayton Street Apizza	Westville	Counter	$15
7.7	Stony Creek Market	Branford	Counter	$15
7.0	Eli's	Multiple locations	Casual	$45
6.7	Wall Street Pizza	South Town Green	Counter	$10
6.7	Mediterranea	South Town Green	Counter	$10
6.7	Alpha Delta Pizza	Broadway District	Take-out	$10
6.5	Brick Oven Pizza	Upper Chapel Area	Counter	$10
6.4	Est Est Est	Upper Chapel Area	Counter	$10
6.1	Amato's	East Rock	Casual	$25
5.9	Bella Haven Pizza	Chapel District	Casual	$15
5.7	Bertucci's	Orange	Casual	$35
5.6	Pizza House	Upper Chapel Area	Counter	$5
5.5	Yorkside Pizza	Broadway District	Casual	$20
4.9	Café Java	South Town Green	Counter	$10
4.8	Aladdin Crown Pizza	Chapel District	Take-out	$15
4.7	Abate Apizza & Seafood	Wooster Square	Casual	$30
4.6	A One Pizza Restaurant	Broadway District	Counter	$10
4.1	Marco Polo Pizza	Ninth Square	Counter	$20
3.8	Brazi's Italian Restaurant	Long Wharf	Casual	$30
3.2	Town Pizza	Audubon District	Casual	$10

Salvadoran

8.5	Sabor Latino	West Haven	Counter	$10
8.0	Restaurante Salvadoreño	West Haven	Casual	$10

Sandwiches

8.3	Atticus	Upper Chapel Area	Café	$10
8.2	Lena's	Westville	Casual	$15
8.1	Book Trader Café	Upper Chapel Area	Counter	$10
7.7	Stony Creek Market	Branford	Counter	$15
7.5	Café George by Paula	Chapel District	Counter	$10
7.4	Judies European Bakery	Audubon District	Counter	$10
7.3	Zoi's on Orange	Audubon District	Counter	$10
7.1	La Cuisine	Branford	Counter	$15
6.7	Alpha Delta Pizza	Broadway District	Take-out	$10
6.6	Roly-Poly	Multiple locations	Counter	$10
6.2	The Owl Shop	Chapel District	Bar	$10
5.3	Celtica	Chapel District	Counter	$15
5.3	Alpine Restaurant	South Town Green	Counter	$10
4.9	Café Java	South Town Green	Counter	$10
4.3	Breakaway Deli	Audubon District	Counter	$10
4.0	Corner Deli	South Town Green	Counter	$10
4.0	Bruegger's Bagel Bakery	Multiple locations	Counter	$10
3.7	Subway	Multiple locations	Counter	$10
2.5	Au Bon Pain	Broadway District	Counter	$10
NR	Bru Café	South Town Green	Café	
NR	Forte's Gourmet Market	Guilford	Market	
NR	JoJo's	Upper Chapel Area	Café	
NR	Koffee on Audubon	Audubon District	Café	
NR	Lulu's	East Rock	Café	
NR	The Publick Cup	Broadway District	Café	
NR	Starbucks	Multiple locations	Café	
NR	Woodland Coffee & Tea	Ninth Square	Café	

Seafood

8.4	The Place	Guilford	Casual	$25
8.3	The Beach House	Milford	Upmarket	$60
8.2	The Blue Cottage	Branford	Casual	$30
8.1	The Stone House	Guilford	Upmarket	$50
8.0	Lenny's Indian Head Inn	Branford	Casual	$30
6.9	Scribner's	Milford	Upmarket	$45
6.8	Chick's	West Haven	Counter	$15
6.7	Martin's	Fair Haven	Upmarket	$50
6.5	Nikkita	Audubon District	Upmarket	$45
6.1	Pacífico	Chapel District	Upmarket	$50
6.0	Jimmies of Savin Rock	West Haven	Upmarket	$40
6.0	The Tymes	Hamden	Upmarket	$50
5.3	USS Chowder Pot III	Branford	Casual	$40
NR	Bud's Fish Market	Branford	Market	
NR	J Mart	Ninth Square	Market	
NR	#1 Fish Market	Hamden	Market	
NR	Star Fish Market	Guilford	Market	
NR	State Fish Farm Market	East Rock	Market	

Southern *includes soul food, Cajun, Creole*

7.0	Uncle Willie's BBQ	West Haven	Casual	$20
7.0	Popeye's	Multiple locations	Counter	$10
6.8	Southern Hospitality	Whalley	Counter	$15
6.4	The Rib House	East Haven	Casual	$30
4.5	KFC	Multiple locations	Counter	$10

Southwestern

7.7	Gerónimo	Chapel District	Upmarket	$50

Spanish

9.3	Ibiza	Chapel District	Upmarket	$80

Spanish _continued_

| 8.9 | Barcelona | Chapel District | Upmarket | $65 |
| 7.8 | Bistro Basque | Milford | Upmarket | $60 |

Steakhouse

8.5	Carmen Anthony	Audubon District	Upmarket	$75
8.3	The Beach House	Milford	Upmarket	$60
6.9	Chuck's Steak House	Multiple locations	Casual	$30
5.9	Central Steakhouse	Ninth Square	Upmarket	$75

Swedish

| 4.9 | IKEA Restaurant | Long Wharf | Counter | $5 |

Taiwanese

| 8.7 | Iron Chef | West Haven | Counter | $15 |

Thai

8.6	The Terrace	Hamden	Casual	$35
8.6	Rice Pot	East Rock	Casual	$30
7.7	Thai Awesome	Hamden	Casual	$25
7.3	Som Siam	Guilford	Casual	$30
7.0	Thai Taste	Upper Chapel Area	Casual	$35
6.9	Bangkok Gardens	Upper Chapel Area	Upmarket	$30
6.8	Jasmine Thai Cart	Audubon District	Take-out	$5
6.6	Thai Awesome Food Cart	Multiple locations	Take-out	$5
6.3	Pad Thai	Upper Chapel Area	Casual	$25
4.9	Indochine Pavilion	Upper Chapel Area	Casual	$25
2.2	Thai Pan Asian	Upper Chapel Area	Casual	$25

Turkish

8.8	Saray	West Haven	Casual	$30
8.7	Turkish Kabab House	West Haven	Casual	$30
7.7	Istanbul Café	Chapel District	Upmarket	$45

Vietnamese

| 5.2 | Pot-au-Pho | Audubon District | Casual | $15 |

Wine store

NR	BevMax	Multiple locations	Market	
NR	Mt. Carmel Wines & Spirits	Hamden	Market	
NR	The Wine Thief	Multiple locations	Market	

By location

Places to eat **listed by neighborhood, suburb, or town, ranked by food rating**. Establishments that don't serve full meals (e.g. cafés, bakeries, grocery stores) appear as "NR" at the bottom of the list.

Audubon Arts District

		Cuisine	Type	Price
8.7	China Great Wall	Chinese	Casual	$15
8.5	Carmen Anthony	Steakhouse	Upmarket	$75
7.4	Judies European Bakery	Baked goods, Sandwiches	Counter	$10
7.3	Zoi's on Orange	Sandwiches, Baked goods	Counter	$10
6.8	Jasmine Thai Cart	Thai	Take-out	$5
6.5	Nikkita	New American, Seafood	Upmarket	$45
5.9	Sitar	Indian	Casual	$35
5.8	Anna Liffey's	Irish, American	Bar	$25
5.7	Clark's Dairy	American	Casual	$15
5.2	Pot-au-Pho	Vietnamese	Casual	$15
4.7	Moe's Southwest Grill	Mexican, American	Counter	$10
4.7	Gourmet Heaven	American, Chinese	Take-out	$10
4.3	Breakaway Deli	Sandwiches	Counter	$10
4.3	The Whole Enchilada	Mexican	Counter	$10
4.0	Bruegger's Bagel Bakery	Sandwiches, Baked goods	Counter	$10
3.7	Subway	Sandwiches	Counter	$10
3.2	Town Pizza	Pizza, Italian, American	Casual	$10
2.1	Dunkin' Donuts	Baked goods, American	Counter	$10
NR	Koffee on Audubon	Baked goods, Sandwiches	Café	

Branford

9.6	Le Petit Café	French	Upmarket	$65
8.2	The Blue Cottage	Seafood	Casual	$30
8.0	Lenny's Indian Head Inn	Seafood, American	Casual	$30
7.7	Stony Creek Market	Pizza, Sandwiches	Counter	$15
7.7	Darbar India	Indian	Upmarket	$35
7.4	Billy's Pasta Così	Italian	Upmarket	$45
7.2	Campania	Italian	Upmarket	$45
7.1	La Cuisine	Baked goods, Sandwiches	Counter	$15
7.1	Foe	New American	Upmarket	$50
7.0	Eli's	American, Italian, Pizza	Casual	$45
6.9	Chuck's Steak House	Steakhouse	Casual	$30
6.8	Su Casa	Mexican	Casual	$30
6.7	Kampai	Japanese	Upmarket	$40
6.6	Jalapeño Heaven	Mexican	Casual	$30
6.2	Assaggio	New American	Upmarket	$45
6.1	Donovan's Reef	American	Casual	$35
5.6	SBC	American	Casual	$30
5.6	McDonald's	American, Burgers	Counter	$10
5.3	USS Chowder Pot III	Seafood	Casual	$40
5.0	Parthenon Diner	American, Greek	Casual	$25
4.5	KFC	Southern	Counter	$10
NR	Ashley's Ice Cream	Ice cream	Counter	
NR	Bud's Fish Market	Groceries, Seafood	Market	
NR	Starbucks	Baked goods, Sandwiches	Café	
NR	Willoughby's	Baked goods	Café	

Broadway District

9.0	Thali Too	Indian	Casual	$35
7.4	Tijuana Taco Company	Mexican	Take-out	$5
7.0	Royal India	Indian	Casual	$25

Broadway District *continued*

6.8	Rudy's Restaurant	American	Bar	$10
6.7	Alpha Delta Pizza	Pizza, Sandwiches, Greek	Take-out	$10
5.6	The Educated Burgher	American, Burgers	Counter	$15
5.5	Yorkside Pizza	Pizza, American, Greek	Casual	$20
5.0	Bulldog Burrito	Mexican	Counter	$5
4.7	Gourmet Heaven	American, Chinese	Take-out	$10
4.6	A One Pizza Restaurant	Pizza, American	Counter	$10
4.4	El Amigo Felix	Mexican	Bar	$25
3.5	Ivy Noodle	Chinese	Casual	$10
3.4	Main Garden	Chinese	Counter	$10
2.9	Patricia's Restaurant	American	Casual	$10
2.5	Au Bon Pain	Sandwiches, Baked goods	Counter	$10
NR	Ashley's Ice Cream	Ice cream	Counter	
NR	The Publick Cup	Sandwiches, Baked goods	Café	

Chapel District

9.3	Ibiza	Spanish	Upmarket	$80
9.1	Union League Café	French	Upmarket	$75
9.1	Bar (Brü Room)	Pizza	Bar	$25
8.9	Barcelona	Spanish	Upmarket	$65
8.7	Prime 16	American, Burgers	Casual	$25
8.5	Gastronomique	French, Burgers	Take-out	$25
8.0	Louis' Lunch	Burgers	Counter	$10
7.8	Sahara	Middle Eastern	Counter	$10
7.7	Gerónimo	Southwestern, Mexican	Upmarket	$50
7.7	Istanbul Café	Turkish	Upmarket	$45
7.7	Lalibela	Ethiopian	Casual	$25
7.6	Sushi on Chapel	Korean, Japanese	Upmarket	$40
7.5	Zinc	New American	Upmarket	$70
7.5	Café George by Paula	Sandwiches, Baked goods	Counter	$10
7.4	Bespoke/Sabor Latino	Nuevo Latino	Upmarket	$80
7.3	Temple Grill	American	Casual	$40
7.1	Soul de Cuba	Cuban, Latin American	Upmarket	$30
6.9	Richter's	American	Bar	$15
6.8	Anchor	American	Bar	$15
6.6	Basta Trattoria	Italian	Upmarket	$60
6.6	Copper Kitchen	American	Casual	$15
6.4	The Playwright	Irish, American	Bar	$30
6.4	S'Wings	American	Casual	$15
6.3	Katz's Restaurant	American	Casual	$20
6.2	The Owl Shop	Sandwiches	Bar	$10
6.1	Pacífico	Nuevo Latino, Seafood	Upmarket	$50
6.1	Buffalo Wild Wings	American	Casual	$25
5.9	Bella Haven Pizza	Pizza, Italian	Casual	$15
5.6	Black Bear Saloon	American	Bar	$30
5.3	Celtica	Irish, Baked goods	Counter	$15
5.2	John Davenport's	American	Upmarket	$65
4.8	Aladdin Crown Pizza	Middle Eastern, Pizza	Take-out	$15
4.7	Kudeta	Pan-Asian	Upmarket	$50
4.2	Landsdowne Bar & Grille	American	Bar	$30
4.1	Claire's Corner Copia	American	Casual	$20
3.8	Downtown @ the Taft	New American	Upmarket	$50
3.7	Subway	Sandwiches	Counter	$10
3.6	Samurai	Japanese	Upmarket	$45
3.4	China King	Chinese	Take-out	$10
2.6	Marius	American	Upmarket	$55
2.1	Dunkin' Donuts	Baked goods, American	Counter	$10
NR	Chow Wine Bar	Pan-Asian	Upmarket	
NR	The Cupcake Truck	Baked goods	Take-out	
NR	Liberry	Ice cream	Counter	
NR	Starbucks	Baked goods, Sandwiches	Café	
NR	The Wine Thief	Wine store	Market	

Derby

8.1	Roseland Apizza	Pizza	Casual	$35
6.7	Archie Moore's	American, Burgers	Bar	$20

East Haven

6.4	The Rib House	Barbecue, Southern	Casual	$30

East Rock

9.4	Caseus	New American	Casual	$40
9.0	Modern Apizza	Pizza	Casual	$20
8.7	Mezcal	Mexican	Casual	$25
8.6	Rice Pot	Thai	Casual	$30
8.2	L'Orcio	Italian	Upmarket	$45
7.6	Christopher Martin's	American, Burgers	Casual	$25
7.5	The Pantry	American	Casual	$15
7.3	Portofino	Italian	Upmarket	$40
6.9	Caffé Bravo	Italian	Casual	$35
6.9	La Carreta	Mexican	Counter	$10
6.8	Contois Tavern	American, Burgers	Bar	$10
6.7	Dolci	New American	Upmarket	$45
6.7	Archie Moore's	American, Burgers	Bar	$20
6.6	Thai Awesome Food Cart	Thai	Take-out	$5
6.5	Café Goodfellas	Italian	Upmarket	$55
6.5	J.P. Dempsey's	American, Burgers	Bar	$30
6.1	Amato's	Pizza, Italian	Casual	$25
6.1	Humphrey's East	American, Burgers	Bar	$20
5.6	McDonald's	American, Burgers	Counter	$10
4.7	C.O. Jones	Mexican	Bar	$20
3.7	Subway	Sandwiches	Counter	$10
2.1	Dunkin' Donuts	Baked goods, American	Counter	$10
NR	Chestnut Fine Foods	Baked goods, Groceries	Market	
NR	Hong Kong Grocery	Groceries, Chinese	Market	
NR	Lulu's	Baked goods, Sandwiches	Café	
NR	Marjolaine	Baked goods	Counter	
NR	Nica's Market	Groceries, Italian	Market	
NR	Romeo & Cesare's	Groceries, Italian	Market	
NR	State Fish Farm Market	Groceries, Seafood	Market	
NR	The Wine Thief	Wine store	Market	

Fair Haven

8.3	Machu Picchu	Peruvian, Latin American	Casual	$25
8.1	Guadalupe La Poblanita	Mexican	Casual	$15
7.8	El Charro	Mexican	Casual	$15
7.7	Adriana's	Italian	Upmarket	$35
7.2	El Coquí	Latin American	Counter	$10
6.7	Martin's	Seafood, American	Upmarket	$50
5.6	McDonald's	American, Burgers	Counter	$10
4.5	KFC	Southern	Counter	$10
3.9	Burger King	American, Burgers	Counter	$10
3.7	Subway	Sandwiches	Counter	$10
NR	Farmer's Market	Groceries, Baked goods	Market	
NR	Ferraro's Foods	Groceries, Italian	Market	
NR	Lucibello's Pastry	Baked goods	Take-out	

Guilford

8.4	The Place	Seafood	Casual	$25
8.1	The Stone House	Seafood, American	Upmarket	$50
7.4	Whitfield's	New American	Upmarket	$55
7.3	Som Siam	Thai	Casual	$30
6.9	Quattro's	Italian	Upmarket	$50
5.1	Chip's II	American, Burgers	Bar	$20

Guilford *continued*

NR	Ashley's Ice Cream	Ice cream	Counter
NR	Bishop's Orchards	Groceries, Baked goods	Market
NR	Forte's Gourmet Market	Groceries, Sandwiches	Market
NR	Four and Twenty Blackbirds	Baked goods	Counter
NR	Star Fish Market	Groceries, Seafood	Market
NR	Take the Cake	Baked goods	Take-out

Hamden

9.0	Szechuan Delight	Chinese	Casual	$25
8.6	The Terrace	Thai	Casual	$35
8.5	Sono Bana	Japanese	Casual	$30
7.7	Glenwood Drive-In	American, Burgers	Counter	$10
7.7	Thai Awesome	Thai	Casual	$25
7.7	Sushi Palace	Japanese	Casual	$35
7.2	Luce	Italian	Upmarket	$55
7.0	Eli's	American, Italian, Pizza	Casual	$45
7.0	Popeye's	Southern	Counter	$10
6.8	Kumo	Japanese	Upmarket	$40
6.4	The Playwright	Irish, American	Bar	$30
6.4	Ixtapa Grille	Mexican	Casual	$25
6.0	The Tymes	American, Seafood	Upmarket	$50
5.6	SBC	American	Casual	$30
5.6	McDonald's	American, Burgers	Counter	$10
5.5	Aunt Chilada's	Mexican	Casual	$30
5.4	Chili's	American, Mexican	Casual	$25
5.1	Brown Stone House	American	Casual	$15
4.5	KFC	Southern	Counter	$10
4.0	Bruegger's Bagel Bakery	Sandwiches, Baked goods	Counter	$10
3.9	Burger King	American, Burgers	Counter	$10
2.8	Applebee's	American	Casual	$25
2.0	TGI Friday's	American	Casual	$30
NR	Ashley's Ice Cream	Ice cream	Counter	
NR	BevMax	Wine store	Market	
NR	Bon Appétit	Groceries, Baked goods	Market	
NR	Mt. Carmel Wines & Spirits	Wine store	Market	
NR	#1 Fish Market	Groceries, Seafood	Market	
NR	Starbucks	Baked goods, Sandwiches	Café	
NR	Wentworth's Ice Cream	Ice cream	Counter	

Long Wharf

6.9	Leon's	Italian	Upmarket	$45
4.9	IKEA Restaurant	Swedish	Counter	$5
3.8	Brazi's Italian Restaurant	Italian, Pizza	Casual	$30

Medical Area

8.6	Mother's	Caribbean	Take-out	$15
7.4	Tijuana Taco Company	Mexican	Take-out	$5
6.6	Thai Awesome Food Cart	Thai	Take-out	$5
5.6	McDonald's	American, Burgers	Counter	$10
3.7	Subway	Sandwiches	Counter	$10
2.1	Dunkin' Donuts	Baked goods, American	Counter	$10
NR	The Cupcake Truck	Baked goods	Take-out	
NR	Medical Area Food Carts		Take-out	

Milford

9.1	East Japanese Restaurant	Japanese	Upmarket	$45
8.3	The Beach House	Seafood, Steakhouse	Upmarket	$60
7.8	Bistro Basque	Spanish, French	Upmarket	$60
7.4	Jeffrey's	New American	Upmarket	$45
7.3	Citrus	New American	Upmarket	$55

Milford *continued*

7.1	Il' Forno	Italian	Upmarket	$50
6.9	Scribner's	Seafood, American	Upmarket	$45
6.8	Rainbow Gardens Inn	New American	Upmarket	$45
6.7	Archie Moore's	American, Burgers	Bar	$20
6.1	Buffalo Wild Wings	American	Casual	$25
5.8	Athenian Diner	American, Greek	Casual	$25
5.6	Black Bear Saloon	American	Bar	$30
5.6	SBC	American	Casual	$30
5.6	McDonald's	American, Burgers	Counter	$10
4.7	Moe's Southwest Grill	Mexican, American	Counter	$10
NR	Cold Stone Creamery	Ice cream	Take-out	
NR	Starbucks	Baked goods, Sandwiches	Café	

Ninth Square

9.1	116 Crown	New American, Burgers	Upmarket	$35
8.4	Thali	Indian	Upmarket	$50
7.8	Royal Palace	Chinese	Upmarket	$30
7.2	Vito's Deli	American, Italian	Counter	$10
7.1	Miso	Japanese	Upmarket	$40
6.8	Bentara	Malaysian	Upmarket	$50
6.5	Café Nine	American	Bar	$15
5.9	Central Steakhouse	Steakhouse	Upmarket	$75
5.8	Skappo	Italian	Upmarket	$40
5.7	Nini's Bistro	New American	Upmarket	$45
4.1	Marco Polo Pizza	Pizza, Italian	Counter	$20
1.8	Foster's	New American	Upmarket	$50
NR	J Mart	Groceries, Seafood	Market	
NR	Woodland Coffee & Tea	Sandwiches, Baked goods	Café	

North Haven

8.4	Juna's Northern Style BBQ	Barbecue	Take-out	$10
7.4	Taste	New American	Upmarket	$45
5.6	McDonald's	American, Burgers	Counter	$10
4.9	Olive Garden	Italian	Casual	$25
2.1	Dunkin' Donuts	Baked goods, American	Counter	$10
NR	Cold Stone Creamery	Ice cream	Take-out	
NR	Libby's Italian Pastry Shop	Baked goods	Counter	
NR	Liuzzi's Cheese Shop	Groceries, Italian	Market	
NR	Starbucks	Baked goods, Sandwiches	Café	

Orange

8.2	Star of India	Indian	Casual	$10
7.9	Coromandel	Indian	Upmarket	$40
7.0	Gabriele's	Italian	Casual	$35
6.8	Wild Ginger	Japanese	Upmarket	$45
6.6	Roly-Poly	Sandwiches	Counter	$10
6.5	Baja's	Mexican	Casual	$25
6.1	China Pavilion	Chinese	Upmarket	$30
5.7	Bertucci's	Italian, Pizza	Casual	$35
5.6	McDonald's	American, Burgers	Counter	$10
4.9	Olive Garden	Italian	Casual	$25
4.5	KFC	Southern	Counter	$10
4.0	Bruegger's Bagel Bakery	Sandwiches, Baked goods	Counter	$10
3.9	Burger King	American, Burgers	Counter	$10
2.8	Applebee's	American	Casual	$25
2.0	TGI Friday's	American	Casual	$30
NR	BevMax	Wine store	Market	
NR	Cold Stone Creamery	Ice cream	Take-out	
NR	Starbucks	Baked goods, Sandwiches	Café	
NR	Trader Joe's	Groceries	Market	

South Town Green

8.0	Soho New Haven	Korean	Casual	$30
6.8	Kumo	Japanese	Upmarket	$40
6.7	Wall Street Pizza	Pizza, American	Counter	$10
6.7	Mediterranea	Middle Eastern, Pizza	Counter	$10
6.6	Roly-Poly	Sandwiches	Counter	$10
6.4	Orangeside Luncheonette	American	Counter	$10
6.3	Katz's Restaurant	American	Casual	$20
6.0	Fresh Taco	Mexican	Counter	$10
5.9	The Blue Pearl	New American	Upmarket	$45
5.3	Alpine Restaurant	Sandwiches, American	Counter	$10
4.9	Café Java	Sandwiches, Baked goods	Counter	$10
4.0	Corner Deli	Sandwiches, Chinese	Counter	$10
NR	Blue State Coffee	Baked goods	Café	
NR	Bru Café	Baked goods, Sandwiches	Café	
NR	Farmer's Market	Groceries, Baked goods	Market	
NR	Willoughby's	Baked goods	Café	

The Hill

8.6	Glen's Bar-B-Q	Caribbean	Take-out	$10
7.0	Sage American Bar & Grill	American	Upmarket	$55

Upper Chapel Area

9.0	Heirloom	New American	Upmarket	$85
8.3	Atticus	Sandwiches, Baked goods	Café	$10
8.3	La Cocinita	Mexican	Counter	$15
8.1	Book Trader Café	Sandwiches, Baked goods	Counter	$10
8.0	Zaroka	Indian	Upmarket	$40
7.6	Tandoor	Indian	Casual	$25
7.3	Miya's	Japanese	Upmarket	$45
7.3	Seoul Yokocho	Korean	Upmarket	$40
7.1	India Palace	Indian	Casual	$25
7.0	Thai Taste	Thai	Casual	$35
6.9	Bangkok Gardens	Thai	Upmarket	$30
6.7	Mamoun's	Middle Eastern	Casual	$10
6.5	Brick Oven Pizza	Pizza	Counter	$10
6.4	Est Est Est	Pizza, Italian	Counter	$10
6.3	Pad Thai	Thai	Casual	$25
6.0	168 York St. Café	American	Casual	$20
5.9	Scoozzi	Italian	Upmarket	$60
5.7	Ahimsa	New American	Upmarket	$55
5.6	Pizza House	Pizza	Counter	$5
5.0	Chap's Grille	American, Middle Eastern	Counter	$15
4.9	Indochine Pavilion	Thai	Casual	$25
4.7	York Street Noodle House	Pan-Asian, Chinese	Casual	$10
4.1	Hunan Café	Chinese	Counter	$10
3.7	Subway	Sandwiches	Counter	$10
3.5	Sullivan's	American	Casual	$20
2.2	Thai Pan Asian	Thai, Pan-Asian	Casual	$25
2.1	Dunkin' Donuts	Baked goods, American	Counter	$10
2.0	Viva Zapata	Mexican	Bar	$25
NR	JoJo's	Baked goods, Sandwiches	Café	
NR	Willoughby's	Baked goods	Café	

West Haven

9.0	Swagat	Indian	Casual	$15
8.8	Saray	Turkish	Casual	$30
8.7	Turkish Kabab House	Turkish	Casual	$30
8.7	Iron Chef	Taiwanese, Chinese	Counter	$15
8.5	Sabor Latino	Salvadoran	Counter	$10
8.4	Zuppardi's	Pizza	Casual	$25
8.0	Restaurante Salvadoreño	Salvadoran	Casual	$10

West Haven *continued*

7.8	Daiko (Jerry-san's)	Japanese	Upmarket	$40
7.6	Warong Selera	Malaysian	Counter	$20
7.6	Taquería Mexicana #2	Mexican	Counter	$10
7.0	Uncle Willie's BBQ	Barbecue, Southern	Casual	$20
6.9	Chuck's Steak House	Steakhouse	Casual	$30
6.8	Chick's	Seafood	Counter	$15
6.0	Jimmies of Savin Rock	Seafood, American	Upmarket	$40
5.6	McDonald's	American, Burgers	Counter	$10
4.5	KFC	Southern	Counter	$10
3.9	Burger King	American, Burgers	Counter	$10
3.7	Subway	Sandwiches	Counter	$10
NR	Starbucks	Baked goods, Sandwiches	Café	

Westville

8.2	Lena's	Sandwiches, Baked goods	Casual	$15
8.1	Bella's Café	American	Casual	$25
8.1	Dayton Street Apizza	Pizza	Counter	$15
7.8	Tropical Delights	Caribbean	Take-out	$10
7.0	Kari	Malaysian	Casual	$30
6.9	Akasaka	Japanese	Upmarket	$35
6.0	Delaney's Grille	American	Casual	$25
5.8	Athenian Diner	American, Greek	Casual	$25
5.6	House of Chao	Chinese	Casual	$15
3.7	Subway	Sandwiches	Counter	$10
NR	Westville Kosher Market	Groceries, Jewish deli	Market	

Whalley

8.3	Caribbean Connection	Caribbean	Take-out	$10
7.9	Five Guys	Burgers	Counter	$15
7.2	Elaine's Healthy Choice	American	Counter	$10
7.0	Popeye's	Southern	Counter	$10
6.8	Southern Hospitality	Southern, Barbecue	Counter	$15
6.0	Edge of the Woods	American, Baked goods	Take-out	$15
5.6	McDonald's	American, Burgers	Counter	$10
4.5	KFC	Southern	Counter	$10
3.9	Burger King	American, Burgers	Counter	$10
3.7	Subway	Sandwiches	Counter	$10
2.1	Dunkin' Donuts	Baked goods, American	Counter	$10
NR	Farmer's Market	Groceries, Baked goods	Market	

Woodbridge

6.3	Katz's Restaurant	American	Casual	$20

Wooster Square Area

9.1	Frank Pepe's	Pizza	Casual	$20
9.1	Sally's Apizza	Pizza	Casual	$20
7.2	Anastasio's	Italian	Casual	$45
7.1	Tre Scalini	Italian	Upmarket	$45
6.8	Consiglio's	Italian	Upmarket	$50
5.8	Tony & Lucille's	Italian	Casual	$35
4.7	Abate Apizza & Seafood	Italian, Pizza	Casual	$30
4.4	Cody's Diner	American	Casual	$15
NR	Farmer's Market	Groceries, Baked goods	Market	
NR	Libby's Italian Pastry Shop	Baked goods	Counter	

By special feature

Ranked by food rating. Establishments that don't serve full meals (e.g. cafés, bakeries, grocery stores) appear as "NR" at the bottom of the list.

Breakfast

		Cuisine	Location	Type	Price
9.0	Heirloom	New American	Upper Chapel Area	Upmarket	$85
8.6	Mother's	Caribbean	Medical Area	Take-out	$15
8.3	Atticus	Sandwiches	Upper Chapel Area	Café	$10
8.3	Caribbean Connection	Caribbean	Whalley	Take-out	$10
8.3	La Cocinita	Mexican	Upper Chapel Area	Counter	$15
8.2	Lena's	Sandwiches	Westville	Casual	$15
8.1	Book Trader Café	Sandwiches	Upper Chapel Area	Counter	$10
8.1	Bella's Café	American	Westville	Casual	$25
7.7	Stony Creek Market	Pizza, Sandwiches	Branford	Counter	$15
7.5	The Pantry	American	East Rock	Casual	$15
7.5	Café George by Paula	Sandwiches	Chapel District	Counter	$10
7.4	Whitfield's	New American	Guilford	Upmarket	$55
7.4	Judies European Bakery	Baked goods	Audubon District	Counter	$10
7.3	Zoi's on Orange	Sandwiches	Audubon District	Counter	$10
7.2	Vito's Deli	American, Italian	Ninth Square	Counter	$10
7.1	La Cuisine	Baked goods	Branford	Counter	$15
7.0	Uncle Willie's BBQ	Barbecue, Southern	West Haven	Casual	$20
6.7	Wall Street Pizza	Pizza, American	South Town Green	Counter	$10
6.6	Copper Kitchen	American	Chapel District	Casual	$15
6.6	Roly-Poly	Sandwiches	Multiple locations	Counter	$10
6.4	Orangeside Luncheonette	American	South Town Green	Counter	$10
6.0	Edge of the Woods	American	Whalley	Take-out	$15
5.8	Athenian Diner	American, Greek	Multiple locations	Casual	$25
5.7	Clark's Dairy	American	Audubon District	Casual	$15
5.6	The Educated Burgher	American, Burgers	Broadway District	Counter	$15
5.6	McDonald's	American, Burgers	Multiple locations	Counter	$10
5.3	Alpine Restaurant	Sandwiches	South Town Green	Counter	$10
5.2	John Davenport's	American	Chapel District	Upmarket	$65
5.1	Brown Stone House	American	Hamden	Casual	$15
5.0	Parthenon Diner	American, Greek	Branford	Casual	$25
5.0	Chap's Grille	American	Upper Chapel Area	Counter	$15
4.9	Café Java	Sandwiches	South Town Green	Counter	$10
4.9	IKEA Restaurant	Swedish	Long Wharf	Counter	$5
4.7	Gourmet Heaven	American, Chinese	Multiple locations	Take-out	$10
4.6	A One Pizza Restaurant	Pizza, American	Broadway District	Counter	$10
4.4	Cody's Diner	American	Wooster Square	Casual	$15
4.3	Breakaway Deli	Sandwiches	Audubon District	Counter	$10
4.1	Claire's Corner Copia	American	Chapel District	Casual	$20
4.0	Corner Deli	Sandwiches	South Town Green	Counter	$10
4.0	Bruegger's Bagel Bakery	Sandwiches	Multiple locations	Counter	$10
3.9	Burger King	American, Burgers	Multiple locations	Counter	$10
3.7	Subway	Sandwiches	Multiple locations	Counter	$10
2.9	Patricia's Restaurant	American	Broadway District	Casual	$10
2.5	Au Bon Pain	Sandwiches	Broadway District	Counter	$10
2.1	Dunkin' Donuts	Baked goods	Multiple locations	Counter	$10
NR	Blue State Coffee	Baked goods	South Town Green	Café	
NR	Bru Café	Baked goods	South Town Green	Café	
NR	Chestnut Fine Foods	Baked goods	East Rock	Market	
NR	Four and Twenty Blackbirds	Baked goods	Guilford	Counter	

Breakfast *continued*

NR	JoJo's	Baked goods	Upper Chapel Area	Café	
NR	Koffee on Audubon	Baked goods	Audubon District	Café	
NR	Lulu's	Baked goods	East Rock	Café	
NR	Marjolaine	Baked goods	East Rock	Counter	
NR	Nica's Market	Groceries, Italian	East Rock	Market	
NR	The Publick Cup	Sandwiches	Broadway District	Café	
NR	Romeo & Cesare's	Groceries, Italian	East Rock	Market	
NR	Starbucks	Baked goods	Multiple locations	Café	
NR	Willoughby's	Baked goods	Multiple locations	Café	
NR	Woodland Coffee & Tea	Sandwiches	Ninth Square	Café	

Brunch

9.0	Heirloom	New American	Upper Chapel Area	Upmarket	$85
8.7	China Great Wall	Chinese	Audubon District	Casual	$15
8.4	Thali	Indian	Ninth Square	Upmarket	$50
8.3	The Beach House	Seafood	Milford	Upmarket	$60
8.2	Lena's	Sandwiches	Westville	Casual	$15
8.1	Bella's Café	American	Westville	Casual	$25
8.1	The Stone House	Seafood, American	Guilford	Upmarket	$50
8.0	Zaroka	Indian	Upper Chapel Area	Upmarket	$40
7.6	Tandoor	Indian	Upper Chapel Area	Casual	$25
7.5	The Pantry	American	East Rock	Casual	$15
7.4	Whitfield's	New American	Guilford	Upmarket	$55
7.0	Sage American Bar & Grill	American	The Hill	Upmarket	$55
6.9	Richter's	American	Chapel District	Bar	$15
6.8	Rainbow Gardens Inn	New American	Milford	Upmarket	$45
6.5	Café Nine	American	Ninth Square	Bar	$15
6.5	Baja's	Mexican	Orange	Casual	$25
6.4	The Playwright	Irish, American	Multiple locations	Bar	$30
6.3	Katz's Restaurant	American	Multiple locations	Casual	$20
6.1	Humphrey's East	American, Burgers	East Rock	Bar	$20
6.1	Donovan's Reef	American	Branford	Casual	$35
6.0	The Tymes	American, Seafood	Hamden	Upmarket	$50
6.0	168 York St. Café	American	Upper Chapel Area	Casual	$20
5.9	Scoozzi	Italian	Upper Chapel Area	Upmarket	$60
5.8	Anna Liffey's	Irish, American	Audubon District	Bar	$25
5.8	Skappo	Italian	Ninth Square	Upmarket	$40
5.2	John Davenport's	American	Chapel District	Upmarket	$65
4.2	Landsdowne Bar & Grille	American	Chapel District	Bar	$30
2.2	Thai Pan Asian	Thai, Pan-Asian	Upper Chapel Area	Casual	$25
NR	Chestnut Fine Foods	Baked goods	East Rock	Market	

BYO

9.0	Swagat	Indian	West Haven	Casual	$15
8.4	The Place	Seafood	Guilford	Casual	$25
8.3	Machu Picchu	Peruvian	Fair Haven	Casual	$25
8.1	Guadalupe La Poblanita	Mexican	Fair Haven	Casual	$15
7.7	Stony Creek Market	Pizza, Sandwiches	Branford	Counter	$15
7.0	Uncle Willie's BBQ	Barbecue, Southern	West Haven	Casual	$20
6.7	Mamoun's	Middle Eastern	Upper Chapel Area	Casual	$10
6.7	Mediterranea	Middle Eastern	South Town Green	Counter	$10
6.5	Brick Oven Pizza	Pizza	Upper Chapel Area	Counter	$10
5.7	Nini's Bistro	New American	Ninth Square	Upmarket	$45
5.6	House of Chao	Chinese	Westville	Casual	$15
4.3	The Whole Enchilada	Mexican	Audubon District	Counter	$10
4.1	Marco Polo Pizza	Pizza, Italian	Ninth Square	Counter	$20

Date-friendly

9.6	Le Petit Café	French	Branford	Upmarket	$65
9.4	Caseus	New American	East Rock	Casual	$40
9.3	Ibiza	Spanish	Chapel District	Upmarket	$80

Date-friendly *continued*

9.1	Union League Café	French	Chapel District	Upmarket	$75
9.1	116 Crown	New American	Ninth Square	Upmarket	$35
9.0	Heirloom	New American	Upper Chapel Area	Upmarket	$85
9.0	Swagat	Indian	West Haven	Casual	$15
9.0	Thali Too	Indian	Broadway District	Casual	$35
8.9	Barcelona	Spanish	Chapel District	Upmarket	$65
8.7	Prime 16	American, Burgers	Chapel District	Casual	$25
8.5	Carmen Anthony	Steakhouse	Audubon District	Upmarket	$75
8.4	The Place	Seafood	Guilford	Casual	$25
8.4	Thali	Indian	Ninth Square	Upmarket	$50
8.3	Atticus	Sandwiches	Upper Chapel Area	Café	$10
8.3	The Beach House	Seafood	Milford	Upmarket	$60
8.2	L'Orcio	Italian	East Rock	Upmarket	$45
8.1	Book Trader Café	Sandwiches	Upper Chapel Area	Counter	$10
8.1	Bella's Café	American	Westville	Casual	$25
8.0	Lenny's Indian Head Inn	Seafood, American	Branford	Casual	$30
8.0	Zaroka	Indian	Upper Chapel Area	Upmarket	$40
7.9	Coromandel	Indian	Orange	Upmarket	$40
7.8	Bistro Basque	Spanish, French	Milford	Upmarket	$60
7.7	Stony Creek Market	Pizza, Sandwiches	Branford	Counter	$15
7.7	Gerónimo	Southwestern	Chapel District	Upmarket	$50
7.7	Istanbul Café	Turkish	Chapel District	Upmarket	$45
7.7	Lalibela	Ethiopian	Chapel District	Casual	$25
7.5	Zinc	New American	Chapel District	Upmarket	$70
7.4	Bespoke/Sabor Latino	Nuevo Latino	Chapel District	Upmarket	$80
7.4	Billy's Pasta Così	Italian	Branford	Upmarket	$45
7.4	Taste	New American	North Haven	Upmarket	$45
7.4	Jeffrey's	New American	Milford	Upmarket	$45
7.4	Whitfield's	New American	Guilford	Upmarket	$55
7.3	Miya's	Japanese	Upper Chapel Area	Upmarket	$45
7.2	Luce	Italian	Hamden	Upmarket	$55
7.2	Campania	Italian	Branford	Upmarket	$45
7.1	Soul de Cuba	Cuban	Chapel District	Upmarket	$30
7.1	Il' Forno	Italian	Milford	Upmarket	$50
7.1	Foe	New American	Branford	Upmarket	$50
7.1	Tre Scalini	Italian	Wooster Square	Upmarket	$45
7.0	Thai Taste	Thai	Upper Chapel Area	Casual	$35
6.9	Richter's	American	Chapel District	Bar	$15
6.9	Caffé Bravo	Italian	East Rock	Casual	$35
6.8	Bentara	Malaysian	Ninth Square	Upmarket	$50
6.8	Anchor	American	Chapel District	Bar	$15
6.8	Rainbow Gardens Inn	New American	Milford	Upmarket	$45
6.8	Rudy's Restaurant	American	Broadway District	Bar	$10
6.8	Su Casa	Mexican	Branford	Casual	$30
6.8	Chick's	Seafood	West Haven	Counter	$15
6.8	Kumo	Japanese	Multiple locations	Upmarket	$40
6.7	Martin's	Seafood, American	Fair Haven	Upmarket	$50
6.7	Dolci	New American	East Rock	Upmarket	$45
6.7	Archie Moore's	American, Burgers	Multiple locations	Bar	$20
6.6	Jalapeño Heaven	Mexican	Branford	Casual	$30
6.5	Café Nine	American	Ninth Square	Bar	$15
6.5	Nikkita	New American	Audubon District	Upmarket	$45
6.2	The Owl Shop	Sandwiches	Chapel District	Bar	$10
6.1	Pacífico	Nuevo Latino	Chapel District	Upmarket	$50
6.0	The Tymes	American, Seafood	Hamden	Upmarket	$50
5.9	Scoozzi	Italian	Upper Chapel Area	Upmarket	$60
5.9	The Blue Pearl	New American	South Town Green	Upmarket	$45
5.9	Central Steakhouse	Steakhouse	Ninth Square	Upmarket	$75
5.8	Anna Liffey's	Irish, American	Audubon District	Bar	$25
5.8	Skappo	Italian	Ninth Square	Upmarket	$40
5.8	Tony & Lucille's	Italian	Wooster Square	Casual	$35
5.7	Nini's Bistro	New American	Ninth Square	Upmarket	$45

Date-friendly *continued*

5.6	SBC	American	Multiple locations	Casual	$30
5.2	John Davenport's	American	Chapel District	Upmarket	$65
4.7	C.O. Jones	Mexican	East Rock	Bar	$20
3.8	Downtown @ the Taft	New American	Chapel District	Upmarket	$50
NR	Chow Wine Bar	Pan-Asian	Chapel District	Upmarket	

Delivery

9.0	Szechuan Delight	Chinese	Hamden	Casual	$25
8.7	Iron Chef	Taiwanese, Chinese	West Haven	Counter	$15
8.5	Gastronomique	French, Burgers	Chapel District	Take-out	$25
8.3	Machu Picchu	Peruvian	Fair Haven	Casual	$25
8.2	Star of India	Indian	Orange	Casual	$10
8.1	Dayton Street Apizza	Pizza	Westville	Counter	$15
7.8	Sahara	Middle Eastern	Chapel District	Counter	$10
7.8	Royal Palace	Chinese	Ninth Square	Upmarket	$30
7.6	Tandoor	Indian	Upper Chapel Area	Casual	$25
7.4	Judies European Bakery	Baked goods	Audubon District	Counter	$10
7.2	Elaine's Healthy Choice	American	Whalley	Counter	$10
7.1	India Palace	Indian	Upper Chapel Area	Casual	$25
7.0	Royal India	Indian	Broadway District	Casual	$25
6.8	Southern Hospitality	Southern, Barbecue	Whalley	Counter	$15
6.7	Mediterranea	Middle Eastern	South Town Green	Counter	$10
6.7	Alpha Delta Pizza	Pizza, Sandwiches	Broadway District	Take-out	$10
6.6	Roly-Poly	Sandwiches	Multiple locations	Counter	$10
6.5	Brick Oven Pizza	Pizza	Upper Chapel Area	Counter	$10
6.4	Est Est Est	Pizza, Italian	Upper Chapel Area	Counter	$10
6.4	S'Wings	American	Chapel District	Casual	$15
6.3	Pad Thai	Thai	Upper Chapel Area	Casual	$25
6.1	Amato's	Pizza, Italian	East Rock	Casual	$25
6.0	Fresh Taco	Mexican	South Town Green	Counter	$10
5.9	Sitar	Indian	Audubon District	Casual	$35
5.9	Bella Haven Pizza	Pizza, Italian	Chapel District	Casual	$15
5.7	Ahimsa	New American	Upper Chapel Area	Upmarket	$55
5.7	Bertucci's	Italian, Pizza	Orange	Casual	$35
5.5	Aunt Chilada's	Mexican	Hamden	Casual	$30
5.0	Chap's Grille	American	Upper Chapel Area	Counter	$15
4.9	Indochine Pavilion	Thai	Upper Chapel Area	Casual	$25
4.8	Aladdin Crown Pizza	Middle Eastern	Chapel District	Take-out	$15
4.7	Abate Apizza & Seafood	Italian, Pizza	Wooster Square	Casual	$30
4.1	Marco Polo Pizza	Pizza, Italian	Ninth Square	Counter	$20
4.1	Hunan Café	Chinese	Upper Chapel Area	Counter	$10
4.0	Corner Deli	Sandwiches	South Town Green	Counter	$10
3.4	Main Garden	Chinese	Broadway District	Counter	$10
3.4	China King	Chinese	Chapel District	Take-out	$10
2.2	Thai Pan Asian	Thai, Pan-Asian	Upper Chapel Area	Casual	$25
NR	Bon Appétit	Groceries	Hamden	Market	
NR	The Cupcake Truck	Baked goods	Multiple locations	Take-out	
NR	Star Fish Market	Groceries, Seafood	Guilford	Market	

Good wine list

9.6	Le Petit Café	French	Branford	Upmarket	$65
9.4	Caseus	New American	East Rock	Casual	$40
9.3	Ibiza	Spanish	Chapel District	Upmarket	$80
9.1	Union League Café	French	Chapel District	Upmarket	$75
9.1	116 Crown	New American	Ninth Square	Upmarket	$35
9.0	Heirloom	New American	Upper Chapel Area	Upmarket	$85
8.9	Barcelona	Spanish	Chapel District	Upmarket	$65
8.5	Carmen Anthony	Steakhouse	Audubon District	Upmarket	$75
8.3	The Beach House	Seafood	Milford	Upmarket	$60
8.2	L'Orcio	Italian	East Rock	Upmarket	$45
7.9	Coromandel	Indian	Orange	Upmarket	$40

Good wine list *continued*

7.7	Istanbul Café	Turkish	Chapel District	Upmarket	$45
7.5	Zinc	New American	Chapel District	Upmarket	$70
7.4	Billy's Pasta Così	Italian	Branford	Upmarket	$45
7.4	Taste	New American	North Haven	Upmarket	$45
7.2	Luce	Italian	Hamden	Upmarket	$55
7.1	Tre Scalini	Italian	Wooster Square	Upmarket	$45
7.0	Sage American Bar & Grill	American	The Hill	Upmarket	$55
6.8	Bentara	Malaysian	Ninth Square	Upmarket	$50
6.7	Martin's	Seafood, American	Fair Haven	Upmarket	$50
6.6	Basta Trattoria	Italian	Chapel District	Upmarket	$60
6.5	Café Goodfellas	Italian	East Rock	Upmarket	$55
6.2	Assaggio	New American	Branford	Upmarket	$45
5.9	Scoozzi	Italian	Upper Chapel Area	Upmarket	$60
5.9	Central Steakhouse	Steakhouse	Ninth Square	Upmarket	$75
5.8	Skappo	Italian	Ninth Square	Upmarket	$40
NR	BevMax	Wine store	Multiple locations	Market	
NR	Mt. Carmel Wines & Spirits	Wine store	Hamden	Market	
NR	Trader Joe's	Groceries	Orange	Market	
NR	The Wine Thief	Wine store	Multiple locations	Market	

Kid-friendly

9.1	Frank Pepe's	Pizza	Multiple locations	Casual	$20
9.1	Sally's Apizza	Pizza	Wooster Square	Casual	$20
9.0	Modern Apizza	Pizza	East Rock	Casual	$20
9.0	Swagat	Indian	West Haven	Casual	$15
8.8	Saray	Turkish	West Haven	Casual	$30
8.7	Turkish Kabab House	Turkish	West Haven	Casual	$30
8.7	Mezcal	Mexican	East Rock	Casual	$25
8.6	Glen's Bar-B-Q	Caribbean	The Hill	Take-out	$10
8.4	The Place	Seafood	Guilford	Casual	$25
8.4	Juna's Northern Style BBQ	Barbecue	North Haven	Take-out	$10
8.4	Zuppardi's	Pizza	West Haven	Casual	$25
8.3	Atticus	Sandwiches	Upper Chapel Area	Café	$10
8.3	Machu Picchu	Peruvian	Fair Haven	Casual	$25
8.2	Lena's	Sandwiches	Westville	Casual	$15
8.2	L'Orcio	Italian	East Rock	Upmarket	$45
8.2	The Blue Cottage	Seafood	Branford	Casual	$30
8.2	Star of India	Indian	Orange	Casual	$10
8.1	Book Trader Café	Sandwiches	Upper Chapel Area	Counter	$10
8.1	Bella's Café	American	Westville	Casual	$25
8.1	Roseland Apizza	Pizza	Derby	Casual	$35
8.1	Dayton Street Apizza	Pizza	Westville	Counter	$15
8.1	Guadalupe La Poblanita	Mexican	Fair Haven	Casual	$15
8.0	Lenny's Indian Head Inn	Seafood, American	Branford	Casual	$30
7.9	Five Guys	Burgers	Whalley	Counter	$15
7.8	Royal Palace	Chinese	Ninth Square	Upmarket	$30
7.7	Stony Creek Market	Pizza, Sandwiches	Branford	Counter	$15
7.7	Glenwood Drive-In	American, Burgers	Hamden	Counter	$10
7.7	Adriana's	Italian	Fair Haven	Upmarket	$35
7.6	Tandoor	Indian	Upper Chapel Area	Casual	$25
7.5	Café George by Paula	Sandwiches	Chapel District	Counter	$10
7.4	Tijuana Taco Company	Mexican	Multiple locations	Take-out	$5
7.4	Judies European Bakery	Baked goods	Audubon District	Counter	$10
7.3	Zoi's on Orange	Sandwiches	Audubon District	Counter	$10
7.3	Som Siam	Thai	Guilford	Casual	$30
7.3	Seoul Yokocho	Korean	Upper Chapel Area	Upmarket	$40
7.1	La Cuisine	Baked goods	Branford	Counter	$15
7.1	India Palace	Indian	Upper Chapel Area	Casual	$25
7.0	Gabriele's	Italian	Orange	Casual	$35
7.0	Uncle Willie's BBQ	Barbecue, Southern	West Haven	Casual	$20
6.9	Leon's	Italian	Long Wharf	Upmarket	$45
6.9	Chuck's Steak House	Steakhouse	Multiple locations	Casual	$30

Kid-friendly *continued*

6.8	Su Casa	Mexican	Branford	Casual	$30
6.8	Chick's	Seafood	West Haven	Counter	$15
6.8	Kumo	Japanese	Multiple locations	Upmarket	$40
6.7	Martin's	Seafood, American	Fair Haven	Upmarket	$50
6.6	Jalapeño Heaven	Mexican	Branford	Casual	$30
6.6	Roly-Poly	Sandwiches	Multiple locations	Counter	$10
6.4	The Rib House	Barbecue, Southern	East Haven	Casual	$30
6.3	Katz's Restaurant	American	Multiple locations	Casual	$20
6.1	Amato's	Pizza, Italian	East Rock	Casual	$25
6.1	Humphrey's East	American, Burgers	East Rock	Bar	$20
6.1	Buffalo Wild Wings	American	Multiple locations	Casual	$25
6.1	China Pavilion	Chinese	Orange	Upmarket	$30
6.0	Jimmies of Savin Rock	Seafood, American	West Haven	Upmarket	$40
5.9	Sitar	Indian	Audubon District	Casual	$35
5.8	Tony & Lucille's	Italian	Wooster Square	Casual	$35
5.8	Athenian Diner	American, Greek	Multiple locations	Casual	$25
5.7	Clark's Dairy	American	Audubon District	Casual	$15
5.7	Bertucci's	Italian, Pizza	Orange	Casual	$35
5.6	McDonald's	American, Burgers	Multiple locations	Counter	$10
5.5	Aunt Chilada's	Mexican	Hamden	Casual	$30
5.5	Yorkside Pizza	Pizza, American	Broadway District	Casual	$20
5.3	USS Chowder Pot III	Seafood	Branford	Casual	$40
5.1	Brown Stone House	American	Hamden	Casual	$15
5.0	Parthenon Diner	American, Greek	Branford	Casual	$25
5.0	Chap's Grille	American	Upper Chapel Area	Counter	$15
4.7	Abate Apizza & Seafood	Italian, Pizza	Wooster Square	Casual	$30
4.1	Claire's Corner Copia	American	Chapel District	Casual	$20
4.1	Marco Polo Pizza	Pizza, Italian	Ninth Square	Counter	$20
4.0	Bruegger's Bagel Bakery	Sandwiches	Multiple locations	Counter	$10
3.8	Brazi's Italian Restaurant	Italian, Pizza	Long Wharf	Casual	$30
2.5	Au Bon Pain	Sandwiches	Broadway District	Counter	$10
2.1	Dunkin' Donuts	Baked goods	Multiple locations	Counter	$10
NR	Ashley's Ice Cream	Ice cream	Multiple locations	Counter	
NR	Bishop's Orchards	Groceries	Guilford	Market	
NR	Cold Stone Creamery	Ice cream	Multiple locations	Take-out	
NR	The Cupcake Truck	Baked goods	Multiple locations	Take-out	
NR	Farmer's Market	Groceries	Multiple locations	Market	
NR	Forte's Gourmet Market	Groceries	Guilford	Market	
NR	Four and Twenty Blackbirds	Baked goods	Guilford	Counter	
NR	Libby's Italian Pastry Shop	Baked goods	Multiple locations	Counter	
NR	Liberry	Ice cream	Chapel District	Counter	
NR	Lucibello's Pastry	Baked goods	Fair Haven	Take-out	
NR	Marjolaine	Baked goods	East Rock	Counter	
NR	Medical Area Food Carts		Medical Area	Take-out	
NR	Take the Cake	Baked goods	Guilford	Take-out	
NR	Wentworth's Ice Cream	Ice cream	Hamden	Counter	

Live music *of any kind, from jazz piano to rock, even occasionally*

8.3	The Beach House	Seafood	Milford	Upmarket	$60
8.2	The Blue Cottage	Seafood	Branford	Casual	$30
8.1	Bella's Café	American	Westville	Casual	$25
8.1	The Stone House	Seafood, American	Guilford	Upmarket	$50
7.4	Jeffrey's	New American	Milford	Upmarket	$45
7.3	Temple Grill	American	Chapel District	Casual	$40
7.2	Anastasio's	Italian	Wooster Square	Casual	$45
7.0	Sage American Bar & Grill	American	The Hill	Upmarket	$55
7.0	Eli's	American, Italian	Multiple locations	Casual	$45
6.9	Leon's	Italian	Long Wharf	Upmarket	$45
6.8	Rudy's Restaurant	American	Broadway District	Bar	$10
6.7	Dolci	New American	East Rock	Upmarket	$45
6.5	Café Nine	American	Ninth Square	Bar	$15
6.4	The Playwright	Irish, American	Multiple locations	Bar	$30

Live music *continued*

6.1	Humphrey's East	American, Burgers	East Rock	Bar	$20
6.1	Donovan's Reef	American	Branford	Casual	$35
6.0	The Tymes	American, Seafood	Hamden	Upmarket	$50
5.9	Scoozzi	Italian	Upper Chapel Area	Upmarket	$60
5.8	Anna Liffey's	Irish, American	Audubon District	Bar	$25
5.7	Ahimsa	New American	Upper Chapel Area	Upmarket	$55
5.6	Black Bear Saloon	American	Multiple locations	Bar	$30
5.6	SBC	American	Multiple locations	Casual	$30
5.3	USS Chowder Pot III	Seafood	Branford	Casual	$40
5.1	Chip's II	American, Burgers	Guilford	Bar	$20
4.2	Landsdowne Bar & Grille	American	Chapel District	Bar	$30
3.8	Downtown @ the Taft	New American	Chapel District	Upmarket	$50
2.6	Marius	American	Chapel District	Upmarket	$55
NR	Chow Wine Bar	Pan-Asian	Chapel District	Upmarket	

Outdoor dining *of any kind, from sidewalk tables to a big backyard patio*

9.4	Caseus	New American	East Rock	Casual	$40
9.0	Thali Too	Indian	Broadway District	Casual	$35
8.6	Glen's Bar-B-Q	Caribbean	The Hill	Take-out	$10
8.4	The Place	Seafood	Guilford	Casual	$25
8.4	Juna's Northern Style BBQ	Barbecue	North Haven	Take-out	$10
8.2	L'Orcio	Italian	East Rock	Upmarket	$45
8.2	The Blue Cottage	Seafood	Branford	Casual	$30
8.1	Book Trader Café	Sandwiches	Upper Chapel Area	Counter	$10
8.0	Lenny's Indian Head Inn	Seafood, American	Branford	Casual	$30
7.8	Bistro Basque	Spanish, French	Milford	Upmarket	$60
7.7	Stony Creek Market	Pizza, Sandwiches	Branford	Counter	$15
7.7	Gerónimo	Southwestern	Chapel District	Upmarket	$50
7.7	Glenwood Drive-In	American, Burgers	Hamden	Counter	$10
7.4	Tijuana Taco Company	Mexican	Multiple locations	Take-out	$5
7.4	Jeffrey's	New American	Milford	Upmarket	$45
7.4	Whitfield's	New American	Guilford	Upmarket	$55
7.3	Temple Grill	American	Chapel District	Casual	$40
7.3	Citrus	New American	Milford	Upmarket	$55
7.2	Luce	Italian	Hamden	Upmarket	$55
7.2	Anastasio's	Italian	Wooster Square	Casual	$45
7.2	Campania	Italian	Branford	Upmarket	$45
7.1	Miso	Japanese	Ninth Square	Upmarket	$40
7.0	Sage American Bar & Grill	American	The Hill	Upmarket	$55
6.9	Leon's	Italian	Long Wharf	Upmarket	$45
6.9	Caffé Bravo	Italian	East Rock	Casual	$35
6.8	Jasmine Thai Cart	Thai	Audubon District	Take-out	$5
6.8	Rudy's Restaurant	American	Broadway District	Bar	$10
6.8	Consiglio's	Italian	Wooster Square	Upmarket	$50
6.8	Su Casa	Mexican	Branford	Casual	$30
6.8	Chick's	Seafood	West Haven	Counter	$15
6.7	Martin's	Seafood, American	Fair Haven	Upmarket	$50
6.6	Basta Trattoria	Italian	Chapel District	Upmarket	$60
6.6	Jalapeño Heaven	Mexican	Branford	Casual	$30
6.6	Thai Awesome Food Cart	Thai	Multiple locations	Take-out	$5
6.5	Café Goodfellas	Italian	East Rock	Upmarket	$55
6.5	J.P. Dempsey's	American, Burgers	East Rock	Bar	$30
6.5	Brick Oven Pizza	Pizza	Upper Chapel Area	Counter	$10
6.4	The Playwright	Irish, American	Multiple locations	Bar	$30
6.3	Pad Thai	Thai	Upper Chapel Area	Casual	$25
6.2	Assaggio	New American	Branford	Upmarket	$45
6.1	Amato's	Pizza, Italian	East Rock	Casual	$25
6.1	Humphrey's East	American, Burgers	East Rock	Bar	$20
6.1	Buffalo Wild Wings	American	Multiple locations	Casual	$25
6.0	Delaney's Grille	American	Westville	Casual	$25
6.0	The Tymes	American, Seafood	Hamden	Upmarket	$50
6.0	168 York St. Café	American	Upper Chapel Area	Casual	$20

Outdoor dining *continued*

5.9	Scoozzi	Italian	Upper Chapel Area	Upmarket	$60
5.9	The Blue Pearl	New American	South Town Green	Upmarket	$45
5.8	Tony & Lucille's	Italian	Wooster Square	Casual	$35
5.7	Nini's Bistro	New American	Ninth Square	Upmarket	$45
5.6	SBC	American	Multiple locations	Casual	$30
5.6	McDonald's	American, Burgers	Multiple locations	Counter	$10
5.5	Aunt Chilada's	Mexican	Hamden	Casual	$30
5.5	Yorkside Pizza	Pizza, American	Broadway District	Casual	$20
5.3	USS Chowder Pot III	Seafood	Branford	Casual	$40
5.0	Chap's Grille	American	Upper Chapel Area	Counter	$15
4.7	Kudeta	Pan-Asian	Chapel District	Upmarket	$50
4.7	C.O. Jones	Mexican	East Rock	Bar	$20
4.7	York Street Noodle House	Pan-Asian, Chinese	Upper Chapel Area	Casual	$10
4.7	Moe's Southwest Grill	Mexican, American	Multiple locations	Counter	$10
3.5	Sullivan's	American	Upper Chapel Area	Casual	$20
2.6	Marius	American	Chapel District	Upmarket	$55
2.5	Au Bon Pain	Sandwiches	Broadway District	Counter	$10
2.2	Thai Pan Asian	Thai, Pan-Asian	Upper Chapel Area	Casual	$25
NR	Bishop's Orchards	Groceries	Guilford	Market	
NR	Forte's Gourmet Market	Groceries	Guilford	Market	
NR	JoJo's	Baked goods	Upper Chapel Area	Café	
NR	Lulu's	Baked goods	East Rock	Café	
NR	Nica's Market	Groceries, Italian	East Rock	Market	
NR	Romeo & Cesare's	Groceries, Italian	East Rock	Market	
NR	Wentworth's Ice Cream	Ice cream	Hamden	Counter	
NR	Willoughby's	Baked goods	Multiple locations	Café	

Wi-Fi

8.5	Carmen Anthony	Steakhouse	Audubon District	Upmarket	$75
8.3	Atticus	Sandwiches	Upper Chapel Area	Café	$10
8.2	Lena's	Sandwiches	Westville	Casual	$15
8.1	Book Trader Café	Sandwiches	Upper Chapel Area	Counter	$10
8.0	Soho New Haven	Korean	South Town Green	Casual	$30
7.2	Campania	Italian	Branford	Upmarket	$45
7.0	Eli's	American, Italian	Multiple locations	Casual	$45
6.8	Rudy's Restaurant	American	Broadway District	Bar	$10
6.7	Mamoun's	Middle Eastern	Upper Chapel Area	Casual	$10
6.7	Mediterranea	Middle Eastern	South Town Green	Counter	$10
6.6	Roly-Poly	Sandwiches	Multiple locations	Counter	$10
6.5	Café Nine	American	Ninth Square	Bar	$15
6.2	The Owl Shop	Sandwiches	Chapel District	Bar	$10
6.1	Buffalo Wild Wings	American	Multiple locations	Casual	$25
5.7	Bertucci's	Italian, Pizza	Orange	Casual	$35
5.6	Black Bear Saloon	American	Multiple locations	Bar	$30
4.7	York Street Noodle House	Pan-Asian, Chinese	Upper Chapel Area	Casual	$10
4.7	Moe's Southwest Grill	Mexican, American	Multiple locations	Counter	$10
4.7	Gourmet Heaven	American, Chinese	Multiple locations	Take-out	$10
4.2	Landsdowne Bar & Grille	American	Chapel District	Bar	$30
4.1	Marco Polo Pizza	Pizza, Italian	Ninth Square	Counter	$20
2.5	Au Bon Pain	Sandwiches	Broadway District	Counter	$10
NR	Blue State Coffee	Baked goods	South Town Green	Café	
NR	Bru Café	Baked goods	South Town Green	Café	
NR	JoJo's	Baked goods	Upper Chapel Area	Café	
NR	Koffee on Audubon	Baked goods	Audubon District	Café	
NR	The Publick Cup	Sandwiches	Broadway District	Café	
NR	Willoughby's	Baked goods	Multiple locations	Café	
NR	Woodland Coffee & Tea	Sandwiches	Ninth Square	Café	

Vegetarian-friendly guide

Places to eat that are **unusually strong in vegetarian options.** This doesn't just mean that there are salads or veggie pastas available; it means that vegetarians will really be happy with the selection at these places. Ranked by **food rating** unless otherwise noted. Establishments that don't serve full meals (e.g. cafés, bakeries, grocery stores) appear as "NR" at the bottom of the list.

All vegetarian-friendly establishments

9.4	Caseus	New American	East Rock	Casual	$40
9.1	116 Crown	New American	Ninth Square	Upmarket	$35
9.1	Bar (Brü Room)	Pizza	Chapel District	Bar	$25
9.1	Frank Pepe's	Pizza	Multiple locations	Casual	$20
9.1	Sally's Apizza	Pizza	Wooster Square	Casual	$20
9.0	Modern Apizza	Pizza	East Rock	Casual	$20
9.0	Swagat	Indian	West Haven	Casual	$15
9.0	Thali Too	Indian	Broadway District	Casual	$35
8.7	Prime 16	American, Burgers	Chapel District	Casual	$25
8.7	China Great Wall	Chinese	Audubon District	Casual	$15
8.6	The Terrace	Thai	Hamden	Casual	$35
8.6	Rice Pot	Thai	East Rock	Casual	$30
8.4	Thali	Indian	Ninth Square	Upmarket	$50
8.4	Zuppardi's	Pizza	West Haven	Casual	$25
8.3	Atticus	Sandwiches	Upper Chapel Area	Café	$10
8.2	Lena's	Sandwiches	Westville	Casual	$15
8.2	L'Orcio	Italian	East Rock	Upmarket	$45
8.2	Star of India	Indian	Orange	Casual	$10
8.1	Book Trader Café	Sandwiches	Upper Chapel Area	Counter	$10
8.1	Bella's Café	American	Westville	Casual	$25
8.1	Roseland Apizza	Pizza	Derby	Casual	$35
8.1	Dayton Street Apizza	Pizza	Westville	Counter	$15
8.0	Soho New Haven	Korean	South Town Green	Casual	$30
8.0	Zaroka	Indian	Upper Chapel Area	Upmarket	$40
7.9	Coromandel	Indian	Orange	Upmarket	$40
7.8	Sahara	Middle Eastern	Chapel District	Counter	$10
7.7	Stony Creek Market	Pizza, Sandwiches	Branford	Counter	$15
7.7	Lalibela	Ethiopian	Chapel District	Casual	$25
7.7	Thai Awesome	Thai	Hamden	Casual	$25
7.7	Darbar India	Indian	Branford	Upmarket	$35
7.6	Tandoor	Indian	Upper Chapel Area	Casual	$25
7.5	The Pantry	American	East Rock	Casual	$15
7.5	Café George by Paula	Sandwiches	Chapel District	Counter	$10
7.4	Billy's Pasta Così	Italian	Branford	Upmarket	$45
7.4	Judies European Bakery	Baked goods	Audubon District	Counter	$10
7.3	Miya's	Japanese	Upper Chapel Area	Upmarket	$45
7.3	Temple Grill	American	Chapel District	Casual	$40
7.3	Zoi's on Orange	Sandwiches	Audubon District	Counter	$10
7.2	Anastasio's	Italian	Wooster Square	Casual	$45
7.2	Campania	Italian	Branford	Upmarket	$45
7.2	Elaine's Healthy Choice	American	Whalley	Counter	$10
7.1	La Cuisine	Baked goods	Branford	Counter	$15
7.1	India Palace	Indian	Upper Chapel Area	Casual	$25
7.0	Thai Taste	Thai	Upper Chapel Area	Casual	$35

All vegetarian-friendly establishments *continued*

7.0	Royal India	Indian	Broadway District	Casual	$25
7.0	Eli's	American, Italian	Multiple locations	Casual	$45
7.0	Gabriele's	Italian	Orange	Casual	$35
6.9	Caffé Bravo	Italian	East Rock	Casual	$35
6.8	Bentara	Malaysian	Ninth Square	Upmarket	$50
6.8	Rainbow Gardens Inn	New American	Milford	Upmarket	$45
6.8	Jasmine Thai Cart	Thai	Audubon District	Take-out	$5
6.7	Dolci	New American	East Rock	Upmarket	$45
6.7	Mamoun's	Middle Eastern	Upper Chapel Area	Casual	$10
6.7	Wall Street Pizza	Pizza, American	South Town Green	Counter	$10
6.7	Mediterranea	Middle Eastern	South Town Green	Counter	$10
6.7	Alpha Delta Pizza	Pizza, Sandwiches	Broadway District	Take-out	$10
6.6	Basta Trattoria	Italian	Chapel District	Upmarket	$60
6.6	Thai Awesome Food Cart	Thai	Multiple locations	Take-out	$5
6.6	Roly-Poly	Sandwiches	Multiple locations	Counter	$10
6.5	Brick Oven Pizza	Pizza	Upper Chapel Area	Counter	$10
6.4	Est Est Est	Pizza, Italian	Upper Chapel Area	Counter	$10
6.2	The Owl Shop	Sandwiches	Chapel District	Bar	$10
6.1	Amato's	Pizza, Italian	East Rock	Casual	$25
6.0	Edge of the Woods	American	Whalley	Take-out	$15
5.9	The Blue Pearl	New American	South Town Green	Upmarket	$45
5.9	Sitar	Indian	Audubon District	Casual	$35
5.9	Bella Haven Pizza	Pizza, Italian	Chapel District	Casual	$15
5.8	Tony & Lucille's	Italian	Wooster Square	Casual	$35
5.7	Ahimsa	New American	Upper Chapel Area	Upmarket	$55
5.7	Bertucci's	Italian, Pizza	Orange	Casual	$35
5.6	Pizza House	Pizza	Upper Chapel Area	Counter	$5
5.5	Yorkside Pizza	Pizza, American	Broadway District	Casual	$20
5.3	Celtica	Irish, Baked goods	Chapel District	Counter	$15
5.2	Pot-au-Pho	Vietnamese	Audubon District	Casual	$15
5.0	Bulldog Burrito	Mexican	Broadway District	Counter	$5
5.0	Chap's Grille	American	Upper Chapel Area	Counter	$15
4.9	Café Java	Sandwiches	South Town Green	Counter	$10
4.9	Indochine Pavilion	Thai	Upper Chapel Area	Casual	$25
4.8	Aladdin Crown Pizza	Middle Eastern	Chapel District	Take-out	$15
4.7	C.O. Jones	Mexican	East Rock	Bar	$20
4.7	York Street Noodle House	Pan-Asian, Chinese	Upper Chapel Area	Casual	$10
4.7	Abate Apizza & Seafood	Italian, Pizza	Wooster Square	Casual	$30
4.7	Gourmet Heaven	American, Chinese	Multiple locations	Take-out	$10
4.6	A One Pizza Restaurant	Pizza, American	Broadway District	Counter	$10
4.3	The Whole Enchilada	Mexican	Audubon District	Counter	$10
4.1	Claire's Corner Copia	American	Chapel District	Casual	$20
4.1	Marco Polo Pizza	Pizza, Italian	Ninth Square	Counter	$20
4.0	Bruegger's Bagel Bakery	Sandwiches	Multiple locations	Counter	$10
3.8	Brazi's Italian Restaurant	Italian, Pizza	Long Wharf	Casual	$30
3.5	Ivy Noodle	Chinese	Broadway District	Casual	$10
3.2	Town Pizza	Pizza, Italian	Audubon District	Casual	$10
2.2	Thai Pan Asian	Thai, Pan-Asian	Upper Chapel Area	Casual	$25
2.1	Dunkin' Donuts	Baked goods	Multiple locations	Counter	$10
NR	Ashley's Ice Cream	Ice cream	Multiple locations	Counter	
NR	Bishop's Orchards	Groceries	Guilford	Market	
NR	Blue State Coffee	Baked goods	South Town Green	Café	
NR	Bon Appétit	Groceries	Hamden	Market	
NR	Bru Café	Baked goods	South Town Green	Café	
NR	Chestnut Fine Foods	Baked goods	East Rock	Market	
NR	Cold Stone Creamery	Ice cream	Multiple locations	Take-out	
NR	The Cupcake Truck	Baked goods	Multiple locations	Take-out	
NR	Farmer's Market	Groceries	Multiple locations	Market	
NR	Ferraro's Foods	Groceries, Italian	Fair Haven	Market	
NR	Forte's Gourmet Market	Groceries	Guilford	Market	
NR	Four and Twenty Blackbirds	Baked goods	Guilford	Counter	
NR	J Mart	Groceries, Seafood	Ninth Square	Market	

All vegetarian-friendly establishments *continued*

NR	JoJo's	Baked goods	Upper Chapel Area	Café
NR	Koffee on Audubon	Baked goods	Audubon District	Café
NR	Libby's Italian Pastry Shop	Baked goods	Multiple locations	Counter
NR	Liberry	Ice cream	Chapel District	Counter
NR	Liuzzi's Cheese Shop	Groceries, Italian	North Haven	Market
NR	Lucibello's Pastry	Baked goods	Fair Haven	Take-out
NR	Marjolaine	Baked goods	East Rock	Counter
NR	Medical Area Food Carts		Medical Area	Take-out
NR	Nica's Market	Groceries, Italian	East Rock	Market
NR	The Publick Cup	Sandwiches	Broadway District	Café
NR	Romeo & Cesare's	Groceries, Italian	East Rock	Market
NR	Starbucks	Baked goods	Multiple locations	Café
NR	Take the Cake	Baked goods	Guilford	Take-out
NR	Trader Joe's	Groceries	Orange	Market
NR	Wentworth's Ice Cream	Ice cream	Hamden	Counter
NR	Willoughby's	Baked goods	Multiple locations	Café
NR	Woodland Coffee & Tea	Sandwiches	Ninth Square	Café

Vegetarian-friendly with top feel ratings

10	The Owl Shop	Sandwiches	Chapel District	Bar	$10
9.5	Caseus	New American	East Rock	Casual	$40
9.5	Atticus	Sandwiches	Upper Chapel Area	Café	$10
9.5	Stony Creek Market	Pizza, Sandwiches	Branford	Counter	$15
9.0	116 Crown	New American	Ninth Square	Upmarket	$35
9.0	Book Trader Café	Sandwiches	Upper Chapel Area	Counter	$10
9.0	Miya's	Japanese	Upper Chapel Area	Upmarket	$45
9.0	Bentara	Malaysian	Ninth Square	Upmarket	$50
9.0	Tony & Lucille's	Italian	Wooster Square	Casual	$35
8.5	Prime 16	American, Burgers	Chapel District	Casual	$25
8.5	Thali	Indian	Ninth Square	Upmarket	$50
8.5	Lena's	Sandwiches	Westville	Casual	$15
8.5	L'Orcio	Italian	East Rock	Upmarket	$45
8.5	Bella's Café	American	Westville	Casual	$25
8.5	Roseland Apizza	Pizza	Derby	Casual	$35
8.5	Thai Taste	Thai	Upper Chapel Area	Casual	$35
8.5	Rainbow Gardens Inn	New American	Milford	Upmarket	$45
8.5	Claire's Corner Copia	American	Chapel District	Casual	$20
8.0	Coromandel	Indian	Orange	Upmarket	$40
8.0	Lalibela	Ethiopian	Chapel District	Casual	$25
8.0	Billy's Pasta Così	Italian	Branford	Upmarket	$45
8.0	Temple Grill	American	Chapel District	Casual	$40
8.0	La Cuisine	Baked goods	Branford	Counter	$15
8.0	Royal India	Indian	Broadway District	Casual	$25
8.0	Jasmine Thai Cart	Thai	Audubon District	Take-out	$5
8.0	Dolci	New American	East Rock	Upmarket	$45
8.0	Mamoun's	Middle Eastern	Upper Chapel Area	Casual	$10
8.0	Basta Trattoria	Italian	Chapel District	Upmarket	$60
8.0	Thai Awesome Food Cart	Thai	Multiple locations	Take-out	$5
8.0	Amato's	Pizza, Italian	East Rock	Casual	$25
8.0	Edge of the Woods	American	Whalley	Take-out	$15
8.0	The Blue Pearl	New American	South Town Green	Upmarket	$45
7.5	Bar (Brü Room)	Pizza	Chapel District	Bar	$25
7.5	Modern Apizza	Pizza	East Rock	Casual	$20
7.5	The Terrace	Thai	Hamden	Casual	$35
7.5	Soho New Haven	Korean	South Town Green	Casual	$30
7.5	Thai Awesome	Thai	Hamden	Casual	$25
7.5	Tandoor	Indian	Upper Chapel Area	Casual	$25
7.5	The Pantry	American	East Rock	Casual	$15
7.5	Zoi's on Orange	Sandwiches	Audubon District	Counter	$10
7.5	Anastasio's	Italian	Wooster Square	Casual	$45
7.5	Campania	Italian	Branford	Upmarket	$45
7.5	Eli's	American, Italian	Multiple locations	Casual	$45

Vegetarian-friendly with top feel ratings *continued*

7.5	Gabriele's	Italian	Orange	Casual	$35
7.5	Caffé Bravo	Italian	East Rock	Casual	$35
7.5	Café Java	Sandwiches	South Town Green	Counter	$10
7.0	Frank Pepe's	Pizza	Multiple locations	Casual	$20
7.0	Swagat	Indian	West Haven	Casual	$15
7.0	Thali Too	Indian	Broadway District	Casual	$35
7.0	China Great Wall	Chinese	Audubon District	Casual	$15
7.0	Zuppardi's	Pizza	West Haven	Casual	$25
7.0	Dayton Street Apizza	Pizza	Westville	Counter	$15
7.0	Zaroka	Indian	Upper Chapel Area	Upmarket	$40
7.0	Darbar India	Indian	Branford	Upmarket	$35
7.0	Wall Street Pizza	Pizza, American	South Town Green	Counter	$10
7.0	Sitar	Indian	Audubon District	Casual	$35
7.0	Ahimsa	New American	Upper Chapel Area	Upmarket	$55
7.0	Pot-au-Pho	Vietnamese	Audubon District	Casual	$15
7.0	Indochine Pavilion	Thai	Upper Chapel Area	Casual	$25

Vegetarian-friendly and date-friendly

9.4	Caseus	New American	East Rock	Casual	$40
9.1	116 Crown	New American	Ninth Square	Upmarket	$35
9.0	Swagat	Indian	West Haven	Casual	$15
9.0	Thali Too	Indian	Broadway District	Casual	$35
8.7	Prime 16	American, Burgers	Chapel District	Casual	$25
8.4	Thali	Indian	Ninth Square	Upmarket	$50
8.3	Atticus	Sandwiches	Upper Chapel Area	Café	$10
8.2	L'Orcio	Italian	East Rock	Upmarket	$45
8.1	Book Trader Café	Sandwiches	Upper Chapel Area	Counter	$10
8.1	Bella's Café	American	Westville	Casual	$25
8.0	Zaroka	Indian	Upper Chapel Area	Upmarket	$40
7.9	Coromandel	Indian	Orange	Upmarket	$40
7.7	Stony Creek Market	Pizza, Sandwiches	Branford	Counter	$15
7.7	Lalibela	Ethiopian	Chapel District	Casual	$25
7.4	Billy's Pasta Così	Italian	Branford	Upmarket	$45
7.3	Miya's	Japanese	Upper Chapel Area	Upmarket	$45
7.2	Campania	Italian	Branford	Upmarket	$45
7.0	Thai Taste	Thai	Upper Chapel Area	Casual	$35
6.9	Caffé Bravo	Italian	East Rock	Casual	$35
6.8	Bentara	Malaysian	Ninth Square	Upmarket	$50
6.8	Rainbow Gardens Inn	New American	Milford	Upmarket	$45
6.7	Dolci	New American	East Rock	Upmarket	$45
6.2	The Owl Shop	Sandwiches	Chapel District	Bar	$10
5.9	The Blue Pearl	New American	South Town Green	Upmarket	$45
5.8	Tony & Lucille's	Italian	Wooster Square	Casual	$35
4.7	C.O. Jones	Mexican	East Rock	Bar	$20

Vegetarian-friendly and kid-friendly

9.1	Frank Pepe's	Pizza	Multiple locations	Casual	$20
9.1	Sally's Apizza	Pizza	Wooster Square	Casual	$20
9.0	Modern Apizza	Pizza	East Rock	Casual	$20
9.0	Swagat	Indian	West Haven	Casual	$15
8.4	Zuppardi's	Pizza	West Haven	Casual	$25
8.3	Atticus	Sandwiches	Upper Chapel Area	Café	$10
8.2	Lena's	Sandwiches	Westville	Casual	$15
8.2	L'Orcio	Italian	East Rock	Upmarket	$45
8.2	Star of India	Indian	Orange	Casual	$10
8.1	Book Trader Café	Sandwiches	Upper Chapel Area	Counter	$10
8.1	Bella's Café	American	Westville	Casual	$25
8.1	Roseland Apizza	Pizza	Derby	Casual	$35
8.1	Dayton Street Apizza	Pizza	Westville	Counter	$15
7.7	Stony Creek Market	Pizza, Sandwiches	Branford	Counter	$15
7.6	Tandoor	Indian	Upper Chapel Area	Casual	$25

Vegetarian-friendly and kid-friendly *continued*

7.5	Café George by Paula	Sandwiches	Chapel District	Counter	$10
7.4	Judies European Bakery	Baked goods	Audubon District	Counter	$10
7.3	Zoi's on Orange	Sandwiches	Audubon District	Counter	$10
7.1	La Cuisine	Baked goods	Branford	Counter	$15
7.1	India Palace	Indian	Upper Chapel Area	Casual	$25
7.0	Gabriele's	Italian	Orange	Casual	$35
6.6	Roly-Poly	Sandwiches	Multiple locations	Counter	$10
6.1	Amato's	Pizza, Italian	East Rock	Casual	$25
5.9	Sitar	Indian	Audubon District	Casual	$35
5.8	Tony & Lucille's	Italian	Wooster Square	Casual	$35
5.7	Bertucci's	Italian, Pizza	Orange	Casual	$35
5.5	Yorkside Pizza	Pizza, American	Broadway District	Casual	$20
5.0	Chap's Grille	American	Upper Chapel Area	Counter	$15
4.7	Abate Apizza & Seafood	Italian, Pizza	Wooster Square	Casual	$30
4.1	Claire's Corner Copia	American	Chapel District	Casual	$20
4.1	Marco Polo Pizza	Pizza, Italian	Ninth Square	Counter	$20
4.0	Bruegger's Bagel Bakery	Sandwiches	Multiple locations	Counter	$10
3.8	Brazi's Italian Restaurant	Italian, Pizza	Long Wharf	Casual	$30
2.1	Dunkin' Donuts	Baked goods	Multiple locations	Counter	$10
NR	Ashley's Ice Cream	Ice cream	Multiple locations	Counter	
NR	Bishop's Orchards	Groceries	Guilford	Market	
NR	Cold Stone Creamery	Ice cream	Multiple locations	Take-out	
NR	The Cupcake Truck	Baked goods	Multiple locations	Take-out	
NR	Farmer's Market	Groceries	Multiple locations	Market	
NR	Forte's Gourmet Market	Groceries	Guilford	Market	
NR	Four and Twenty Blackbirds	Baked goods	Guilford	Counter	
NR	Libby's Italian Pastry Shop	Baked goods	Multiple locations	Counter	
NR	Liberry	Ice cream	Chapel District	Counter	
NR	Lucibello's Pastry	Baked goods	Fair Haven	Take-out	
NR	Marjolaine	Baked goods	East Rock	Counter	
NR	Medical Area Food Carts		Medical Area	Take-out	
NR	Take the Cake	Baked goods	Guilford	Take-out	
NR	Wentworth's Ice Cream	Ice cream	Hamden	Counter	

Vegetarian-friendly delivery

8.2	Star of India	Indian	Orange	Casual	$10
8.1	Dayton Street Apizza	Pizza	Westville	Counter	$15
7.8	Sahara	Middle Eastern	Chapel District	Counter	$10
7.6	Tandoor	Indian	Upper Chapel Area	Casual	$25
7.4	Judies European Bakery	Baked goods	Audubon District	Counter	$10
7.2	Elaine's Healthy Choice	American	Whalley	Counter	$10
7.1	India Palace	Indian	Upper Chapel Area	Casual	$25
7.0	Royal India	Indian	Broadway District	Casual	$25
6.7	Mediterranea	Middle Eastern	South Town Green	Counter	$10
6.7	Alpha Delta Pizza	Pizza, Sandwiches	Broadway District	Take-out	$10
6.6	Roly-Poly	Sandwiches	Multiple locations	Counter	$10
6.5	Brick Oven Pizza	Pizza	Upper Chapel Area	Counter	$10
6.4	Est Est Est	Pizza, Italian	Upper Chapel Area	Counter	$10
6.1	Amato's	Pizza, Italian	East Rock	Casual	$25
5.9	Sitar	Indian	Audubon District	Casual	$35
5.9	Bella Haven Pizza	Pizza, Italian	Chapel District	Casual	$15
5.7	Ahimsa	New American	Upper Chapel Area	Upmarket	$55
5.7	Bertucci's	Italian, Pizza	Orange	Casual	$35
5.0	Chap's Grille	American	Upper Chapel Area	Counter	$15
4.9	Indochine Pavilion	Thai	Upper Chapel Area	Casual	$25
4.8	Aladdin Crown Pizza	Middle Eastern	Chapel District	Take-out	$15
4.7	Abate Apizza & Seafood	Italian, Pizza	Wooster Square	Casual	$30
4.1	Marco Polo Pizza	Pizza, Italian	Ninth Square	Counter	$20
2.2	Thai Pan Asian	Thai, Pan-Asian	Upper Chapel Area	Casual	$25
NR	Bon Appétit	Groceries	Hamden	Market	
NR	The Cupcake Truck	Baked goods	Multiple locations	Take-out	

What's still open?

This is our late-night guide to New Haven food. These places claim to stay open as follows; still, we recommend calling first, as the hours sometimes aren't honored on slow nights. Establishments that don't serve full meals (e.g. cafés, bakeries, grocery stores) appear as "NR" at the bottom of the list.

Weekday food after 10pm

9.1	116 Crown	New American	Ninth Square	Upmarket	$35
9.1	Bar (Brü Room)	Pizza	Chapel District	Bar	$25
9.0	Modern Apizza	Pizza	East Rock	Casual	$20
8.8	Saray	Turkish	West Haven	Casual	$30
8.7	Prime 16	American, Burgers	Chapel District	Casual	$25
8.7	Turkish Kabab House	Turkish	West Haven	Casual	$30
8.7	Iron Chef	Taiwanese, Chinese	West Haven	Counter	$15
7.8	Sahara	Middle Eastern	Chapel District	Counter	$10
7.7	Gerónimo	Southwestern	Chapel District	Upmarket	$50
7.7	Darbar India	Indian	Branford	Upmarket	$35
7.7	Adriana's	Italian	Fair Haven	Upmarket	$35
7.6	Christopher Martin's	American, Burgers	East Rock	Casual	$25
7.6	Tandoor	Indian	Upper Chapel Area	Casual	$25
7.3	Miya's	Japanese	Upper Chapel Area	Upmarket	$45
7.1	India Palace	Indian	Upper Chapel Area	Casual	$25
7.0	Royal India	Indian	Broadway District	Casual	$25
6.9	Leon's	Italian	Long Wharf	Upmarket	$45
6.8	Anchor	American	Chapel District	Bar	$15
6.8	Rudy's Restaurant	American	Broadway District	Bar	$10
6.8	Kumo	Japanese	Multiple locations	Upmarket	$40
6.7	Martin's	Seafood, American	Fair Haven	Upmarket	$50
6.7	Mamoun's	Middle Eastern	Upper Chapel Area	Casual	$10
6.7	Archie Moore's	American, Burgers	Multiple locations	Bar	$20
6.7	Mediterranea	Middle Eastern	South Town Green	Counter	$10
6.7	Alpha Delta Pizza	Pizza, Sandwiches	Broadway District	Take-out	$10
6.5	Café Nine	American	Ninth Square	Bar	$15
6.5	Nikkita	New American	Audubon District	Upmarket	$45
6.5	J.P. Dempsey's	American, Burgers	East Rock	Bar	$30
6.5	Brick Oven Pizza	Pizza	Upper Chapel Area	Counter	$10
6.4	Est Est Est	Pizza, Italian	Upper Chapel Area	Counter	$10
6.4	S'Wings	American	Chapel District	Casual	$15
6.2	The Owl Shop	Sandwiches	Chapel District	Bar	$10
6.1	Humphrey's East	American, Burgers	East Rock	Bar	$20
6.1	Buffalo Wild Wings	American	Multiple locations	Casual	$25
6.0	Delaney's Grille	American	Westville	Casual	$25
6.0	Fresh Taco	Mexican	South Town Green	Counter	$10
5.8	Skappo	Italian	Ninth Square	Upmarket	$40
5.8	Athenian Diner	American, Greek	Multiple locations	Casual	$25
5.6	Pizza House	Pizza	Upper Chapel Area	Counter	$5
5.6	McDonald's	American, Burgers	Multiple locations	Counter	$10
5.5	Aunt Chilada's	Mexican	Hamden	Casual	$30
5.5	Yorkside Pizza	Pizza, American	Broadway District	Casual	$20
5.4	Chili's	American, Mexican	Hamden	Casual	$25
5.1	Chip's II	American, Burgers	Guilford	Bar	$20
5.0	Parthenon Diner	American, Greek	Branford	Casual	$25

Weekday food after 10pm *continued*

4.8	Aladdin Crown Pizza	Middle Eastern	Chapel District	Take-out	$15
4.7	Kudeta	Pan-Asian	Chapel District	Upmarket	$50
4.7	C.O. Jones	Mexican	East Rock	Bar	$20
4.7	Gourmet Heaven	American, Chinese	Multiple locations	Take-out	$10
4.6	A One Pizza Restaurant	Pizza, American	Broadway District	Counter	$10
4.5	KFC	Southern	Multiple locations	Counter	$10
4.4	Cody's Diner	American	Wooster Square	Casual	$15
4.4	El Amigo Felix	Mexican	Broadway District	Bar	$25
4.1	Hunan Café	Chinese	Upper Chapel Area	Counter	$10
3.9	Burger King	American, Burgers	Multiple locations	Counter	$10
3.7	Subway	Sandwiches	Multiple locations	Counter	$10
3.5	Sullivan's	American	Upper Chapel Area	Casual	$20
3.5	Ivy Noodle	Chinese	Broadway District	Casual	$10
3.4	Main Garden	Chinese	Broadway District	Counter	$10
3.4	China King	Chinese	Chapel District	Take-out	$10
2.8	Applebee's	American	Multiple locations	Casual	$25
2.6	Marius	American	Chapel District	Upmarket	$55
2.5	Au Bon Pain	Sandwiches	Broadway District	Counter	$10
2.1	Dunkin' Donuts	Baked goods	Multiple locations	Counter	$10
2.0	Viva Zapata	Mexican	Upper Chapel Area	Bar	$25
2.0	TGI Friday's	American	Multiple locations	Casual	$30
NR	Ashley's Ice Cream	Ice cream	Multiple locations	Counter	
NR	The Publick Cup	Sandwiches	Broadway District	Café	
NR	Starbucks	Baked goods	Multiple locations	Café	

Weekday food after 11pm

9.1	116 Crown	New American	Ninth Square	Upmarket	$35
9.1	Bar (Brü Room)	Pizza	Chapel District	Bar	$25
7.8	Sahara	Middle Eastern	Chapel District	Counter	$10
7.7	Gerónimo	Southwestern	Chapel District	Upmarket	$50
7.6	Christopher Martin's	American, Burgers	East Rock	Casual	$25
6.8	Anchor	American	Chapel District	Bar	$15
6.8	Rudy's Restaurant	American	Broadway District	Bar	$10
6.7	Martin's	Seafood, American	Fair Haven	Upmarket	$50
6.7	Mamoun's	Middle Eastern	Upper Chapel Area	Casual	$10
6.7	Archie Moore's	American, Burgers	Multiple locations	Bar	$20
6.7	Alpha Delta Pizza	Pizza, Sandwiches	Broadway District	Take-out	$10
6.5	Café Nine	American	Ninth Square	Bar	$15
6.5	Brick Oven Pizza	Pizza	Upper Chapel Area	Counter	$10
6.4	Est Est Est	Pizza, Italian	Upper Chapel Area	Counter	$10
6.2	The Owl Shop	Sandwiches	Chapel District	Bar	$10
6.1	Humphrey's East	American, Burgers	East Rock	Bar	$20
6.1	Buffalo Wild Wings	American	Multiple locations	Casual	$25
6.0	Delaney's Grille	American	Westville	Casual	$25
5.8	Skappo	Italian	Ninth Square	Upmarket	$40
5.8	Athenian Diner	American, Greek	Multiple locations	Casual	$25
5.6	McDonald's	American, Burgers	Multiple locations	Counter	$10
5.5	Aunt Chilada's	Mexican	Hamden	Casual	$30
5.5	Yorkside Pizza	Pizza, American	Broadway District	Casual	$20
5.0	Parthenon Diner	American, Greek	Branford	Casual	$25
4.8	Aladdin Crown Pizza	Middle Eastern	Chapel District	Take-out	$15
4.7	Gourmet Heaven	American, Chinese	Multiple locations	Take-out	$10
4.6	A One Pizza Restaurant	Pizza, American	Broadway District	Counter	$10
4.5	KFC	Southern	Multiple locations	Counter	$10
4.4	Cody's Diner	American	Wooster Square	Casual	$15
3.9	Burger King	American, Burgers	Multiple locations	Counter	$10
3.5	Sullivan's	American	Upper Chapel Area	Casual	$20
3.5	Ivy Noodle	Chinese	Broadway District	Casual	$10
3.4	Main Garden	Chinese	Broadway District	Counter	$10
2.5	Au Bon Pain	Sandwiches	Broadway District	Counter	$10
2.1	Dunkin' Donuts	Baked goods	Multiple locations	Counter	$10
2.0	TGI Friday's	American	Multiple locations	Casual	$30

Weekday food after 11pm *continued*

NR	The Publick Cup	Sandwiches	Broadway District	Café	
NR	Starbucks	Baked goods	Multiple locations	Café	

Weekday food after midnight

6.8	Rudy's Restaurant	American	Broadway District	Bar	$10
6.7	Mamoun's	Middle Eastern	Upper Chapel Area	Casual	$10
6.7	Alpha Delta Pizza	Pizza, Sandwiches	Broadway District	Take-out	$10
6.5	Café Nine	American	Ninth Square	Bar	$15
6.5	Brick Oven Pizza	Pizza	Upper Chapel Area	Counter	$10
6.4	Est Est Est	Pizza, Italian	Upper Chapel Area	Counter	$10
6.2	The Owl Shop	Sandwiches	Chapel District	Bar	$10
6.1	Buffalo Wild Wings	American	Multiple locations	Casual	$25
5.8	Athenian Diner	American, Greek	Multiple locations	Casual	$25
5.6	McDonald's	American, Burgers	Multiple locations	Counter	$10
5.5	Aunt Chilada's	Mexican	Hamden	Casual	$30
5.5	Yorkside Pizza	Pizza, American	Broadway District	Casual	$20
5.0	Parthenon Diner	American, Greek	Branford	Casual	$25
4.8	Aladdin Crown Pizza	Middle Eastern	Chapel District	Take-out	$15
4.7	Gourmet Heaven	American, Chinese	Multiple locations	Take-out	$10
4.6	A One Pizza Restaurant	Pizza, American	Broadway District	Counter	$10
4.4	Cody's Diner	American	Wooster Square	Casual	$15
3.9	Burger King	American, Burgers	Multiple locations	Counter	$10
3.5	Ivy Noodle	Chinese	Broadway District	Casual	$10
3.4	Main Garden	Chinese	Broadway District	Counter	$10
2.1	Dunkin' Donuts	Baked goods	Multiple locations	Counter	$10

Weekday food after 1am

6.7	Mamoun's	Middle Eastern	Upper Chapel Area	Casual	$10
6.7	Alpha Delta Pizza	Pizza, Sandwiches	Broadway District	Take-out	$10
6.5	Brick Oven Pizza	Pizza	Upper Chapel Area	Counter	$10
6.1	Buffalo Wild Wings	American	Multiple locations	Casual	$25
5.8	Athenian Diner	American, Greek	Multiple locations	Casual	$25
5.6	McDonald's	American, Burgers	Multiple locations	Counter	$10
5.0	Parthenon Diner	American, Greek	Branford	Casual	$25
4.8	Aladdin Crown Pizza	Middle Eastern	Chapel District	Take-out	$15
4.7	Gourmet Heaven	American, Chinese	Multiple locations	Take-out	$10
4.6	A One Pizza Restaurant	Pizza, American	Broadway District	Counter	$10
4.4	Cody's Diner	American	Wooster Square	Casual	$15
3.9	Burger King	American, Burgers	Multiple locations	Counter	$10
3.5	Ivy Noodle	Chinese	Broadway District	Casual	$10
2.1	Dunkin' Donuts	Baked goods	Multiple locations	Counter	$10

Weekday food after 2am

6.7	Mamoun's	Middle Eastern	Upper Chapel Area	Casual	$10
6.7	Alpha Delta Pizza	Pizza, Sandwiches	Broadway District	Take-out	$10
6.5	Brick Oven Pizza	Pizza	Upper Chapel Area	Counter	$10
5.8	Athenian Diner	American, Greek	Multiple locations	Casual	$25
5.6	McDonald's	American, Burgers	Multiple locations	Counter	$10
5.0	Parthenon Diner	American, Greek	Branford	Casual	$25
4.7	Gourmet Heaven	American, Chinese	Multiple locations	Take-out	$10
4.6	A One Pizza Restaurant	Pizza, American	Broadway District	Counter	$10
4.4	Cody's Diner	American	Wooster Square	Casual	$15
2.1	Dunkin' Donuts	Baked goods	Multiple locations	Counter	$10

Weekend food after 10pm

9.6	Le Petit Café	French	Branford	Upmarket	$65
9.1	116 Crown	New American	Ninth Square	Upmarket	$35
9.1	Bar (Brü Room)	Pizza	Chapel District	Bar	$25
9.1	East Japanese Restaurant	Japanese	Milford	Upmarket	$45
9.1	Sally's Apizza	Pizza	Wooster Square	Casual	$20

Weekend food after 10pm *continued*

9.0	Heirloom	New American	Upper Chapel Area	Upmarket	$85
9.0	Modern Apizza	Pizza	East Rock	Casual	$20
9.0	Thali Too	Indian	Broadway District	Casual	$35
9.0	Szechuan Delight	Chinese	Hamden	Casual	$25
8.9	Barcelona	Spanish	Chapel District	Upmarket	$65
8.8	Saray	Turkish	West Haven	Casual	$30
8.7	Prime 16	American, Burgers	Chapel District	Casual	$25
8.7	Turkish Kabab House	Turkish	West Haven	Casual	$30
8.7	Iron Chef	Taiwanese, Chinese	West Haven	Counter	$15
8.5	Carmen Anthony	Steakhouse	Audubon District	Upmarket	$75
8.5	Gastronomique	French, Burgers	Chapel District	Take-out	$25
8.4	Thali	Indian	Ninth Square	Upmarket	$50
8.4	Zuppardi's	Pizza	West Haven	Casual	$25
8.3	The Beach House	Seafood	Milford	Upmarket	$60
8.3	Machu Picchu	Peruvian	Fair Haven	Casual	$25
8.2	L'Orcio	Italian	East Rock	Upmarket	$45
8.1	The Stone House	Seafood, American	Guilford	Upmarket	$50
8.1	Dayton Street Apizza	Pizza	Westville	Counter	$15
8.0	Louis' Lunch	Burgers	Chapel District	Counter	$10
8.0	Zaroka	Indian	Upper Chapel Area	Upmarket	$40
7.9	Coromandel	Indian	Orange	Upmarket	$40
7.8	Bistro Basque	Spanish, French	Milford	Upmarket	$60
7.8	Daiko (Jerry-san's)	Japanese	Multiple locations	Upmarket	$40
7.8	Sahara	Middle Eastern	Chapel District	Counter	$10
7.8	Royal Palace	Chinese	Ninth Square	Upmarket	$30
7.7	Gerónimo	Southwestern	Chapel District	Upmarket	$50
7.7	Istanbul Café	Turkish	Chapel District	Upmarket	$45
7.7	Lalibela	Ethiopian	Chapel District	Casual	$25
7.7	Darbar India	Indian	Branford	Upmarket	$35
7.7	Sushi Palace	Japanese	Hamden	Casual	$35
7.7	Adriana's	Italian	Fair Haven	Upmarket	$35
7.6	Christopher Martin's	American, Burgers	East Rock	Casual	$25
7.6	Tandoor	Indian	Upper Chapel Area	Casual	$25
7.6	Sushi on Chapel	Korean, Japanese	Chapel District	Upmarket	$40
7.4	Bespoke/Sabor Latino	Nuevo Latino	Chapel District	Upmarket	$80
7.3	Miya's	Japanese	Upper Chapel Area	Upmarket	$45
7.3	Temple Grill	American	Chapel District	Casual	$40
7.3	Portofino	Italian	East Rock	Upmarket	$40
7.3	Seoul Yokocho	Korean	Upper Chapel Area	Upmarket	$40
7.1	Soul de Cuba	Cuban	Chapel District	Upmarket	$30
7.1	Il' Forno	Italian	Milford	Upmarket	$50
7.1	Foe	New American	Branford	Upmarket	$50
7.1	Miso	Japanese	Ninth Square	Upmarket	$40
7.1	India Palace	Indian	Upper Chapel Area	Casual	$25
7.0	Sage American Bar & Grill	American	The Hill	Upmarket	$55
7.0	Thai Taste	Thai	Upper Chapel Area	Casual	$35
7.0	Royal India	Indian	Broadway District	Casual	$25
7.0	Gabriele's	Italian	Orange	Casual	$35
7.0	Kari	Malaysian	Westville	Casual	$30
6.9	Leon's	Italian	Long Wharf	Upmarket	$45
6.9	Bangkok Gardens	Thai	Upper Chapel Area	Upmarket	$30
6.9	Akasaka	Japanese	Westville	Upmarket	$35
6.8	Bentara	Malaysian	Ninth Square	Upmarket	$50
6.8	Anchor	American	Chapel District	Bar	$15
6.8	Rainbow Gardens Inn	New American	Milford	Upmarket	$45
6.8	Rudy's Restaurant	American	Broadway District	Bar	$10
6.8	Su Casa	Mexican	Branford	Casual	$30
6.8	Wild Ginger	Japanese	Orange	Upmarket	$45
6.8	Kumo	Japanese	Multiple locations	Upmarket	$40
6.7	Martin's	Seafood, American	Fair Haven	Upmarket	$50
6.7	Dolci	New American	East Rock	Upmarket	$45
6.7	Mamoun's	Middle Eastern	Upper Chapel Area	Casual	$10

Weekend food after 10pm *continued*

6.7	Archie Moore's	American, Burgers	Multiple locations	Bar	$20
6.7	Kampai	Japanese	Branford	Upmarket	$40
6.7	Mediterranea	Middle Eastern	South Town Green	Counter	$10
6.7	Alpha Delta Pizza	Pizza, Sandwiches	Broadway District	Take-out	$10
6.6	Jalapeño Heaven	Mexican	Branford	Casual	$30
6.5	Café Nine	American	Ninth Square	Bar	$15
6.5	Café Goodfellas	Italian	East Rock	Upmarket	$55
6.5	Nikkita	New American	Audubon District	Upmarket	$45
6.5	J.P. Dempsey's	American, Burgers	East Rock	Bar	$30
6.5	Brick Oven Pizza	Pizza	Upper Chapel Area	Counter	$10
6.4	Ixtapa Grille	Mexican	Hamden	Casual	$25
6.4	The Rib House	Barbecue, Southern	East Haven	Casual	$30
6.4	Est Est Est	Pizza, Italian	Upper Chapel Area	Counter	$10
6.4	S'Wings	American	Chapel District	Casual	$15
6.3	Pad Thai	Thai	Upper Chapel Area	Casual	$25
6.2	The Owl Shop	Sandwiches	Chapel District	Bar	$10
6.1	Pacífico	Nuevo Latino	Chapel District	Upmarket	$50
6.1	Amato's	Pizza, Italian	East Rock	Casual	$25
6.1	Humphrey's East	American, Burgers	East Rock	Bar	$20
6.1	Buffalo Wild Wings	American	Multiple locations	Casual	$25
6.1	China Pavilion	Chinese	Orange	Upmarket	$30
6.0	Delaney's Grille	American	Westville	Casual	$25
6.0	Jimmies of Savin Rock	Seafood, American	West Haven	Upmarket	$40
6.0	Fresh Taco	Mexican	South Town Green	Counter	$10
5.9	The Blue Pearl	New American	South Town Green	Upmarket	$45
5.9	Central Steakhouse	Steakhouse	Ninth Square	Upmarket	$75
5.8	Skappo	Italian	Ninth Square	Upmarket	$40
5.8	Athenian Diner	American, Greek	Multiple locations	Casual	$25
5.7	Nini's Bistro	New American	Ninth Square	Upmarket	$45
5.7	Bertucci's	Italian, Pizza	Orange	Casual	$35
5.6	SBC	American	Multiple locations	Casual	$30
5.6	Pizza House	Pizza	Upper Chapel Area	Counter	$5
5.6	McDonald's	American, Burgers	Multiple locations	Counter	$10
5.5	Aunt Chilada's	Mexican	Hamden	Casual	$30
5.5	Yorkside Pizza	Pizza, American	Broadway District	Casual	$20
5.4	Chili's	American, Mexican	Hamden	Casual	$25
5.1	Chip's II	American, Burgers	Guilford	Bar	$20
5.0	Bulldog Burrito	Mexican	Broadway District	Counter	$5
5.0	Parthenon Diner	American, Greek	Branford	Casual	$25
4.9	Olive Garden	Italian	Multiple locations	Casual	$25
4.8	Aladdin Crown Pizza	Middle Eastern	Chapel District	Take-out	$15
4.7	Kudeta	Pan-Asian	Chapel District	Upmarket	$50
4.7	C.O. Jones	Mexican	East Rock	Bar	$20
4.7	York Street Noodle House	Pan-Asian, Chinese	Upper Chapel Area	Casual	$10
4.7	Gourmet Heaven	American, Chinese	Multiple locations	Take-out	$10
4.6	A One Pizza Restaurant	Pizza, American	Broadway District	Counter	$10
4.5	KFC	Southern	Multiple locations	Counter	$10
4.4	Cody's Diner	American	Wooster Square	Casual	$15
4.4	El Amigo Felix	Mexican	Broadway District	Bar	$25
4.1	Hunan Café	Chinese	Upper Chapel Area	Counter	$10
3.9	Burger King	American, Burgers	Multiple locations	Counter	$10
3.8	Brazi's Italian Restaurant	Italian, Pizza	Long Wharf	Casual	$30
3.8	Downtown @ the Taft	New American	Chapel District	Upmarket	$50
3.7	Subway	Sandwiches	Multiple locations	Counter	$10
3.6	Samurai	Japanese	Chapel District	Upmarket	$45
3.5	Sullivan's	American	Upper Chapel Area	Casual	$20
3.5	Ivy Noodle	Chinese	Broadway District	Casual	$10
3.4	Main Garden	Chinese	Broadway District	Counter	$10
3.4	China King	Chinese	Chapel District	Take-out	$10
2.8	Applebee's	American	Multiple locations	Casual	$25
2.6	Marius	American	Chapel District	Upmarket	$55
2.5	Au Bon Pain	Sandwiches	Broadway District	Counter	$10

Weekend food after 10pm *continued*

2.2	Thai Pan Asian	Thai, Pan-Asian	Upper Chapel Area	Casual	$25
2.1	Dunkin' Donuts	Baked goods	Multiple locations	Counter	$10
2.0	Viva Zapata	Mexican	Upper Chapel Area	Bar	$25
2.0	TGI Friday's	American	Multiple locations	Casual	$30
1.8	Foster's	New American	Ninth Square	Upmarket	$50
NR	Ashley's Ice Cream	Ice cream	Multiple locations	Counter	
NR	Cold Stone Creamery	Ice cream	Multiple locations	Take-out	
NR	The Publick Cup	Sandwiches	Broadway District	Café	
NR	Starbucks	Baked goods	Multiple locations	Café	

Weekend food after 11pm

9.1	116 Crown	New American	Ninth Square	Upmarket	$35
9.1	Bar (Brü Room)	Pizza	Chapel District	Bar	$25
9.0	Heirloom	New American	Upper Chapel Area	Upmarket	$85
9.0	Modern Apizza	Pizza	East Rock	Casual	$20
9.0	Thali Too	Indian	Broadway District	Casual	$35
8.5	Gastronomique	French, Burgers	Chapel District	Take-out	$25
8.3	The Beach House	Seafood	Milford	Upmarket	$60
8.0	Louis' Lunch	Burgers	Chapel District	Counter	$10
7.8	Sahara	Middle Eastern	Chapel District	Counter	$10
7.7	Gerónimo	Southwestern	Chapel District	Upmarket	$50
7.7	Adriana's	Italian	Fair Haven	Upmarket	$35
7.6	Christopher Martin's	American, Burgers	East Rock	Casual	$25
7.3	Miya's	Japanese	Upper Chapel Area	Upmarket	$45
7.3	Temple Grill	American	Chapel District	Casual	$40
6.8	Anchor	American	Chapel District	Bar	$15
6.8	Rudy's Restaurant	American	Broadway District	Bar	$10
6.7	Martin's	Seafood, American	Fair Haven	Upmarket	$50
6.7	Dolci	New American	East Rock	Upmarket	$45
6.7	Mamoun's	Middle Eastern	Upper Chapel Area	Casual	$10
6.7	Archie Moore's	American, Burgers	Multiple locations	Bar	$20
6.7	Mediterranea	Middle Eastern	South Town Green	Counter	$10
6.7	Alpha Delta Pizza	Pizza, Sandwiches	Broadway District	Take-out	$10
6.5	Café Nine	American	Ninth Square	Bar	$15
6.5	Nikkita	New American	Audubon District	Upmarket	$45
6.5	J.P. Dempsey's	American, Burgers	East Rock	Bar	$30
6.5	Brick Oven Pizza	Pizza	Upper Chapel Area	Counter	$10
6.4	Est Est Est	Pizza, Italian	Upper Chapel Area	Counter	$10
6.4	S'Wings	American	Chapel District	Casual	$15
6.2	The Owl Shop	Sandwiches	Chapel District	Bar	$10
6.1	Humphrey's East	American, Burgers	East Rock	Bar	$20
6.1	Buffalo Wild Wings	American	Multiple locations	Casual	$25
6.0	Delaney's Grille	American	Westville	Casual	$25
5.8	Skappo	Italian	Ninth Square	Upmarket	$40
5.8	Athenian Diner	American, Greek	Multiple locations	Casual	$25
5.6	Pizza House	Pizza	Upper Chapel Area	Counter	$5
5.6	McDonald's	American, Burgers	Multiple locations	Counter	$10
5.5	Aunt Chilada's	Mexican	Hamden	Casual	$30
5.5	Yorkside Pizza	Pizza, American	Broadway District	Casual	$20
5.4	Chili's	American, Mexican	Hamden	Casual	$25
5.0	Bulldog Burrito	Mexican	Broadway District	Counter	$5
5.0	Parthenon Diner	American, Greek	Branford	Casual	$25
4.8	Aladdin Crown Pizza	Middle Eastern	Chapel District	Take-out	$15
4.7	Kudeta	Pan-Asian	Chapel District	Upmarket	$50
4.7	Gourmet Heaven	American, Chinese	Multiple locations	Take-out	$10
4.6	A One Pizza Restaurant	Pizza, American	Broadway District	Counter	$10
4.5	KFC	Southern	Multiple locations	Counter	$10
4.4	Cody's Diner	American	Wooster Square	Casual	$15
4.4	El Amigo Felix	Mexican	Broadway District	Bar	$25
3.9	Burger King	American, Burgers	Multiple locations	Counter	$10
3.8	Downtown @ the Taft	New American	Chapel District	Upmarket	$50
3.7	Subway	Sandwiches	Multiple locations	Counter	$10

Weekend food after 11pm *continued*

3.6	Samurai	Japanese	Chapel District	Upmarket	$45
3.5	Sullivan's	American	Upper Chapel Area	Casual	$20
3.5	Ivy Noodle	Chinese	Broadway District	Casual	$10
3.4	Main Garden	Chinese	Broadway District	Counter	$10
3.4	China King	Chinese	Chapel District	Take-out	$10
2.8	Applebee's	American	Multiple locations	Casual	$25
2.6	Marius	American	Chapel District	Upmarket	$55
2.5	Au Bon Pain	Sandwiches	Broadway District	Counter	$10
2.1	Dunkin' Donuts	Baked goods	Multiple locations	Counter	$10
2.0	Viva Zapata	Mexican	Upper Chapel Area	Bar	$25
2.0	TGI Friday's	American	Multiple locations	Casual	$30
NR	The Publick Cup	Sandwiches	Broadway District	Café	
NR	Starbucks	Baked goods	Multiple locations	Café	

Weekend food after midnight

9.1	116 Crown	New American	Ninth Square	Upmarket	$35
9.0	Thali Too	Indian	Broadway District	Casual	$35
8.5	Gastronomique	French, Burgers	Chapel District	Take-out	$25
8.0	Louis' Lunch	Burgers	Chapel District	Counter	$10
7.8	Sahara	Middle Eastern	Chapel District	Counter	$10
6.8	Rudy's Restaurant	American	Broadway District	Bar	$10
6.7	Mamoun's	Middle Eastern	Upper Chapel Area	Casual	$10
6.7	Archie Moore's	American, Burgers	Multiple locations	Bar	$20
6.7	Mediterranea	Middle Eastern	South Town Green	Counter	$10
6.7	Alpha Delta Pizza	Pizza, Sandwiches	Broadway District	Take-out	$10
6.5	Café Nine	American	Ninth Square	Bar	$15
6.5	Nikkita	New American	Audubon District	Upmarket	$45
6.5	J.P. Dempsey's	American, Burgers	East Rock	Bar	$30
6.5	Brick Oven Pizza	Pizza	Upper Chapel Area	Counter	$10
6.4	Est Est Est	Pizza, Italian	Upper Chapel Area	Counter	$10
6.4	S'Wings	American	Chapel District	Casual	$15
6.2	The Owl Shop	Sandwiches	Chapel District	Bar	$10
6.1	Humphrey's East	American, Burgers	East Rock	Bar	$20
6.1	Buffalo Wild Wings	American	Multiple locations	Casual	$25
6.0	Delaney's Grille	American	Westville	Casual	$25
5.8	Athenian Diner	American, Greek	Multiple locations	Casual	$25
5.6	Pizza House	Pizza	Upper Chapel Area	Counter	$5
5.6	McDonald's	American, Burgers	Multiple locations	Counter	$10
5.5	Aunt Chilada's	Mexican	Hamden	Casual	$30
5.5	Yorkside Pizza	Pizza, American	Broadway District	Casual	$20
5.0	Parthenon Diner	American, Greek	Branford	Casual	$25
4.8	Aladdin Crown Pizza	Middle Eastern	Chapel District	Take-out	$15
4.7	Gourmet Heaven	American, Chinese	Multiple locations	Take-out	$10
4.6	A One Pizza Restaurant	Pizza, American	Broadway District	Counter	$10
4.5	KFC	Southern	Multiple locations	Counter	$10
4.4	Cody's Diner	American	Wooster Square	Casual	$15
3.9	Burger King	American, Burgers	Multiple locations	Counter	$10
3.5	Ivy Noodle	Chinese	Broadway District	Casual	$10
3.4	Main Garden	Chinese	Broadway District	Counter	$10
2.1	Dunkin' Donuts	Baked goods	Multiple locations	Counter	$10
2.0	TGI Friday's	American	Multiple locations	Casual	$30

Weekend food after 1am

9.0	Thali Too	Indian	Broadway District	Casual	$35
8.5	Gastronomique	French, Burgers	Chapel District	Take-out	$25
8.0	Louis' Lunch	Burgers	Chapel District	Counter	$10
6.8	Rudy's Restaurant	American	Broadway District	Bar	$10
6.7	Mamoun's	Middle Eastern	Upper Chapel Area	Casual	$10
6.7	Alpha Delta Pizza	Pizza, Sandwiches	Broadway District	Take-out	$10
6.5	Café Nine	American	Ninth Square	Bar	$15
6.5	Brick Oven Pizza	Pizza	Upper Chapel Area	Counter	$10

Weekend food after 1am *continued*

6.4	Est Est Est	Pizza, Italian	Upper Chapel Area	Counter	$10
6.4	S'Wings	American	Chapel District	Casual	$15
6.2	The Owl Shop	Sandwiches	Chapel District	Bar	$10
6.1	Buffalo Wild Wings	American	Multiple locations	Casual	$25
5.8	Athenian Diner	American, Greek	Multiple locations	Casual	$25
5.6	McDonald's	American, Burgers	Multiple locations	Counter	$10
5.5	Aunt Chilada's	Mexican	Hamden	Casual	$30
5.5	Yorkside Pizza	Pizza, American	Broadway District	Casual	$20
5.0	Parthenon Diner	American, Greek	Branford	Casual	$25
4.8	Aladdin Crown Pizza	Middle Eastern	Chapel District	Take-out	$15
4.7	Gourmet Heaven	American, Chinese	Multiple locations	Take-out	$10
4.6	A One Pizza Restaurant	Pizza, American	Broadway District	Counter	$10
4.4	Cody's Diner	American	Wooster Square	Casual	$15
3.9	Burger King	American, Burgers	Multiple locations	Counter	$10
3.5	Ivy Noodle	Chinese	Broadway District	Casual	$10
3.4	Main Garden	Chinese	Broadway District	Counter	$10
2.1	Dunkin' Donuts	Baked goods	Multiple locations	Counter	$10

Weekend food after 2am

6.7	Mamoun's	Middle Eastern	Upper Chapel Area	Casual	$10
6.7	Alpha Delta Pizza	Pizza, Sandwiches	Broadway District	Take-out	$10
6.5	Brick Oven Pizza	Pizza	Upper Chapel Area	Counter	$10
6.4	Est Est Est	Pizza, Italian	Upper Chapel Area	Counter	$10
6.4	S'Wings	American	Chapel District	Casual	$15
5.8	Athenian Diner	American, Greek	Multiple locations	Casual	$25
5.6	McDonald's	American, Burgers	Multiple locations	Counter	$10
5.5	Yorkside Pizza	Pizza, American	Broadway District	Casual	$20
5.0	Parthenon Diner	American, Greek	Branford	Casual	$25
4.8	Aladdin Crown Pizza	Middle Eastern	Chapel District	Take-out	$15
4.7	Gourmet Heaven	American, Chinese	Multiple locations	Take-out	$10
4.6	A One Pizza Restaurant	Pizza, American	Broadway District	Counter	$10
4.4	Cody's Diner	American	Wooster Square	Casual	$15
3.9	Burger King	American, Burgers	Multiple locations	Counter	$10
2.1	Dunkin' Donuts	Baked goods	Multiple locations	Counter	$10

Top tastes

Baked pork buns, China Great Wall
Banana tres leches, Bespoke/Sabor Latino
Beef patty, Tropical Delights
Bloody Mary and oysters, Sage American Bar & Grill
Bottle of wine, The Wine Thief
Bread basket, Atticus
Broccoli cheese croissant, Marjolaine
Buffalo wings, Archie Moore's
Caciocavallo, Liuzzi's Cheese Shop
Carrot cake, Take the Cake
Cauliflower masala, Coromandel
Cheese works, Louis' Lunch
Chicken soup with lemon, El Amigo Felix
Chocolate fondue, The Blue Pearl
Cigars and whiskey, The Owl Shop
Corned beef hash, Lena's
Crab cakes, Carmen Anthony Steakhouse
Creamed spinach, Chuck's Steak House
Crusty burger, Gastronomique
Doner kebab, Turkish Kabab House
Duck confit, Union League Café
Eggplant parmesan pizza, Modern Apizza
Espresso, Romeo & Cesare's
French fries with Belgian mayonnaise, Rudy's Restaurant
French toast, Bella's Café
Fried calamari, Adriana's
Fried calamari, Martin's Riverside Restaurant
Goat curry, Mother's Homestyle Kitchen
Grilled meat platter, Saray
Haldiram chole bathura, Thali Too
Half-price wine on Tuesday, Scoozzi
Half-yard, Richter's
Hot dog well done, Glenwood Drive-In
Hunkar begendi (Sultan's delight), Istanbul Café
Indian pudding ice cream, Ashley's Ice Cream
Jalapeño kampachi, East Japanese Restaurant
Jerk chicken, Glen's Bar-B-Q
Key lime tart, Jeffrey's
Lion's head, Szechuan Delight
Lithuanian coffee cake, Claire's Corner Copia
Lobster roll, Chick's
Margarita, Gerónimo
Masala dosa, Star of India
Mashed potato, bacon, and onion pizza, Bar (Brü Room)
Mofongo, El Coquí
Moo nam tok (grilled pork salad), Rice Pot
Morcilla (blood sausage), Barcelona

Number Two Sandwich (turkey, brie, apple), Gourmet Heaven
Osso buco, Anastasio's
Oxtail soup, Soul de Cuba
Parmesan truffle fries, 116 Crown
Pastrami, Katz's Restaurant
Pizza with sweet-potato dough, Stony Creek Market and Pizza
Pizza with tomato and garlic, Sally's Apizza
Pulled-pork burrito, Tijuana Taco Company
Pupusa platter, Restaurante Salvadoreño
Pupusas, Sabor Latino
Roast suckling pig, Ibiza
Roasted lobster, The Place
Sashimi, Sono Bana
Sausage pizza, Zuppardi's
Scones, Book Trader Café
Shrimp Casino pizza, Roseland Apizza
Small draft beer, Contois Tavern
Soft-shell crab sandwich, Lenny's Indian Head Inn
Steak frites, Le Petit Café
Stuffed mushroom burger, Prime 16
Tacos, Guadalupe La Poblanita
Tacos al pastor, La Cocinita
Tacos de barbacoa, Taquería Mexicana #2
Terrace curry, The Terrace
Three-cup chicken, Iron Chef
Txipirones, Bistro Basque
Uttapam, Swagat
Vanilla ice cream, Wentworth's Homemade Ice Cream
Water beef, Royal Palace
Wenzel's sub, Alpha Delta Pizza
White clam and bacon pizza, Frank Pepe's
Yook-gae-jang, Soho New Haven
Zeppole, Caseus

Fearless Critic

Reviews

A One Pizza Restaurant

4.6 Food   **3.5** Feel

If it's 3am and you want some mediocre pizza or serviceable sandwiches, this is your place

Pizza, American

Counter service   **$10** Price

24 hours

Bar None
Credit cards Visa, MC
Veg-friendly

Broadway District
21 Broadway
(203) 865-8888

At least you can say that A One (also known as 21 Broadway) pleases the night owls of New Haven. The all-night schedule is certainly A One's most distinguishing feature; otherwise, it's just a little storefront with some tables, a place that hawks okay (at best) food and overpriced cigarettes. The atmosphere is strangely antiseptic, like a simple neighborhood pizzeria-sandwich shop without any of the friendliness or charm. But at 4am, long after most other establishments have turned out the lights, we'll take what we can get.

The food itself is nothing more than standard diner fare. There's breakfast night and day; there are also grinders, hot and cold wraps, and edible but uninspired pizza. Crusts are fairly thin, and ingredients seem fresh enough, but there's some taste and tang missing here. Sandwiches, similarly, are tolerable but not noteworthy. The steak-and-cheese sandwich, with lettuce, tomato, mayonnaise, and hot peppers, is a perfectly good version, with a high taste-to-grease ratio, but accompanying fries aren't worth the carbs. Omelettes are basic and large. French toast is sliced thick, in the typical New York diner style.

Nothing here will impress you. But chances are, in the wee hours, you're not in the most discriminating mood. Inexplicable is the interminable wait between ordering and actually being served food, but then, where are you rushing off to at this hour?

Abate Apizza & Seafood

4.7 Food   **4.0** Feel

An Italian-American gorgefest, served up by a warm, fuzzy staff

Italian, Pizza

Casual restaurant

$30 Price

Mon–Thu 11am–9pm
Fri 11am–10pm
Sat noon–10pm
Sun noon–9pm

Bar Beer, wine, liquor
Credit cards Visa, MC, AmEx
Reservations Accepted
Delivery, kid-friendly, veg-friendly

Wooster Square Area
129 Wooster St.
(203) 776-4334

For years, Abate has been a proud member of the old gang of Wooster Street Italian restaurants, kept in business not just by the stream of overflow customers from the nearby Frank Pepe and Sally's, but also by the generations of families that know the place and return year after year. Service is definitely friendly; you'll feel welcome, perhaps even loved, as Bill and Hillary seemed to when they frequented the Wooster Street joint during their days at Yale Law School.

But it seems like the food is still stuck in that time period, too. Dishes like chicken marsala are too rich, overcooked, and bland. Just about everything comes with well-done pasta, which fares scarcely better. Others, like the combo Florentine (veal, chicken, and shrimp sautéed with lemon and spinach over pasta), are over-ambitious, diluting whatever individual flavors might otherwise be in evidence. This is not to mention the daily all-you-can-eat buffet, which is just plain overwhelming.

Pizza is probably your best bet, with fried seafood and veal a not-so-distant second. The "Captain's Platter" has fried scallops, clams, and shrimp with fries, cole slaw, and toast—not a bad choice, but if you're after seafood, there are plenty of *better* choices around. We recommend avoiding all fish that's not fried, and all chicken. Portions are huge, so you might not want to order more than one main dish for every two people. Prices are not as high as some of the more upscale Wooster Street competition, but they're none too low either. The atmosphere is equally unexciting—a big, open space of mostly empty tables and an incongruous atrium area.

But there's any easy solution to that: delivery.

Adriana's

7.7 Food   **6.5** Feel

A classic gem of a Grand Avenue Italian-American restaurant—now back from the fire

Italian

Upmarket restaurant   **$35** Price

www.adrianasrestaurant.net

Mon–Fri 11:30am–2:30pm,
5pm–10:30pm
Sat 5pm–11:30pm
Sun 1pm–10pm

Bar Beer, wine, liquor
Credit cards Visa, MC, AmEx
Reservations Accepted
Kid-friendly

Fair Haven
771 Grand Ave.
(203) 865-6474

Neither a devastating fire nor inhospitable economic conditions can stop Adriana's. The restaurant reopened its doors after six months (and much renovation) following a November 2008 fire. The post-facelift digs are shiny and new. A sleek bar, one of the more "modern" additions, is a nice place for a pre-dinner drink.

And we're glad that Adriana rose from the ashes, because we can't imagine New Haven without her. This is American-style Italian the way it's supposed to be—the quintessential old-school family restaurant, with a menu that's longer, more interesting, and tastier than most other Italian options in town. Perhaps this is in part because of its location: across the tracks, down Grand Avenue toward Fair Haven. As such, the place is off the beaten path, at least if the path is downtown. The restaurant's wonderfully friendly management depends on word of mouth rather than proactive marketing, so the place tends to host local families rather than tourists or Yale parents in town for just one evening.

Everything about Adriana's feels genuine. Fried calamari, the ultimate litmus test for Italian-American food, are superb. The savory batter is remarkably crisp, and the squid achieves a wonderful balance between firm and tender. Even the marinara sauce is just right. Pane cotto is just decent, but there's also a bewildering array of veal dishes and some authentic Italian pasta selections (all'amatriciana, for example, the traditional Roman red sauce, with pancetta and onions).

An almost impossibly friendly attitude has long been one of the hallmarks of New Haven's great tradition of Italian-American restaurants, and Adriana's is no exception: the welcome is warm, and the service is professional yet genuine in a very rare way. This is gracious hospitality incarnate.

Thank goodness *that* wasn't lost in the fire.

Ahimsa

A multiregional effort toward healthy eating turns sour at these prices

5.7 Food

7.0 Feel

New American

Upmarket restaurant

$55 Price

www.ahimsainc.com

Mon–Thu 11:30am–2:30pm, 5:30pm–9:30pm
Fri–Sat 11:30am–2:30pm

Bar Beer, wine, liquor
Credit cards Visa, MC, AmEx
Reservations Accepted
Delivery, live music, veg-friendly

Upper Chapel Area
1227 Chapel St.
(203) 786-4774

Everywhere you look, they're popping up: restaurants that are not just vegetarian, but actually vegetable-focused. These two concepts are actually quite different: macaroni and cheese, bean burritos, and mashed potatoes may be vegetarian, but their flavors are built around the immediate gratification of starches and fats. The new breed of vegetable-focused restaurant, instead, resists both heavy carbs and veggie imitation of meats, and instead does wondrous things by merely reshaping the elements of nature's simplest bounty.

At first blush, Ahimsa, a kosher-and-vegetarian "tapas bar" focusing on raw and vegan foods, looks like a restaurant squarely in this new school. To wit: one of the Indian founders was just 18 years old when the restaurant opened in 2007—it's hard to get more new-school than that. The founding family hails from India, a country whose cuisine often teases remarkable complexity from vegetables and spices. And indeed, the best things we've sampled here have been South Asian: puri and curry, pakoras and samosas.

Unfortunately, on the menu, these are mostly crowded out by the worst sort of vegan dish: nut-cheese imitations of Italian-American dishes like "fettucine alfredo," "manicotti," and "lasagne," for example, or ill-fated pan-world renderings of "soft taco," "spring roll," "mushroom medley," and "nut loaf."

The extraordinarily expensive lunch buffet (which has disappeared and then reemerged), at one visit, consisted largely of pasta with marinara sauce, one dal, a green mesclun salad with balsamic vinaigrette, and a couple of lukewarm samosas. We wish we could report that ordering à la carte yields better results, but it doesn't. Empanadas boast a meaty nut-cheese filling and a salsa with some kick, but they're brought down by skin that's soggy from incompetent deep-frying. "Raw" lasagna has crisp, thinly sliced zucchini, but its overbearing sun-dried tomato paste evokes tomato paste straight from the can, and worse still are the thick slices of mealy, unripe raw tomato—spectacularly embarrassing at a restaurant that prides itself on serving raw vegetables.

What's even less excusable than the sadly banal raw-and-vegan fare here is the high prices: even *lunch* main courses are price-gouged up to $18. With restaurants like Napa Valley's Ubuntu and Chicago's Green Zebra springing up around America, even omnivorous, pork-fat-loving chefs have been exploring the possibilities brought about by mere vegetables. They're extraordinary; don't be deceived into thinking that Ahimsa properly represents this movement.

Akasaka

Decent sushi and Japanese food at reasonable prices from a welcoming staff in costume

6.9 Food **6.0** Feel

Japanese

Upmarket restaurant **$35** Price

Sun–Thu 11am–3pm, 4:30pm–10pm; Fri–Sat 11am–3pm, 4:30pm–11pm

Bar Beer, wine, liquor
Credit cards Visa, MC, AmEx
Reservations Accepted

Westville
1450 Whalley Ave.
(203) 387-4898

Akasaka is a Westville neighborhood favorite for reliable sushi and cooked Japanese classics that are better than the norm. The best pieces of nigiri sushi have been the basics, salmon and tuna, along with fluke and red snapper. There are some faults: yellowtail and mackerel have been more variable, and we'd get our sea urchin elsewhere, as it has the right texture but some strong off-notes.

There are also some interesting modern Japanese concoctions, including a miso-marinated cod misoyaki, which is well marinated, tender, rich, and peppery, served with a side of almost raw asparagus. We also like the interesting preparation of "green mussels," baked with a flavorful mix including mayonnaise and tobiko. Soft-shell crab, when in season, has soft meat and is delicately fried. Chuka hotate, a marinated scallop salad, is chewy but with a nice soy-sauce flavor. These are all dishes that it would be hard to find at most area Japanese restaurants.

Prices are reasonable at Akasaka, if not particularly cheap. The place lies well outside downtown New Haven, although it's no further by car than Daiko or Hama, two of the other local sushi champions. We also like the attitude; the servers, who are clad in bright red traditional Japanese garb (it's hard to decide if the outfits are cheesy or charming), welcome you with open arms and then dote on you.

Although we tend to prefer dim, buzzing haunts, Akasaka is located in a supremely suburban stretch up Whalley Avenue, out a bit past Westville, nestled jarringly amidst car dealerships and fast-food chains. But it doesn't aspire to be anything more than a simple, friendly Japanese restaurant that serves reasonable sushi at reasonable prices to a local crowd. And it does so. None of which is anything at all to complain about.

Aladdin Crown Pizza

Average Middle Eastern food in an unavoidably prime location with late, late, late hours

4.8 Food	**3.0** Feel

Middle Eastern, Pizza

Take-out **$15** Price

Mon–Wed 11am–2am; Thu–Sat 11am–3am; Sun 2pm–midnight

Bar None
Credit cards Visa, MC, AmEx
Delivery, veg-friendly

Chapel District
260 Crown St.
(203) 773-3772

This late-night favorite on Crown Street does some of its best business after the bars close, when throngs of ungratified young people, irate at Connecticut's puritanical alcohol curfew, seek to soothe their sorrows with pizza and falafel. Aladdin serves very average pizza by the slice, along with an array of Middle Eastern short-order specialties such as gyros, the standby falafel sandwich (ask for hot sauce), and a few more unusual preparations, such as Damascus moujadarah (steamed lentils with fried onions).

The lamb shawarma, strips of rotisserie-roasted lamb with lettuce, tomato, parsley, and onion, topped with tahini and served on pita, is a standard version, not bad but not remarkable either. The stuffed pizza, which might be filled with some combination of broccoli, spinach, tomato, basil, ricotta, and mozzarella, has a following; we concede that it's better than the regular pizza, but it's also inexplicably expensive for late-night take-out grub. Ditto for the rest of the menu—it's monopoly (or perhaps oligopoly) pricing, and so the tab for a handful of small Middle Eastern dishes can really add up.

The location, speed, variety, and hours make Aladdin Crown a great favorite among undergraduates, and its success along those axes is well deserved. Late-night delivery is also a welcome surprise. In terms of atmosphere, it's nothing more than a brightly lit take-out joint with a few token tables; unless the weather is unforgiving, most choose the Crown Street sidewalk as the preferred venue for frenzied consumption.

Alpha Delta Pizza

A good sub and gyro purveyor that is open spectacularly late, although the pizza is just okay

6.7 Food | **3.5** Feel

Pizza, Sandwiches, Greek

Take-out | **$10** Price

Mon–Wed 3pm–3am; Thu–Sat 3pm–4am; Sun 3pm–midnight

Bar None
Credit cards Visa, MC, AmEx
Delivery, veg-friendly

Broadway District
371 Elm St.
(203) 787-3333

Alpha Delta is a conveniently situated late-night take-out option for subs, gyros, or slices, outlasting the competition on Thursday through Saturday by staying open until 4am. Alpha Delta sits at a crossroads of sorts, across from Rudy's, where Elm meets Howe. It's close to Broadway, Yale, and the beginning of Whalley Avenue, and near the university's small but loud frat scene. But Alpha Delta is also close to the Howe Street neighborhood where a lot of New Haven's reasonably priced apartments sit. The joint's large sign is unmistakable as you pass that corner; it has become a New Haven landmark of sorts.

And for good reason. Subs are the best choice here, followed by gyros and slices, in that order. The Wenzel's sub, a buffalo chicken sandwich with the works, including mayo and hot peppers, is a rich, spicy, textured delight with some interesting flavor counterpoints. It's their best work. Other subs and standard gyros are average or a bit above.

The pizza, however, which figures into the name of the place, is somewhat greasy—it's far from the best in town. We wonder why so many of the drunken post-party Yalies looking to satiate their late-night appetites choose the pizza. Granted, it's cheaper. But subs are still reasonably priced, so much better, and a large one can easily be split between two people. We highly recommend taking out rather than eating in: you'll want to avoid sitting in the drab, bluish room adjacent to the counter. But of course this place isn't about atmosphere. It's about late-night grub. So enjoy.

Alpine Restaurant

Just an extremely basic downtown cafeteria, with a
mediocre catch-all Chinese-American buffet

5.3	5.0
Food	Feel

Sandwiches, American

Counter service

$10
Price

Mon–Fri 6:30am–2:30pm,
6am–4pm

Bar None
Credit cards Visa, MC, AmEx

South Town Green
100 Elm St.
(203) 776-6117

This is just another downtown breakfast and lunch spot, appropriately
located in the ground floor of an office building. The simple, white room
is furnished with institutional-style blond-wood tables and cheaply framed
photos of cities and pastoral scenes, making the Alpine Restaurant feel
like nothing so much as a hospital cafeteria. It's improved, though, by
well-lit views of the downtown buildings through picture windows.

The space is curiously divided up into two sections by a frilly, painted-
glass barrier with plants. One side is table service only, and its tables have
place settings and bottles of ketchup. On the other side of Alpine, bare
tables await your counter-service trays. It's rather like an airplane divided
into first and coach, divider and all. And as in an airplane, most people
choose the simpler option (though in this case, it's just to save tip money).

The best things at Alpine are the inexpensive, eminently standard deli
sandwiches and breakfast fare (omelettes and so on). A bacon, egg, and
cheese sandwich, for instance, is perfectly competent, with the white
American cheese well melted, the bacon fried for the right amount of
time, and the egg as runny as you request it. The coffee's not bad either.

After 11am, there is also a catch-all Chinese-American buffet evocative
of the New York bodega concept: fried rice, assorted stir-fry plates with
broccoli and the like, Chinese noodles…and then comes the fried chicken,
boiled chicken breasts, vaguely Italian pasta dishes, sliced sausage, and so
on. As a rule, places that try to do absolutely everything do virtually
nothing well, and Alpine is no exception. The haphazard buffet is like a
culinary minefield, with one item overcooked and tasteless, the next dried
out from sitting in the buffet for so long. Stick to the printed menu.

Amato's

A solid State Street standby for subs and pizza by
the slice, with unbelievably welcoming service

6.1 *Food* **8.0** *Feel*

Pizza, Italian

Casual restaurant **$25** *Price*

www.amatosapizza.com

Mon, Wed 11am–10pm
Thu–Sat 11am–11pm
Sun noon–10pm

Bar Beer, wine
Credit cards Visa, MC, AmEx
Reservations Not accepted
Delivery, kid-friendly, outdoor
dining, veg-friendly

East Rock
858 State St.
(203) 562-2760

Amato's is a State Street neighborhood pizzeria that's an old standby for
the East Rock folk. Inside, the atmosphere is nothing special; the place
feels like a comfortable neighborhood joint. The welcoming staff here
makes you feel as if you've chosen wisely by shunning the much-hyped
Modern just a block away.

Although that may not be true culinarily—Modern makes better pies—
Amato's is a good place to go if there's too long a wait down the street.
It's also a solid choice—especially during the day—for take-out pizza by
the slice, an option not available at Modern. And don't worry; the reliably
good pizza at Amato's does justice to its New Haven appellation.

Subs, including the chicken parmesan and Italian cold cut versions, are
equally good—it's easily the best place on State Street for that sort of
fare. There are some traditional Italian-American pasta dishes served as
well, though, a few of them quite elaborate: zuppa di pesce, for example,
combines clams, mussels, scallops, calamari, and shrimp, over pasta with
red or white sauce. We think there are plenty of better places in town to
enjoy more ambitious Italian-American mains such as those, especially
when they involve fish. Salads come overdressed and watery—skip them.

But Amato's has nice homemade cannoli, and the service is dazzlingly
open-armed—they'll know your name by your third or fourth visit. So
don't overlook this place: the pizza is tasty, the price is right, and the
people are outstanding.

Anastasio's

This newcomer is better than its predecessor, and
it's got a charmingly urban back patio

7.2	7.5
Food	Feel

Italian

Casual restaurant

$45
Price

www.anastasiosrestaurant.com

Sun–Thu 11am–9pm
Fri–Sat 11am–10pm

Bar Beer, wine
Credit cards Visa, MC, AmEx
Reservations Accepted
Live music, outdoor dining,
veg-friendly

Wooster Square Area
127 Wooster St.
(203) 776-4825

A newcomer to the Wooster Street Italian-American scene, Anastasio's
picks up where Perrotti's left off. The small dining room is still *way* too
bright, with the glass and mauve-and-black accents that evoke a 1980s
hair salon, but as of this moment, they are jerry-rigging quite the cute
little scene out back. This is the only place to sit if you come here; you
wouldn't really come for the Italian-American food alone, although it's
not bad (and it's certainly better than Perrotti's before it). With a simple
strand of lights and a view of the back end of an old tenement, it's about
as inner-city romantic as it gets. When they put on Dean Martin to cover
up the noisy fan in the corner of the patio, it's totally "Lady & the
Tramp."

There are some nice touches here, like the bread basket that includes
some mighty tasty spinach and cheese stromboli—careful, you will fill up.
The benchmark of basic performance, broccoli rabe and sausage (you
gotta have special talent to mess this one up), is beyond the usual "good"
here. There's an ideal amount of salt, garlic, and acidity from the greens.
Not so for the boring, overdressed, yet watery salads. Penne amatraciana
has a red sauce that's fresh, not sugary in the least, but it's a bit liquidy
and doesn't bind properly to the (somewhat overcooked) pasta; it's
inoffensive, but utterly forgettable, like a Josh Hartnett performance. But
the osso buco (among the highest benchmarks) is splendid, tender and
rich, with just the right balance of saffron rice and light tomato broth.
Watch for landmines in this menu, like a flavorless calamari pasta whose
fava beans underneath are lost in the same watery soup that seems to
have drowned any purported anchovy taste.

For dessert, there are homemade gelati, tiramisù, and perfunctory
chocolate cake, but nothing beats the melty little curds of a ricotta
cheesecake. Forfeit the mostly American and New World-Italian wine list
in favor of the Barbera sitting on each table, if it's there (they're usually
inside). It's quite a steal at less than $20. Service is adorable—the Italian-
American version of Flo. But sitting outside makes a world of difference.

Anchor

The dive bar to end all dive bars, equally beloved by locals and students for its time-frozen charm

6.8	8.5
Food	Feel

American

Bar **$15**

Price

Daily 11:30am–midnight

Bar Beer, wine, liquor
Credit cards None
Date-friendly

Chapel District
272 College St.
(203) 865-1512

Where have all the grad students gone? On weekdays, the Anchor doesn't have the human energy it once had. Are kids these days getting less edgy? Are they losing their taste for kitsch, a jukebox, a wink, and a smile? Are they becoming beer snobs, and getting tired of drinking cheap, crappy bottled plonk?

Yet for a regular drink at a real bar in the very heart of town, any night you please, the Anchor is still the obvious choice. There may be no better-preserved, no more self-consciously hip postwar watering hole in New Haven. And no local bar is such a perennial and reliable crowd-pleaser.

The Anchor serves passable, well-priced comfort food at lunchtime, which is more classic American diner food than typical bar food: a well-executed tuna melt; good club sandwiches; liver, bacon, and onions (cheers to that); a reasonably priced cheeseburger; and hot, crisp French fries.

The Anchor still comes into its own on weekend nights, as the crowd slowly starts to assemble. The last shifts of Union League kitchen staff and bleary-eyed architecture students sidle up to the bar. Regulars have commandeered their usual tables, and the jukebox is stacked with classics. People squirm in their plastic booths, sitting knee to knee in observance of some irrational fire code prohibiting more comfortable configurations.

The newer "mermaid room," in the basement, doesn't really seem to have caught on; it's usually empty, and it's missing the dive-bar energy of the main floor. People don't seem to hang out down there much except to wait in line for the bathroom. It's kind of a network-effects issue: everybody wants to be around other people, and nobody wants to be the trend-setter.

The bartenders turn into psychotic last-call drill sergeants at the untimely hour of 12:45. (Anchor closes a little early. Always. Even the clock on the wall is at least 10 minutes fast.) As regulars whine and guzzle while intimidated novices file out obediently, the jukebox calmly spins its classic tunes. Life is as it should be at the Anchor, and we only wish that the soundtrack could follow us home.

Anna Liffey's

An authentic, subterranean Irish pub whose vibe is much more worthwhile than the food

5.8	9.0
Food	Feel

Irish, American

Bar **$25**
Price

www.annaliffeys.com

Daily 11:30am–9:30pm	**Bar** Beer, wine, liquor	**Audubon Arts District**
abbreviated menu served late	**Credit cards** Visa, MC, AmEx	17 Whitney Ave.
Sunday brunch until 2pm	Date-friendly, live music	(203) 773-1776

We haven't been thrilled with the Irish-American food lately at this classic local hangout. The place still feels as fun as ever, but ugh, that shepherd's pie: not only does it taste obviously frozen, but it's come with a center that was still icy—and topped with grainy instant mashed potatoes. And although it's hard to complain about free food, the happy-hour chafing dishes are so bad that it's warranted (cooling, congealing mozzarella sticks with marinara, for instance).

If you do eat at Anna Liffey's, giant burgers are still the best way to go: they're usually juicy, not overcooked, and served with fresh, clean cole slaw. The place is also overlooked as a brunch option; an artery-clogging Irish breakfast, featuring Irish sausage, is among several compelling options. With that, you'll definitely need a pint, or a Bloody Mary.

Otherwise, Anna Liffey's is pretty authentic as Irish pubs go. The waitstaff and bartenders, for example, hail from the homeland. You'll have to descend a flight of stairs to enter the pub, where you'll find yourself in a subterranean Irish wonderland, a dark haunt with wooden tables and benches, properly poured Guinness, and a gregarious town-gown mix among patrons. Smithwick's, a tasty bitter, is on tap, along with Harp; they'll make good Irish coffee, and even hot grog, if you ask nicely. In short, the place feels like a real pub—there's sometimes live Irish music, trivia night (Tuesday) is an entertaining ritual that's taken damn seriously, there's live Irish music on Fridays, and soccer games are on TV (the schedule is posted on the web site).

In fact, even though it's not really in a neighborhood, Anna Liffey's comes off more like a neighborhood bar than most of New Haven's real neighborhood bars (e.g. Archie Moore's) do. It's an easy place to strike up conversations, and it's also a great place for big groups on weeknights.

When some of us were law students, this pub was dear to our hearts as the Wednesday night gathering place. Our classmates may have worked their way up to seven-figure law firm partner salaries and Obama administration posts, but we can still be found slugging pints of Smithwick's in the corner, talking about local restaurants, fearing for the future of journalism.

Applebee's

Exactly the sort of chain that gives the suburbs a bad name

2.8	6.5
Food	Feel

American

Casual restaurant

$25
Price

www.applebees.com

Mon–Thu 11am–11pm
Fri–Sat 11am–midnight
Sun 11am–10pm

Bar Beer, wine, liquor
Credit cards Visa, MC, AmEx
Reservations Not accepted

Hamden
2400 Dixwell Ave.
(203) 288-8521

Orange
526 Boston Post Rd.
(203) 795-5762

The first hint that "Neighborhood Grill and Bar" is a misnomer for Applebee's is its location: you'll generally find it only on the most franchise-ridden stretches of the 'burbs. As low as your expectations might be for this sort of chain joint, with its "Eatin' Good in the Neighborhood" motto and the self-consciously quirky Americana adorning its walls, Applebee's will still disappoint. It's one of the worst of the major casual-dining chains.

The laminated, illustrated menu is laughable. That is, it's hard not to laugh at Applebee's when you encounter such ludicrous ingredient descriptions as "Mexi-ranch dressing" and "quesadilla burger." The basics are generally prepared poorly. French fries tend to be soggy; "riblets" have a super-sweet BBQ sauce and taste like processed meat; as for the congealed-on-the-inside mozzarella sticks, we've had better from the supermarket frozen-foods section. Marinara sauce is just as bad.

Boneless Buffalo wings are at least competent, and creamy spinach-and-artichoke dip with tortilla chips is passable—it's hard to go wrong with that much fat. Vegetarian options are almost comically absent: incredibly, not one of the seven "Fresh Crisp Salads" is even vegetarian. If you're on a diet, the Weight Watchers section of the menu tempts you by substituting in reduced-fat cheese.

Every now and then, Applebee's comes out with a new gimmick; their latest is the "Realburger," perhaps an attempt to compete with In 'n' Out and Five Guys. Get this: Applebee's is advertising heavily that the "best new burger on the block" is made with "100% fresh ground beef and seasonings." One shudders to imagine how the *old* burgers must have been made. Were they not fresh? Not 100% ground beef? Not "Real"?

Steaks are USDA Select-grade—the lowest you're likely to find commercially. Some dishes read like a dystopian nightmare vision of New American cuisine, like "Cajun Lime Tilapia," "Citrus Teriyaki Sauce," "Crispy Orange Chicken Bowl," or "Fiesta Lime Chicken" (a name their lawyers have actually trademarked, believe it or not).

And then there some dishes that are even more dated and disgusting than that dystopian nightmare: the ill-fated attempts at 1980s fusion with a 1970s sensibility, like "Orange Glazed Salmon" and "Oriental Chicken Salad" (with its accompanying "Oriental Vinaigrette"). Who uses the word "oriental" anymore?

Amazingly, Applebee's is just that out of touch with reality.

Archie Moore's

An archetypal American watering hole with a local feel, bar food, and a Coca-Cola fetish

6.7	7.5
Food	Feel

American, Burgers

Bar $20
Price

www.archiemoores.com

Sun–Thu 11:30am–midnight
Fri–Sat 11:30am–1am

Bar Beer, wine, liquor
Credit cards Visa, MC, AmEx
Date-friendly

East Rock
188 Willow St.
(203) 773-9870

Derby
17 Elizabeth St.
(203) 732-3255

Milford
15 Factory Ln.
(203) 876-5088

If you are a grad student, chances are you will come here in a giant group your first week of classes to bond. And our advice to you would be to do so over the menu's bar basics—not any of the fancy-sounding specials.

That's because Archie Moore's is a leading example of the classic New Haven/American bar-and-grill model, which is as appealing today as it was 50 years ago. No nonsense here. As bar food goes, Archie Moore's, generally speaking, is a slight notch below Christopher Martin's, and significantly better than Sullivan's. But they're all in the same general ballpark.

Archie's, unique among the pub-food mainstays, has an improbable residential East Rock location that draws in a large contingent of students to complement the regulars that grew up in the neighborhood. It's one of the classic spots to meet a bunch of the guys for a burger and a beer—to watch the playoffs, perhaps, or just for a night of inane banter. (The Milford and Derby locations don't have quite the neighborhood feel, but the concept is similar—the chain is rapidly expanding throughout Connecticut.)

Generally speaking, the kitchen comes through on the burgers. Our favorite incarnations are the cracked peppercorn and horseradish versions; the latter's roasted garlic and "creole spread" make surprisingly good burger-fellows. Bacon has been less reliable.

Many come here for the Buffalo wings, which have quite a reputation. To wit: you can get bottled buffalo sauce from Archie Moore's at the local grocery stores. But we must report that they're a bit overrated. On the other hand, we have to give props for the buffalo calamari, which are pulled off quite nicely. Nachos aren't bad either (the more they have on them, the better). And don't forget the steak and cheese with pepper and onions, or the pitchers of pretty good beer at pretty good prices.

In addition to the requisite televisions everywhere, the walls reveal a unique Coca-Cola fetish, with Coke paraphernalia covering virtually every inch. The signs can be amusing, but if you're frightened by the evil empire, then the inundation of signs and plaques, white script on a red field—you know the drill—might just induce seizure.

Ashley's Ice Cream

A popular pit stop that rotates through more than
150 rich, sweet flavors

Ice cream

Counter service

www.ashleysicecream.net

Mon–Sat 11am–11pm
Sun noon–11pm

Bar None
Credit cards Visa, MC, AmEx
Kid-friendly, veg-friendly

Broadway District
280 York St.
(203) 776-7744

Guilford
942 Boston Post Rd.
(203) 458-3040

Branford
1016 Main St.
(203) 481-5558

Hamden
2100 Dixwell Ave.
(203) 287-7566

Still as popular as ever, and still proclaiming to serve "Connecticut's Best
Ice Cream," Ashley's is worth a visit in any season, whether you choose
the New Haven, Guilford, Branford, or Hamden branch. Even if the motto
smacks of puffery, the little shop serves about 20 choices of quite decent
ice cream, sorbet, and frozen yogurt, including one fat-free and sugar-
free option. (In our opinion, though, such healthful choices do not
deserve to be called ice cream.) The derivative options run the usual
gamut—milkshakes, sundaes, cups, and cones of various sizes.

The ice cream is rich, sweet (but not too sweet), and very creamy.
Flavors span from traditional to adventurous; if you are lucky with your
timing, "White Russian" may be among the flavors on offer—try it. You
also can't go wrong with "Bittersweet Chocolate." It really is
bittersweet—not cloying and not icy—with tiny chips studding a mousse-
like, melty ice cream. Other great flavor finds—when on special—are
Grape-Nuts and Indian pudding. The latter is a molasses-based wonder;
it's New England in a cup. The hot fudge topping is delicious, too.

The décor at the New Haven branch, which is patronized by undergrads
and Yale Law students, is a pleasant combination of blond wood, high
round bar tables, and corresponding stools. The atmosphere is good
enough for the year-round enthusiasts. Still, most people take out,
especially in good weather. This particular York Street storefront has a
checkered history of food-service failures—honk if you remember
Whimsels, the ill-fated crêpe place.

Ashley's, however, seems to be the best idea yet for the space, perhaps
because ice cream is something (unlike crêpes) that many people are able
to eat just about every day. And for variation, Ashley's ice cream also
comes shaped into cakes, which are prized for birthdays and other
celebrations (order ahead). Baked goods include some allegedly famous
and incredibly rich chocolate fudge. If you like to get your daily allowance
of sugar and fat in one sitting, this is one way to do it. There's a stable of
permanent flavors; others rotate daily in summer months, permuting
through a total of at least 150 varieties. Cheers (or licks?) to that.

Assaggio

Middling, dated Italian-American food in an upmarket environment

6.2	8.0
Food	Feel

New American

Upmarket restaurant

$45
Price

www.assaggiobranford.com

Sun–Fri 11am–9pm
Sat 5pm–9pm

Bar Beer, wine, liquor
Credit cards Visa, MC, AmEx
Reservations Accepted
Good wines, outdoor dining

Branford
168 Montowese St.
(203) 483-5426

Assaggio is the consummate upscale Connecticut restaurant: Jazz. Little red candles. Swervy track lighting. Cool mirrors. A happy atrium with exposed windows. In good weather, there are even outdoor seats, although they're a bit close to the road for our taste. Dinner will likely begin with the habit of dipping the bread into the plate of olive oil. They don't do this in Italy, but they do it here; it's one of the many tidbits that have made Italian restaurants in America into a unique genre: not authentic, but not bad either.

Assaggio's menu is absurdly long, which is a warning sign. A crêpe stuffed with ricotta, broccoli rabe, and sausage, covered by tomato cream sauce, comes undersalted; all that's left is richness. That's a widespread problem; uneven seasoning has plagued both fish and meat preparations. We appreciate a few authentic touches—tortellini in chicken broth, homemade gnocchi—but the menu is riddled with over-sauced banalities: grilled chicken breast with shiitake mushrooms and gorgonzola; pennette with "julienned chicken," portabella mushrooms, roasted peppers, and pine nuts; scallops in Madeira cream sauce; or those same pennette with chicken (this time "grilled"), asparagus, and sun-dried tomatoes. Tossing chicken strips with pasta isn't just a totally late-1980s move; it's something you'd literally never see at a serious Italian restaurant these day. Not to mention the "iced shrimp with cocktail sauce."

And what about pricing duck breast, Chilean sea bass, and New York strip at "market"? At this sort of restaurant? Give us a break. This just looks like a lame attempt to conceal the high prices.

Assaggio has been cited by the state of Connecticut for having fruit flies in their liquor bottles. On the other hand, fruit flies in liquor won't hurt you, and there's quite a good, and decently priced, Italian wine list; there are some good Oregon Pinot Noir and Spanish producers on the list, as well.

It's not that the food's bad, exactly—just frustratingly dated and unexciting. We still love Assaggio's atmosphere, but it's frustrating when fairly high prices and pretense aren't backed up by technical proficiency, careful seasoning, or any commitment to doing something more authentic or interesting than the norm.

Athenian Diner

Its figure may be less than Greek, but at least it's open all night

5.8 Food

4.0 Feel

American, Greek

Casual restaurant

$25 Price

www.atheniandiner.com

24 hours

Bar Beer, wine, liquor
Credit cards Visa, MC, AmEx
Reservations Accepted
Kid-friendly

Westville
1426 Whalley Ave.
(203) 397-1556

Milford
1064 Boston Post Rd.
(203) 878-5680

The Athenian Diner is Connecticut's very own late-night mini-chain, keeping state residents fed 24 hours a day, seven days a week. (Okay, maybe people aren't traveling from *all* over for the fare; in fact, we're fairly confident that most patrons have come from within a five-mile radius.)

But the look and feel, especially of the location in New Haven proper, is pretty classic. You might be on Whalley Avenue in Westville, but you'll swear you're in Queens. All of it could hardly be any more typical: there are the tinted-glass windows; the big, incongruous pink neon lines; the colorful assortment of customers from every imaginable walk of life, especially late at night, after the bars close; and the diner's very shape, a boxy apparition in a lonely parking lot. Then there are the brightly lit booths and the big, glossy everything-but-the-kitchen-sink menus, which you are apparently expected to have speed-read in the 45 seconds before the waiter or waitress arrives, expectantly tapping pen on pad.

Or maybe they don't even expect you to order off the menu. After all, the whole process reinforces our deep sense of bafflement at these sorts of menus at these sorts of places: does anyone ever *really* order the $24.95 twin lobster tail special? What about the elaborate Italian-American veal dishes? When was the last time they sold an order of the baked red snapper? Who in their right mind would spend that kind of money at an all-night diner rather than at a restaurant with some ambiance? It really boggles the mind.

We prefer to stick to the diner classics, such as a well-executed Reuben, with beefy slices of meat that stand up to the properly fried bread, decent sauerkraut, and Russian dressing. Good also are the few available Greek-ish dishes, which can be hard to find in the New Haven area—a rich, creamy, and indulgently satisfying moussaka, for example, which comes with a simple, if uninspiring, salad whose herbed dressing has a subtle sprinkling of feta. Stick to the basic diner fare, and you won't be disappointed.

Atticus

New Haven's classic bookstore-café, newly renovated and as great as ever

8.3 Food

9.5 Feel

Sandwiches, Baked goods

Café

$10 Price

www.atticusbookstorecafe.com

Mon–Sat 7am–10pm
Sun 8am–9pm

Bar None
Credit cards Visa, MC, AmEx
Date-friendly, kid-friendly,
veg-friendly, Wi-Fi

Upper Chapel Area
1082 Chapel St.
(203) 776-4040

Bring together good books, good coffee, a great bakery, and a warm, open space, and you've set the stage for a legendary institution. Warm yet studious, hip yet professorial, intellectual yet flirtatious, Atticus is a college-town classic that became a true American pioneer in the bookstore-café genre when it added a café section in 1986.

In more recent times, the space has been newly renovated and slightly modernized to accommodate more tables, and—as makes sense given the café's success—it has become as much a place to eat and drink as it is a bookstore. But the feeling hasn't changed much. For that, we're glad, because there's something magical about Atticus. An academic buzz permeates the place from dawn until closing. There's scarcely an hour in the day when Atticus isn't hopping with everyone from book-signing authors to travel-guide browsers to over-caffeinated, pre-exam collegians.

The black-bean soup is always a winner (say yes to the dash of sour cream and chopped fresh onions proffered), but almost all of the soups here are tempting; they're served with hot slices of delicious, locally produced Chabaso bread. Even on its own, we love the cranberry nut bread, which is best served toasted with butter. The garden salad comes with Atticus' trademark shredded carrots and a notable Dijon dressing.

Panini, while slightly pricey, are served on those great breads, too, and are uniformly good. A standout is the tacchino (turkey) version, which is like Thanksgiving on a roll but warm and gooey, so—in fact—an improvement on most of our Thanksgivings. The Cuban panino on brioche is also very satisfying.

Pastries and desserts are also as good as ever. Bread pudding is rich, decadent, and delicious—which is perhaps not surprising, considering the bread it begins with.

The two-floor independent bookstore is formidable in its own right, with one of New Haven's best selections of fiction and nonfiction and one of the city's best lineups of readings by well-known authors, with a particular focus on those with Yale and New England affiliations. It's yet another feather in this classic establishment's culiniterary cap.

Au Bon Pain

2.5 Food **4.0** Feel

A sketchy but well-located McSandwich joint—skip
the food and steal the outdoor seats

Sandwiches, Baked goods

Counter service

$10 Price

www.aubonpain.com

Mon–Sat 7am–midnight
Sun 8am–midnight

Bar None
Credit cards Visa, MC, AmEx
Kid-friendly, outdoor dining, Wi-Fi

Broadway District
1 Broadway
(203) 865-5554

This McSandwich café-restaurant chain is hyper-convenient to Yale Law
School, which is part of why ABP perennially contends with the Law
School Dining Hall (along with Yorkside and Koffee Too?) in the battle for
lunchtime hegemony over lawyers-to-be. This can make for a considerable
queue at peak times. Problem is, it's pretty gross. It smells bad, it often
feels filthy, and the food is processed to the max.

The best place to sit here—weather permitting—is outdoors, where a
few metal tables and chairs are frequented by some of New Haven's more
legendary street characters. You probably won't even get caught if you
bring over something better from one of the local food carts.

The bright and bustling but fast-food-style room is updated in simple
shades of yellow, in line with ABP's new look, but the vibe remains the
same, with tables and booths that are as likely to be occupied by a laptop
date as by a friendly couple or gregarious group. The service is nothing
more than perfunctory, but if you position yourself right, you can monitor
the person assembling your sandwich, making last-minute requests for
more of this or none of that.

The baked goods are hit-or-miss. We don't mind the stuffed croissants,
particularly the ham and cheese, spinach and cheese, and raspberry and
cheese versions; they're satisfying, if reheated and overpriced. Scones,
bagels, and plain croissants are less impressive. Strangely, ABP seems to
get worse each year.

The sandwiches are the other focus of the menu, but the yearly
innovations don't seem to be going anywhere interesting, even if prices
have remained relatively reasonable. Soups rotate daily, and they can be
okay, but the watery coffee does not impress. In the end, your only use
for ABP might be when you've got an absolute coffee craving and Publick
Cup has no seats left (as is frequently the case). Even then, you might as
well try bootlegging some take-out contraband from Publick and free-
riding on ABP's outdoor tables.

Aunt Chilada's

A festive Tex-Mex mecca better for the free-flowing margaritas than the grub

5.5	7.5
Food	Feel

Mexican

Casual restaurant

$30
Price

www.auntchilada.com

Sun–Thu 11am–1am
Fri–Sat 11am–2am

Bar Beer, wine, liquor
Credit cards Visa, MC, AmEx
Reservations Accepted
Delivery, kid-friendly, outdoor
dining

Hamden
3931 Whitney Ave.
(203) 230-4640

This used to be one of our favorite trips to make—go way out on Whitney Avenue, walk around Sleeping Giant for a while, and get a better-than-decent margarita and a bowl of spinach-queso dip at Aunt Chilada's. But the slipping quality of the food has recently changed this. What used to be a fun, kitschy outing when we craved Tex-Mex has turned into a bland, greasy, expensive proposition.

The menu of this enormous suburban Tex-Mex restaurant and bar is just what you'd expect: huge portions of enchiladas, burritos, and tacos overflowing with cheese, rice, and refried beans; giant appetizer platters of artery-clogging New-England-meets-border food; easy-to-drink margaritas; and a raucous bar that caters largely to the frat crowd from nearby Quinnipiac College and other local schools.

There's cavernous seating in the huge, two-floor wooden house, so even when it hops on weekends, it's not hard to get a seat. We recommend sitting in the room to the left as you enter the restaurant, because it has a fireplace and a cozier feel. The atmosphere, regardless, is festive, perhaps because so many of the patrons are sipping the sweet margaritas (the house version is fine).

Food tends to come with a generous helping of grease, and we have our suspicions that it's not the freshest. As mains go, we recommend sticking to the Mexican combinations or the fajitas rather than the "dinners," which have recently included an habanero pasta with muenster cheese. Yikes.

Prices are startlingly high, but go to the web site and you can find coupons for a free appetizer. In the end, Aunt Chilada's delivers Tex-Mex comfort food basically as expected. No more, no less.

Baja's

Once an exciting find for authentic Northern
Mexican in Orange; now it's resting on its laurels

6.5	5.0
Food	Feel

Mexican   Casual restaurant   **$25**
                                                                     Price

Mon 11:30am–9pm; Tue–Thu   **Bar** Beer, wine, liquor   **Orange**
11:30am–9:30pm; Fri   **Credit cards** Visa, MC, AmEx 63 Boston Post Rd.
11:30am–10pm; Sat noon–   **Reservations** Accepted   (203) 799-2252
10pm; Sun noon–9pm

Sigh. This is another former favorite gone downhill, while prices went up.
How did a place known for its four-alarm salsas and terrific fish tacos turn
into such a run-of-the-mill dive? We loved the Cal-Mex feel of this place
and would go when we were craving the closest approximation of a
Mission burrito we could get. Now, though, the dishes just seem
carelessly oversized and underseasoned.

It's still stuck in the middle of a nondescript strip mall on that very
suburban Route 1, which is why it was so cool that Baja's was rocking out
some of the most legitimate regional Mexican food in the area. It was real
Northern Mexico/Baja California/dusty borderland grub. Now it's leaning
heavily to the gringo side.

Everything still tastes fresh, and chicken mole is still good. Burritos have
definitely been beefing up since our last review, though, and it seems to
have become a reason to charge people in the neighborhood of $15 for
them. $15? The product cost on a burrito doesn't vary that much, even if
it did get bigger. What's in it now, Périgord truffles?

As can be the case in strip malls, Baja's atmosphere can seem a little
strange and depressing, especially if you show up when no one else
happens to be around. That said, there are colorful murals of Baja
California, and an equally colorful bartender hawking gargantuan
margaritas at the improbably-placed central bar. Everything is supremely
casual, and there's a salsa bar with endless toppings for tortilla chips,
ranging from mild to picante.

There is also still the illustrious lineup of Mexican beers—down-and-
dirty and prestigious alike. It's still one of the best chances you have in
Orange of getting good Mexican, but where we once got kind of worked
up about this place, it seems to have just blended in with all the rest.

Bangkok Gardens

Sit in the atrium, and you'll survive—but time has
left this decent Thai-American food behind

6.9 Food

6.5 Feel

Thai

Upmarket restaurant

$30 Price

Mon–Fri 11:30am–10pm
Sat noon–11pm
Sun noon–10pm

Bar Beer, wine
Credit cards Visa, MC, AmEx
Reservations Accepted

Upper Chapel Area
172 York St.
(203) 789-8684

The aptly named Bangkok Gardens can be thought of as the date restaurant of downtown New Haven Thai: it's the nicest looking (although that's not saying much), and it's compatible with even the most cash-strapped grad student's budget. And it is something of an icon, serving the same Thai-American dishes that pass for authentic in most of the US—but at least these versions taste a bit better than average. But only a bit.

At a minimum, you can't fault Bangkok Gardens for any shortage of options. The lunch buffet has a dizzying array of dishes. Hoa mouk, which features on the bargain-priced lunch menu, is a tender cake of chopped chicken, cabbage, basil leaf, and aromatic kaffir lime leaf, covered with a homemade sauce that includes coconut. It's a totally authentic dish that you'll almost never see elsewhere, but, sadly, we've slowly noticed the cake becoming drier and the sauce more scarce. While just about everything else on the menu—lunch or dinner—is at least reliable, we've noticed variability in drunken noodle and yum nua (beef salad infused with citrus and cilantro).

In spite of the slightly upmarket vive, there's something unsatisfying about dining here. Maybe it's the atmosphere; too much glass and the formal, blackbowtied waitstaff make you much less comfortable than you should be. Or maybe it's the bland décor and starchy tablecloths. A sunny atrium in the front area of the restaurant provides warm respite from the day, especially welcome in winter. At lunch, when the sun is out, the room bustles with midday energy, and the price is right. It's a good way to go if you are lucky enough to find seating in the atrium. In the evenings, the shortcomings of décor and lighting are harder to ignore, and prices are higher. Take-out is always an option.

But with Thai Taste having improved and better Thai now available—Rice Pot, The Terrace—the reasons to patronize Bangkok Gardens are vanishing.

Bar (Brü Room)

Craft beer, top-echelon thin-crust pizza, and ever-irritating service that can't stop us from loving it

9.1	7.5
Food	Feel

Pizza

Bar **$25**

Price

www.barnightclub.com

Mon–Tue 5pm–11:30pm
Wed–Thu 11:30am–2:30pm,
5pm–11:30pm
Fri–Sat 11:30am–midnight
Sun 11:30am–11:30pm

Bar Beer, wine, liquor
Credit cards Visa, MC, AmEx
Veg-friendly

Chapel District
254 Crown St.
(203) 495-8924

Our position may be controversial, but we won't beat around the bush, and we won't apologize for it: the New Haven Pizza Triumvirate needs to expand to include a fourth. Bar is every bit in the same league as Frank Pepe and Sally's—and it's better than Modern.

Back in the day, Pepe's and Sally's crusts were considered thin. Now, even your mom makes thin-crust pizza, but Bar takes it to the next level. The crust is so delicate that it's almost invisible, the tomatoes are fresh, and the balance is superb. The white pizza with mashed potato, bacon, and extra garlic is an absolute hoot, one of the first New Haven foods we feed our visitors from afar. You can't knock it unless you've tried it. We also love the spinach-and-bacon and sausage-and-hot-pepper pies.

Prices are reasonable, so why not start with Bar's classic New American formula salad (greens, sliced pears, caramelized pecans, crumbled blue cheese, and a light vinaigrette— works like a charm), and get a pitcher of microbrewed Pale Ale, a hoppy American classic. Seasonal beers are great, too; the brewmaster here is a genius, a true beer nerd who has been known to lead beer tours of England.

There seems to be a hard-and-fast rule that great New Haven pizza comes with snotty and indifferent service. Bar is no exception, but its approach is different, anyway: instead of charmingly salty old servers, your fate is placed in the hands of a gaggle of self-important hostesses who seem to seat cute guys they know first, intimidating thugs second, and (unless you're in one of the first two groups) you, after an hour or two.

On weekends, you can throw velvet-rope cover-charge preposterousness into the mix, too (the adjoining club has a crawling pick-up scene). It's all a recipe for ruining your night before it's even begun. However, if there's a long wait, you can always order a pie at the counter and enter the anarchic self-service fray of the bar room, which is preferable, at least, to dealing with that bitchy front of the house. Do keep in mind, however, that Bar pizza has a very short half-life in cool air, so don't bother with the after-hours slices that are sitting there, asymptoting.

In spite of all this, once you're seated, Bar has an enjoyable post-hip vibe. The place has long ago graduated into an age when the microbrewery concept is no longer novel, an age when exposed brick and steel pipes are no longer the revelation they were in the early '90s. But Bar still wears them well. Now if only they'd start treating their customers like human beings. That principle should be timeless.

Barcelona

Tapas dressed up for a sexy (if chainish) night on the town

8.9	9.0
Food	Feel

Spanish

Upmarket restaurant

$65
Price

www.barcelonawinebar.com

Sun–Thu 5pm–10pm
Fri–Sat 5pm–11pm

Bar Beer, wine, liquor
Credit cards Visa, MC, AmEx
Reservations Accepted
Date-friendly, good wines

Chapel District
155 Temple St.
(203) 848-3000

Connecticut's chain-tapas empire is built around a tried-and-true formula: fashion, flash, and the lucre wrought from your consumption of endless numbers of tapas and pitchers of sangría. Even if Yale students get a 15% weekday discount, Barcelona is still, to be blunt, a money machine.

The beautiful, almost-too-dark space has a classy-urban-meets-Austin-Powers vibe, with sleek mahogany panels, warm lighting, an airy kitchen. Some of the floor-to-ceiling glass windows are covered by walls of wine. Clearly, Barcelona is heavily capitalized. But the food shatters chain expectations. Start with jamón serrano (cured ham), which is coaxed into unusually appropriate thinness by a clear professional with the meat slicer. Pair it with roasted garlic cloves and charcoal-grilled, olive-oil-rubbed bread, and you've got a starter of unusual power and elegance.

Caña de oveja, a silky, earthy sheep's milk cheese, pairs well with the crisp tartness of green apples. We also love the slightly over-sweet but addictive chorizo with figs; deep, rich morcilla (blood sausage); properly cooked, flavorful (if hardly tender) hanger steak; Brussels sprouts a la plancha, redolent of bacon and thyme; and coca del día, a tiny pizza with a cracker-crisp crust whose ingredients rotate daily. Gambas al ajillo—garlicky shrimp cooked in good olive oil and leavened by the spicy energy of hot peppers—are served without their heads on, contrary to Spanish tradition, thus robbing customers of the shrimpiest juices. Regardless, ask for an extra ration of the hot, crusty bread to soak up the sauce.

Among mains, the Spanglish "Half Chicken al Pimientos" stands out boldly. Its succulent meat and crisp skin are supported by a layer of thinly sliced roasted potatoes and a bright, lemony cherry-pepper sauce. If Barcelona can do chicken like this, why must it also lower itself to serving Caesar salad with grilled chicken? And why must grilled white asparagus, dressed with a slimy truffle vinaigrette, be so tough? Caldo gallego, a white-bean stew, is bland in spite of its chorizo, bacon, and winter greens. Flan is dreamily delicate, but carrot cake is uninspired. We like Barcelona's competent sangría, though, and the heavily Spanish wine list, full of Sherries and underappreciated reds, although we wish older Rioja vintages were marked up more reasonably.

The service is spotty, profit-minded, and irritatingly chainy ("Welcome to Barcelona, my name is Jenny and I'll be taking care of you this evening; have you dined with us before? Let me tell you a little about what tapas are…."). Water is rarely refilled, yet empty tapas plates are cleared with aggressive efficiency, even when you're still sopping. Don't let the profit principle impede your pleasure: just say no!

Basta Trattoria

6.6 Food | **8.0** Feel

Italian

Upmarket restaurant | **$60** Price

www.bastatrattoria.com

Mon–Fri 5pm–10pm	**Bar** Beer, wine	**Chapel District**
Sat noon–10pm	**Credit cards** Visa, MC, AmEx	1006 Chapel St.
Sun 1pm–10pm	**Reservations** Essential	(203) 772-1715
	Good wines, outdoor dining, veg-friendly	

First, the good news: this Italian restaurant—which is next door to, and under the same ownership as, Claire's, New Haven's vegetarian/kosher college-town eclecticopia on the corner of Chapel and College Streets—has reinvented itself as a "trattoria," with an informality more appropriate for the space. There's still the commitment to local produce and sustainable food.

But there's some bad news, too: first, the kitchen hasn't improved. Most of the menu is still underwhelming, and still overpriced. Second, gone from the menu, sadly, is our favorite thing here—the wood-fired pizza. It had only been offered at lunch, but now that there's no lunch service, they seem to have gotten rid of the one thing they did really well. Why?

Fried calamari aren't bad—we like the hot cherry peppers—but this $14 appetizer is stunningly dear. We like the sweet-savory balance (okay, more sweet than savory) in the less pricey "ricotta di' natale" (we have no explanation for the apostrophe after the "di"), made with local, hand-packed, artisanal cheese; toasted almonds and berries; and lemon-rosemary honey. We'd like it even more as dessert.

Among mains, we favor "Sunday Dinner," which brings together well-constructed meatballs, hot sausage that's hard to argue with, cheesy eggplant rollatini, and mushy rigatoni. (Virtually every pasta comes overcooked.) Carbonara fares considerably worse, made with cream and thus heavier than it should be, and topped with mealy, horrendously overcooked shrimp. Fish mains tend to be cooked too much, too, especially salmon, which requires a light touch.

The space feels lunchy and casual, better suited to the new concept than it was to the more pretentious previous version. We enjoy the view into the bustling little kitchen, which is barely wider than an Amtrak railway car. Service is folksy and friendly. As fans of organic and local produce, it pains us to complain about Basta's value proposition. We know how expensive these ingredients are. But we also know what people expect from a restaurant when they're paying a lot, and it's something more than this.

The Beach House

Sexy, intimate, and upscale steak and seafood that won't break the bank

8.3	9.0
Food	Feel

Seafood, Steakhouse

Upmarket restaurant

$60
Price

www.beachhousemilford.com

Mon–Wed 11:30am–10pm
Thu–Sat 11:30am–midnight
Sun 11am–3pm, 4pm–9pm

Bar Beer, wine, liquor
Credit cards Visa, MC, AmEx
Reservations Accepted
Date-friendly, good wines, live music

Milford
141 Merwin Ave.
(203) 877-9300

From the outside, it looks morose and generic, like the beige leasing office for the housing development across the street. You have to off-road to park in the torn-up lot. But once inside, the world utterly changes. This is the mark of a good restaurant.

The dining room has the feeling of a Hamptons or Newport Beach dinner party. The windows are shaded (and there aren't really any in the bar), which helps shut out the outside world. Off to one side, a small enclave with a fireplace and armchairs also fits a few tables, so diners feel like they're in the family room of a house. White linens, preset wine glasses, candles on every table, and hurricane lamps set among stones and shells set the mood, which is intimate and a little sexy. Further back, a huge wooden saloon back bar is flanked by softly glowing blue lights, which could look cheesy and nightclubby if they were just a shade brighter. A mini-rotunda with library ladder stores the wines, and a totally open kitchen sizzles and jumps off to one side.

The menu is half seafood and half steak. Oysters are available by the single piece, which gives diners the chance to sample Blue Points, or the daily changing Eastern or Pacific oyster without committing to a whole dozen. They are beautifully shucked, the lip of the shell so smooth you could cut paper on it, and the body lies, unperturbed, like a pink-beige pool within. Don't dare touch that cocktail sauce! Calamari are fried to a non-greasy, feather-light crispness and come with ample cherry peppers and olives.

Seafood mains, however, tend to come somewhat overcooked, and they take an awfully long time to get to you. This problem seems to be more seriously addressed on the steak page of the menu, where cooking temps are described, from "Pittsburgh-style" ("seared, red, and cool inside") to well done ("not responsible").

The wine list is a veritable tome that seems pretty savvy, but is filled with amateurish descriptions and misleading conceits. ("Albariño" is in parentheses next to "Spanish Pinot Grigio.") Domestics are mostly boring mass producers, with a few Central Coast gems here and there, but the imports are more exciting and chosen with obvious passion. Prices are a little inflated, but there's a decent half-bottle selection.

This is a fantastic place for date night, or to impress clients and guests. Just to be safe, ask for your grilled fish "undercooked." We're sure they know how to oblige.

Bella Haven Pizza

5.9 **3.0**
Food *Feel*

The best of the recent quick-and-late purveyors in this spot—but that's not saying much

Pizza, Italian

Casual restaurant

$15
Price

Mon–Wed 11am–midnight; Thu 11am–2am; Fri–Sat 11am–3am; Sun noon–midnight

Bar None
Credit cards Visa, MC
Reservations Not accepted
Delivery, veg-friendly

Chapel District
240 College St.
(203) 777-7775

Thank goodness for small mercies.

This narrow space was once occupied by Original Falafel, one of the lowest-rated establishments in the second edition of this guide. Then it was King Falafel, which was scarcely better. Now it's Bella Haven pizza, which is less bad. Way less bad.

That doesn't mean it's good, though. When you name yourself after a particular food item—pizza, in this case—it's strange not to pay enough attention to that food item to make it culinarily worthwhile. Yet the pizza by the slice, at this joint, sits around for ages, getting congealed. Who wants to go out to a restaurant for the equivalent of leftover pizza reheated in your oven?

Bizzarrely, that pizza is also the most overpriced thing on the menu: $16.75 for a mediocre large veggie pie? In this town of great, affordable pizza? Are they kidding?

Calzones, fried seafood, wings, baked ziti, seafood pasta (like the doomed shrimp alfredo), and such don't do much better; mains like chicken broccoli, chicken piccata, and chicken cacciatore do much worse. But that's probably not a shocker.

A steak-and-cheese sandwich with grilled onions, lettuce, tomato, hot peppers, and mayo, on the other hand—comfort food for the ages—rings in at under six bucks; in a nice touch, the pizza oven is employed to melt the cheese into the roll. (Bella Haven takes their time with preps, for better or worse.) The strangely chosen romaine lettuce is a throwaway, but the meat is well seasoned, the bread fresh, and the sandwich above average.

All of this happens in a fairly depressing, usually empty, fast-food-ish space that can't be rescued by the cheeriness of its red and orange walls. The people are friendly, and there's late night delivery, but with so-so pizza, that sounds so much less exciting. In the end, this place might be a small improvement over its disastrous predecessors, but that doesn't mean it's worth seeking out.

Bella's Café

One of New Haven's best brunch spots is now dabbling in dinner

8.1	8.5
Food	Feel

American

Casual restaurant

$25
Price

www.bellascafect.com

Tue–Thu 7am–3pm
Fri 7am–3pm, 5:30pm–10pm
Sat 8am–3pm, 5:30pm–10pm
Sun 8am–3pm, 5:30pm–9pm

Bar Beer, wine
Credit cards Visa, MC, AmEx
Reservations Not accepted
Date-friendly, kid-friendly, live music, veg-friendly

Westville
896 Whalley Ave.
(203) 387-7107

Watch out, Pantry: Westville is becoming quite the brunch destination for New Haven proper. Lena's does a lovely brunch and breakfast, but Bella's (formerly Bella Rosa) has long been considered the best. It all begins with the cheery neighborhood atmosphere—the small room is lovely and informal, bright and airy, cozy and intimate, as if Parisian and American at the same time. And now that there's wine and beer here, a mimosa will put it over the top, for sure.

Specials vary from day to day, and the brunch menu changes weekly. It's worth the wait—and the SuperCatholic décor—to breakfast on such loveliness as pumpkin pancakes stuffed with cinnamon mascarpone, or gigantic omelettes filled with smoked salmon, dill, and crème fraîche. Bella's also makes the best French toast in New Haven, hands down. There are several incarnations, and often a special like panettone French toast with orange crème anglaise—a concoction that, when we tried it, might have been too rich for breakfast, but was also a soft and buttery treat that was worth every indulgent bite.

Here's the big news: dinner is now served on Friday and Saturday nights (with live jazz on the former), with a menu that glides somewhat haphazardly over Italian, Middle Eastern, Indian, and classic American preps. There's a dated lack of creativity on this menu—tuna-wasabi combinations and such—but the execution is generally there to make up for the uninspired recipes.

The service here tends to be friendly, but—especially at peak times— almost intolerably slow. Still, with these yellow walls, this brunch, and this vibe, it barely matters. You want the experience to last. Waits at prime time on weekend mornings can be considerable, but interestingly, Bella's still seems unknown to many downtowners—like so many places in Westville, it's only a ten-minute drive from the center of New Haven. In a neighborhood that conceals many gems, Bella's Café must be its crowning achievement.

Bentara

Still the beauty queen of Ninth Square, but the
kitchen is no longer executing

Malaysian

Upmarket restaurant

www.bentara.com

Sun–Thu 11:30am–2:30pm,
5pm–9:30pm; Fri–Sat
11:30am–2:30pm, 5pm–
10:30pm

Bar Beer, wine, liquor
Credit cards Visa, MC, AmEx
Reservations Accepted
Date-friendly, good wines,
veg-friendly

Ninth Square
76 Orange St.
(203) 562-2511

It is with great sadness that we are obligated to report the decline of this
great restaurant. For years, Bentara was one of the most dependable
spots in New Haven for an excellent meal, but it also deserved great praise
for its role as a Ninth Square pioneer—the first smart restaurant to
venture into this struggling old neighborhood. Bentara was a landmark in
New Haven's history, a gleaming beacon of a new urban renaissance.

It's still impossible to argue with the warm, hip, beautiful space; the
relatively reasonable prices; or the suitability of Bentara to large parties
(you can order family-style and share everything) and to vegetarians (the
menu is packed with meatless options). And although the hefty wine list
doesn't accurately describe what's in the cellar, it is still studded with fairly
priced, hard-to-find Burgundies and Super-Tuscans.

But this kitchen has lost its way. Even roti murtabak, which was always
a reliable way to start—griddle-fried bread, rendered rich with ghee, filled
with ground beef, onion, and egg, and served with curry lentil sauce and
a sweet-and-sour red onion relish—arrives soggy and lukewarm. Beef
kerutuk, a curry-stew preparation with potatoes and coconut milk, has
come with unbelievably chewy chunks of meat. Nasi lemak has gone
downhill, too, with tough anchovies, and beef or chicken two soy—long
one of our favorites—seems to have gotten sweeter and less complex.
These tasting notes have been consistently confirmed on multiple visits by
multiple critics.

The service has suffered, too, especially with respect to the wait for
your food. We've had lunch take two and a half hours when we'd hoped
to get out in one. Orders have frequently come out wrong, and rudeness
has been a frequent problem, too (especially when one orders a wine
from the wine list that isn't in stock, which seems to be most of the time).
Although there are still occasionally some flashes of deliciousness, we
have no idea how this restaurant has descended from such greatness to
such averageness. Who is in charge here these days? Hyde?

Bertucci's

One of the few chains that we've long loved to love—but can't they ditch those pastas?

5.7 *Food*   **6.4** *Feel*

Italian, Pizza

Casual restaurant   **$35** *Price*

www.bertuccis.com

Sun–Thu 11am–10pm
Fri–Sat 11am–11pm

Bar Beer, wine, liquor
Credit cards Visa, MC, AmEx
Reservations Accepted
Delivery, kid-friendly, veg-friendly, Wi-Fi

Orange
550 Boston Post Rd.
(203) 799-6828

It's nice when one of the McFamilyRestaurant chains turns out to serve reasonably good food in a reasonably pleasant atmosphere. For a long time Bertucci's did so—and made Olive Garden look really, really bad in the process—both aesthetically (Bertucci's doesn't try as hard to be fake Italian, and thus comes off less awkward, although we can't get with the new logo, whose pizza-slice apostrophe looks accidentally un-curly) and taste-wise (they make good use of that oven and don't overcook pasta as much). Even if it's a family "casual dining" chain at its heart, it's a unique New England version of one (the chain calls the Boston area home), and an exposed kitchen gives the place a surprisingly upscale flair.

If you can look past the mass-produced aesthetic of the menus, they also show spikes of sophistication. Three-cheese focaccia, on the menu for years, is a crispy starter that comes with a winning sauce of smoky tomatoes. Among mains, we strongly favor the pizza (traditional, not deep-dish). There's a real brick oven here, and it can turn out some enjoyable pies. Crusts are pleasingly crispy, cheese is well handled, and ingredients taste fresh. Meat eaters will find the "Sporkie," with mild ricotta and sweet sausage, easy to love. The segmented "Ultimate Bertucci" also fares well; one quarter of the disc boasts fragrant rosemary ham. For those less carnivorous, the "Lestina" deep-dish pizza, with sun-dried tomatoes, mushrooms, and roasted garlic, can be nice, especially when it's not overwhelmed with a carpet of chewy sage leaves.

Lunch begins with a free salad; you can get one for $2 with dinner. Here, though, you get what you pay for: a curious mix of iceberg lettuce and bell peppers, shredded American cheese, and a gloopy supermarket-style vinaigrette. Then there are the famous Bertucci's dinner rolls (they're served at lunch as well)—warm, bagel-dense doughballs that have built up a cult following, perhaps in large part because they arrive hot enough to melt butter, a quality that has undeniable appeal. We don't like many of the huge-portioned pasta dishes, especially the ones with shrimp, lobster, or any sort of chicken. The trend there is that they either perish in a sea of cream or are bland and dry. Worse yet is the expanded menu of "dinners," which are abominations like "balsamic chicken" (which comes with broccoli and mashed potatoes) or (yikes) breadcrumb-crusted tilapia on a bed of spinach. Here they're trying to compete with Olive Garden. Don't buy it. Locals in the know stick to the pizza, and so should you.

Bespoke/Sabor Latino

Roomba's displaced successor is just as exciting and sexy, but not as good

7.4	9.5
Food	Feel

Nuevo Latino   Upmarket restaurant

$80
Price

www.bespokenewhaven.com

Mon–Thu 5pm–9:30pm
Fri–Sat 5pm–10:30pm
Sun 4:30pm–8:30pm

Bar Beer, wine, liquor
Credit cards Visa, MC, AmEx
Reservations Accepted
Date-friendly

Chapel District
266 College St.
(203) 562-4644

This dual-personality restaurant on the choicest block in town comes from the team behind the beloved Roomba, which closed after a real estate dispute. It occupies more or less the entirety of a spectacularly renovated townhouse, a true labor of love that took years to finish. It was worth the wait. On the ground floor, the bar—open fully to the street in warm months—twinkles with skinny chandeliers and lights embedded in the wood-covered walls; a trendy flirtation turns into an all-out love affair when you see the candle-lit, wine-cellarish back room. Every floor is themed differently, and the open-air rooftop bar is absolutely sensational.

Although the new restaurant feels just as sexy as Roomba did, and there are still some high culinary points, the execution in the kitchen isn't consistently there—in part because the menu suffers from such an identity crisis. The place first opened with different menus for the different floors: if you wanted to order off the New American menu, you had to sit in one area, below, called Bespoke; if you wanted to order the old Roomba food, you had to sit in another area, above, called Sabor Latino. At some point, they realized the ridiculousness of these artificial menu/space restrictions, so now it's really all just one restaurant—but one that tries to do too much, with too little focus. The portions are too big, too complicated, and too expensive; without restraint and balance, bold flavors tussle for attention and turn into a muddy mess. The New American side of the menu commits this sin more frequently than does the Nuevo Latino.

Our favorite starters come from the Sabor Latino menu. Ceviche of shrimp and scallops with onion, chipotle, cilantro and tomato is still good, although there's less citrus kick than we remember in the past. A terrine-like "arepa" of shrimp and crab with grilled sweet corn cake, avocado, and Mexican crema, has a pleasant mix of flavors and textures…but $14?

Among mains, we've also loved a correctly rare hanger steak in a smoky chile sauce that's not bullied by its Cabrales blue cheese. Unfortunately, most other proteins have come horribly overcooked. Not even interesting flavors like tamarind, chipotle, fufu, and chayote slaw can rescue chalky mahi-mahi or leathery pork shoulder. A side of asparagus and salsify shows up in a useless sauce, reddish and watery.

Above all, this is a great place for a drink on the ground floor or up on the roof, perhaps accompanied by dessert; banana tres leches, a carryover from Roomba, is still sublime. But the dinner menu's latest incarnation of confusion fusion is generally not as sweet.

BevMax

Why do they call them convenience stores when they're so small? This is much more convenient.

Wine store

Market

www.bevmax.com

Mon–Thu 9am–8pm
Fri–Sat 9am–9pm
Hours vary by location

Bar Beer, wine, liquor
Credit cards Visa, MC, AmEx
Good wines

Hamden
2165 Dixwell Ave.
(203) 281-0784

Orange
528 Boston Post Rd.
(203) 795-8302

With a wide selection of wines and liquors in two locations convenient to the main Hamden and Orange commercial zones, BevMax is handy if you need wine that's better than grocery-store level at a steal. Because they order in such large quantities, they get a discount and can pass the savings on to the consumer. And there is a good range of regions and varietals represented. Within each, there's plenty of the tried-and-true big names, plus a few surprises.

In a smart, economy-minded move, BevMax's website lists the bottles they carry for under $20 that the critics like. There are also liquors, mostly bottom-shelf but with a few high-minded producers. The vodka selection is comprehensive, and they've got Hendrick's, one of our favorite gins. As for beer, keep an eye out for Rogue, a tasty microbrewery out in Oregon.

Staff here are friendly and patient. There are frequent tastings and events, plus loads of accessories and gift ideas. There are stores all over Connecticut, including two in the greater New Haven area, making sure dinner party guests don't show up empty-handed.

Billy's Pasta Così

7.4 | **8.0**
Food | Feel

A mix-and-match Italian hotspot that's newly—and wisely—located on Branford's main drag

Italian

Upmarket restaurant

$45
Price

www.pastacosi.com

Tue–Fri 11:30am–3pm, 5pm–10pm
Sat 5pm–10pm
Sun 4pm–10pm

Bar Beer, wine, liquor
Credit cards Visa, MC, AmEx
Reservations Accepted
Date-friendly, good wines, veg-friendly

Branford
1018 Main St.
(203) 483-9397

Don't get us wrong: we do understand Billy's popularity. Apparently, so does the restaurant, whose ownership clearly sensed that there might be a bigger market for the concept right on the edge of the Branford Green rather than the more out-of-the-way location in Indian Neck.

It's looking like an inspired decision; this restaurant is now perpetually packed with everyone from daters to families, from bigwigs to scenesters, some of whom come just to hang out and drink wine at the bar. This stems in part from the fact that the atmosphere is better at the new spot; the cheesy soundtrack, dim lighting, and sense of glossy, tablecloth-free restaurant-catalog chic mimic the old Billy's, but there's something more urban about the lively buzz (okay, urban for Branford, anyway).

We haven't been impressed by "Billy's Roasted Red Peppers," which have been served too cold to appreciate the many layers of flavors advertised. Nor can we get into the mix-and-match pasta-plus-sauce principle. Our position is that the chef should choose what pasta pairs with what sauce, and not the customer; certain sauces are built to match with certain shapes and textures, and when you're paying to go out to eat, the expectation is that you're hiring the services of someone in the kitchen whose expertise in such matters exceeds your own.

Some of the possibilities, in fact, are downright scary. Would they honor an order of gorgonzola-and-walnut ravioli topped by red clam sauce? How about chicken alfredo over slightly granular lobster ravioli?

We're not sure why Billy's sauces are considered worthy of being bottled and sold, but pasta puttanesca is a competent preparation, and capricciosa is interesting, with wild mushrooms, sun-dried tomatoes, olives, capers, and a balsamic reduction; it sounds like too much, but it's not. The classic, and most convincing, order here is "Pasta Così," which features white beans, sausage, broccoli rabe, sun-dried tomatoes, and a garlicky broth. The short, carefully salted tubes of pasta glisten with oil. The pairing of beans with pasta—starch with starch—is unusual, but the plate is good, elemental, even if its coherence flutters in and out from bite to bite. Among meat courses, braciola has come dry but endowed with a sweetness from raisins and a crunch from chubby pine nuts.

Even if the atmosphere is more memorable than the food, we salute Billy's for its new location and for its interesting wine list, which is still well priced at the bottom end—if not so much at the top.

Bishop's Orchards

A lovely market that sells specialty groceries and
even (don't tell) Connecticut wine on Sundays

Groceries, Baked goods

Market

www.bishopsorchards.com

Mon–Sat 8am–7pm
Sun 9am–6pm

Bar Wine
Credit cards Visa, MC
Kid-friendly, outdoor dining,
veg-friendly

Guilford
1355 Boston Post Rd.
(203) 453-2338

This long-established farmer's market has expanded to selling gourmet
foods and local wine. The choo-choo train running around the ceiling will
delight kids, and families still arrive by the vanload during the growing
season to pick their own produce (apples, peaches, blueberries, and
strawberries are favorites).

There's also an impressive collection of specialty groceries. D'Artagnan
products make up a quarter of the meat case, and you can find several
varieties of Connecticut-produced Nodine's bacon there as well. There are
also well-chosen artisanal cheeses from local, domestic, and international
cheese farms; breads from Judy's and Chabaso bakeries, and—most
striking of all—a good selection of Connecticut wines, including the
farm's own fruit wines. (Bonus! Because it's technically and legally a farm,
Bishop's is able to circumvent Connecticut's outdated blue laws
prohibiting the sale of alcohol on Sundays.) Try one of their own fruit
wine blends (honey peach melba wine, anyone?), farm-made hard ciders,
or a bottle of wine from one of about a dozen other Connecticut
producers. So shop local—after all, where else are you going to see a sign
at the megamart reading "Our Own Macoun Apples"? Bishop's is the
kind of place that makes us proud to be New Englanders.

Bistro Basque

Even if the tapas are like Russian roulette, you'll
never want to leave

7.8	8.5
Food	Feel

Spanish, French

Upmarket restaurant

$60
Price

www.bistrobasqueusa.com

Mon–Thu 4pm–10pm
Fri–Sat 11:30am–11pm
Sun 11:30am–9pm

Bar Beer, wine, liquor
Credit cards Visa, MC, AmEx
Reservations Accepted
Date-friendly, outdoor dining

Milford
13 River St.
(203) 878-2092

You enter Bistro Basque through a barrier of heavy, Baroque curtains.
Beyond that is a bar area filled with dark wood, crystal chandeliers, and
casual Thonet chairs at small tables. Then there's the cozy dining room,
with its paprika-colored walls, rectangular acoustic baffles on the ceiling,
and tiny glass pots of wheatgrass at each table, which radiates warmth
and feels like a chic secret. In warm weather, the back patio allows diners
to enjoy their meals within earshot of Milford's downtown waterfall.

The Basque region is a fascinating one; despite having its land split
between French and Spanish regimes over the centuries, it adheres
vehemently to its indigenous, ancient traditions. So does Bistro Basque's
menu, which is split into tapas and main courses. But beware—the tapas
are larger than usual and very filling.

We're coming back again and again for txipirones, ideally toothsome
squid cooked in a deep, garlicky squid-ink sauce, served with a scoop of
creamy, salty rice. This is one of the best dishes Milford has to offer.

Otherwise, we hate to say it, but quantity often trumps quality here,
and seasoning is a rampant problem. A white asparagus gratin with
Serrano ham has come both flavorless and overcooked—a real danger
with white asparagus, whose firm texture is its main delight. A mushroom
flan sounds great, but it's a curdled mass of monotony; the accompanying
sauce tastes like little more than reduced cheap beef stock.

Many dishes are plated identically, making the unsexy suggestion that
the kitchen is something of a mechanized tapas factory: everything comes
on square plates, tapas at the corners, pile of greens in center, garnished
with diced tomato. And none of these are memorable; crispy lamb ravioli
taste like glorified wontons, and pork toasts are too squishy and bready to
deserve the moniker (although the meat is moist and nicely cooked).
Paella is made with overcooked, bland chicken and shrimp, and the
saffron gets lost in the overpoweringly bell-peppery sofrito, making it
taste like generic Mexican-restaurant rice.

A dessert of blueberry clafouti, though buttery and rich, suffers from
the same surprisingly dull flavors that plague the savory menu. They do
make a delicious, fresh, and vibrant white sangría, which we will be
enjoying on the back patio—with extra txipirones.

Black Bear Saloon

A mini-chain that delivers a good beer selection and party vibe to both corporate and coed masses

5.6	7.5
Food	Feel

American

Bar **$30**
Price

www.blackbearnh.com

Sun–Thu 11am–10pm
Fri–Sat 11am–10pm

Bar Beer, wine, liquor
Credit cards Visa, MC, AmEx
Live music, Wi-Fi

Chapel District
124 Temple St.
(203) 562-2327

Milford
1201 Boston Post Rd.
(203) 301-0778

It's hard to make a new place look old and lived in, so we sympathize with Black Bear's plight. It does boast wood paneling and shutters, a polished bar, brass fixtures and such, but the restaurant catalog-looking booths and barstools can't muster the nostalgic charm of, say, Rudy's. The Temple Street location plays host to a very lively happy hour/business lunch crowd from the neighboring Omni Hotel, as well as college students. It becomes quite the sports bar scene when a good game is on one of its several flat-screen TVs (positioned cleverly so that you can watch comfortably from just about any angle).

The undistinguished menu is full of the usual suspects of bar food, and ranges from forgettable to decent. An extraordinarily bland chili is really nothing more than ground beef and beans. When it's purveyed as a hamburger topping, it's particularly silly, like topping a solid burger with a mashed-up one. The burgers do come reasonably rare on request, and when they're rare, they taste like meat, thankfully.

Fries are crispy and pretty good, even if they don't look like much. They're actually kind of similar to McDonald's fries (we mean that as a compliment, of course). Curiously, there's also a kids' menu, which you can access online right next to photos of coeds doing shots—quite the family-friendly move for a place voted "Best Place to Get Lucky" in *Fairfield County Weekly's* 2007 reader's poll.

The liquor selection is middle-tier, and while there's a more extensive selection of beer on draft than you see at most places of this ilk, "extensive" doesn't necessarily translate to "interesting." These are run-of-the-mill domestic and borderline microbrews—UFO and such. There's a Black Bear-labeled ale that's not bad, but not the best thing here, either. Karaoke, nightly specials, and friendly service that isn't sports-bar-bitchy make this a perfectly acceptable hangout, if not exactly the most charming or delicious.

The Blue Cottage

Fresh fish and excellent crab cakes in newer-than-Lenny's digs

8.2 Food

7.5 Feel

Seafood

Casual restaurant

$30 Price

www.thebluecottage.net

Mon–Thu 11:30am–9:30pm
Fri–Sat 11:30am–10pm
Sun 1pm–9pm

Bar Beer, wine, liquor
Credit cards Visa, MC, AmEx
Reservations Accepted
Kid-friendly, live music, outdoor dining

Branford
2 Sybil Ave.
(203) 481-2583

While it might seem a little ambitious to offer a seafood-heavy menu at a brand-new restaurant across the street from local legend Lenny's Indian Head Inn, The Blue Cottage presents a completely different vibe. While Lenny's has an old-school, varnished-wood, checkered-tablecloths feel, The Blue Cottage is clean, crisp, and nautical, almost to the point of seeming empty, like a house that's just been moved into.

We suspect a different crowd comes here: Lenny's is a bit of a destination and a sentimental favorite, but The Blue Cottage seems more aimed at the immediate neighborhood, with a bar that occupies a major chunk of the space (though not obtrusively so), and late-night hours that are almost unheard of on this sleepy part of the Shoreline (the bar is usually open until midnight on weekdays and 1am on weekends).

Seafood and pasta dishes dominate the menu, though there are many less-expensive bar standbys and sandwiches, as well as a couple cursory steaks. A clam pane cotto with escarole and white beans—a shoreline dish if there ever was one, fusing New Haven's Italian-American tradition with New England's seafood staple—is hearty and nourishing, perfect for a raw, wind-whipped winter afternoon. Fries with Old Bay seasoning pair well with steamers. We love the name of the slightly terrifying "Man vs. Food Burger," but whoever tries to tackle two bacon cheeseburgers squished between two grilled cheese sandwiches had better be able to afford the medical bills.

Fish and chips are light, crisp, appealing, and better with malt vinegar. Best of all is the crab cake sandwich, served on a toasted ciabatta roll dripping with butter, and slathered in a homemade lemon tartar sauce. The cakes taste exclusively of large lumps and flakes of sweet crabmeat, and the sandwich is a bargain.

One can also order whole shellfish "pots"—lobster, shrimp, or King crab legs—for a summery clam-bake feel. Portions here are substantial, and service is efficient and eager to please. In warm weather, the outdoor patio makes a gorgeous place to eat and listen to live music. We have high hopes that the Blue Cottage will stick around as a low-key local favorite for its Indian Neck and Pine Orchard clientele.

The Blue Pearl

Stick to chocolate fondue and martinis in this airy, vibey space

5.9	8.0
Food	Feel

New American

Upmarket restaurant

$45
Price

www.thebluepearlnewhaven.com

Tue–Thu 5pm–10pm
Fri–Sat 5pm–11pm abbreviated
menu until midnight

Bar Beer, wine, liquor
Credit cards Visa, MC, AmEx
Reservations Accepted
Date-friendly, outdoor dining,
veg-friendly

South Town Green
130 Court St.
(203) 789-6370

The Blue Pearl just tries a little too hard. It misses the style bull's-eye, looking somewhat like a giant marshmallow in the sky. And the menu is eclectic but poorly harmonized, and can't jibe with a sexy bar vibe.

The décor comes off like New Haven's answer to New York's Asia de Cuba and Miami's Delano, a fantasy of flowing curtains in pale shades, ultra-hip lighting and Art Deco furniture, a place clearly meant to attract beautiful people for strong martinis and successful dates. When in season, the backyard offers an edgy-yet-romantic spot for drinks or dessert. Given how close it is to the State Street station, it's also an excellent spot for happy hour. The fairly ambitious menu brings a broad palate of fondues to New Haven and riffs on traditional American comfort food.

The best-selling savory fondue, with artichoke, Parmesan and crème frâiche, is underwhelming. Its lumpy texture, meager ration of cheese, and inflated price betray the hearty, fill-me-up-right pretensions of genuine fondue. There's something of a racket going on here: for $5 more, you can order a partial fondue refill when your (small) bowl runs dry. Hmm. The white bread for dipping is pretty blah, but we enjoy the rye and nicely blanched broccoli. On the dessert side, the bittersweet chocolate fondue with roasted hazelnuts and frangelico is smooth, delicious, and easily replicable at home at a third the price (but unless your apartment sports exclusively Scandinavian furniture and stainless appliances, you'll probably feel sexier at The Blue Pearl than in your living room).

Among the non-fondue offerings, we love the fried oysters; they're fresh, plump, and spicy. We've also had a decent lobster roll with tarragon mayonnaise. In general, it's so hit-or-miss with the savories that you'd best stick to appetizers, drinks, and dessert.

The location, though central, is another downer: the entrance spills out onto a desolate corporate alleyway rather than a hopping hangout spot. Unlike Matt Damon, The Blue Pearl is too self-aware to score full sexy points, yet just might satisfy a high roller's lust for mediocre food, kitschy atmosphere, and inflated prices.

Blue State Coffee

A hot, progressive community organizer that
represents Kona, Kenya, and Indonesia

Baked goods

Café

www.bluestatecoffee.com

Mon–Fri 7am–10pm
Sat–Sun 9am–10pm

Bar None
Credit cards Visa, MC, AmEx
Veg-friendly, Wi-Fi

South Town Green
84 Wall St.
(203) 764-2632

The independent coffee shop is about as iconic of blue America as the
gun shop is of red America. Indeed, many of Europe's own political
revolutions saw their geneses in cafés. Even in an achromatic
Obamamerica, Blue State Coffee flaunts its political colors, serving up
good coffee on deeply brewed progressive "grounds."

The coffee, like the shop's mission, is both audacious and hopeful. A
strong roast gives it a zesty, earthy punch that is passionate, but not
combative. All of the beans are fair trade (most are organic), and if you
bring your own mug, they charge you the price of a small—with a little
discount.

If you were still unsure of its political allegiances, Blue State pays
homage to the president in more ways than one. A spirited quote from
Obama's inaugural address runs the counter front wall, while the "Hope
Blend" made from Kenyan, Kona, and Indonesian beans, enshrines him in
every biodegradable cup. Espresso pulls are red-state-supersized,
however—their "small" cappuccino would be laughed out of Italy—but
when you want a huge mug of soy caramel latte, you're in business.

Blue State Coffee is, naturally, community-oriented. This focus is not
limited to the Yale population, which will find its huge interior, free Wi-Fi,
plethora of power outlets, and the bonhomie of the staff and owners
extremely appealing. Five percent of their profits are donated to a New
Haven charitable organization (e.g., Dwight Hall, CitySeed) that you vote
for every time you buy a cup, while leftover pastries, soups, and
sandwiches (which are brought in fresh each morning from the above-
average La Cuisine in Branford) are given to food pantries at the end of
the day. Of course, napkins, utensils, and cups are compostable.

Blue State is a paragon of sustainable and ethical business, a
portmanteau of profit and progress. So "drink liberally," as their slogan
says, and soothe your conscience with every last, delicious drop.

Bon Appétit

Make gift baskets or covet these tasty treats for
yourself; grab the wine from right next door

Groceries, Baked goods

Market

www.bonappetitct.com

Mon–Sat 10am–6pm

Bar None
Credit cards Visa, MC, AmEx
Delivery, veg-friendly

Hamden
2979 Whitney Ave.
(203) 248-0648

This pretty, well-appointed little store sits way back in the parking lot next
to Mt. Carmel Wine & Spirits and Luce Italian Restaurant.

Front and center, there's a wonderful cheese selection, with imports
from Denmark, France, Italy, England, Wales, Holland, and Switzerland,
plus domestic cheeses from small farms, like Green Hill in Massachusetts,
and Lazy Lady Farms in Vermont. The latter produces some charming
cow's milk cheeses, like the "Barick Obama," a washed rind, double
cream cheese with a cheddary, nutty finish.

In another case, you can find D'Artagnan products and all manner of
cured meat. Also listed as "available upon request" are game and poultry
like rabbit, elk, pheasant, boar, and so on. Chocolates, crackers, and
cookies from Europe are alluring, and jars of pickled everything, olives,
caviar, rose water, and oils all have pretty labels for gift baskets. The tea
selection is small, but they will try their best to accommodate you if you
want to order a certain kind. Whole-bean coffee is available from the
Jamaican Gourmet Coffee Company, a Connecticut roaster that sources
the legendary Blue Mountain beans.

Bon Appétit can make gift baskets on the spot (for any purpose you can
think of: sympathy, recovery, new birth...whatever), or call ahead if you
think you might need something special-ordered for it. They also will
deliver all over the greater New Haven area. That should whet your
appetite.

Book Trader Café

We can't stop loving this casual, veggie-friendly
used bookstore

8.1 Food
9.0 Feel

Sandwiches, Baked goods

Counter service

$10 Price

www.booktradercafe.com

Mon–Fri 7:30am–9pm
Sat 9am–9pm
Sun 9am–7pm

Bar None
Credit cards Visa, MC, AmEx
Date-friendly, kid-friendly, outdoor
dining, veg-friendly, Wi-Fi

Upper Chapel Area
1140 Chapel St.
(203) 787-6147

The years go by, but there are some delightful constants in this great city:
the cycle of the academic year, the crisp autumns and steamy summers,
and the pleasure of coffee or lunch in Book Trader's expansive, sunny
atrium. It's one of the best places in New Haven for that great American
college-town tradition—the casual solo lunch with a book, or its modern
cousin, a laptop.

A Yale-heavy crowd of budding intellectuals and artists sidle up to the
counter and place orders for good dark-roast coffee (they call it the
"Black Cow"), a muffin, or one of an array of pun-heavy sandwiches
scrawled across a chalkboard. Lately, we've been enjoying the "Jane
Rare," a roast beef sandwich with a very snappy horseradish cream.
We've long enjoyed the field greens with a superlative balsamic
vinaigrette, whose syrupy, emergent sweetness works well with the add-
on chicken salad. Salads come with good, fresh, whole-grain bread.

Perhaps predictably, Book Trader is also a haven for vegetarians and
vegans; soy chicken (which is surprisingly firm and flavorful) and oven-
roasted vegetables with caramelized onions are among the sandwich
fillings. There's always a vegetarian or vegan soup on the menu, and
many of them are very good—the African peanut and butternut-squash-
and-leek bisque have been recent winners. Prices are right for the area,
given that the place is across the street from the School of Architecture.
Perhaps it's for that reason, too, that the atrium gets so crowded at
lunchtime—so much so, in fact, that there's a sign discouraging people
from lingering or studying from noon to 3pm.

At other times, perhaps it's the atrium's easy acoustics that lend Book
Trader a certain talking-across-tables aspect among the contingent of
single Yalies. You're well advised to avert your gaze if you aren't in the
mood for a late afternoon flirtation—or for the classically awkward
exchange of credentials and summer plans.

Brazi's Italian Restaurant

A garden-variety Italian-American place popular
for the friendly service—it couldn't be the food

3.8	6.5
Food	Feel

Italian, Pizza

Casual restaurant

$30
Price

www.brazis.com

Mon–Thu 11:30am–9:30pm
Fri–Sat 11:30am–10:30pm
Sun noon–9pm

Bar Beer, wine, liquor
Credit cards Visa, MC, AmEx
Reservations Accepted
Kid-friendly, veg-friendly

Long Wharf
201 Food Terminal Plaza
(203) 498-2488

A rather popular restaurant, Brazi's brings in a large cadre of regulars
even for weekday lunches. Why? We have no idea. It couldn't be for the
watery pasta—a bland, undersalted dish of penne, for example, whose
red sauce is largely dissociated from the pasta itself.

Nor is it likely that the crowds would flock in for the predictable dinner
salads, with olives and cherry tomatoes, or for the tough meats like "veal
caprese," with seemingly unsalted red sauce and basil that's cooked so as
to sap it of all flavor. One vegetable side has featured peas, not-so-fresh
green beans, carrots, onions, and zucchini—all as limp, watery, and
underseasoned as hospital food.

If you do end up at Brazi's, stick with the pizza, which is made in a brick
oven, resulting in a decent crust. The tomatoes aren't bad, and (unlike in
the veal caprese) the basil is fresh. But the cheese falls short flavor-wise,
especially by the standards of this pizza town.

The mystery remains. Why do they come? Is it for the atmosphere? We
suppose it's possible that the cafeteria-fancy furnishings and muzak
appeal to some people, or that certain people have a particular taste for
dated ceiling fans, mirrors, and big, canopied columns that lie somewhere
in the aesthetic middle ground between Las Vegas' Caesar's Palace and
the restaurant of a Holiday Inn.

At least the service is very friendly, in a folksy kind of way. You might
see the regulars in playful banter with the staff, asking for another free
refill of the hot but chewy salami rolls. Sometimes a smile of recognition
goes a long, long way.

Breakaway Deli

A cheap lunch stop with cafeteria-style food that's below average even within its short-order category

4.3	5.5
Food	Feel

Sandwiches

Counter service

$10
Price

Mon–Fri 8am–4pm

Bar None
Credit cards None

Audubon Arts District
24 Whitney Ave.
(203) 865-5946

If you're a good, upstanding fan of New England sports teams (as you should be—times are good for the Red Sox and Celtics), you'll be (mostly) happy with the décor here. Otherwise, it's hard to sign onto the pink-and-purple program.

The Breakaway Deli, conveniently located next to the FedEx office on Whitney, is one of those kinds of short-order deli and lunch counters, in a certain part of New Haven, that's geared to a certain kind of crowd. Within this group of lunch spots, price ranges and menu offerings are often essentially similar, and it can be hard to distinguish one place from the next. That's where we come in. And we'll say it: Breakaway Deli isn't among our top choices within this genre.

The prices are low, but the food misses the mark. To begin with, it's hard to prepare things that should be cooked on a skillet without such a skillet—all they have is a little electric contraption, and so the eggs in the breakfast sandwiches are pre-cooked and then microwaved. Cold cuts, too, are below average, basic and cheap; get "the works" on a sandwich, and it becomes an incoherent mess with things like raw mushrooms (why?) and insufficient condiment application. Provolone is tasteless and the tomatoes are often unripe. Hard rolls, meanwhile, are soft, a tad chewy, not the best but not exactly bad. Chicken noodle soup is well seasoned, but the chicken within is hard to find and the noodles so mushy that they barely taste like pasta.

There's a "low-carb menu" that features things such as no-sauce pizza and "meatwiches" (vegetables wrapped inside the meat). But we don't advise trying such unusual dishes at a place that executes so poorly on the basics.

Brick Oven Pizza

Reliable thin-crust pizza and unexpectedly good
subs—even at 2:45am

6.5	3.0
Food	Feel

Pizza

Counter service

$10
Price

Mon–Wed 11am–3am; Thu–Sat
11am–4am; Sun 3pm–3am

Bar BYO
Credit cards Visa, MC
Delivery, outdoor dining,
veg-friendly

Upper Chapel Area
122 Howe St.
(203) 777-4444

Brick Oven Pizza scores points with consistently good thin-crust pizza and decent chicken subs (here they're called grinders, in the small-town New England style). And it's open daily until 3am, making it one of the best late-night take-out options in the city.

We make reference to take-out for a reason, though: the atmosphere inside the restaurant is fast-food style. Bright lights and an array of empty tables are backed by an incongruous wall of bricks with an oven. It's not our favorite place to sit. Even the sign outside has a distinct 1990s fast-food aesthetic that makes you want to get in and get out. And while it's not far from downtown and fairly near the late-night post-bar scene, Brick Oven Pizza is also in a neighborhood that can sometimes feel deserted in the wee hours. For take-out pies in those hours, though, Brick Oven is a welcome surprise.

The pies here are fairly thin, with a crust that is generally well seared. Although the sauce and cheese aren't in the league of New Haven's champions, they're a sizeable notch above the norm. Along with the usual pizza repertoire, there are some unusual combinations here, like the "Sweetie Pie" (with peas, tomatoes, mozzarella, ricotta, parsley, and basil) and the "Black Sea" (shrimp and garlic). The grilled chicken grinder with lettuce, tomato, cheese, and mayo is better than you'd expect for a mostly-take-out pizza joint: the chicken is moist, with charcoal flavor in evidence; vegetables are fresh; and the mayo adds another layer of texture. It all sits on very fresh bread. We recommend adding hot sauce.

There's also a very cheap dinner special that comes with pasta and a salad. It's not the best pasta, but at 2:45am, you can't ask for much more.

Brown Stone House

Like a simple museum of Americana, with a menu
that seems not to have changed since the 1950s

5.1	6.5
Food	Feel

American   Casual restaurant   **$15**
                                                               Price

Mon–Fri 6am–3pm   **Bar** None   **Hamden**
Sat–Sun 6am–2pm   **Credit cards** None   2365 Whitney Ave.
                         Reservations Not accepted   (203) 281-0446
                         Kid-friendly

At one of the main intersections of sleepy downtown Hamden, the Brown
Stone House is a treasure of Americana, a relic from another era. Here
you can have an open-faced turkey sandwich with gravy, or a vanilla
milkshake—both of which are in all likelihood identical to what you would
have gotten in 1955.

That doesn't mean that America hasn't made culinary advances since
that era, however, and a lot of the food is pretty unexciting. In order to
appreciate a meal at the Brown Stone House, you need to have a taste for
the simple, even the bland—and for nostalgia. The soda fountain, for
starters, is no replica—it's been here all along. In addition to the menu, all
the paraphernalia and appliances behind the counter, and even the sign
on the door, are unselfconsciously frozen in a dreamlike postwar America.

And so are the customers. The years show up more dramatically on a
man's face than on a stainless-steel refrigerator. You'll notice such a
theme among the clientele, who all seem to be (not coincidentally) on a
first-name basis with the servers. For all these reasons, if you're a
youngster, it might be hard not to feel out of place here. But you also
won't feel anything less than warmly welcomed—and, when you leave,
perhaps also heartsick for a kinder, simpler age that may never have been.

Bru Café

A great space for working and studying if you're
downtown—but the coffee disappoints

Baked goods, Sandwiches

Café

www.brucafe.net

Mon–Fri 7am–6pm	**Bar** None	**South Town Green**
Sat 8am–6pm	**Credit cards** Visa, MC, AmEx	141 Orange St.
	Veg-friendly, Wi-Fi	(203) 752-0052

This coffee shop, formerly Koffee on Orange (and before that, Moka), is
another fledgling spin-off from the now almost defunct New Haven
coffee empire spelling its shops' names with that annoyingly egregious
"K." Aside from the pretentious orthographic conceits (a macron, which
we could not reproduce here without lavish, expensive pains, hangs over
the "u" in brazen indication that it is indeed a long vowel), this is one of
the best coffeeshops in town.

But this fact has nothing to do with the coffee. Free Wi-Fi and about
two dozen outlets; a ton of mismatched, café-shabby chairs (both soft
and hard); and the slightly later hours make this a terrific place to spread
out books and papers and get some serious work done. But don't come
for the coffee.

The decaf can be tepid and flavorless, and the regular has the distinct
burnt, metallic flavor that's evocative of the pot that sits on a diner's hot
plate all day. Either way, even if it is fairly traded and organic, the coffee is
just not as good as Blue State's or Willoughby's. The same is true for
specialty drinks. The Nutella latte, which sounds amazing—when isn't
Nutella amazing?—loses something in the translation. In fact, there's no
actual Nutella in it; it's simply hazelnut flavoring and Ghirardelli chocolate
syrup. Cappuccino sometimes tastes funky, too, as if the milk has nearly
turned or the wands aren't properly cleaned. The long list of Rishi teas will
treat you better.

The pastries are culled from Koffee on Audubon and are fair to
middling. A cranberry-bran muffin has the consistency of leftover gruel,
but a raspberry chocolate bar is buttery and delicious. Panini, cold
sandwiches, and salads are made to order, and are pretty good. Still,
studying or reading is the best excuse for coming here.

Bruegger's Bagel Bakery

4.0 Food   **3.0** Feel

A chain gang of doughy McBagels and more-than-McUnhealthy sandwiches

Sandwiches, Baked goods

Counter service   **$10** Price

www.brueggers.com

Daily 6am–8pm
Hours vary by location

Bar None
Credit cards None
Kid-friendly, veg-friendly

Audubon Arts District
1 Whitney Ave.
(203) 773-3199

Hamden
2425 Dixwell Ave.
(203) 287-9559

Orange
263 Boston Post Rd.
(203) 795-1300

"In a year's time," boasts the company's fact sheet, "Bruegger's will produce approximately 70 million bagels. That's enough to make a stack higher than the Empire State building and have plenty left over!" In an age in which consumers are increasingly coming to see the value of small, artisanal, and local, Bruegger's is *boasting* of this fact?

At least the bagel chain seems to have finally realized that its doughy, below-average bagels don't make great sandwiches: as of 2009, they've increased the number of non-bagel sandwich platforms to five. These include the wrap, the ciabatta, the "Softwich" (not bad; we favor the asiago parmesan version), and—new for 2009—good, old-fashioned bread ("hearty white" or honey wheat). There are grilled panini, too.

"Signature sandwiches" are edible but unexciting; options include turkey chipotle club and tarragon chicken salad, which sound light and lunchy but pack in 770 and 800 calories, respectively. The tuna-and-cheddar melt rings in at 1,020 calories—that's the equivalent of more than four McDonald's hamburgers. Beware even the sesame chicken salad; between its disgusting "chow mein noodles" and a sugar-spiked "Asian dressing," it's got 480 calories—more than a Mickey D's double cheeseburger.

Dense, pasty bagels are baked in the store, but they won't exactly transport you to New York (although the rude service might). Smoked-salmon spread and chive cheese are both perfectly acceptable. We like the bacon-and-scallion cream cheese best, especially with a garlic or onion bagel. Most unimpressive are the breakfast options, made with prefabricated slabs of "egg patty (whole egg, water, soybean oil, modified food starch, whey, salt, calcium caseinate, liquid pepper extract, citric acid)" that are peeled out of little plastic baggies, then paired with cold, processed bacon and cheese. Eew.

The New Haven Bruegger's gets a lot of mileage from its location on Church Street, which sits just a few steps from Yale and the Green. You won't forget that it's a fast-food chain—booths and countertops are hopelessly plasticky—but it's a bit brighter and airier than most; the corner location and big plate-glass windows onto Church Street brighten things up. Given the mediocrity, we can only surmise that it's the convenience and the airiness that keep the crowds reliable. If it's coffee you're after, you certainly have no excuse for stopping here instead of Willoughby's across the street.

Bud's Fish Market

A wide selection of quality seafood, plus spreads, sauces, and sausage

Groceries, Seafood

Market

www.budsfishmarket.com

Tue–Sat 10am–6pm	**Bar** None	**Branford**
Sun 10am–4pm	**Credit cards** Visa, MC, AmEx	4 Sybil Ave.
		(203) 488-1019

Since 1948, the family behind Bud's Fish Market has been keeping this part of the coastline stocked with local, fresh seafood. The family's son now runs the joint, and they boast an impressive selection.

They'll ship pretty much anywhere in the nation, via FedEx, which is handy if you want to send Maine lobsters to your newly transplanted, forlorn friends in Oklahoma City.

Depending on the season, they carry Irish, Scottish, *and* Atlantic salmon, as well as the ever-delicious Arctic Char. Also from Iceland, there's haddock. American goodies like Alaskan king crab, Maine lobster, and Rhode Island-caught swordfish round out the list. A nice, ruby red loin of sushi-grade ahi tuna is ready for sushi parties or simple searing—if you can get it home without taking a big bite out of it.

Any sort of bivalve or crustacean you could ever want to squirt lemon juice on is here: Littlenecks, shrimp (cooked and raw), steamers, razor clams, and oysters, all of which you can dip in the spicy cocktail sauce that's sold here, too.

In addition, there are seafood sausages and spreads, which go above and beyond the usual fish market offering.

Prices are a little high here, but for this kind of quality, it seems appropriate. Call ahead to see when lobsters are coming in and get them that day. It will be well worth it.

Buffalo Wild Wings

Wacky flavors for decent wings from a big-time chain

6.1	7.0
Food	Feel

American

Casual restaurant

$25
Price

www.buffalowildwings.com

Daily 11am–2am
Hours vary by location

Bar Beer, wine, liquor
Credit cards Visa, MC, AmEx
Reservations Accepted
Kid-friendly, outdoor dining, Wi-Fi

Chapel District
74 Church St.
(203) 789-9453

Milford
1201 Boston Post Rd.
(203) 877-9453

Since when did Buffalo wings mean wings with mango-habanero sauce? Or parmesan and garlic? We like our Buffalo wings as they're meant to be: with Buffalo sauce and blue cheese. Buffalo Wild Wings, a nationwide mega-chain, might be one big homage to that greatest of American bar-food inventions, but its proliferation of wacky flavors leaves us scratching our heads. Regardless of the intentions, by offending our collective Buffalo-wing sensibilities, are they doing more harm than good?

Perhaps that's a philosophical question. In any case, the wings here are good, and come not only in a myriad of flavors, but also at different spice levels—great for those who don't want tears streaming down their faces as they eat. They also come with or without the bone. Culinary purists will, of course, want bone-in wings; infidels will choose the Buffalo-tender version (here they're called "boneless wings," but it's white meat). Buffalo Wild Wings can be a bit stingy with the sauce, and presentation is subpar, but you can ask for more sauce and blue cheese to remedy the former situation; as for the latter, who cares? We are sometimes annoyed by the service, which is generally far more what-can-you-do-for-me than what-can-I-do-for-you; due to chronic understaffing, tracking down your waitperson can be next to impossible.

Stray from the wings, and the menu is a minefield. Burgers are notoriously bad, and ribs disappoint. Given that Buffalo Wild Wings is also a bar, you should have a beer, though the beer selection isn't the greatest in town. The interior is cavernous, but in an oddly deliberate way; lighting is strangely bright. The crowd tends to be young, and composed primarily of early-twenty-somethings, for whom wings are a staple. There's also a distinct sports-bar need being filled here, with numerous well-endowed TVs consistently screening whatever games matter.

For the older (or nerdier) crowd, the TV trivia games are also popular—you ask your waitperson for a little game computer and compete against other teams at the bar and at other bars across the country. Trust us, it's fun. This place feels like a bar in the suburbs anyway, so you might as well distract yourself with some trivia. We don't quite get Buffalo's inordinate popularity, but, somehow we do seem to find ourselves here from time to time, watching sports, playing trivia, and eating wings. There's something to it.

Bulldog Burrito

Competent burritos that keep hungry students from passing out, little more

5.0	5.5
Food	Feel

Mexican

Counter service

$5
Price

www.bulldogburrito.com

Mon–Thu 11am–10pm
Fri–Sat 11am–midnight
Sun noon–10pm

Bar Beer, wine
Credit cards Visa, MC
Veg-friendly

Broadway District
320 Elm St.
(203) 495-8600

Like most vaguely Mexican joints in this country, Bulldog Burrito doesn't do justice to the variety and intensity of Mexican cuisine. There are no organ meats, no super-hot pickled vegetables, no moles or authentic chilies. Yet just as unskillful Chinese-American cuisine can, on occasion, taste just right, Bulldog Burrito is comforting and satisfying.

As you might guess from the name, Bulldog caters directly to Yalies, especially undergrads stuck in the limbo times between dining-hall meals. The burritos are competent if you like the Californian everything-but-the-kitchen-sink approach to fillings. The burrito setup is Chipotle-esque: a super-huge flour tortilla, the offspring of Sonoran 24-inch wheat tortillas, is flash-steamed and stuffed with rice, beans, salsa, lettuce, cheese, and sour cream. "El Bulldog," with marinated chicken, isn't inspirational; "El Vaquero" is a bit better, bringing a good deal of beefiness to the party. With sturdy tortillas, the burritos maintain their structural integrity down to the last bite—a simple attribute that's not to be ignored. We like the creamy chipotle sauce, which adds another layer of flavor. Curiously, this condiment isn't always volunteered to customers as an option; don't let yourself forget that it's there, particularly in the light of the anemic one-trick-pony salsa bar.

If you're more of a minimalist, try the soft tacos with surprisingly boisterous shredded beef and tangy salsa. The bean-and-cheese quesadilla is utterly devoid of distinctiveness, but hey, it's beans and cheese in a tortilla: it tastes good. And the price is right; the regular burrito—a steal in the $5-6 range—really fills you up. Still, adamant aficionados would rather brave the elements at one of the many burrito carts poking around Yale's campus—especially the Tijuana Taco Company, which far outclasses this place.

Eating in at Bulldog—which not so many people do—means claiming a table and tackling your burrito in a bright, modern room with hanging photo art. Here's the kicker, though: Bulldog used to have late-late hours that were well-suited to the post-party wind down (a.k.a. drunk food). But now they close much earlier—which gives the place a lot less of a unique hook.

Burger King

It's more than just a 1,260-calorie sandwich—it's an anti-intellectual way of life

3.9	1.0
Food	Feel

American, Burgers

Counter service

$10
Price

www.burgerking.com

Sun–Wed 6am–2am
Thu–Sat 6am–3am
Hours vary by location

Bar None
Credit cards Visa, MC, AmEx

Whalley
1329 Whalley Ave.
(203) 397-8426

Orange
140 Boston Post Rd.
(203) 795-3646

West Haven
644 Campbell Ave.
(203) 932-6274

Additional locations
and more features at
www.fearlesscritic.com

"Have it your way." Burger King (sorry, "BK")'s new marketing pitch is all about appealing to patriotic American populism, in its rawest, most anti-intellectual, anti-healthy, anti-foodie, anti-organic, anti-ingredient movement. Here it's not "coffee," it's "joe," a "hard-working cup of coffee," and in a dig at Starbucks, it "comes in three easy-to-say sizes." It's amazing when a fast-food chain positions itself so far downmarket that it actually resorts to painting other fast-food chains as effete.

We don't discuss nutrition much within these pages—we generally prefer to leave that to others—but BK is so extreme that we're willing to make an exception. Amazingly, even as America gains health-consciousness, the menu items here just get worse and worse. There's now a Triple Whopper with Cheese, which on its own sports a spectacular 1,260 calories and 85 grams of fat. Make it into a meal by adding a large fries and large Coke, and you're up to 2,248 calories—more than most people's entire recommended daily caloric intake—and 118 grams of fat. Might the word "whopping" be in order here?

There are garden salads on the menu, but they're so bad that they're not worth discussing. Going back to the things that people actually order, what's almost as stunning about BK's menu is how many calories it is possible for you to consume before you even start the day. How about a breakfast of the "Enormous Omelet Sandwich," large hash browns, and an orange juice? How about 1,480 calories and 86 grams of fat? For *breakfast*?

In recent years, the oblique way about talking about the cooking method for BK's burgers has gone from "flame broiled" to "fire grilled" back to "flame broiled." Whatever. The burgers are microwaved. And they're not just microwaved—they're microwaved right in front of you! Just how stupid do they think we are? BK's customer service line, in response to our incredulous query, informed us that the microwave was necessary "only to melt the cheese."

It does seem that Burger King manifests a desire—however hidden or under-utilized—to beat McDonald's. But BK executes so poorly on its innovations—from "French toast sticks" to the new "baguettes" to the infamous Whaler—that McDonald's doesn't even have to keep up. Even the atmosphere at BK is one of the least inspiring of all chains, with an aesthetic of flashy sleaze that has all the subtlety of Saturday morning TV. If this is "having it your way," then we feel pretty sorry for you.

C.O. Jones

Strong, easy-to-down margaritas keep this place
packed—as does the free (bad) food

4.7	6.0
Food	Feel

Mexican

Bar

$20
Price

www.c-o-jones.com

Mon–Sat 4:30pm–11pm
Sun 5pm–10pm

Bar Beer, wine, liquor
Credit cards Visa, MC, AmEx
Date-friendly, outdoor dining,
veg-friendly

East Rock
969 State St.
(203) 773-3344

Perhaps it's because the margaritas are so potent and easy to drink that you always come away with warm (if foggy) memories of this East Rock Tex-Mex bar and grill with the double-entendre name (if you don't get it, ask a Spanish speaker). A lively mélange of grad students and a smattering of locals and suburban denizens flocks into the dimly lit, sombrero-laden bar mostly just for drinks, although there's also a menu of burritos and border-style appetizers. Weekend nights hop with jolly carousers, as do nightly happy hours from 4:30pm–7pm—with half-price house margaritas—and Mondays, when happy hour continues until 10pm.

It bears mention that the house margarita recipe isn't the best, with a sticky-sweet, sour-mix-type flavor. We're more convinced by the pricier versions on the menu. During non-happy hour, you should definitely try some of the more inventive options like the prickly-pear margarita—or savor a top-shelf tequila like limey Tarantula or Herradura Reposado (one of our favorites). For budding connoisseurs, the tequila samplers are a good deal. Service is distracted at best, downright rude at worst. People don't seem to care, as the place is generally pretty packed.

But here's the kicker: if you have good timing, C.O. Jones offers the cheapest meal in all of New Haven. That's because weeknight happy hours also feature a free, all-you-can-eat buffet of bean burritos, with lettuce, tomato, sour cream, and salsa to accompany your drinks. With just one small half-price 'rita as the minimum, a starving student can actually pile up the free burritos and eat a two-dollar dinner. That said, the food, burritos in particular, is less than stellar. Still, it's a fun place, a good pickup scene, and a mainstay on the New Haven bar-and-grill map.

Café George by Paula

An office-building hideaway that delights us with
its superior cafeteria skills

7.5 Food   **6.0** Feel

Sandwiches, Baked goods

Counter service

$10 Price

www.cafegeorgebypaula.com

Mon–Fri 7am–3pm

Bar None
Credit cards Visa, MC, AmEx
Kid-friendly, veg-friendly

Chapel District
300 George St.
(203) 777-1414

Look down the alleyway between South Frontage and George Street for
the little purple awning. This café is surreptitiously located inside an office
building. It's easy to miss, but that hasn't deterred Paula's business, which
is largely dependent on (and reputed for its) catering functions. A reliable
crowd still shows up for breakfast and lunch at this weekday-only,
cafeteria-style operation.

The service at Café George by Paula could hardly be any more friendly
or welcoming; if you're a first-timer, you may well be acknowledged as
such, helped through the menu, encouraged to come back.

The key to Paula's success is consistently skillful execution of simple
favorites. There are prepared foods ready to go, which range from deli
sandwiches on croissant and ciabatta to several kinds of salad and pasta
dishes, cold or for reheating. They also make fresh any sandwich you
dream possible.

We are still fans of the house-breaded chicken cutlet sandwich with
bacon, smoked mozzarella, and a peppery, creamy chipotle sauce. It is a
challenging blend of flavors, but Paula's hand is steady. Ditto for the
salads, whose vegetables are some of the freshest around. The extensive
breakfast spread is a treat here; eggs are handled with ease.

The atmosphere reminds us of a really swank hospital cafeteria: burnt
pumpkin-colored walls, matte-framed photographs, and catalogue-nice
furnishings. Or maybe it's the Jell-O parfaits for sale in the deli case.

If you can find your way here, through the tinted glass doors and
office-building lobbies, you'll be richly rewarded.

Café Goodfellas

An upmarket East Rock joint with decent food and a winning attitude

6.5	**7.5**
Food	Feel

Italian

Upmarket restaurant

$55
Price

www.cafegoodfellas.com

Mon–Thu 11:30am–10pm
Fri–Sat 10:30am–11pm
Sun 1pm–10pm

Bar Beer, wine, liquor
Credit cards Visa, MC, AmEx
Reservations Accepted
Good wines, outdoor dining

East Rock
758 State St.
(203) 772-3415

Café Goodfellas is a caricature of a caricature of a caricature of mafia life. In the restaurant and on its website, scenes from Martin Scorsese's *Goodfellas* are mixed with Dean Martin tunes and such. Quotes from the film flash across your screen. Another page brags about all the VIPs that have visited: Deniro and Pacino. John Leguizamo. And, of course, "many other *Soprano* cast members."

So, when the time comes for you to pay a visit to Café Goodfellas, make sure to wear your Sunday best. You never know who you'll run into. (You'll most certainly run into those same big names on the screen, anyway, which plays throughout your dinner.)

At a minimum, the über-friendly servers will make you feel mighty special. Attention is given to every small detail, but with minimal fuss. Plates that are meant to be shared among a group are split by the server without your having to ask. Suggestions are given carefully—you won't just be steered to the most expensive items on the menu. The space is casual, with exposed brick and easy vibes. White tablecloths look clean and sharp. A nice sidewalk seating area is pleasant on a beautiful spring day (although the rush of cars along State Street isn't).

The menu is exactly as you would expect it to be, with all the big Italian-American players present. Fried calamari are fine, but we can't understand how a $14 price tag is justified for "New York Style" (which is brightened by cherry peppers but made soggy by tomato sauce). Eggplant rollatini is comfort food for the ages, with the vegetable crispy, marinara tasty, and ricotta fine.

Among mains, we would steer you toward pasta dishes. Pappardelle with "Sunday gravy" is slightly overcooked, not firm enough, but comes with tender braised meat. Meat mains vary. A pork chop has come wildly overcooked, while tilapia has been properly cooked and moist, but muddy in flavor.

That's an offer we can refuse.

Café Java

A simple lunch joint, geared toward take-out, with underperforming panini but passable pizza

4.9	7.5
Food	Feel

Sandwiches, Baked goods, Pizza   Counter service

$10
Price

www.cafejavanh.com

Mon–Fri 7am–4pm

Bar None
Credit cards Visa, MC, AmEx
Veg-friendly

South Town Green
59 Elm St.
(203) 624-1275

The décor at Café Java is warm and inviting. The stucco walls of this downtown lunch spot are coated in a rich acrylic burgundy, and every table bears a collage of guidebook clippings from a different European country.

In the event that your mind was wandering, a glimpse at the café's menu offerings reminds you that you're still squarely on this side of the Atlantic. You can choose from a half-dozen sandwiches and a sampling of pizzas, plus a few standard pastries. After a taste of the overripe fruit or dry bagels, however, even a package of Skittles begins to look like a viable lunch option.

Despite their promising nomenclature, the panini have little to recommend them. A soupy mess of ingredients—only some of them fresh—are layered between two slices of sourdough bread that are then embossed with defining grill marks. The sandwich tends to fall apart long before it can be consumed in full.

Yet Café Java is well located near New Haven's business district, which provides it with a steady stream of suited customers. The place is not terrible for a quick lunch or a morning coffee; just skip the brown, watery espresso, and don't expect marvels. The atmosphere is pleasant, but the café's saving grace is its pizza: although oily and not on par with this town's finest, the personal pies make a satisfying meal. The crust is appropriately crisp, and the pizzas are cooked for each customer on the spot (expect to wait about 10 minutes). It's nice to be reminded of what New Haven does best: for pizza, even this little corner of downtown beats a Parisian bistro, any day.

Café Nine

A classic dive with reasonable bar food and a deep
commitment to the local music scene

6.5	9.0
Food	Feel

American

Bar

$15
Price

www.cafenine.com

Sun–Thu 11am–1am
Fri–Sat 11am–2am

Bar Beer, wine, liquor
Credit cards Visa, MC, AmEx
Date-friendly, live music, Wi-Fi

Ninth Square
250 State St.
(203) 789-8281

Café Nine (named for its Ninth Square location) has got more than a few
appealing features. Free Wi-Fi (something that you would expect to be
more commonplace than it actually is) makes it a good workspace by day,
and live music makes it a good entertainment spot by night. Some of it is
laid-back—like acid jazz with a deep groove—and some of it is just plain
loud. Either way, as a venue, this place is just right. The crowd lies at the
awkward nexus of working-class seniors, vintage-clothed Ivy League
rockers, and goth suburbanites that can make the edges of New Haven
into such a fascinating scene.

The staff is friendly and unpretentious, and the well-worn, well-stocked
bar runs along one side of the room. Even the cheap furniture feels right
at home; for feel, we give it a Nine. Café Nine also functions as an eating
place of sorts, with a tiny kitchen that turns out a standard menu of
comfort food, which you order at the bar and eat either right there (as
many do) or at a table. There's a popular pulled-pork sandwich, which has
come oversalted, causing parched diners to reach for their drinks more
often than usual. It's a shame, because the sandwich is otherwise
impressive—tender and exceptionally flavorful, if closer to roast pork than
smoky barbecue.

No fries are in sight, but the potato salad—"Jody's Famous"—is. Except
for needing salt, Jody's concoction is a good representative of the skin-on,
medium-mayo school of potato salad. Macaroni and cheese doesn't fare
as well; while the cheese sauce is at least average and properly seasoned,
the noodles are often overcooked and soggy.

But you should realize that this is all beside the point. This is a bar, not
a restaurant, and the food is there because bar patrons sometimes get
hungry. Come to Café Nine to drink, come to listen, and let yourself relax
into the rhythm of whatever band happens to be rocking the house.

Caffé Bravo

A neighborhood cult favorite whose serviceable
Italian is better outdoors

6.9 Food	**7.5** Feel	

Italian

Casual restaurant

$35 Price

www.caffebravo.com

Mon–Wed 11:30am–2:30pm,
5pm–9pm; Thu–Fri 11:30am–
2:30pm, 5pm–9:30pm; Sat
5pm–9:30pm

Bar Beer, wine
Credit cards Visa, MC, AmEx
Reservations Accepted
Date-friendly, outdoor dining,
veg-friendly

East Rock
794 Orange St.
(203) 772-2728

When we learned that Caffé Bravo was trading in its BYO status for a
wine and beer list, we thought: *that's it, it's doomed*. BYO keeps the price
of dinner down, but it also allows diners to bring in much more
interesting and well-made wines than a lot of restaurants are carrying
(sad, but true).

We're pleased to see that this isn't entirely the case with Bravo, which
has taken some care in the selection of its wine list, which is split evenly
between New and Old World bottles. That "some care" refers to only half
of the Italians, and one or two of the domestics. Still, it's better than you
might expect for such a laid-back place.

Caffé Bravo's straightforward Italian-American food doesn't have much
innovation or regional authenticity, though they do display a particular
skill in preparing pasta. Penne and filled pastas alike are carefully done
and refreshingly al dente.

Pane cotto is a good way to start. The white beans have an appropriate
texture, cooked exactly the right amount, while the bread is soft and rich;
it's like a casserole. More complex dishes aren't bad either—peppery veal
marsala, for instance, is tender, with a sweet and well-developed brown
sauce and deliciously fresh mushrooms; at last visit, it needed an extra
touch of salt, but it was still satisfying. Gnocchi with tomato sauce,
unfortunately, lack the softness that one would expect from a homemade
preparation. The tomato sauce tends to be undersalted; plenty of
parmesan helps.

There's not much to say about the atmosphere. It has a certain
neighborhood charm, but orderly rows of nameless, faceless tables with
cafeteria-style furnishings stare up at you in bright boredom—so keep in
mind that this restaurant is a good take-out option. Summer dining is a
welcome treat, when luck and patience may grant you one of the few
outdoor tables. Sit in the evening warmth, and share a bottle of Barolo
with a few friends. Above-average espresso makes a good finish; so does
the cognac pumpkin cheesecake.

Campania

Decent Italian-American fare served up in a cozy little Branford house

7.2	7.5
Food	Feel

Italian

Upmarket restaurant

$45
Price

www.campaniaristorante.com

Mon noon–9pm
Wed–Sat noon–10pm
Sun 1pm–9pm

Bar Beer, wine, liquor
Credit cards Visa, MC, AmEx
Reservations Accepted
Date-friendly, outdoor dining,
veg-friendly, Wi-Fi

Branford
283 E. Main St.
(203) 483-7773

Branford isn't the most densely populated restaurant town, which is why we're happy about Campania's arrival on the scene. The space is quite comfortable, although it's not close to the town green. The building (actually an old house) is located more on the whizzing-road section of East Main Street, but it's tucked far enough back that there's no annoying noise or visuals. A few outdoor tables are nice, too, and they manage to avoid the dreaded eating-on-a-highway syndrome.

Inside, the restaurant is warm and cozy. This is a family operation (with the husband manning the back of the house, and the wife womaning the front), and it shows. Careful touches make you feel pretty much as if you've been plopped down in their home, casually posted up next to the fireplace. We're not so sure about their claims that we'll be convinced we're in Italy, but perhaps we're just a tougher sell than most.

Like an unsung version of Billy's Pasta Così, Campania is quietly serving up a menu that's pretty good for typical East coast Italian-American. There are some questionable moves—Italian egg rolls (eep!)—and some pleasantly challenging ones, like veal tripe and veal hearts. The menu is long (perhaps longer than necessary) and protein-centric. Pastas make up a considerable chunk of it. "Gnocchi Woodsmen" combines arugula, mushroom, roasted peppers, and rosemary into an earthy dish that works pretty well. Not so for "Vitello Mediterranean," which combines a lot of pricey ingredients—veal, lobster, crab, cognac cream sauce—into a dish that is more style than substance. This is the sort of overpriced, everything-but-the-kitchen-sink prep that Shoreline diners are ready to move away from.

Our biggest beef with Campania is their failure to observe their own hours. We were once turned away on a Sunday evening, even though we arrived well before closing time. The excuse was a "private party," of which there was obviously no evidence—just a couple quietly finishing dinner. Campania has such a lovely space…can we be blamed for wanting to spend time in it during their supposed business hours?

Nonetheless, we're happy about the restaurant's addition to the local dining scene. As for you, arrive early.

Caribbean Connection

One of New Haven's tiniest—and best—Jamaican take-out spots

Caribbean

8.3 Food

5.5 Feel

Take-out

$10 Price

Mon–Sat 1pm–9pm

Bar None
Credit cards None

Whalley
364 Whalley Ave.
(203) 777-9080

It can be easy to miss if you're driving down Whalley Avenue between downtown and Westville with tunnel vision, but this stretch of road is quite a culinary melting pot, from soul food to new-age vegetarian to Chinese to Eastern European Jewish. Caribbean Connection, next door to Stella's kosher bakery, is a representative of New Haven's Jamaican community—and one of the easiest of all to miss. The storefront is barely wider than the entrance to an apartment building.

The tiny take-out window inside the door, where there's barely enough room for two or three people to stand and order at the little counter, offers some of the best Jamaican even in a town of excellent Jamaican finds. Jerk chicken, not always available, is top-notch, with a good kick and moist texture. Oxtail is soft and rich, just as it should be, even if it isn't quite up to the gold standard of Mother's. Curry goat and stew chicken benefit from well-balanced seasoning, and plenty of sauce. (Note that the curry might be gone by 7pm or so.) They even serve breakfast— eggy ackee (the Jamaican national fruit) and saltfish with a fried dumpling and callaloo (a leafy green).

Plenty of sauce is something that can't be taken for granted at these sorts of Jamaican places—there's significant variation in how generously the liquid from the stew is ladled over the meat and allowed to permeate through the rice-and-peas accompaniment as well. With cooking by extraction (stewing, for instance), much of the flavor seeps from the meat into the liquid, and the sauce is where it's at. Caribbean Connection clearly understands this. Meat patties, too, are reliable, and service comes with a smile. And don't forget to consult the list of daily specials at this little treasure.

Carmen Anthony

An outstanding, high-priced steakhouse that
follows a well-tested formula—but follows it well

8.5	8.5
Food	Feel

Steakhouse

Upmarket restaurant

$75
Price

www.carmenanthony.com

Mon–Wed 11:30am–4pm,
5pm–9pm; Thu–Fri 11:30am–
4pm, 5pm–10pm; Sat 5pm–
11pm; Sun 4pm–8:30pm

Bar Beer, wine, liquor
Credit cards Visa, MC, AmEx
Reservations Accepted
Date-friendly, good wines, Wi-Fi

Audubon Arts District
660 State St.
(203) 773-1444

In keeping with the chain restaurant theme, the building that houses
Carmen Anthony—not far from downtown but on a lonely stretch of
State Street—is strictly office-park material. But looks can be deceiving,
especially in the restaurant business. Inside, the design is careful and
understated; globe lamps, which might be left too bright in less able
hands, are dimmed enough to turn into friendly orbs, removing the
blemishes from your date's face. Such elaborate place settings,
uncontained, might be stuffy, but here they're protected by the
gregarious, clubby buzz of the humanity that inhabits them.

Clubby is really the point here, after all; we understand that we really
should be starting out with martinis (excellent), jumbo shrimp cocktail
(good), or perhaps an iceberg lettuce wedge (superb, with homemade
blue cheese dressing masterfully paired with warm pieces of bacon). Crab
cakes are a must—they're exemplary, crusted with shredded potato, and
delicious.

But what's even more exciting is that this is one of New Haven's few
restaurants where rare orders are fully honored. The beef is not dry-aged,
but it is still flavorful, juicy, and well crusted with spices. The New York
strip and the fattier ribeye are equally good (skip the filet). Even the
tricked-out "specialty steaks," a category that we generally try to avoid at
steakhouses, were much better than expected: the "sliced New York
Florentine" is redolent of garlic and drizzled with olive oil that seeps into
every flavorful flap of the slices, like in a rustic Italian tagliata di manzo.

That's not to say that you'll get out cheaply. Even the excellent wine list
is one of the most expensive in New Haven—but, like everything else,
worth every penny.

Caseus

New Haven's new big cheese is a transportative
trip through culinary space-time

9.4 Food
9.5 Feel

New American

Casual restaurant

$40 Price

www.caseusnewhaven.com

Mon–Tue 11:30am–3:30pm
Wed–Thu 11:30am–3:30pm,
5:30pm–9pm
Fri–Sat 11:30am–3:30pm,
5:30pm–10pm

Bar Beer, wine, liquor
Credit cards Visa, MC, AmEx
Reservations Accepted
Date-friendly, good wines, outdoor
dining, veg-friendly

East Rock
93 Whitney Ave.
(203) 624-3373

One of the best things about New Haven's most exciting new restaurant
in a decade is that it doesn't act the part. Caseus, which inhabits the old
Miya's space, looks at first like it's just the city's best cheese shop. And it
is that. But then you notice a few casual tables set up around the bar—
and a few squeezed in by the shop below. And then, if you're there
around lunch or dinner hours, you notice that you can't have one,
because they're all reserved. (Clearly, the word is out.) There's bustle and
warmth, but the prices aren't particularly high, and there's no pomp, no
circumstance, no tablecloths, and certainly no calling you sir.

The relentlessly modern, well-edited menu—along with the expertly
constructed wine list that's equally at ease in Alsace, Rioja, or the better
nuggets of the New World—is the first real clue to how special this place
is. And then there's the food. Oh, the food. Poutine comes with french
fries crisped to such an ideal deep brown that they stand up to the
moisture of cheese curds and the thickly reduced brown gravy. A brioche
cheeseburger is honest and direct. Pig's foot, the "offal special" at one
visit, had richness seeping from every crevice of melting cartilage.
Macaroni and cheese is anchored by gruyère, but that cheese works in
complex tandem with several others; unfortunately, the dish suffers from
undersalting, one of the few consistent problems here. A creamy plate of
homemade pappardelle with lemon zest and Parmigiano exists at the very
intersection of richness and lightness, but it, too, is undersalted. Lamb
sliders have come a touch overcooked, but still bursting with flavor and
moistness. Caseus is not perfect—yet.

The kitchen's early versatility is impressive. These guys have almost as
much of a way with mussels, with crab-and-grapefruit salad, and with fish
as they do with the organ meats. Zeppole—crisp, melting balls of fried
dough, sprinkled with powdered sugar—come in a brown paper cone,
like something you once tasted at the county fair, only much, much
better. Your memory has been scanned in, the pubescent haze
Photoshopped out, the image sharpened and saturated.

Caseus inhabits that subjunctive place, that anachronistic childhood,
that counterfactual culinary space-time. Its haute nostalgia is for a
pastoral American cuisine that never really existed, so it had to be
invented. As this restaurant matures, it will be an exquisite pleasure for us
to have the chance to watch its kitchen change, grow, explore the further
reaches of its prodigious potential, and continue to rewrite the early
chapters of America's fictional culinary biography.

Celtica

A pleasant stop for tea and scones

5.3	6.5
Food	Feel

Irish, Baked goods, Sandwiches

Counter service

$15
Price

www.gotirish.com

Mon–Sat 11:30am–4pm
Sun noon–4pm

Bar None
Credit cards Visa, MC, AmEx
Veg-friendly

Chapel District
260 College St.
(203) 785-8034

Take a hint from the domain name: your Irish fetish will be well fed by the downtown Celtica store and its little tea room in the back, whose friendly service and calming vibe create a little world apart from the bustle of College Street.

This place is just as much store as it is tea room. The store itself, which you will walk through along the way, peddles all manner of Irish curios—Celtica, if you will. The tea room, too, aside its few brown tables and chairs and a counter in back, has walls that are lined with boxes of Irish this and Irish that—boxes of Bewley's Irish Tea, biscuits, and so on. There's even a blooming shamrock, like an Irish chia pet.

It's a pleasant place to duck in for a spell. Gone are the days when you could order sandwiches, soups, salads, and quiches (not a loss we spent too much time lamenting). Now scones are the only staple available. The room itself is cute, if a little kitschy—it feels a bit as if you're taking your high tea in the home of a slightly older, slightly batty Irish woman.

Not that we're complaining. The feel is warm and soothing, much like the pot of Irish tea, which is served in a French press. And that's why you're here, right? That and to pick up a Shamrock onesie with a hat and bib, which is advertised on the website for only $29.95.

Central Steakhouse

Go to the neighboring steakhouse competition—
it's cheaper *and* better

5.9	8.0
Food	Feel

Steakhouse

Upmarket restaurant

$75
Price

www.centralsteakhouse.com

Mon–Thu 5pm–10pm
Fri–Sat 5pm–11pm

Bar Beer, wine, liquor
Credit cards Visa, MC, AmEx
Reservations Accepted
Date-friendly, good wines

Ninth Square
99 Orange St.
(203) 787-7885

Central Steakhouse was exciting when it first opened, but these days we don't get it. For one thing, the hours are a guessing game (website says open Monday, but we've found it closed then; arrive at 8:30 pm on a Tuesday, in spite of the supposed hours, and you might be out of luck again). On some nights, they even manage to run out of potatoes. How does a steakhouse run out of potatoes? It's not like they're a terribly perishable item. Mostly, though the food is just plain bad. And what prices!

We don't know how long a steakhouse can survive with an iceberg wedge salad as poor as this. They will riot in the streets, won't they? Overcooked, tough bacon and watery blue cheese that tastes more like ranch?

There's a law of steakhouse averages that says that, even if everything else the kitchen offers is blah, the steak will be the sure thing. Central defies it utterly, with cheap cuts of unevenly cooked, underseasoned (though reasonable quality) meat. A porterhouse for $39 has been the thinnest we've ever seen, medium-rare in some parts and medium-well in others.

You're actually better off, for once, with non-steak dishes. Scallops with soy sesame "wakame seaweed" (think seaweed salad from a sushi place with a pineapple-Riesling reduction) is not bad; the scallops are at least cooked properly. Carbonara with asparagus tips and bacon is too heavy, since they make the tacky decision to use cream and not just egg, à la Olive Garden. Still, it doesn't taste bad, and the spaghetti isn't overcooked. The other steakhouse standard, creamed spinach, is served in a crockpot, but the cream doesn't integrate with the spinach. Where others traditionally use béchamel, this didn't taste at all like it. Grilled asparagus is, likewise, just eh.

The one redeeming feature here is the wine list, which is extensive and interesting. The prices are fairer than those of the food. We've enjoyed a funky, pleasantly oxidized old Touraine that we hadn't seen anywhere else. However, wine service detracts: the untrained staff can't help you at all, and they pour too much into the glass.

Central, perhaps; a steakhouse, barely.

Chap's Grille

It's well located and open late...but we don't really have any other good news for you

5.0 Food

2.5 Feel

American, Middle Eastern

Counter service

$15 Price

Daily 7:30am–10pm

Bar None
Credit cards Visa, MC, AmEx
Delivery, kid-friendly, outdoor dining, veg-friendly

Upper Chapel Area
1174 Chapel St.
(203) 562-3966

Part lunchroom, part diner, part delivery service (within a limited area, of course), Chap's Grille is centrally located and open late. The space is a quiet, tiled dining area with cheesy picket-fence detail by the window and an uneventful short-order menu. The atmosphere, as a glance inside from the street quickly reveals, is not exactly depressing, but neither is there much to write about. There are a few simple tables and chairs, and that's just about it.

If food means little more than sustenance to you, then Chap's may fit the bill. Almost everything about Chap's is average, although the offerings make erratic forays into unlikely territory. There's "Egyptian-style" moussaka and a version of Indian chicken tikka. Hmm. At least there are also some specifically vegan options.

For sheer nourishment, the best option here is breakfast. The breakfast special, served until 11am, offers two eggs, toast, and hash browns for $2.65. Other morning options include the "Big Breakfast" with all the usuals: French toast (thickly cut, thankfully), a stack of pancakes, or an omelette with hash browns and bacon. Of the breakfast standards, all are good except the hash browns, which are too soft and somewhat soggy, as though they've been heated and reheated endlessly. For lunch and dinner, the sandwich wraps are as good a choice as any—try the chicken wrap with couscous. Or try nothing at all.

Chestnut Fine Foods

A pretty Victorian shop for baked goods, prepared
foods, and catering

Baked goods, Groceries

Market

www.chestnutfinefoods.com

Mon–Fri 9am–7pm
Sat 9am–5pm

Bar None
Credit cards Visa, MC, AmEx
Veg-friendly

East Rock
1012 State St.
(203) 782-6767

Since our last review of Chestnut Fine Foods and Confections, the café
has given way almost completely to its catering and retail business. It's a
smart move for the shop, which has been well known to New Haven for
almost two decades. We still like the precious 19th-century building up
State Street, whose interior is replete with low-hanging feathered lamps,
pale pink walls, and other aunt's-house frills. It feels like a whimsical
tearoom.

The once-nonchalant service is gone, too, and what remains is a more
competent, familial vibe. Indeed, this vibe has even gone so far as to
provide Sunday brunch couples therapy with a licensed therapist (on their
website; by reservation only). While it sounds like the plot of an NBC
sitcom—*nothing makes a man open up like quiche!*—we applaud the
innovative community involvement. What's *your* bakery done for you
lately?

Speaking of which, there's still an abundance of very good artisanal
breads and rolls, the shop's best work. They bake a few every day,
including flavors like carrot-tarragon and spinach-feta. There's also a nice
selection of imported and domestic cheeses from small farms.

The catering operation still plays within outdated borders, resting
heavily on the time when Americans couldn't get enough sugar. Think
pork tenderloin with roasted nectarines (far sweeter than the more-often
paired apricots) and glazed ham with brown sugar-roasted pineapple
(Insulin! Bring us insulin!).

If you prefer your confections in a paper doily instead of on a duck
breast, you're still in luck. Chestnut's cases are filled with glistening tarts,
pies, and cookies (including some rather macabre hand-shaped ones with
chocolate "fingernails"). These can get pretty pricey, but their gorgeous
cakes, like chocolate ganache, can be a good deal (if you don't eat them
all by yourself).

They also make gift baskets out of their specialty goods, many of which
are locally made for housewarmings, birthdays, and wedding showers.
Not to be cynical, but it wouldn't hurt to slip in a certificate good for one
couples brunch…

Chick's

A Shoreline seafood shack where the nostalgia, not
the greasy fried food, is worth the price

6.8	7.0
Food	Feel

Seafood

Counter service

$15
Price

Mon–Thu 11am–8:45pm	**Bar** None	**West Haven**
Fri–Sat 11am–9:45pm	**Credit cards** None	183 Beach St.
	Date-friendly, kid-friendly, outdoor dining	(203) 934-4510

As long as New Englanders keep their insatiable appetites for clams,
Chick's will be here, doling them out. They're well-loved steamed, in a
chowder, or on a pizza (just ask Frank Pepe), but old-school New
Englanders love them fried most of all. Though Chick's purports to be just
the place for that preparation, we find the quality has deteriorated over
time while the prices keep climbing.

Come for nostalgia's sake, if anything: this is a timeless Shoreline
seafood shack with a beach right across the street and an autographed
photo of Marilyn Monroe over the register.

Chick's is strictly downmarket—it looks like the sign has been there for
ages, and the whole place has a sort of run-down-beach-town feel, like
the place you might have gone as a little kid for fried clams after a day on
the sand along Boston's South Shore.

Aside from the fried clams, Chick's dishes out hot Connecticut-style
lobster rolls, New England clam chowder, and soft-shell crabs, when in
season. Lobster rolls are just decent (the meat is a bit more shredded than
we prefer), and the fried food can be rather greasy. But this is nothing
new: the preparations here are eminently typical, deeply in touch with
regional tradition, for better or worse.

The service is at the counter only; you can sit at any of the informal
tables inside, or, in good weather, outside, across from the water.
Although the amply outfitted parking lot (they don't call it "drive inn" for
nothing) figures prominently into the view from Chick's proper, it's just as
easy to take your paper boxes and bags across the street and enjoy their
spoils while actually sitting on the beach. Still, some people do the truly
old-school thing and eat the clams and fries in their car. A convertible, of
course, is best.

Chili's

Everybody knows it, no matter who you are

5.4 Food **7.0** Feel

American, Mexican

Casual restaurant

$25 Price

www.chilis.com

Sun–Thu 11am–11pm
Fri–Sat 11am–midnight

Bar Beer, wine, liquor
Credit cards Visa, MC, AmEx
Reservations Not accepted

Hamden
2100 Dixwell Ave.
(203) 248-2283

Like its namesake dish, this suburban "casual dining" mainstay is more just-plain-American than it is Mexican or Southwestern, so it's no coincidence that it tends to hang out along the most suburban-style stretches of America. After all, strip centers are more American than almost anything else. Populated in equal numbers by families and frat boys, Chili's has certainly hit on a successful formula.

The main reason it works is its Disneyesque version of Tex-Mex iconography. The fact that Chili's is packed during peak dinner hours, especially on weekends, adds to the atmospheric effect and makes it a fun place in which to hang out.

One of our major gripes about Chili's concerns the price-gouging margaritas: they're too sweet, they have too much ice, and they are far too weak—it feels as if barely a stingy airport-bar shot has dissipated through a a tub of sickly sour mix. Otherwise, generally speaking, the food is actually not as bad as some people say it is; try not to be too put off by the glossy, mass-produced menus or dishes with intentionally cute titles.

But you do have to be careful what you order. Stick to things that are either fried or slathered in sauce or cheese. The surfeit of flavor compensates for bland and overcooked primary ingredients. Grilled baby back ribs with barbecue sauce, though expensive and unrelated to any actual Southern barbecue sauce, are a good example of this rule—they might not be subtle or down-home authentic, but who would come to Chili's expecting authenticity?

Avoid the steaks and fajitas, where beef and chicken are liable to be overcooked and dry. Burgers, including the chipotle blue cheese bacon burger, are fine, although the beef isn't very flavorful. Aside from the fajitas, chicken might actually be the best category, particularly the boneless Buffalo wings and "southwestern egg rolls," which are flour tortillas wrapped around smoked chicken, black beans, corn and jalapeño jack cheese with red peppers, spinach, and an avocado-ranch dipping sauce. Delicious. Otherwise, avoid fish at all costs.

Appetizers are generally better than main courses, but that's almost needless to say; at Chili's, you know what you're going to get, and you get what you come for: typical suburban-chain fun.

China Great Wall

The best Chinese restaurant in New Haven has
earned its own space—finally

8.7	7.0
Food	Feel

Chinese

Casual restaurant

$15
Price

Mon–Fri 11am–9:30pm; Sat
10am–9:30pm; Sun 10am–9pm

Bar Beer, wine
Credit cards Visa, MC
Reservations Not accepted
Veg-friendly

Audubon Arts District
67 Whitney Ave.
(203) 777-8886

Great Wall used to be concealed within the dark depths of Hong Kong
Grocery, behind aisles of persimmons, ginger, and green onions in
cardboard boxes. The restaurant was uncannily reminiscent of short-order
restaurants in Beijing: the snappy women demanding your order and
yelling in dialect, the chef in back chopping huge cuts of pork, the
Styrofoam containers and plastic bags with juices and fats seeping out,
the impossibly cheap prices, the Chinese clientele sitting at scattered
tables and plastic chairs busily eating with little chatter. The food, as we
remember it then, was delicious.

Perhaps reacting to the influx of savvy diners who knew the secrets of
Great Wall, the grocery has been moved next door, and the restaurant
has expanded to fill the entire space. Pleather booths, clean linoleum
floors, and striped wallpaper give the place a cafeteria-like sterility. The
menu has expanded as well—sometimes for the worse. The Fujianese
working there now try their hand, not always successfully, at the Chinese
culinary kaleidoscope, with a huge list of Szechuan fare and Cantonese
dim sum.

Fish-flavored Chinese eggplant, deep-fried and coated in a garlic bean
sauce, is tasty as usual. But gongbao jiding, a stir-fry of chicken, red
chilies, and fried peanuts, is greasy and bland, not fiery and energetic as it
should be. Ma po tofu is silky and able to retain its shape, but seriously
lacks the peppery numbing spice that lends the dish its name.

Cantonese dishes and dim sum (carts roll around on weekend mornings
and afternoons) are mostly successful, and certainly the best in New
Haven. Chicken feet melt in the mouth. BBQ pork steamed buns are light
and sweet, but the baked buns are even better, with a savory-sweet
balance between pork and eggy bread. Steamed rice in lotus leaf is
evocative and redolent of deep pork flavor.

As before, the buffet caters simultaneously to Chinese-American
traditionalists and to those seeking more authentic experiences. Four
choices with rice for $6.99 is still one of the best lunch deals in the area.
But as with any food kept warm by chafing dishes and heat lamps,
proceed with caution (see Gourmet Heaven at 1am).

At press time, a beer and wine license was expected any day. That, plus
fresh-baked pastries every morning, ensure we will be here all the time.

China King

Predictably bad Chinese-American take-out with a
prime location but little else to recommend it

3.4 Food

2.5 Feel

Chinese

Take-out

$10 Price

Sun–Thu 11am–11pm
Fri–Sat 11am–midnight

Bar None
Credit cards Visa, MC
Delivery

Chapel District
942 Chapel St.
(203) 776-8807

It's hard to write about little Chinese take-out spots like China King. On
the one hand, you understand the value proposition—more food than
two people could possibly eat for somewhere between four dollars (at
lunch) and six or seven dollars (at dinner). There are a couple of tables,
but most customers take out. China King is right on the Green, and it fills
you up cheaply and satisfyingly if you're starving at an off hour.

The even more frustrating thing is that there is clearly some skill and
talent in the kitchen, and yet it goes to waste on these Chinese-American
brown-sauce preparations. We once watched the cook, in a virtuoso
performance, carefully scramble an egg inside the bowl of his large metal
spoon before dropping it into a peppery hot and sour soup, which turned
out pretty well.

But another time, when we asked for a recommendation and were told
by the cashier that General Tso's chicken was the best choice on the
menu, we had to wonder whether he just took us for Americans without
taste buds. The thick, syrupy brown sauce, which is too sweet, also saps
any crunch from the pieces of curiously spongy deep-fried chicken. It's a
heavy and cloying dish. Fried rice is well seasoned and properly textured, if
unexciting; an egg roll is properly crispy, but its bland filling features those
little red bits of pork similar to the ones in the fried rice.

People once craved the sort of Chinese-American glop that proliferated
at these sorts of joints throughout the 20th century. But the American
palate has turned a corner, and places like China King must now consider
that they could be so much more than what they are.

China Pavilion

Fairly typical suburban Chinese food with a devoted following and Peking duck

6.1	6.5
Food	Feel

Chinese

Upmarket restaurant

$30
Price

www.chinapavilion.net

Mon–Thu 11:30am–10pm
Fri–Sat 11:30am–11pm
Sun 12:30pm–10pm

Bar Beer, wine, liquor
Credit cards Visa, MC, AmEx
Reservations Accepted
Kid-friendly

Orange
Hitchcock Plaza, 185
Boston Post Rd.
(203) 795-3555

We're not sure why this place gets so many awards. China Pavilion is little more than a welcoming suburban restaurant with some curious quirks. The décor is pink, pink, pink, while the service is friendly but sometimes scarce, especially considering the number of people working here.

Most distinctive, perhaps, are the signature drinks and their intriguing descriptions. These fruity, punchy concoctions are fairly guaranteed to pack a wallop. Nor are they short on drama and ingenuity; a cocktail for two arrives in a large bowl adorned with ceramic figures of topless hula dancers, with a blue flame flickering in the middle of it all. The "special straws" might transport you directly back to childhood.

The menu offers a recitation of Chinese restaurant standards. Vegetable dumplings have soft skin; they're doughy with a bland filling, not much different from their equivalent at your basic corner Chinese restaurant, although the sauce with scallion and chili is a notch above the norm.

We suggest that you go for the Peking duck, which is carved tableside with a flourish. Its skin is crisp, the meat succulent. At our last visit, however, our expert carver disappeared and we waited many minutes while the glistening meat sat just a foot away, cooling. Another complaint: the moo shu-style pancakes are bland and starchy. The menu offers a one-course and a two-course version of the Peking duck; for the second course, if requested, they stir-fry the rest of the duck with celery in a basic Szechuan preparation, which is nothing to write home about. Still, the duck meat, as in the first course, is tender, and the dish has a nice sweetness.

While China Pavilion may not be worth the trip to Orange, it's not a bad stop if you happen to be in the area.

Chip's II

A great pub for Sox fans and popcorn-fiends—but that's about it

5.1	7.0
Food	Feel

American, Burgers

Bar

$20
Price

Daily 11:30am–11pm

Bar Beer, wine, liquor
Credit cards Visa, MC, AmEx
Live music

Guilford
725 Boston Post Rd.
(203) 453-0615

Some polls have listed Chip's II Pub in Guilford as having the best burger arpund. It certainly has the usual characteristics of such an honor: it's hidden in back of a strip mall on Route 1, with a sign whose '70s kelly-green font reminds us of Cheers.

Inside, there's a hopping bar scene, complete with bits of free popcorn strewn all over the floor. Lots of license plates and other not-quite-memorabilia hang on the wood-paneled walls, and there's a long, but fairly standard, beer list. It could have been the model for TGI Friday's.

The space is divided almost evenly—half dining room, half bar (with big TVs playing the game)—but the noise at the bar makes the dining room feel like just an extension of that area. You won't find a better place in town to watch a Sox or Patriots game, though.

The menu is long, with cutesy, punny names for dishes, and the waitstaff is very friendly and quick to refill your popcorn bowl. Even if one excludes the city of New Haven (and its powerhouses, Prime 16 and Caseus) from the best-burger-on-the-shoreline competition, the burger at Chip's II is not a contender. It's always overcooked, no matter how you order it, and comes coated in too much of some kind of mystery seasoning involving a great deal of black pepper. And it's full—*full*—of gristle. Like, crunchy cartilage. This is not quality meat, and it is definitely not a quality burger. The fries it comes with are even worse, battered and frozen-tasting. Other options include giant salads with lots of cheese, sprouts, and avocadoes (which tastes reasonably fresh), as well as other casual staples like a daily pasta special and a pork chop. Pass on these overpriced underperformers.

If it's a great burger you're looking for, keep looking. If what you're looking for, on the other hand, is a hospitable bar full of sports fans and endless popcorn right off I-95, then look no further.

Chow Wine Bar

Disastrous Asian fusion that shares a kitchen (and some foibles) with Zinc

Pan-Asian   Upmarket restaurant

call for hours

Bar Beer, wine, liquor
Credit cards Visa, MC, AmEx
Reservations Accepted
Date-friendly, live music

Chapel District
966 Chapel St.
(203) 772-3002

At press time, we learned that Chow was closing to revamp, with a reopening that promised a menu of local, sustainable ingredients. The following review reflects the previous Chow concept, but we have removed our numerical ratings in advance of the new version. Check fearlesscritic.com for an update.

Chow labels itself a "dim sum wine bar," immediately calling to mind disaster. Surely, one or the other must suffer in such an arrangement. The immediate suspicion is that this place is disguising yet another tired Asian-fusion small-plates concept in a cuter package.

The best thing about Chow is its patio on the alleyway that connects the Taft with the Liberty, which makes for lots of summertime easy-drinking fun. Inside, the place sports cheap Christmas lighting (which we like under the right circumstances), scratched wooden tables, and dirt-colored walls, making the place feel like an underground grunge dive—a bit incongruous given that people are sipping wine and eating food with lofty menu descriptions.

The driving philosophy of the kitchen seems to be that the mere use of Chinese ingredients makes a dish dim sum, and it's used here with mindless abandon. Salmon rice-paper rolls are doused in chili sauce, completely overpowering the fish. What's more, it's not just salmon, but gravlax…what's the point of curing it if you're going to kill it? Five spice appears in everything from the ribs to the dipping sauces, and finally gets its starring role in a chicken bowl—and promptly overpowers it. It chews the scenery worse than Pacino.

Fortunately, five spice is not cast in the sweet potato dumplings, which are delicious in their simplicity. Desserts, though, have been convoluted both in concept and execution. Steamed buns with chocolate filling are innovative, but then served with a confusing passion fruit coulis. Ginger in a honey cheesecake is more jarring than juxtaposing.

The main draw here seems to be the cocktails and wine, which show more innovation than usual, but are still not up to the standards set by more ambitious beverage programs, like the one at 116 Crown. How long are we going to continue to exalt Smirnoff-and-juice elixirs as "specialty cocktails"?

Christopher Martin's

A big screen, a local vibe, great bar food, and a
strange upscale Italian restaurant next door

7.6	8.5
Food	Feel

American, Burgers

Casual restaurant

$25
Price

www.christophermartins.com

Daily 11:30am–midnight

Bar Beer, wine, liquor
Credit cards Visa, MC, AmEx
Reservations Accepted

East Rock
860 State St.
(203) 776-8835

This is a strange wedding of the classic big-screen TV sports bar serving
good, unambitious pub grub with an adjacent upmarket Italian restaurant
that has an ambitious menu whose mains go as high as $25.

The restaurant side of things attracts fewer customers, it seems, than
does the bar. Not that there's anything wrong with it; they feature
Connecticut-made "Black Ledge" blue cheese, and they do a nice job
with a fusiony dishes, but we're not sure if the atmosphere there justifies
the prices.

For us, though, the bar is where it's at. Christopher Martin's is probably
the best place in town to watch the Celtics, Red Sox, or Pats win another
championship. You'll always be joined by a lively local crowd, gregarious
but rarely raucous. This is the sort of place in which a hamburger should
be savored for the wonder that it is.

To our delight, the food is about as good as you can get in town for bar
fare, and you can get it until midnight. The "sloppy fingers" (called
"buffalo tenders" at less dignified places) are absolutely addictive—
they're breaded, fried crisp, and tossed in a great (and spicy) sauce.
Burgers here are tender, made with high-quality beef, and filled with fresh
cheese, lettuce, and tomato, and the right mix of condiments.

The "appetizer" chicken burrito is massive—it's more of a main than a
starter. Onion rings—if you can call them rings—are delicious, and you
get a portion about as big as your head for $5. They're the shoestring-
fries equivalent of onion rings, and it is impossible to keep from shoving
handful after handful in your mouth. Curly fries are crispy and tangy, too.
Even the grilled chicken sandwich, too often a bland choice, is a winner
here.

The draft beer is also just so, a tour of America's best smaller mass-
market breweries: Sam Adams, Sierra Nevada, and the like. Christopher
Martin's is enough to make you stop and appreciate one of the proudest
culinary traditions in America: bar food done right.

Chuck's Steak House

A time-frozen 1970s chain steakhouse with bargain-priced meals and correct creamed spinach

6.9 Food

7.0 Feel

Steakhouse

Casual restaurant

$30 Price

www.chuckssteakhouse.com

Tue–Thu 4:30pm–9pm
Fri–Sat 4:30pm–10pm
Sun 4pm–9pm
Hours vary by location

Bar Beer, wine, liquor
Credit cards Visa, MC, AmEx
Reservations Accepted
Kid-friendly

West Haven
1003 Orange Ave.
(203) 934-5300

Branford
377 E. Main St.
(203) 483-7557

Luckily, the damage caused by a fire in early 2009 wasn't enough to put Chuck's Steak House out of commission; after a brief closure, they were up and running again. And this is a good thing, because Chuck's holds a special place in New England history. It's now a big chain, but the West Haven branch was the first of all.

It's hard to resist the heroic $15.95 "Economic Stimulus Menu" that includes an all-you-can-eat salad bar, a steak (or other main), a side dish of potatoes, a dessert, and even coffee. There's a clubby bar that's straight out of the past, and there are a few different rooms that are intermittently inhabited by local families, West Haven boys' nights out, and older boys ready to finish with a cigar.

All-you-can-eat salad bars are not our favorite thing in the world, but this one's fun: you can make your own iceberg wedge salad, with a creamy if mild blue cheese dressing, and bacon bits that are actually chopped up pieces of bacon—not those disgusting little brown things that look like grape nuts and pass for bacon at a less worthy salad bar. Next, to our delight and surprise, a sirloin steak ordered black and blue came exactly that way—extremely rare. The steaks taste good and beefy, with a satisfying texture.

Creamed spinach is a dish that can so often go awry, with watery leaves that don't bind to the béchamel, or clumpy stuff that tastes industrial; but Chuck's version is exactly as it should be. The wine selection is not much, with nothing above cheap California cabs. But what do you expect? This is, after all, a suburban chain steakhouse. And it's a great one.

At Chuck's newer Branford location, called "Chuck's Steakhouse and Margarita Grill," there's mediocre Tex-Mex in the mix to go along with the steaks, and the salad comes to your table—no more bar. Speaking of bar, it's got more of a sports-bar concept, too. We prefer the West Haven original.

Citrus

A bizarrely designed restaurant with an interesting
menu but little to recommend it at this price range

7.3	6.5
Food	Feel

New American

Upmarket restaurant

$55
Price

www.citrus-ct.com

Bar Beer, wine, liquor
Credit cards Visa, MC, AmEx
Reservations Accepted
Outdoor dining

Milford
56 S. Broad St.
(203) 877-1138

We're not sure that anyone really likes or "gets" the design of Citrus.
Granted, both the restaurantgoers and those who are there just to grab a
drink at the bar (a fairly common practice, actually) must appreciate the
variation between rooms, the architectural twists and turns. But other
touches are just plain weird, like the ceiling, which looks like congealed
gobs of black goo. It makes you wonder if the otherworldly substance will
drip down onto your plate, or if Sigourney Weaver is hiding around the
corner.

There's outdoor dining, too, but it's like a Home Depot garden, and the
indoor window seats look out onto little more than cars zooming by. Even
the parking lot is strange: have you ever seen a restaurant with main
courses in the $30s that sternly declares a two-hour parking limit? What is
this, Walgreens?

The food is fine, more or less what you'd expect from a New American
place with high-end pretensions. Fried calamari are tender, but not crispy
enough; they come with cucumber, lemon, onion, and a side of chipotle
aioli. The dish is satisfying in that way that calamari tend to be. Spring
rolls are more inspired, well executed if not subtle, with a strange
bedfellow—wasabi mashed potatoes. Aren't we over that fad?

We still don't really find any sort of generalized citrus theme; most
things here are traditional comfort dishes that have been given some sort
of modern twist. Take, for instance, the tilapia, which comes with a
cilantro-lime gastrique. But $21 for this dud of a fish?

In the end, Citrus underperforms within its genre and price range; and
nowhere is this more evident than in the wine list, which reads like a
catalog of advertisements in *Wine Spectator*. Foreign wines like
Châteauneuf-du-Pape and Chianti are better values, but however you
figure it, your tab at the end of the night is going to be fairly steep.

Claire's Corner Copia

A pan-ethnic vegetarian restaurant whose
popularity owes almost exclusively to the cake

4.1	8.5
Food	Feel

American

Casual restaurant

$20
Price

www.clairescornercopia.com

Mon–Thu 8am–9pm
Fri 8am–10pm
Sat 9am–10pm
Sun 9am–9pm

Bar None
Credit cards Visa, MC, AmEx
Kid-friendly, veg-friendly

Chapel District
1000 Chapel St.
(203) 562-3888

Claire's must be the most polarizing restaurant in New Haven. There's no place for which a negative review has brought us so many compliments: "I knew when I read the Claire's review that you guys really know food"; "you earned my trust with the low ratings for Claire's review"; "thank you so much for being honest—somebody had to say it!" At the same time, the people who disagree with the review disagree with it vehemently—Claire's is often one of their favorite places in town.

We attribute this, first and foremost, to a major disparity in what people are ordering. Upon further questioning, it turns out that many—if not most—of the people that fall into the latter category only go to Claire's for dessert. A good number of them, in fact, only go to Claire's for *one* dessert: the rich, buttery, sour-cream-based Lithuanian coffee cake. We've said it before, and we'll say it again: the Lithuanian coffee cake is delicious.

But the cake is one small part of this enormous menu, and the rest of the menu is as bad as ever. Have these Claire's fans actually tried, and liked, the disastrous pan-ethnic items that sit around all day in the glass case? Have they tried the burritos, with their shocking proliferation of boring, underseasoned beans? The flavorless quiches? The stir-fry dishes, with their giant chunks of tough, stalky, woody vegetables?

How about the buffalo-fake-chicken sandwich? Seitan and other forms of pressed gluten are not inherently problematic: we've had wonderful forms of soy meat. But here, it comes seemingly unsalted, smothered in utterly flavorless cheese, with more cheese spread on the bread, along with some underseasoned sautéed peppers.

Wonderful vegetarian dishes are found as natural subsets of indigenous culinary traditions all over the world. But the bland fare that proliferated as a result of the 1970s and '80s development of "Vegetarian Food" as a distinct culinary category, emphasizing haphazard fusion, was a misstep in the history of American cooking and a disservice to vegetarians everywhere.

There is still much to like about Claire's, and it goes beyond the cake. There's the attractively bustling, airy college-town vibe. There's the enviable location on one of downtown's most convenient corners. And there's the fact that the genial owner is a bona fide community figure in New Haven who has done much for the city's organic food movement. But we're food critics, and we are bound by our duty to our readers to report that it's no longer 1977, and vegetarians no longer have to settle for this kind of food.

Clark's Dairy

A time-frozen treasure of a local diner, even if the food's not the best

5.7	7.0
Food	Feel

American

Casual restaurant

$15
Price

Mon–Sat 7am–8pm	**Bar** None	**Audubon Arts District**
Sun 9am–8pm	**Credit cards** None	74 Whitney Ave.
	Reservations Not accepted	(203) 777-2728
	Kid-friendly	

We love that this place never changes. The diner is one of our national treasures, a dying artifact that's rarely found in city centers anymore. Clark's Dairy has been around for a long while. It's family-run, it's filled with regulars, and with its 1950s appliances, menu of old standards, and warm, fuzzy service, the place is a nod to that tradition—but it's the white-bread version, without as much character as the great diner, and chances are it will leave you still thirsting for something more nostalgic or tasty.

With a central kitchen island and lunch counter, Clark's feels half diner, half Friendly's. But sit at the counter and your experience will be largely diner; you'll also be closer to the staff, who are kind and welcoming in a "What'll it be, hon?" kind of way.

The fare is comfort food, delivered quickly. Grilled cheese is always the right thing to order (anytime, anywhere). Square-cut fries are appropriately crispy. Try the cheeseburger deluxe, relentlessly traditional, with bacon, lettuce, and tomato, served with french fries and cole slaw. The tuna melt gets high marks. Milkshakes, malted if you please, are top-notch. Not so for the chicken Caesar salad, a sad, greasy mess.

Ice cream sundaes, though, are sublime, and will make even the most grown-up adult feel eight years old (better with a cherry on top). For breakfast, it's cool to see greasy, crispy hash browns, instead of home fries, which can run dry and tasteless.

Adjacent to the Dairy is Clark's Restaurant (or "Clarks' Restaurant," as the sign says), an emptier, vaguely more elaborate room under the same ownership but with its own kitchen. This Clark's serves a similar menu, but adds pizza, subs, and old-school dinners like meatloaf and mashed potatoes. We're not sure what the deal is with that place. By all means stick to the Clark's Dairy room—after all, you're here for the chrome-and-Formica diner aesthetic, right?

Cody's Diner

A 24/7 spot for great, edgy local atmosphere and respectable diner food

4.4	5.0
Food	Feel

American　　　　　　　　　　　Casual restaurant

$15
Price

24 hours

Bar None
Credit cards Visa, MC, AmEx

Wooster Square Area
95 Water St.
(203) 562-0044

Cody's Diner has never really had much of an eye turned toward décor. It's all done up in the tasteless cafeteria school of thought, from the outside to the inside. Mirrors that seem to have been recently spiffed up are the most aesthetically pleasing objects in the entire place, although we miss the old grab-game machine.

Given that it's one of a small group of 24-hour food options in the whole city, it's surprising that Cody's diner is still so little known among the downtown crowd. The main reason is its location. Buried across from a highway overpass on Water Street, Cody's is actually not far from Wooster Square, but you'll need a car to get there from most of the city. This is definitely a forgotten corner of New Haven. Maybe another reason for this diner's relative obscurity is the fact that it's a big late-night hangout for cops—what, are the Yalies afraid of being arrested for staying up too late?

We like this place. It's got a great local atmosphere and respectable, if a bit greasy, diner food. That's exactly what you want at 4am. Prices are reasonable, and the service is vintage diner. It's hard to go wrong with Cody's big breakfast, which arrives on two plates: three pancakes, two eggs, sausage, bacon, and toast. But a bacon cheeseburger with onions is also fine, as is the grilled cheese, and the obligatory milkshake is appropriately thick and sweet.

Cold Stone Creamery

An ice cream chain with plans to take over the
country, one scoop at a time

Ice cream   Take-out

www.coldstonecreamery.com

Mon–Thu noon–10pm   **Bar** None   **North Haven**
Fri noon–11pm   **Credit cards** Visa, MC, AmEx 102 Universal Dr. N.
Sat 11am–11pm   Kid-friendly, veg-friendly   (203) 239-7300
Sun 11am–10pm

Orange   **Milford**
297 Boston Post Rd.   1201 Boston Post Rd.
(203) 795-4911   (203) 783-0860

Cold Stone is the big daddy of the ice-cream-chain genre, scooping
disturbingly large quantities of industrial-style ice cream into oversized
waffle cones, along with a good dose of dramatic action from the staff.
Expect ensemble singing upon certain cues and melodious thank-yous of
variable enthusiasm, depending on the mood of the staff.

There's also a good deal of action behind the counter for those who
decide on a custom ice cream "mix-in" made with a choice of ingredients
including fruit, nuts, candy pieces, and crushed cookies. Your choice of ice
cream is then slathered flat on a cold, granite stone (hence the name);
these ingredients are incorporated in a process that, to us, is curiously
reminiscent of the signature smoosh-ins at the legendary Herrell's ice
cream shops in Massachusetts. Coincidence?

Whatever the process, though, the ice cream is woefully deficient
compared with Herrell's—or compared with Ashley's, the local favorite.
It's bland, it's mass-produced, it's…just plain boring. But they do seem to
have good lawyers: "Apple Pie à la Cold Stone," like most "Cold Stone
Originals," is studded with a Federal trademark registration notice; it's
sweet cream ice cream—a sweet and otherwise benign flavor—combined
with Graham cracker pie crust, cinnamon, caramel, and apple pie filling.
Most of these "Originals" (inexplicably, another trademarked term) have
at least four ingredients in them.

Nowadays, perhaps in an attempt to size upon the ludicrous Sex and
the city fueled cupcake craze, there are ice cream cupcakes, which, by
April 15, 2009, had sold more than 1.75 million units nationwide. If you
think you've come across a Cold Stone elsewhere, chances are you're
right. This hyper-corporate franchise has, thus far, opened 1,450 stores in
12 countries around the world. The formula seems to be working well.
For them, that is—less so for us.

Consiglio's

Family-owned Wooster Street classic Italian with
huge portions

6.8 Food   **7.5** Feel

Italian

Upmarket restaurant   **$50** Price

www.consiglios.com

Mon–Thu 11:30am–2:30pm,
4:30pm–9pm; Fri 11:30am–
2:30pm, 4:30pm–10pm; Sat
3pm–10pm; Sun 1pm–9pm

Bar Beer, wine, liquor
Credit cards Visa, MC, AmEx
Reservations Essential
Outdoor dining

Wooster Square Area
165 Wooster St.
(203) 865-4489

We humbly submit that New Haven is not a great town for Italian food
other than pizza. While the legendary pizzerias have endured, the
downward momentum at elegant Italian restaurants is palpable.

The legendary Consiglio's has long vied for supremacy with its Wooster
Street rival, Tre Scalini, in the league of high-end New Haven Italian-
American restaurants. A perennial favorite, Consiglio's gets consistently
rave reviews from the local and regional press and other polls. It's a New
Haven restaurant with a history going back to 1938. And it's a food
destination that has pleased local families for generations. Fond memories
of celebrations have made space for Consiglio's in many hearts. This is an
enduring icon, a footnote in the history of American restaurants.

But the reality is that what you get here is simply well-executed versions
of suburban Italian-American food that do their best to mix in expensive-
sounding ingredients. For example, veal might be sautéed with shiitake
mushrooms, shrimp, and broccoli in a lobster champagne sauce. An
unimpressive braciola, meanwhile, is tough and chewy.

While we cannot deny the sentimental appeal, the dining experience at
Consiglio's is at best uninspiring, and at worst disappointing— especially
when you're paying $33.95 for a main course like "Filet Italiano": "An
8oz aged filet, topped with roasted red peppers, spinach and mozzarella
cheese, finished in a bacon, red wine onion demi-glaze sauce, served with
roasted potatoes." Incidentally, this is in a portion of the menu labeled as
"El Secondo." Isn't "El" Spanish, not Italian? Or is this just a nostalgic
reference to A Tribe Called Quest's hip-hop masterpiece "I Left My Wallet
in El Segundo"? For this much money elsewhere, you could get true
culinary excellence. Granted, the portions are enormous—enough to take
home the leftovers and feed yourself for the next day—but the problem
is, not everyone wants to do that.

And the atmosphere at Consiglio's is just as predictable as the menu,
with overdressed tables, although the considerable crowd adds ambiance.
The place enjoys neither the old-school Italian kitsch value of a Tony &
Lucille's nor the regional menu of a L'Orcio. Here's hoping for more
creative or authentic regional Italian food in New Haven.

Contois Tavern

A charmingly gruff East Rock classic since 1934: old men, cheap beer, and occasional burgers

6.8	9.0
Food	Feel

American, Burgers

Bar

$10
Price

Daily 11am–2pm

Bar Beer, wine, liquor
Credit cards None

East Rock
150 Nicoll St.
No phone

The cult following of this humble, no-frills bar off State Street seems to grow every year, even as (or perhaps because) the place doesn't change a bit. Contois is an unapologetic local, a place that's been in New Haven since 1934, a squat, square, brick building on a residential block that avoids hype to such an extent that it hides beneath almost imperceptible dark wood signage over the door. It's quintessentially an old-man bar, and that's what the staff is used to.

Don't look here for a swinging scene, late-night hours, or witty postmodernisms. Don't look, in fact, for anyone that's not a 40-to-70-year-old male slugging a bottle of Bud Light or Michelob—or a *New Haven Advocate* editor. But for a quiet beer (they come in dainty little glasses, too, for just a couple of bucks) and conversation; for some great, basic, and inexpensive lunchtime dining; or to observe a true slice of old New Haven life, this is your spot.

Knowing that anyone who sits for long enough on a bar stool will eventually become hungry, Contois has the good sense to serve food. In fact, the lunch counter serves one of the better burgers in town, available daily as long as the grill is on. It's as classic as the bar itself. The burger comes on a paper plate, and on request, it comes with blackened onions and tomato, too. The beef patty is big and tasty, if browned a bit much; if you're looking for rare, you've come to the wrong place. The cheese is melted beautifully.

The schedule at Contois is as erratic as the menu; generally, food is available at lunchtime until 2pm, but occasionally it's still being served at 3:30, depending on the traffic. Hot dogs are always available, but roast beef sandwiches usually appear later in the week. Pepperoni soup has a particular following. This is not nouvelle cuisine, nor should it be. Just stop by, pull up a stool, and enjoy a taste of living history.

Copper Kitchen

A storybook greasy-spoon diner, right downtown

6.6 **6.5**
Food Feel

American

Casual restaurant

$15
Price

Mon–Sat 6:30am–6pm	**Bar** None	**Chapel District**
Sun 8am–4pm	**Credit cards** None	1008 Chapel St.
	Reservations Not accepted	(203) 777-8010

One of New Haven's only true downtown diners, Copper Kitchen, with its mid-century appliances, milkshake blenders, soda fountains, and coffee pitchers, is almost too typical, reducing visiting foreigners to giddy giggles. They can now die happy, having just seen a carbon copy of the diner set from whichever American TV show was dubbed into their language growing up. The evidence is in the postcards from loyal customers around the world tacked up by the register.

It's not bad food, either. Lunches are quite good, with daily specials being the main draw. We particularly like the "fish cakes"—white fish mixed with potato, formed into patties, breaded, and deep-fried—and the macaroni and cheese (which is still bubbling when it gets to the table).

As for breakfast, they serve straightforward omelettes, with friendly service and a bottomless cup of coffee, and they're not particularly trying to pull anything off. Breakfast is definitely the way to go—and unlike certain places up State Street, you won't have to wait in line or deal with opening-hours hijinks. The weekday breakfast is an especially good deal for those up and about before 11am. Just don't ask for anything elaborate—all the tea here is Lipton's, and it's all caffeinated.

Copper Kitchen is not great for groups, since most tables seat four at most. But anyway, counter service is the most fun for your buck. Order eggs, order fried, order traditional. Order the bacon, egg, and cheese sandwich, one of America's greatest culinary achievements. Watch it be prepared, and revel in it. When you are telling your grandkids about the way things used to be, Copper Kitchen may just be what comes to mind.

Corner Deli

Below-average Chinese, about-average short-order grill food, and a strange grocery-store vibe

4.0 Food

4.0 Feel

Sandwiches, Chinese

Counter service

$10 Price

Mon–Fri 7am–7pm
Sat 7:30am–5pm

Bar None
Credit cards Visa, MC, AmEx
Delivery

South Town Green
181 Orange St.
(203) 772-1611

Corner Deli probably has the least attractive signage among all the lunch spots in downtown New Haven—and also, arguably, the least attractive interior. The place feels like a glorified grocery store, filled with soft-drink fridges, some fairly grungy tables and chairs, a few assorted retail items for sale, and a big central Chinese buffet with piles of Styrofoam and plastic containers in which to scoop its contents (sold by the pound).

It's certainly a jarring juxtaposition—not just the Chinese buffet, but also a full Chinese-American menu, along with the standard short-order grill fare (the egg sandwiches, the burgers, the deli offerings, and so on). It's not so often, after all, that eggplant parm, beef curry, strawberry pancakes, a liverwurst sandwich, a bagel with cream cheese, and General Tso's chicken all share the space on one little folded paper menu. Welcome to America.

The problem is that the Chinese food at Corner Deli is awful. It's all lukewarm, the fried items are soggy and limp, the sweet sauce on the tough spare ribs tastes like cherry cough syrup, and so on. The only tasty thing we've tried from the buffet was a sort of Chinese meatloaf drowned in gummy gravy. You're much better off ordering something more American, like a well-executed steak-and-cheese sandwich, whose hard roll is good, pliable, and fresh, and whose tender steak is shredded into small pieces that absorb melted cheese into their many nooks and crannies.

Maybe the lack of focus is the whole point here. For instance, if you need a cosmetic break between your first course of steamed dumplings and your second course of a tuna melt, then Corner Deli will even sell you a hairbrush. Now that's full service.

Coromandel

Multi-regional Indian served elegantly in a somewhat dated-hip setting

7.9 Food

8.0 Feel

Indian

Upmarket restaurant

$40 Price

www.coromandelcuisine.com

Mon–Thu noon–2:30pm, 5pm–
10pm; Fri noon–2:30pm, 5pm–
10:30pm; Sat noon–3pm, 5pm–
10:30pm; Sun noon–3pm,
5pm–10pm

Bar Beer, wine
Credit cards Visa, MC, AmEx
Reservations Accepted
Date-friendly, good wines,
veg-friendly

Orange
185 Boston Post Rd.
(203) 795-9055

Coromandel is a coastal region in Southeast India, but the food at this Connecticut-based minichain is a panoply of influences from all over the Subcontinent. So it follows that the menu is not only lengthy, but rich in flavors not seen in the lunch buffets that comprise most Americans' experience with Indian.

One of those flavors is sugar. A dish touted as the "chef's signature special," shaam savera, sees spinach and cottage cheese dumplings served with a "tangy tomato honey sauce" that is more like sticky-sweet brown salad dressing. Sambar vadai dresses up dense, heavy lentil dumplings (they're supposed to be light and crispy) with sambar, Southern India's staple, a curried lentil stew that lacks the kick it wants. The greatest triumph in this area is a cauliflower masala that is deliciously spiced, with strong cumin notes and an oily, wonderful texture. (Get it with yogurt.) We also like their more kozhambu, okra in yogurt and southern spices, mustard seed, curry leaf, red chili. It reminds us of the fried pickles we've scarfed down in Texas (these, too, get old after several bites).

Their best work is with lamb, especially ghustaba, New Zealand tandoori lamb chops with yogurt, scented with nutmeg and ajwain. This Kashmiri specialty is tender, with a nice sear and served sizzling atop chickpeas, onions, and tomatoes that remind us rather of some favored Italian dishes. Also good are the kori kebab, bright red ground lamb "sausages" with cumin, coriander, mint, and cilantro. But turf trumps surf when badami jhinga shrimp are overcooked, then served in a bright orange, sugary goo that's a bit like Chinese sweet-and-sour sauce.

The space is strip-mall elegant, following the theorem that Indian restaurants tend to be prettier than other ethnic holes-in-the-wall. Most prominent above the high-backed booths in this small space are these small, blown-glass lighting fixtures in twisting, conic shapes and primary colors that were the apex of style...in 1995. Still, the lighting is warm, and the place is very likeable. The service is impeccable—soft-spoken, patient, performing an elegant sleight of hand with a wine bottle (try India's sweet but interesting Sula Chenin Blanc).

Although we usually applaud innovation, when this kitchen takes liberties with saag paneer, it obliterates it with cardamom (at least it's not more sugar). In Coromandel's case, perhaps less is more.

The Cupcake Truck

Drooling hordes give chase to this travelling
cupcake pusher

Baked goods   Take-out

www.followthatcupcake.com

Mon–Sat 1pm–5pm (hours vary   **Bar** None   **Medical Area**
daily; check website)   **Credit cards** Visa, MC, AmEx   Cedar St. and York St.
                              Delivery, kid-friendly, veg-friendly   (203) 675-3965

Chapel District
College St. between Elm and
Chapel
(203) 675-3965

It's not that we have a problem with cupcakes in principle. It's that we
take issue with this whole Sex-and-the-City-inspired craze surrounding
them. At least the Cupcake Truck adds some element of originality: they
announce their location via their blog and Twitter, giving a treasure-hunt
appeal to the whole experience. How 21st Century.

Despite how jaded we are becoming with the cupcake craze, we admit
that the Cupcake Truck's are really pretty good. The truck offers different
cupcakes each day of the week. But as of late, they seem to have
concentrated on their delivery business (mainly to office ladies downtown
and Yale functions) at the expense of their loyal foot soldiers, some of
whom stand in line for 20 minutes in the summer heat just to gobble
down a $2 cupcake, then spread the word to all their friends.

The cupcakes' bases are delicate and fluffy, though not as moist as a
steaming cake right out of the oven. We love the red velvet (with white
chocolate cream cheese frosting, to follow tradition), as well as the
coconut cupcakes, which automatically come with extra coconut sprinkled
on top. The sweet potato and hummingbird cakes are more naturally
sweet, almost deceptively healthy-tasting, and a better base for more
cloying frostings. Chocolate with marshmallow frosting is like a miniature
Whoopie Pie. Frostings are made with buttercream, not that greasy, vapid
Crisco stuff you find on airbrushed cakes at the grocery store.

Toppings range from gourmet (candied organic violets) to the usual
(M&Ms and rainbow sprinkles). Use your time in line to devise some
winning combinations: chocolate cake with caramel frosting and fleur de
sel create a seductive marriage of salty and sweet; lemon cake (which
seems to be the moistest base) pairs well with vanilla frosting and candied
violet. The fruitiness of the lemon and richness of the buttercream is
piqued by the subtle fragrance of the flower.

Frosting availability may change with the seasons. Despite our
frustration with their delivery focus, we wish these guys the best and
hope they make scads of money. After all, they made us excited about
cupcakes again.

Daiko (Jerry-san's)

Fresh sushi, personable chefs, and the most embarrassing birthday salute ever

7.8	7.5
Food	Feel

Japanese

Upmarket restaurant

$40
Price

www.jerrysans.com

Mon–Thu 11:30am–3pm, 5pm–10pm; Fri–Sat 11:30am–3pm, 5pm–11pm; Sun 4pm–10pm

Bar Beer, wine, liquor
Credit cards Visa, MC, AmEx
Reservations Accepted

West Haven
400 Derby Ave.
(203) 392-3626

West Haven
220 Captain Thomas Blvd.
(203) 931-1990

So beloved is Jerry-san that he's now opened a second branch near Savin Rock, and added a pan-Asian thing to the sushi he's already famous for. The interior is a little cheesy, over-the-top "hi, you're in Japan!"—but, that said, some of the dishes here give people access to Malaysian in a sexier setting than Warong Selera's take-out hovel. There are even some rarer delicacies that will lead food-lovers to rejoice, like monkfish liver, herring roe, and spicy green mussels.

The original Daiko (Jerry-san's) still shouts theatrically from among the car dealerships and green plastic storefronts. Opt for the rotating selection of lesser-known fish for more interesting flavors that you won't automatically want to drown in wasabi and soy sauce; otherwise you're relegated to crab stick and some reliable, but prosaic, maguro and ika. There's also the usual maki: soft-shell crab, crunchy spicy tuna, and such. Sit in front of the sushi chefs to get recommendations catered to your tastes and level of adventurousness.

Don't expect too much in the way of atmosphere, and you won't be disappointed. The small, curtained room with tables spanning its edges, surrounding a central sushi bar, can seem cozy on a good night (when you have dining companions), or uncomfortably weird on a bad one. Still, Daiko's small size keeps it from feeling too empty and suburban. Oh, and if it's your birthday, or if you say it is, they bang on a drum with a cat symbol on it; then they take a photo of everyone at the table. The photos, of which there are hundreds, go on the wall, where they stay for years. Prices are reasonable, the fish is fresh, and the service is really friendly, making it one of the best choices in the area for sushi. Kanpai!

Darbar India

The prices are hard to beat, but the authenticity can't keep up with the competition

7.7	7.0
Food	Feel

Indian

Upmarket restaurant

$35
Price

www.darbarindia.com

Sun–Wed 11:30am–3pm, 5pm–10:30pm
Thu–Sat 11:30am–3pm, 5pm–11pm

Bar Beer, wine, liquor
Credit cards Visa, MC, AmEx
Reservations Accepted
Veg-friendly

Branford
1070 Main St.
(203) 481-8994

The days of Darbar's supremacy are over. Don't get us wrong—the place is still much loved, but lately it feels overshadowed by some of the more authentic Indian in town (Thali, Thali Too, Swagat, even Star of India). But its location in Branford has its advantages: if you're a Yalie on the run, you're far less likely to bump into that teaching assistant who thinks you're deathly ill or the ex who thinks you're questioning your sexuality.

The location is pleasant, right on the town green. The feeling is very classic suburban Indian restaurant, with bright lighting, deferential service, and zealous attention to the level of your water glass. The menu is also very standard for the genre—don't come here expecting to sample any unusual new regional dishes.

Food comes in little silver metal soup bowls with lids instead of the standard open platter. The stuff-you-see-on-every-Indian-menu dishes are satisfying, including the shrimp tandoori masala and the mixed grill. Classics like chicken tikka masala are reliable, and there is a great selection of vegetarian-dishes-after-saag-paneer; try the baigan bhartha, eggplant cooked with green peas, onions, and tomatoes with ginger and spices. The mango lassi is superb.

Portions are not particularly large for an Indian restaurant, which we actually find refreshing. Prices are quite reasonable from top to bottom, but the best value are the lunch specials, which hover under ten dollars, and a great all-you-can-eat buffet on Fridays, Saturdays, and Sundays.

But the New Haven area has seen that indian food can be more than this standard menu, and there may be no looking back.

Dayton Street Apizza

8.1 | 7.0
Food | Feel

A little Westville gem of a pizzeria, with well-executed, sweetly thin-crusted pies, best taken out

Pizza

Counter service

$15
Price

Mon–Thu 11:30am–10pm; Fri 11:30am–11pm; Sat–Sun 11:30am–10pm

Bar None
Credit cards Visa, MC
Delivery, kid-friendly, veg-friendly

Westville
60 Dayton St.
(203) 389-2454

This is little more than a take-out spot, but it's one that makes extraordinarily good pizza. In fact, it's been compared to the giants of Wooster Street in the literature. We wouldn't go nearly that far, but the pizza is quite nice, while fuss and waits are completely nonexistent. The hallmark at Dayton is the thin crust, which is well textured with a gentle sweetness, although we'd prefer a couple more minutes of cooking. The sauce, too, is excellent, but unremarkable grated cheese on the basic mozzarella pie is too abundant. The overall effect is still great; it reminds us of the very best style of New York pizza, such as that served at the late and great Joe's on Carmine Street, only more liberally seasoned.

But here's the thing: even better—both in terms of texture and taste—is the more basic marinara pie that is simply sprinkled with parmesan cheese. It allows that wonderful crust to shine without all that mozzarella moisture. As for the rest of the menu, there are subs, which are well executed and quite worthwhile. There's also a range of pasta dishes, from gnocchi to spaghetti with clam sauce to lobster ravioli—the folks at Dayton Street bottle and sell their pasta sauce, in fact, which they dub "Bobo's"—but in our mind, the pasta dishes (and appetizers—fried mozzarella, calamari, and so on) are far less notable than the delicious pizza.

You won't want to spend too much time hanging out in the little room, which is lined with fake bricks and has a couple of soda machines for a centerpiece. Unfortunately, the pies here (as with most good pizza) have a short half-life; if you're traveling a fair distance with the box, keep it closed, and hurry!

Delaney's Grille

A Westville institution, with good feelings and
great drinks, even if the food is just okay

6.0	8.5
Food	Feel

American

Casual restaurant

$25
Price

www.delaneystaproom.com

Sun–Thu 11:30am–midnight
Fri–Sat 11:30am–1am

Bar Beer, wine, liquor
Credit cards Visa, MC, AmEx
Reservations Accepted
Outdoor dining

Westville
882 Whalley Ave.
(203) 397-5494

Delaney's is a Westville neighborhood legend, pure and simple. No fewer
than three are the sections of Delaney's: the Pub Dining Room, with a
restored art-deco bar that pays homage to the 1939 World's Fair; the Tap
Room, which is more of a bar, with a limited late-night menu; and the
Main Dining Room, which is brighter and, in our view, less atmospheric
than the other two. Great also is the expansive outdoor patio, which sits
right on Westville's main drag.

First and foremost, the bar's the thing, from the dark wood paneling to
the darts to the clientele to the spectacular service, which really couldn't
be nicer. But, boy, it can be loud. It is often crowded, too crowded, with
people with various agendas—drinking themselves sick, playing pool,
watching sports, eating dinner, screeching along with the jukebox.
Delaney's list of libations is expansive beyond belief, beginning with more
than 20 single malts and no fewer than 35 vodkas, continuing with a
spectacular beer list that takes you around Europe with more than 50
options on tap, and finishing with cordials from Gammal Dansk Bitters to
cachaça (can you imagine drinking it straight?) to Baronjager Honey
Liqueur. That's not to mention the Ports, the Cognacs, the Bourbons,
including one that's 124 proof. So many ways to get sauced!

As for food, Delaney's tends to execute competently on the basics,
beginning with the Buffalo wings, which have a good balance of sauce.
Blue cheese dressing is chunky and flavorful. Calamari with cherry
peppers, on the other hand, are soggy and inedible. Burgers are fine, but
don't justify their reputation or merit a trip all the way out to Westville,
unless Westville is where you live, in which case get a burger but eat it
outside on the patio. Onion rings are thickly battered and pleasantly
crispy, and french fries are of a specific bar-food type—that is, fried with
some seasoning beyond just the plentiful salt—and sufficiently crispy.

A steak sandwich isn't bad—you'll want to keep eating it—but it's also
problematic: our view is that every bite that's presented between two
pieces of bread should be edible. Here, on the other hand, there are
periodic bites of gristle, interfering with the sandwich-eating process. Still,
the gorgonzola adds a welcome kick. As for the even more ambitious
main courses—seafood and the like—keep in mind that this is just a bar.

Dolci

Small plates and desserts don't do as much to
distinguish Dolci as its lovely setting

6.7	8.0
Food	Feel

New American

Upmarket restaurant

$45
Price

Sun–Thu 3pm–10pm
Fri–Sat 3pm–midnight

Bar Beer, wine, liquor
Credit cards Visa, MC, AmEx
Reservations Accepted
Date-friendly, live music,
veg-friendly

East Rock
932 State St.
(203) 764-2069

This stylish bar and lounge on State Street certainly looks as delicious as its
name would suggest. Set back from and raised slightly higher than the
sidewalk, it's a little slice of Los Angeles inside. Plum-colored walls
adorned with sculptural panels, low light, and a long, sleek bar provide
welcome respite from louder haunts of this type, while a floor-to-ceiling
window in front frames chic diners (and drinkers) seated at the two-tops
near the door. On weekends, a DJ spins, and the mood is more sleek and
seductive than raucous and rowdy; on Wednesdays, the place becomes a
piano bar, by reservation only. A small dining room of about six tables at
the end of the bar can be reserved for parties.

Dolci serves a full menu of candyish stripper drinks, but don't let that
put you off—the bartenders here can make a decent Gibson, too, and
interesting wines are available by the glass.

The kitchen has high aspirations, and an adjective-filled menu proudly
presents a number of small, trendy, expensive dishes meant to be ordered
in multiples, tapas-style. Many of the menu items are gluten-free
(indicated by the initials GF). Among the better dishes are a Caesar salad,
cavatelli pasta with mushroom and truffle sauce, and a confit leg of duck.
Much less successful are the Asian-inspired dishes; something described as
"sesame-seared rock shrimp" has come as nothing more than battered,
fried shrimp bits tossed in sweet-and-sour sauce, and a pork spring roll
(with "soy foam") might as well have been brought over from
neighboring Chinese takeout joint Blessings II Go. At prices averaging
more than $10 per small plate, you'd expect that the food would, at the
very least, come to the table as described.

While dinner is a major component of the menu, we sense that the
main focus of Dolci—hence the name—is its dessert menu. Connecticut's
own Knipschildt Chocolates are displayed in a case like little jewels.
Besides chocolates, though, the sweets are standards like crème brûlée,
roasted apple tart, and molten chocolate cake; the most interesting might
be the artisanal cheese plate. In general, we're disappointed in the lack of
innovation—it makes the whole thing feel a bit like a sweet little gimmick.

Donovan's Reef

A big, open American bar and grill, pure and simple

6.1 Food

7.0 Feel

American   Casual restaurant **$35** Price

www.donovans-reef.com

Daily 11:30am–9pm

Bar Beer, wine, liquor
Credit cards Visa, MC, AmEx
Reservations Accepted
Live music

Branford
1212 Main St.
(203) 488-5573

Are you a sucker for trivia night? If so, Donovan's is the place for you on a Wednesday evening. But don't be deceived; this isn't a seafood specialist, it's a reference to *Donovan's Reef*, a 1963 John Wayne film, in which a bunch of ex-sailors are settled on a South Pacific island, one hot chick shows up, and all hell breaks loose.

Ironically enough, at one visit, the entire second and third floor ("the loft") of the airily terraced indoor space was filled only with women (it was a baby shower).

The big, open room—the building once belonged to the Yale Lock company—has a soaring roof; it reminds us of a base lodge bar and grille at a ski resort. Live bands come and go, and the place is also quite a Branford bar scene at peak hours, when it feels more like your local watering hole than a restaurant.

Donovan's is a self-described "American grill," which should clue you in to what's on the menu: Buffalo wings, steak, shrimp, ribs, chili, and so on. They're also known for the Sunday brunch, which is pretty standard but not bad. Generally, preparations are competent; scallops, for instance, are browned with a deep, dark crust, and served over an extremely lemony but good sauce. Crab cakes, too, are above average; it's not lump crabmeat, but it's decent shredded crab, not too bready but still well crisped on the outside, although the sweet salad beneath the cakes comes over-dressed.

The more unusual "surf and turf burger" is less successful: the delicate taste and texture of lobster meat, which is placed between burger and bun, is completely drowned out by stronger tastes and textures—the good but underseasoned meat, the enormous bun, the lettuce and tomato, the remoulade. In retrospect, we should have known better than to wander away from the American basics at such a deeply American place.

Downtown @ the Taft

Great new name, same low standards!

3.8	5.5
Food	Feel

New American

Upmarket restaurant

$50
Price

www.downtownatthetaft.com

Mon–Wed 11:30am–3pm,
4pm–10pm; Thu 11:30am–
3pm, 4pm–11pm; Fri 11:30am–
3pm, 4pm–midnight; Sat 4pm–
midnight; Sun 4pm–10pm

Bar Beer, wine, liquor
Credit cards Visa, MC, AmEx
Reservations Accepted
Date-friendly, live music

Chapel District
261 College St.
(203) 624-6331

Hot Tomato's has become Downtown @ the Taft, which seems a more fitting name given the elegant, stately atmosphere. It's still in the grand ballroom of what was once the Taft Hotel in the heart of downtown, with exceedingly high ceilings and brass railings. The space is divided into the pricey, Italian-influenced New American restaurant—most of which spreads out over second-floor balconies—and a ground-floor bar that doesn't seem as popular as it once did. Competent cocktails are made with medium-shelf call liquors.

Although the restaurant menu has evolved somewhat, the concept hasn't. Seared scallops, blackened tuna, recognizable pastas, and steaks anchor a dated menu that evokes wedding food. There is a new brick oven churning out pizzas downstairs, and although the crust is properly thin, and the sauce fresh and naturally sweet, the pies come out gummy and under-fired. Much better pizza can be had across the street at Bar.

Beyond that, most dishes here are so uniformly miserable these days that to come across one that you want to finish is more thrilling than it ought to be. You might kvell over a bisque that is skillfully proportioned between lobster and mildly sweet butternut squash, with just a touch of citric acidity, only to suffer through a white-bean bruschetta whose flavor is fine, but whose topping-to-bread ratio is a joke. Salad dressing has come out so aggressively acidic that it lights up your mouth like an electric eel dance party. But this is the sort of thing you might expect from a place whose menu, in a goombah-like touch, lists a "Chef the Cuisine." It continues with unevenly cooked and chewy steak, thin chicken breast with the consistency of chalk, and vodka sauce like a cheap Chinese sweet-and-sour (with a $6 upcharge to add what looks like half an ounce of aforementioned chalky chicken).

Downtown @ the Taft is an exercise in baffling opposites, a place where Barolo is cooked into a sauce, but Blackstone Merlot is served to patrons in a glass; where the most prosaic dish, seared tuna, is the only one worth its salt; where the digs are regal and sexy, but the service is so bad that you'll often find yourself not just wandering the floor but even descending a staircase in search of a waitperson you haven't been able to find for 45 minutes.

And although many restaurants add gratuity for larger parties, it's only the rare scam artist that does so without a heads-up of any kind, verbal or otherwise. This restaurant's attitude is an embarrassment to our fair city.

Dunkin' Donuts

You know the drill—thousands of locations, okay donuts, worse savories

2.1 Food
1.0 Feel

Baked goods, American

Counter service

$10 Price

www.dunkindonuts.com

24 hours

Bar None
Credit cards Visa, MC, AmEx
Kid-friendly, veg-friendly

Audubon Arts District
54 Whitney Ave.
(203) 789-0380

Upper Chapel Area
1179 Chapel St.
(203) 624-1107

Chapel District
770 Chapel St.
(203) 497-9250

Additional locations
and more features at
www.fearlesscritic.com

Business still chugs along for the chain that survived the explosion of the Krispy Kreme empire. Dunkin' Donuts' main marketing response to its chief competitor seems to have been to focus on the freshness of its coffee rather than to attempt to challenge the sublime taste and texture of a Krispy Kreme doughnut taken hot out of the oven. We think the coffee at Dunkin' Donuts is okay, better than some, worse than others. It does seem to be brewed frequently.

Before ordering food, ask yourself one question: is it a doughnut? The doughnuts themselves are fine, just what you'd expect, although we think they're baked in too-large batches, and not often enough, hurting their freshness. We favor the basic jelly-filled and glazed varieties. Crullers and crumb doughnuts have a less exciting texture, a bit too dry and cakey, and we find the cream-filled options too rich.

Apart from doughnuts, pickings are slim indeed. The breakfast sandwiches, of the frozen-and-reheated-egg-from-the-plastic-wrapper variety, are boring and chewy. (At least they're better than the ones at Bruegger's.) Bagels and muffins are not much better. Of late, there has been some innovation in the frou-frou coffee-drink realm, but your calories are best spent elsewhere.

But at least for now, New Haven is still Dunkin' Donuts country. Believe it or not, there are actually 16 branches in New Haven proper. It's the closest thing to a fast-food empire in town—this is truly staggering coverage, folks. There are two in Union Station alone. For better or for worse, sooner or later, you'll probably find yourself at one of these outlets, if only for a cup of perfectly passable coffee. But unless you're desperate, get your food elsewhere.

East Japanese Restaurant

9.1 Food

6.0 Feel

Lonely strip-mall sushi and Japanese fusion that's still the best in the area—by far

Japanese

Upmarket restaurant

$45 Price

Sat 5pm–11pm	**Bar** Beer, wine, liquor	**Milford**
Sun 5pm–10pm	**Credit cards** Visa, MC, AmEx	17 Turnpike Square
	Reservations Accepted	(203) 877-7686

At our last visit to this excellent sushi and Japanese fusion restaurant along an unlikely stretch of Milford strip mall, its bland blond-wood interior felt lonelier than ever. There was the stale air of a restaurant in decline. What had gone wrong, we wondered? Where was the energy? Where were the customers?

We were surprised, thus, to find its kitchen and sushi bar firing on all cylinders, from bracingly fresh Washington State oysters on the half shell to jalapeño kampachi that's as melty and fresh as ever, sprinkled with copious Osetra caviar (although we weren't quite sure what a strawberry was doing on the plate). Sweet live scallop sits on a bed of lemon, with the muscles showing up in a separate pile, chewy but good, with an abalone-like texture, in a soy-vinegar dressing. Toro tartare in a salty, flavorful soy-wasabi sauce, at one visit, was accompanied by a syrupy bayberry, a rarely-encountered fruit. The combination simultaneously activated receptors sweet and salty, taste and touch; the crunch of the shallots amplified the ethereal softness of the toro. And almost flawless are the crispy, comforting duck spring rolls with citrus, oil, and soy sauce, like a brilliantly executed Peking duck—but with an edge.

Even the basic nigiri are excellent at East; they come at the proper room temperature, with sushi rice that's beautifully vinegared, with ideal sweetness. You can't find anything like this in New Haven. Try silky hiramasa (Australian golden amberjack), when available. Ask for yellowtail, and you might get a nice, oily belly piece with impeccable flavor and richness. King salmon is sometimes flown in from New Zealand, and bursts with freshness. Uni (sea urchin) is lovely and creamy, sweet, as good a specimen as we've had in the area.

In short, East still serves the best sushi in the area. But they need a new marketing pitch. The cafeteria-style tables and office-style ceilings aren't really cutting it anymore. And prices are high. Good sea urchin is always expensive, but $18 for an uni appetizer (wrapped with fluke and served with lemon yuzu) probably prices out most customers. The $12 price tag on the plate of jalapeño kampachi is steep, too. Perhaps they should offer half-portions of such dishes for half the price. Lunches are much more reasonably priced, but don't give you the chance to taste the kitchen at its best. Management has also been sending some mixed messages about discontinuing lunch and weekday hours; call ahead before you go.

The message is that get what you pay for. Here's hoping people will come to see the value proposition here, even at the high end. If only they'd do something about the atmosphere.

Edge of the Woods

Vegetarian, kosher, healthy, and not bad at all

6.0 Food **8.0** Feel

American, Baked goods

Take-out **$15** Price

Mon–Fri 8:30am–7:30pm; Sat 8:30am–6:30pm; Sun 9am–6pm

Bar None
Credit cards Visa, MC
Veg-friendly

Whalley
379 Whalley Ave.
(203) 787-1055

For those seeking health-conscious take-out food, Edge of the Woods is definitely on the short list. Like Claire's downtown, the place is also kosher. Attached to an excellent whole-foods store of the same name, this café, storefront, and caterer offers vegetable pastries, vegan soups, whole-grain breads, pies, pastas, and dessert. There are, however, a few tables to sit at, and they get nice light in the atrium-style enclosure.

Some items on the buffet spread have perhaps been sitting there a bit too long, and thus tend toward the limp and crusty. There are some standard dishes, like eggplant parmesan, a garden-variety version here, battered and fried eggplant in a red sauce with melted parmesan and mozzarella on top. There are some slightly more interesting soups.

But Edge of the Woods also tends to freestyle. Vegan shepherd's pie features soy "un-sausage," corn, carrots, and celery in gravy topped with vegan mashed potatoes. Hmm. We prefer naturally vegetarian or vegan dishes to the sort of ill-advised attempts to simulate meat dishes that proliferated as "vegetarian cuisine" during the 1980s; along those lines, we'd prefer the tofu vegetable lasagne if it didn't have the tofu, even if it is a good source of protein.

Look carefully at the dishes before selecting, and if you fear bland fare, seek out well-spiced options. For liquid nutrition, there's a serious juice bar for wheatgrass shots, beet juice, and so on. Alternatively, you can skip directly to dessert, the equal-opportunity option, but avoid the vegan chocolate cake unless you've long since forgotten what the real thing tastes like.

The Educated Burgher

A predictable American breakfast-and-lunch spot
that caters to Yale, but doesn't impress

5.6 Food

7.0 Feel

American, Burgers

Counter service

$15 Price

www.educatedburgher.com

Mon–Sat 7am–10pm
Sun 9am–10pm

Bar Beer
Credit cards None

Broadway District
53 Broadway
(203) 777-9198

Now that Yankee Doodle across the street is gone, this classic spot, known for its kitschy spelling and generations of Yalie patrons, is at the top of a weak short-order-breakfast-and-lunch-counter field in the Broadway area. Unfortunately, the Burgher's fare isn't nearly as melt-in-your-mouth good as the Doodle's was (in part due to the more judicious, artery-sparing use of butter here).

The Burgher does have other advantages. Seating is plentiful, relaxed, and good for a conversation, and the menu is varied. The Burgher serves salads, for example, including a large bowl of Greek salad (although it's better at Yorkside around the corner). In addition to the standard selection of burgers, grilled cheese sandwiches, and their progeny, there are hot deli sandwiches (including a good pastrami special on rye toast with Swiss cheese, bacon, mushroom, and grilled onion), Greek-style gyros, and the like. The basics are best, though; leave the complex salads and ethnic food for elsewhere.

The room is simple and classic, if a bit dingy, with assorted Yale memorabilia and books (which no one ever has read, or ever will read) lording over a bright array of basic booths. There's very little natural light—a problem for a breakfast and lunch place—and perhaps too many mirrors. Ordering and food delivery both happen at the counter. During busy weekday lunches, this arrangement can sometimes lead to the tragic choice between a tedious standing wait and a seated wait at your table in a limbo state (neurotically glancing over your shoulder toward the kitchen every few seconds in anticipation of your order).

The Burgher might be best for breakfast, when lines are not an issue, standards like eggs over-easy with home fries, toast, and bacon are prepared reliably well, and the playful academic setting sets a light tone for the day ahead.

El Amigo Felix

More of a fratty scene than a foodie scene, with
bad Tex-Mex food and fat margaritas

4.4 **5.0**
Food *Feel*

Mexican

Bar **$25**
Price

Tue–Thu 3:30pm–11pm; Fri–Sat
noon–11:30pm; Sun noon–
10pm

Bar Beer, wine, liquor
Credit cards Visa, MC, AmEx

Broadway District
8 Whalley Ave.
(203) 785-8200

Where we once had nothing good to say about El Amigo Felix's food, we
now have reason to raise its score modestly: the chicken soup. It's all
brothy, with rice, tomatoes, and cilantro; when you squeeze lemon in it,
you could eat buckets. While this dish is hardly revelatory, it takes a really
special place to make a bad chicken soup, and this is not that place. This,
however, is the place to screw up most Tex-Mex dishes pretty completely.
Before the soup, this was one of the lowest-scoring restaurants in our
book. Both of the first two editions.

Your best bet is to drink some planet-sized margaritas (on the rocks is
better) and eat the serviceable chips and salsa. If you're lucky, the chips
might even come warm. Spend more money, however, and you'll find
enchiladas whose sauce have the texture of paint cracking off the tortilla,
the beef within implausibly tasteless, with a texture that seems generated
by a hair dryer. Certainly you can skip the appetizer of chile con queso,
whose surface is a thick, plasticky skin, and whose cheese taste is worse
than that of any microwaved version we've ever tried.

The service is friendly and helpful, and it's far more charming than the
food or décor, which is in the Tijuana-frat-bar vein. This is perfectly fine if
you've come, as most do, to consume lots of generic alcohol. Because El
Amigo Felix isn't really about the food. It's a party for the college students
who come here to drink, to flirt, and to drink more. Hey, late into the
evening, there are probably some worse decisions made here than eating
the food.

El Charro

A true slice of Mexico in the middle of Fair Haven

7.8 Food

5.0 Feel

Mexican

Casual restaurant

$15 Price

Wed–Mon 10am–9pm

Bar Beer, wine
Credit cards None
Reservations Not accepted

Fair Haven
262 Grand Ave.
(203) 498-7354

Those with wheels who are willing to make the trek into what to some may be unfamiliar territory—the middle of Fair Haven, up Grand Avenue, which ultimately amounts to little more than five minutes from the Green—will be well rewarded with some of the best, most authentic Mexican food around. One of the glorious, little-known Mexican champions that hide out in nooks and crannies of the New Haven area (Guadalupe La Poblanita and Taquería Mexicana #2 also come to mind), El Charro is the closest to downtown New Haven but also easy to miss amidst pawn shops, bodegas, and stereo-equipment resellers.

El Charro is a funny, bright little place, and it really feels like a slice of Mexico—all is conducted in Spanish (though English is spoken), and you're even wont to find the most traditional Mexican scene of all: the cadre of down-and-out middle-aged men in the corner, good-naturedly teasing the waitress, drowning their sorrows in jukebox tunes and 40s of Tecate. The low prices feel like Mexico too (order individual antojitos rather than the plates that come with rice and beans—they're much cheaper).

Chorizo tacos and enchiladas are good choices. There are some more sophisticated combinations, like a seafood stew that integrates lobster, clams, mussels, fish, octopus, shrimp, in a broth of shrimp stock and dry red pepper sauce, served with tostadas on the side. Everything is good, even the Mexican beer selection, although this might not quite be your spot for boozing. In all, El Charro is very much worth the trip, wherever you're coming from.

El Coquí

A Fair Haven take-out find with authentic Puerto Rican preparations and the best mofongo in town

7.2 Food

7.0 Feel

Latin American

Counter service

$10 Price

Daily 10:30am–8:30pm

Bar Beer, wine
Credit cards Visa, MC

Fair Haven
286 Grand Ave.
(203) 562-1757

The sign outside this shabby-looking Fair Haven joint, which is basically a take-out place, advertises "Spanish food," but really, the cuisine is Latin American, with a clear focus on Puerto Rican specialties. The menu changes regularly; there is always an assortment of fried foods, various stews, chicken, and above all, pork dishes (from fried pork rinds to roast pig), most displayed behind the counter. Unless you're familiar with the dishes, even if you're a Spanish speaker, you might just want to point, rather than trying to figure out the names and ingredients of the different dishes. Ordering at El Coquí can be humbling and disorienting—but very worthwhile.

For us, the truly superlative dish at El Coquí is the mofongo; this one you can request by name. It's a famous Cuban and Caribbean dish of mashed plantain with garlic that is formed into a ball, seasoned, fried, and then covered with another topping. There are higher-priced versions of mofongo in town—at Pacifico, for instance—but with all due respect, we believe that El Coquí's is the best in town. It's like a showcase for garlic, with that flavor deeply infused into the moist but not wimpy starch, and a broth that's generously spooned on (you choose which kind; we love the beef broth) adds another dimension. It's a unique experience in the New Haven area.

Plantains are also good in their other fried forms. We've been less impressed by the empanadas, which sometimes sit around for a while and will be in your bag yet longer, cooling off, if you order take-out. Better are the moister stews, roast meats, and such. There's even beer for sale. The incredibly low prices are yet another reason to make it to this easy-to-miss food counter.

Elaine's Healthy Choice

7.2 Food   **6.0** Feel

Good, fast vegan food on the cheap...that's right, we said "good"

American

Counter service   **$10** Price

www.elaineshealthychoice.com

Mon–Thu 11am–8:30pm
Fri 11am–3pm
Sun 11am–6:30pm

Bar None
Credit cards Visa, MC
Delivery, veg-friendly

Whalley
117 Whalley Ave.
(203) 773-1897

It is hard not to like Elaine's Healthy Choice. Everything about it is bright, from the clean tangerine-colored walls to the smiling proprietor, Elaine. She greets you with angelic grace, like a demigoddess out of some bucolic Caribbean dream. Fortunately for New Haven, she somehow found herself here. Because Elaine makes good food at unthinkably low prices—even though it's 100% vegan.

It is the concept of mock meat that makes vegan cuisine hard to swallow for carnivorous customers. A menu listing of "vegetarian fish ham" causes sweats and tremors. But even if Textured Vegetable Protein (TVP) doesn't exactly entice you as much as, say, a bacon double cheeseburger, one taste of Elaine's cooking might just have you shaking your head in incredulous delight. "Chicken" is cooked in a well-developed, nicely seasoned curry sauce and has a striated complexion, like real breast meat, but with a stringier texture. It is served with good homemade whole wheat bread and a heaping portion of white rice and beans or sesame brown rice, an incredible deal for $6.95.

Macaroni and "cheese" is made from dairyless cheese, some of which Elaine makes herself from cashews and cardamom. It is surprisingly creamy, with a pleasantly smoky and nutty flavor. A side of beans and corn is soupy and flavorful, made heartier by the addition of TVP. For dessert, Elaine bakes moist carob "chocolate" brownies, not merely passable facsimiles, but tasty in their own right, if a little dense. Elaine's does an entirely take-out business, so don't plan on staying long—though you may want to because of her (and her husband's) warmth and hospitality.

The problem with vegetarian/vegan cuisine is that it often fails to meet the demands of big appetites. But Elaine's is unexpectedly satisfying. For vegans, this is the best option in New Haven, beating out Edge of the Woods, Claire's, and Ahimsa handily—and at cheaper prices.

Eli's

With one in Hamden and one in Branford, you have no reason to go to Applebee's

7.0	7.5
Food	Feel

American, Italian, Pizza

Casual restaurant

$45
Price

www.elisonthehill.com

Mon–Sat 11:30am–10pm
Sun 11:30am–9pm
Hours vary by location

Bar Beer, wine, liquor
Credit cards Visa, MC, AmEx
Reservations Accepted
Live music, veg-friendly, Wi-Fi

Hamden
2392 Whitney Ave.
(203) 287-1101

Hamden
Eli's Brick Oven
2402 Whitney Ave.
(203) 288-1686

Branford
624 W. Main St.
(203) 488-2700

The Eli's on Whitney (har har) location in Hamden is the hunter-green, above-ground version of Cheers, a tight neighborhood haunt without the blaring music, Budweiser posters, or haute décor that attracts the younger crowds. Nevertheless, on weekends, it gets packed, which totally obliterates the relaxed, mellow vibe. A large horseshoe bar is the center of all the action, with a sectioned-off dining room that looks wilted and marginally elegant, like the dining room in a rest home. Behind this is an even more generic, antiquated room for banquets, post-funeral luncheons, and—a more depressing prospect—wedding receptions. Stick to eating in the bar, which is vibrant (especially during a game), but not obnoxious until after about 10pm on Fridays and Saturdays.

The appetizers consist of typical pub fare: they're steamed, stuffed, fried, and cheesy. For some reason, Andy Boy-brand broccoli rabe is proudly featured (with Italian sausage) on the menu, as if it's something exclusive that a supermarket wouldn't carry. Buffalo tenders (here called "Lazy Man's Wings") are pretty greasy; most things coming out of the fryer here follow suit. But the "Whitney Burger," made from meatloaf, is anything but standard. It's very moist and flavorful, and we appreciate the inventiveness. The pizza is surprisingly terrific for these parts—not in the same league as the New Haven big boys, perhaps, but boasting super-thin crusts and burnt semolina edges. If you love the pizza but hate the pubby atmosphere, Eli's Brick Oven is just across the street.

The Branford (Eli's on the Hill) location is newer and looks a little better in the dining room, but service has been spottier there. The trick is not to see Eli's as a restaurant, but rather as a bar that serves better-than-average bar food, plus expensive, over-sauced main courses if you absolutely must have one (you mustn't).

In the bar, service is friendly and sincere, and they seem to know their regulars, like your neighborhood pub ought to. The beers here are standard, with a few on draft. But it's more about the neighborhood vibe: this is the kind of place you want to go where…you know…everybody knows your name.

Est Est Est

New York-style pizza in the wee hours at this
spiffed-up joint—oh, and subs too

6.4	**4.0**
Food	Feel

Pizza, Italian

Counter service

$10
Price

Sun–Thu 10am–1am
Fri–Sat 10am–3am

Bar None
Credit cards Visa, MC, AmEx
Delivery, veg-friendly

Upper Chapel Area
1176 Chapel St.
(203) 777-2059

Est Est Est has prettied itself up from the outside in. A snazzy new façade
with shiny, pretty wood (and warm red brick above) and gold lettering is a
marked improvement, and the interior, too, has seen a facelift that now
makes it a nicer place to spend some time in. (Back in the day, you would
be hard-pressed to see anyone do anything but take their pizza and run.)

Granted, it's still hardly a date place, and delivery is a popular option.
Most of the clientele is starving grad students (especially art and
architecture students, whose headquarters are right nearby). They come
especially for the low prices and late hours. On Friday and Saturday
nights, Est Est Est is open until 3am, and other weeknights it closes at
1am, so it's a viable late-night option right on Chapel Street. As for the
slices, the plain cheese variety is better than average. The crust is crispy in
a balanced way; sauce is just tangy enough; and it's not overwhelmed
with cheese (although unfortunately, what cheese there is is mediocre).

All in all, it's what you'd expect at a solid New York-style joint, which is
nothing to be ashamed of. There are also some daring combinations that
are not for the faint of heart. For instance, the "Chicken Paisano" pizza is
topped with mozzarella, grilled chicken, mushrooms, tomatoes, artichoke
hearts, and capers, the pizza equivalent of one-pot cooking. Est Est Est
also serves up garden-variety Italian subs. There's certainly enough going
on there to command your attention, though pizza purists may shudder at
the thought. To each his own.

Farmer's Market

The horn of plenty is available to all now, thanks to CitySeed's efforts

Groceries, Baked goods

Market

www.cityseed.org/city_markets

Sat 9am–1pm
Hours vary by location

Kid-friendly, veg-friendly

Wooster Square Area
Russo Park, corner of Chapel St. and DePalma Ct.

Whalley
Edgewood Park, corner of Whalley and West Rock Ave.

South Town Green
Church St. at the Green

Fair Haven
Quinnipiac River Park, corner of Front St. and Grand Ave.

CitySeed keeps expanding the New Haven Farmer's Market every year, and now there are four locations—in Fair Haven, in Edgerton Park, in front of City Hall, and the main one in Wooster Square. In Wooster, the market is held every other weekend from winter through early spring, increasing to every weekend from May through the fall. See the website for each market's schedule.

These markets are a shining success, as several name-brand vendors have set up booths here. Beltane Farms' goat cheese (try their fresh chêvre rolled in dill) is terrific, as are the delicious pastries—many with seasonal fruit—and breads from the SoNo Baking Company. If you're one of those people who always gets stuck with a bag of salad greens going bad in the fridge because you're forced to buy enough for a family of four and you're still soltero/a (for now), Two Guys sells hydroponic greens still alive, with roots in a very small pot of dirt, which prevents them from dying. You can keep them in your fridge for several weeks, and they will still be extremely fresh when you cut them off the plant (and they are great company). Elsewhere, there's great whipped honey, if you can shell out the cash for it.

You'll find an abundance of local, organically raised heirloom varietal vegetables and meats, including dry-aged grass-fed beef, goat, and lamb. The lamb farmers also sell their own cheeses, and some prepared foods like world-class sausage, shepherd's pie, and pasta sauce. There's also pasture-raised chickens and their eggs (if you've never had farm-fresh eggs, you are missing a transcendent experience), and unpasteurized fresh milk (if you've never had raw, fresh milk...see above).

Probably the coolest thing about the CitySeed project is the fact that they accept food stamps. Eating farm-to-table should never be a luxury—it should be an everyday fact of life—but we've gotten ourselves so deeply entrenched in processing and mass production that eating healthy has long been considered a privilege too expensive for those who need it the most (kiddos, of course). Way to go, CitySeed. Way to go, farmers. Way to go, cows and chickens and goats and things.

Ferraro's Foods

A cheap, dumpy market that's got meat, meat, and basic staples...and meat

Groceries, Italian

Market

Mon–Sat 8:30am–6pm

Bar None
Credit cards Visa, MC, AmEx
Veg-friendly

Fair Haven
664 Grand Ave.
(203) 772-4926

The hulking warehouse down the street from what looks suspiciously like a mob front (we've seen *The Godfather* trilogy too many times) is Ferraro's Fine Foods. Not what you'd expect, given the city's plethora of fancy-schmancy truffle-oil-pushing Italian specialty groceries. But this is why we like it.

Inside, Ferraro's would be a pretty standard, slightly sorry grocery store were it not for two things: (1) the signs depicting actual neighborhood streets that designate each aisle, and (2) the phenomenal butchers. If you live in New Haven and you need meat—any kind, any cut—you come here. If they don't have it, they'll get it for you. Pig's feet? Got it. Pig's *head*? Check. Stay in the store long enough and you'll hear loud, Italian-accented men bellowing their specials over the PA system: *I gotcher veal chops over here. Nice loin chops. $11.99 a pound. Don't everyone run over at once.*

Produce is kind of bare bones, and the rest of the groceries in the store may have dust on them, but they're also way cheap. It's all about the meat and fish, anyway. They even make their own sausages. Seafood is also plentiful, though not as extensive as Bud's in Branford (but much cheaper here).

But we have one big beef with Ferraro's: closing at 6pm every day doesn't leave anyone enough time after getting off work to stop in for groceries. Needless to say, this place is a zoo on Saturdays. As for the help they offer with getting your stuff out to your car? You might want to take them up on it, if you had to park a block away.

Five Guys

Meat haiku

7.9 Food
6.0 Feel

Burgers

Counter service

$15 Price

www.fiveguys.com

Daily 11am–10pm

Bar None
Credit cards Visa, MC
Kid-friendly

Whalley
71 Amity Rd.
(203) 285-3016

To commune with flesh.
To feel it fall like pleasure
from your lips. Five Guys

strips your hunger raw.
Hedonistic animal
possessed. Get some now.

Five Guys gets you in
your gut. Feeds your empty with
hope and calories.

The whole room is bare.
Ordering is like high school.
It doesn't matter.

Get yours like we get
ours: Two plump patties, cheese, stuffed
between seeded buns.

The secret is the
better bread. Buttery sweet.
Changing everything.

Like a meat grilled cheese
Candies drip. And forbidden flesh
(bacon) taut and crisp.

You can never get
enough. You will never get
enough. Die happy.
(*Guest review by Lil' G*)

Foe

A flabby menu that needs tightening if it wants to
keep up with the competition

7.1	7.5
Food	Feel

New American

Upmarket restaurant

$50
Price

www.foebistro.com

Tue–Thu 11:30am–2:30pm,
5pm–9:30pm
Fri–Sat 5pm–10:30pm
Sun 5pm–9pm

Bar Beer, wine, liquor
Credit cards Visa, MC, AmEx
Reservations Accepted
Date-friendly

Branford
1114 Main St.
(203) 483-5896

Foe may be more accessible in its new digs closer to the Branford Green, but it's lost the cozy charm of the old building to a space that is somewhat sterile. It's pale and clean, often seen with more people at the small bar watching sports (with the sound turned off) than in the dining room. It's not for lack of service, which is friendly and attentive; warm sourdough bread arrives at the table along with a whipped honey butter (whose sweetness would be better suited to a true Southern cornbread).

What seems to keep the throngs at bay, rather, is a menu that may have once been interesting, teeming with adjectives and gourmet ingredients, but now comes across as derivative and unfocused. Among main courses alone, there are half a dozen choices each of seafood, poultry, and meat. Each entails a description nearly biblical in proportion.

Execution isn't the problem here; concept is. An appetizer of corn flan has correctly seared scallops, but should only be offered in summer, when there is fresh, sweet corn. Otherwise, it tastes rather like eggy canned corn. Roasted Blue Point oysters with bacon, lemon, and thyme have shown restraint, allowing the briny meat to shine through. In general, meats and fish are cooked properly, but sometimes paired with ingredients that overwhelm the proteins. Greens and potatoes have tasted like old cooking oil; whipped brie and meaty mushrooms have smothered delicate veal. Crab-cake-encrusted tilapia and aioli-baked cod are like the Versailles of fish dishes. How about grilled filet mignon with melted gorgonzola *and* Merlot reduction? Not much here is refreshing and delicate.

The beverage program (if you can call it that) is subpar. The wines are of the sort that you might expect to see discarded in a paper bag in some park. The cocktails are hideous chimeras of sugar-addict-tailored syrups.

Of the boring-sounding sweets, the best one has the worst name: the "Double Gooey Chocolate Butter Cake." It's actually a surprisingly restrained, elegant cupcake of chocolate, salty and sophisticated, with a tender crust that soaks up its cappuccino gelato beautifully. This dessert is, ironically, less cloying than either the honey butter or the drinks list.

Forte's Gourmet Market
Italian specialty market with nearly any cut of meat
you desire

Groceries, Sandwiches   Market

www.fortesmarket.com

Mon–Fri 9am–6pm   **Bar** None   **Guilford**
Sat 8:30am–5:30pm   **Credit cards** Visa, MC, AmEx   1153 Boston Post Rd.
                          Kid-friendly, outdoor dining,   (203) 453-4910
                          veg-friendly

With Bishop's Orchards in one direction and Star Fish Market in the other,
Forte's faces some steep competition in the small world of Guilford
gourmet food shops. In addition to being the only truly Italian market
(right down to their hours: they're closed on Sundays), Forte's literally
carves out its niche by serving as Guilford's only full-service butcher. If
they're out of a cut, they'll recommended good alternatives and cut them
to size for you. Fresh chicken livers, beef ground to order, and less-
common cuts of pork point to butchers who know what they're doing
and who their customers are. An advance call will likely yield just about
any cut of any animal you wish to cook.

The grocery selection is small, and the produce nearly non-existent, but
the selection of prepared foods (mostly Italian) is impressive and fresh. The
freezers hold lamb from local farmers like Sankow's Beaver Brook Farm,
individually frozen beef Wellingtons, and sorbets. The selection of butters
is wide-ranging, including Irish Kerrygold, black truffle butter, and a
variety made with the leftover cream from Parmesan cheese production.
Several shelves are stocked with Italian canned vegetables, sauces, and
dried pastas. You can also bring your own container and stock up on bulk
olive oil and balsamic vinegar.

Forte's may be small, and you need to check their hours before
stopping by, but it's a worthy Route 1 resource for all your meat needs.

If, while running errands, you found that you've forgotten to eat, they
make good sandwiches, salads, and wraps for you to munch on in the
store or (more common) to take with you to your next shopping stop.

Foster's

Awful execution and strained style take the "fun" out of "fusion"

New American

Upmarket restaurant

$50 Price

www.fostersrestaurant.com

Mon–Thu 11:30am–2:30pm, 5pm–10pm; Fri 11:30am–2:30pm, 5pm–11pm; Sat–Sun 5pm–11pm

Bar Beer, wine, liquor
Credit cards Visa, MC, AmEx
Reservations Accepted

Ninth Square
56 Orange St.
(203) 859-6666

Asian fusion is like American Idol: few people have really been able to make it work, but that doesn't stop everyone and their grandmother from trying.

From décor to menu to execution, Foster's is a confused disaster. For starters, each wall of the nightclubbish interior is different: red, black, exposed white brick, faux granite. There are Buddha statues, big white curtains that conceal columns of light, and huge white ceiling pads that sit weirdly beneath fluorescent bulbs, muting the light but also effectively inducing chuckles and eye-rolling.

The menu reads like it was composed by throwing darts at a chart of multinational ingredients. To call it unfocused is to downplay how utterly freakish the range of flavors is, and how destructive are the combinations within each dish. If a simple salad of romaine hearts (with the tacky offer to add chicken or grilled shrimp) manages to be dry to the point of inedibility, how can you trust a "filet of sole cashew crusted with a key lime sherry cream sauce, brown rice and okra croquettes"?

You can't. Polenta-crusted, bone-dry tuna with wasabi mashed potatoes is horrendous; the tough, low-quality fish tastes suspect, and sits under a candyish orange ginger glaze that reminds us of a certain Lean Cuisine. You can't taste the wasabi in the crumbly mashed potatoes, though corn kernels add a bit of texture and sweetness. A harmless-sounding lamb and smoked gouda quesadilla comes in a wheat tortilla whose texture feels sort of toasted or baked, not grilled. Though the lamb tastes sort of braised and has a good, slightly gamy flavor like barbacoa, it's too sinewy, making some parts just plain hard to chew. We had to spit out one bite (and then struggle not to spit out the others). The seasoning was decent, but served with a dish of useless ice-cold sour cream with a couple of scallion slices. The whole thing reminded us of Chili's.

The service is lovely and personal here, and the presentations are as carefully plotted as the interior, but this self-proclaimed "eccentric American" is just a poorly executed mess. It's the kind of restaurant that, through overambition, manages to be worse than even the lowliest lunch counters.

Four and Twenty Blackbirds

Easily the best bakery in Guilford...many would say
the best anywhere

Baked goods

Counter service

Tue, Thu, Sat 7:30am–4pm
Fri 7:30am–5pm

Bar None
Credit cards None
Kid-friendly, veg-friendly

Guilford
610 Village Walk
(203) 458-6900

If you took a poll on the Guilford Green asking town residents what the
best things about living in Guilford are, you'd get three responses more
than any others: the rugged coastline, Bishop's Orchards, and Four and
Twenty Blackbirds. Aside from having what may be the most charming
name for a bakery we've ever heard, this local favorite draws residents
from up and down the shoreline with its high-quality, low-frills breads,
cakes, cookies, scones, and all manner of tarts and pies. Savory and sweet
goods are given equal attention here, pleasing those who crave a saltier
breakfast of leek and black pepper biscuits or a hunk of rustic, yeasty
focaccia topped with tomato and ricotta salata.

If you're here to satisfy your sweet tooth, though, look no further than
the sour cream-pecan muffin, piled high with buttery brown sugar
streusel, or one of the bakery's famed coconut macaroons. Seasonal fruit
tarts here are exceptional, as is a cooling slice of the key lime pie on a hot
summer day. Enjoy these with a cup of nearby Ashlawn's organic, farm-
roasted coffee. Call well ahead to reserve a dessert for a special occasion,
as this place tends to sell out early. Erratic hours also make it worth your
while to call before making the trip.

Frank Pepe's

The gold standard for pizza is going chain—get it while it's still good

9.1 Food

7.0 Feel

Pizza

Casual restaurant

$20 Price

www.pepespizzeria.com

Daily 11:30am–10pm
Hours vary by location

Bar Beer, wine
Credit cards Visa, MC
Reservations Not accepted
Kid-friendly, veg-friendly

Wooster Square Area
157 Wooster St.
(203) 865-5762

Wooster Square Area
The Spot, 163 Wooster St.
(203) 865-7602

Frank Pepe, one of the two most famous pizzerias in New Haven and among the best known in all New England, is chaining it up. Branches in Fairfield and Manchester are already open, and branches in (wince) Yonkers, and (double wince) Mohegan Sun casino are on the way. Although we wish them the best, it's hard not to feel a bit slighted by this news, like finding out from your brilliant humanities-scholar son that he's decided to pursue a career in management consulting.

At least the new branches won't be the same as this one. An icon of the old Wooster Street Neapolitan community, this inimitable pizzeria has held its ground since 1925. You'll have quite a while to ponder its illustrious history during your epic wait for seating (come between 3 and 4pm on a weekday to sit immediately), but superior quality demands commitment.

Pepe's master dough pullers maneuver pies within a gargantuan coal-fired brick oven with 10-15 foot-long peels. The flaky, bubbly crust is superb: thin and crisp, with a delightful hint of "burnt." The famed white clam and bacon pie—still our favorite—sports freshly shucked whole clams and the earthiness of bacon fat.

For your pie #2 (two mediums feed 4), forego the plain tomato-and-mozzarella version—it has come too greasy and cheesy lately—and arrest your palate with meaty, wonderful sausage. Don't forget to order the local Foxon cream soda or root beer—it's classic, as is the cheap American beer.

The place feels cozy, with plenty of comfortable wooden booths and, although whitewashed, the room feels appropriately historic. Your order is taken with good-natured brusqueness (it's more charming once you've sat down than during your hour's wait). Pepe's refusal to take reservations is understandable yet annoying, especially when one's I-95 detour into the Elm City centers exclusively upon a visit here. Their next door offshoot The Spot, offers similar pizza, with shorter lines, in a drab room that lacks the nostalgic appeal of the mothership.

On your way out, mosey over to the open-air kitchen and watch the pizzas being made. It's so simple: dough, sauce, toppings, heat. Frank Pepe gets each exactly right.

Fresh Taco

An Asian-run lunch stop with fast, no-frills Tex-Mex
that's built upon homemade tortillas (roti?)

6.0 Food

6.0 Feel

Mexican

Counter service

$10 Price

Mon–Thu 10:30am–10:30pm;
Fri–Sat 10:30am–11pm; Sun
noon–10:30pm

Bar None
Credit cards Visa, MC, AmEx
Delivery

South Town Green
39 Elm St.
(203) 777-3068

Visually, Fresh Taco is an experience in cultural dissonance. The little place
screams Chinese take-out, from the Asian staff to the narrow storefront
and photo-board menu overhead to the alpha-numeric listings on the
fold-out menu (complete with a "no MSG" assurance). But if you look
more closely, things take an unexpected turn: this little shop packs up not
Chinese but rather Mexican food—burritos, tacos, refried beans,
guacamole, and so on. The shop caters to a lunch-break crowd, with
equal parts take-outers and solo sit-down diners. Prices are low; the $10
delivery minimum means feeding at least two people.

Perhaps because of the heritage of the staff and perhaps not, things
taste a little bit different here than at your standard Tex-Mex quick stop.
That is not necessarily a bad thing. The flour tortillas are homemade in a
press, not taken out of a package, which is a most welcome touch. Their
texture is somewhat unusual, more doughy than most, and almost
evocative of...well...roti. Nowhere is the roti resemblance quality stronger
than in the extra-puffy tortillas used for the quesadillas sincronizadas
(pressed with meat and jack cheese).

Among fillings, chicken is fully flavored but crunchy around the edges,
and cumin-forward "Tex-Mex chili" is okay if unusually soft. Lettuce and
tomato are fresh, but the little plastic tub of salsa that's served with
almost everything is subpar. And we're not sure what to make of the
french fries and Buffalo wings.

Guess there's something for everybody.

Gabriele's

Reliable, humble Italian far from the Wooster fuss and budget

7.0	7.5
Food	Feel

Italian

Casual restaurant

$35
Price

www.gabrielect.com

Mon–Thu 11am–10pm
Fri–Sat 11am–11pm
Sun noon–9pm

Bar Beer, wine, liquor
Credit cards Visa, MC, AmEx
Reservations Accepted
Kid-friendly, veg-friendly

Orange
326 Boston Post Rd.
(203) 799-2633

Though the restaurant goes by many names—Gabriele's Restaurant, Gabriele's Ristorante Italiano, Gabriele's Ristorante Italiano & Bar—this eatery has no identity issues. It's solidly a family-style operation, offering everything you would expect from an East Coast Italian-American restaurant (bad wine list included).

Weekends bring the expected flocks of families, as well as couples both young and old. The usual suspects crowd the menu, and are served in gigantic portions. While the service is warmly genuine, the ambience strikes a note somewhere between family-owned and a family chain. The tagline is "When you're here, you're family."

Warm, chewy bread arrives immediately. Crab cakes are crispy and well-seasoned, but not worth transgressing the Italian experience, as they lack either rich lumps of meat or other interesting flavor nuggets. Grilled Portobello mushrooms topped with Gorgonzola strike a solid earthy note, but it's not a transcendent flavor combination. A heap of penne comes cooked al dente, dotted with a healthy dose of slippery porcini mushrooms whose taste unfortunately gets obscured by the snap of too many sundried tomatoes. The penne is favored even by the staff, who recommends it as the noodle of choice with velluto, a chicken dish whose vodka cream sauce has more depth than the average rendition, and is enlivened by the smokiness of prosciutto. Pizza has a flexible, thinnish crust that gets soggy when topped with watery vegetables like broccoli rabe.

Desserts made in-house trump those that are purchased from elsewhere. Of the former, a brick-sized tiramisù does an admirable job of combining judiciously soaked lady fingers with mascarpone cream in a balance between sweet and savory and dense and light. The outsourced mud pie with chocolate and peanut butter filling, however, is boring and gummy.

Overall, it's a not objectionable, but not extraordinary, experience. For its many die-hard fans, Gabriele's has more of a homey feel than do the crazy-busy Wooster Street icons. Certainly it doesn't claim—with high prices, attempts at haute creations, or self-aggrandizing websites—to be so glorious. For families are rarely looking for glory; they're looking for good feelings and easy eating. On both of these counts, Gabriele's delivers.

Gastronomique

Some of New Haven's best and most artful cuisine
is served out of its tiniest restaurant

8.5 Food

6.5 Feel

French, Burgers

Take-out **$25** Price

Mon–Thu 10am–9pm; Fri–Sat
10am–2am; Sun 11am–5pm

Bar None
Credit cards Visa, MC, AmEx
Delivery

Chapel District
25 High St.
(203) 776-7007

At press time, Gastronomique was operating as a catering-only
establishment, with the promise of resuming à la carte service soon. Let's
hope the hiatus is as short as possible, as there's a lot to like about this
tiny take-out place.

Mark Woll, a veteran of some of New York's most serious kitchens,
opened Gastronomique with awesome chops and his entire life savings of
$22,000. In a space the size of a VW bus, Woll creates superb food—both
mundane comfort grub and upscale specialties—with only four burners,
an oven, and six feet of counter space. It's impressive.

A chalkboard outside announces the steaming, glistening seasonal daily
specials, which might include roasted chestnuts, macaroni casserole,
braised short ribs, or duck confit. Creations are sort of French bistro,
ranging from a rich, velvety, cheesy French onion soup in the traditional
style to a fabulous lobster bisque. The Provençal rack of lamb, on one
visit, was a triumph, tender, sweetly crusted with forest spices and olive
tapenade, and served with a creamy potato tart, dried tomato, and
shredded fennel. Woll's sandwiches are spectacular: the steak and cheese
is beyond the pale, made with hefty chunks of excellent beef pilled onto a
toasted ciabatta role with Cheddar. The juice drips down your arm. A
simple crêpe, judiciously filled with haricots verts, cured olives, tomato,
and anchovy, makes a perfect light lunch.

All this genius makes the missteps that much more baffling. We once
had a spinach salad whose ingredients included—in addition to
understandable spinach, vinaigrette, cranberries and orange slices—cream
cheese, chocolate chips, crushed graham crackers and raw onion. It
wasn't terrible, but it wasn't remotely recognizable, either. A risotto with
saffron, spinach, parmesan, and roasted red pepper has tasted like a Hot
Pocket. Yet we love the creamy chicken pâté sandwich, accompanied by
fresh greens with a subtle vinaigrette; fruit smoothies, composed of
wondrously fresh fruit and vegetable combinations; and French toast that
makes for a decadent mid-morning breakfast.

Gastronomique is well suited for dinner-party augmentation or a
candlelight dinner for two, brought home with no prep required. The wry
chef, who comes to High Street by way of the Culinary Institute of
America and a bevy of prestigious restaurants, also somewhat amusingly
thumbed his nose at Yale Dining Services by offering a "student meal
plan" of 30 meals per month at discounted prices.

If Gastronomique stays an all-catering operation—which would be a
great loss to the city—then you owe it to yourself to have something
catered.

Gerónimo

The best margaritas around, pretty good food, and a patio where you can meet your next mate

7.7 Food
9.0 Feel

Southwestern, Mexican

Upmarket restaurant

$50 Price

www.geronimobarandgrill.com

Sun–Thu 5pm–11:30pm
Fri–Sat 5pm–midnight

Bar Beer, wine, liquor
Credit cards Visa, MC, AmEx
Reservations Accepted
Date-friendly, outdoor dining

Chapel District
271 Crown St.
(203) 777-7700

If your timing is right and your luck is good, you can have a nice night at this loud, lively hotspot. Antler-sprouting light fixtures look like something straight out of any old bar or resto in the Southwest (atmospheric authenticity—check). Lighting is low, colors are warm, and pretty woods dominate; it all combines to create a rather comforting effect. But if your luck is bad, you can have a pretty unpleasant experience here. To wit: we were once shuffled around the bar *three times* to accommodate a corporate party. Service can be spotty. And the meat-market scene on the patio in summer is a major turn-off for some (and a major turn-*on* for others).

But no matter. All is forgiven because they do a very good job with the food—despite their over-reliance on the adjective "hatch" for their chiles (a reminder, perhaps, that their shtick is more New Mexico than Nuevo México)—and the margaritas. Oh, the margaritas. A spicy passion fruit margarita is one of the best in New Haven; its jalapeño-infused tequila is not hot and sweet like a candied jalapeño, but rather hot and sweet in a very grown-up kind of way. A "Smokin' Margarita," made with Del Maguey San Luis del Río mezcal (hence the smokiness), Grand Marnier, and lime juice, is beautifully balanced. A version with blood orange juice has only a whisper of sweetness; it's genius. Even the simple "Gerónimo Margarita" is good stuff. And keep in mind that this is New Haven—we don't do good margaritas!

As for food, the different variations of chiles rellenos are quite good—a quinoa version is decent, but we prefer ours stuffed with barbecue shredded pork; it's roasted to an even smoothness, and it's surprisingly good. A chorizo chop—a double cut pork chop stuffed with chorizo stuffing and served atop a three bean ragout—is decadent and flavorful. Gerónimo's shot at the haute mac and cheese fad (we're not-so-secretly very happy that this trend isn't over yet) comes with hatch green chile, Cheddar, Chihuahua cheese, and gruyère and is "topped with (indetectable) Mexican corn 'truffle' oil." This common euphemism for huitlacoche, which is actually a fungus that grows on corn, is a marketing trick that makes us giggle (and roll our eyes) every time we see it on a menu.

But it's one we're willing to forgive, especially after another round of margaritas. Cheers.

Glenwood Drive-In

A time-frozen roadside hot dog stand and more—
bring your classic car

7.7	7.5
Food	Feel

American, Burgers

Counter service

$10
Price

www.glenwooddrivein.com

Daily 11am–9pm winter, 11am–
10pm summer

Bar None
Credit cards Visa, MC
Kid-friendly, outdoor dining

Hamden
2538 Whitney Ave.
(203) 281-0604

Here's what you order: the hot dog. How do you want it cooked? A little?
A lot? Split and deep-fried? They will do any of these things for you, and
the teenager who takes your order will shout it to the cooks: "One Dog!
Well-done! Rings!" (This is how you should order, mind you).

It is a little bit breathtaking, in an everyday way, to witness this
seemingly anarchic system working so well—kind of like the post office.
You get what you ordered, every time, and the only thing that takes a
little while is the line, because this place is no secret. The postwar diner
feel has been perfectly preserved; to this day, there are vintage auto
shows at 6pm every Wednesday night in summer—bring your classic and
join in the fun.

It's really all about the hot dogs, though. The more cooking of the hot
dog, of course, the more browning and crisping of the skin. This may be
the first and last time within these pages that we recommend ordering
any meat "well done," but here it adds a welcome new dimension. We
recommend the hot dog with American cheese (it's placed between the
hot dog and the bun, where it melts somewhat beneath the heat). Skip
the merely average chili topping, but don't miss the condiment station off
to the side, where you'll pile on sauerkraut, chopped onions, and a nice
hot pepper sauce along with the other usual suspects. The bun is
wonderfully browned, and the overall effect is memorable. The best hot
dog in America? Who knows. The best hot dog we've had in recent
memory? Easily. A steal at less than three dollars? Absolutely.

The rest of the menu—which includes seafood preparations like the
classic Connecticut hot lobster roll, clam strips, and so on—might not be
as superlative as the hot dogs, but the fries are crispy and well prepared
and the burgers get good marks. Soft-shell crabs are another specialty
when in season. Finish with the superb vanilla ice cream from the adjacent
Kelly's Kone Konnection.

Glen's Bar-B-Q

Some of the best Jamaican food around comes out of a truck on the Boulevard

8.6 Food   **8.0** Feel

Caribbean

Take-out   **$10** Price

Tue–Sun 11:30am–6pm

Bar None
Credit cards None
Kid-friendly, outdoor dining

The Hill
Near 624 Ella Grasso Blvd.
No phone

We were hungry, and we'd pulled into a parking lot on Ella Grasso Boulevard (still just "The Boulevard" to old-school locals), trying to turn around in search of—well, something. Then the smell crept in the car: a snap of smoke, spice and blackened meat. This was our something. But we hadn't found it. The jerk chicken at Glen's Bar-B-Q had found us.

The promise of wonderful food where you'd expected only pavement is a good reason to keep your eyes off the road. But at Glen's Bar-B-Q, you can drive safely. Just roll down your window.

"It was a family thing, man," Glen James says, explaining how he started cooking jerk chicken. He grew up in Ocho Rios, a now-popular tourist town on Jamaica's northern coast, where his parents have a stand selling jerk and other Jamaican specialties. James grew up working in the family business, and when he rolled out his own stand in New Haven a little over five years ago, he had a lifetime of preparation.

It hasn't hurt. The jerk chicken, smoky and moist with a perfectly sharpened sauce, is superb, and at press time, it started at just $6 for a small order. The oxtail stew—rich, sumptuous, crowded with flavor—is every bit as good. Either is available with sides of rice and beans and lightly cooked shredded cabbage, delicious with a dousing of sauce.

This wasn't James's original plan, though. He wanted to market the steel smoker he uses: compact, deep-bottomed, crowned with a small chimney, all hammered out and welded together by James himself. He still hopes to patent it someday.

The ingenious grills weren't selling, though, so James took one out himself. He hasn't stopped working it since. The Jamaican community is strong in New Haven, as James will remind you, and a sizable percentage seem to pass through Glen's Bar-B-Q. There's a Bob Marley freedom flag flying high above the smoker, calling out to cars on Ella Grasso. It's the stand's most visible sign.

Gourmet Heaven

A 24/7 deli with two locations in town, but only use them in emergency

4.7	4.0
Food	Feel

American, Chinese

Take-out | **$10**
Price

24 hours
deli buffet ends at 2am

Bar None
Credit cards Visa, MC, AmEx
Veg-friendly, Wi-Fi

Broadway District
15 Broadway
(203) 787-4533

Audubon Arts District
44 Whitney Ave.
(203) 776-0400

The buffet at Gourmet Heaven is like Hulk Hogan: both are way past their prime, browning and toughening under heat lamps, and slathered in oil to look fresh both day and night (well, it's a rumor, at least in the case of Gourmet Heaven). But where our affections for the Hulkster are the result of nostalgia, the occasional 1am trip to the overpriced steam trays here seems to be the product of much alcohol consumption.

Here you'll find hideous renditions of such global fare as fried plantains, crab Rangoon, mac and cheese, and yakisoba. We can't put the blame solely on the fact that these have been sitting around for hours; we suspect a few things probably weren't particularly tasty to begin with. Stir-fried beef tends to be tough, and pasta with cream sauce is overly creamy, bland, and undersalted.

Salads are palatable, diverse, and a slightly better value; the fresh fruit, though expensive (a handful of grapes is heavier than one might imagine), is also okay. There are also deli sandwiches, and some basic eat-in seating offered upstairs. The loft upstairs (at the Broadway location) has little to no air circulation and a low ceiling, making every meal taken here seem like it will probably be your last. (The deli buffet ends at 2am, so it just might be—at least for the night.)

If you're looking for packaged food, Gourmet Heaven delivers—albeit at a premium—from cheeses to dried fruits and nuts, upmarket sauces, and the requisite instant ramen. This is also the place for various and sundry items that you won't find elsewhere at 3am, whether fresh-cut flowers or prophylactics.

Gourmet Heaven's second branch is on Whitney, next to Moe's SW Grill. It's more of the same, but with less of a college crowd. Unless you're in a dire late-night situation, try to avoid these places.

Guadalupe La Poblanita

8.1 Food **4.0** Feel

New Haven's best Mexican food has settled into new digs...again

Mexican

Casual restaurant

$15 Price

Mon 11am–5pm
Wed–Sun 11am–8pm

Bar Beer, BYO
Credit cards None
Reservations Not accepted
Kid-friendly

Fair Haven
136 Chapel St.
(203) 752-1017

In four years, Guadalupe has occupied three different locations, most recently (and finally, we hope) on Chapel Street, in a cheery turquoise building near the bridge in Fair Haven. In terms of taste, this rivals La Cocinita for best Mexican in town. Everything on the menu is good. Where some downtown haunts tend to evoke packaged, processed Old El Paso, Guadalupe serves up truly authentic dishes to those in the know. Don't make the mistake of coming here for a romantic night out, though; depressing, white lights and tinny music bear down on bright plastic abominations that pass for booths.

But Guadalupe is all about the food. The cheese is the real thing—Mexican queso fresco, not Cracker Barrel shredded Monterey Jack. The chicken with chocolate-tinged mole, which might be the best dish on the menu, is an excellent balance of sweet and savory, and it comes with rice, beans, and homemade tortillas. Never take tortillas for granted.

Tostadas are fantastic; chiles rellenos, which used to be texturally a little tough, have been sublime lately. The tamales, which come in different flavors, are as good as you'll find in town, but not outstanding in their own right. They're made with good masa, and the accompanying salsa can be as spicy or mild as you like, but they're not especially flavorful. And oh boy, are they expensive—if we told you that in West Texas, we've gotten them for 3 for $1, would you riot?

Simpler, but well executed, are the roast pork and anything with chorizo, and there's also an impressive selection of Mexican-beer-after-Corona, including the delicious Bohemia and even—if you're lucky—Sol.

Portions are large, so order less rather than more; even the smaller antojitos will satisfy most appetites. Some English is spoken, though remembering your high school Spanish would be useful if you don't want accidental animal parts—although it might be the best thing that ever happened to you.

Heirloom

A restaurant with all the chic urbanity of the hippest hotel in town—and a price tag to match

9.0	8.5
Food	Feel

New American

Upmarket restaurant

$85
Price

www.studyhotels.com

Mon–Thu 7am–10am,
11:30am–2:30pm, 5:30pm–
10pm; Fri–Sat 7am–10am,
11:30am–2:30pm, 5:30pm–
11:30pm; Sun 11:30am–3pm,
5:30pm–10pm

Bar Beer, wine, liquor
Credit cards Visa, MC, AmEx
Reservations Accepted
Date-friendly, good wines

Upper Chapel Area
1157 Chapel St.
(203) 503-3900

Heirloom is in the new Study hotel, the hippest lodging New Haven has ever seen. The feel is very Soho-Grand-ish—and it's pulled off remarkably well. There's warm lighting, sleek glass, and silky wood; in short, you'll feel important dining here. But all this cool luxury doesn't come cheap. It's an expense-account destination, to be sure, but even if the experience doesn't quite match the prices, it's nice to see this type of urban sensibility here in New Haven. To compare Heirloom to its predecessor, Olde Blue Publick House, is to compare apples to Buffalo-wing sauce.

Start your evening off here with some interesting cocktails at the lively bar—the setting is beautiful. In fact, some just choose to sip a libation, munch on an app or two, soak in the vibe, and leave it at that. Otherwise, a stiff drink will help you feel better about all the money you're about to spend.

At dinner, the concept is 21st-century Italian-influenced New American—the sort of seasonal menu that makes a big deal about ingredients, seeks out nostalgic throwbacks, and embraces fats and innards. In other words, it's the kind of stuff we like. Your first wise purchase would be what amounts to a preparation of mozzarella sticks made with burrata; the cheese is deep-fried, served with marinara, and fun to eat. Bacon-wrapped dates are good, too. Macaroni and cheese with smoked ham hock is unsurprisingly popular, and addictive, too.

A New York strip comes out just as requested, not cooked a touch beyond medium-rare. The accompanying fries are absolutely excellent, some of the best in the city. "Brick chicken" (cooked under a brick in the oven) turns out to be a happy life partner for its Brussels sprouts leaves. There have been execution problems with fish, however, and halibut has arrived inexcusably overcooked. The wine list would be fairly well thought out—if the thinking didn't involve the price column. Finding something decent under $50 requires a sharp eye indeed.

Hotel breakfasts are generally aimed only at the poor saps who are stuck with few other options, but in the case of Heirloom, we'd recommend eating here even if you're not a key-carrying guest of the hotel. Steel-cut oatmeal is delicious, and comes with a delightful brown sugar that melts over the top. Eggs are faithfully served as ordered. Coffee is good, as it should be; it's the cornerstone of a good breakfast.

It is hard to argue that this is one of New Haven's best new restaurants. But at these prices, we might expect a room, too.

Hong Kong Grocery

A lovely little escapist trip—pretend you are in Asia for the afternoon

Groceries, Chinese

Market

Daily 9am–10pm

Bar None
Credit cards Visa, MC

East Rock
67 Whitney Ave.
(203) 777-8886

Hong Kong Grocery is an overwhelmingly aromatic Asian market on Whitney Avenue. Gone are the days when you could duck into China Great Wall, the restaurant in the back, for a $5 meal that could effectively feed you for days. Now you have to go all the way next door for such pleasures.

The restaurant is now its own entity, and Hong Kong Grocery is exactly that—a grocery. Needless to say, the atmosphere, even for a supermarket, is still about as uncharming as it gets. Aside from David Grewal, the clientele is still largely Chinese, but word is getting out, and it seems that soon enough just about everyone will be coming here for the cheap and interesting produce. "Service" remains surly.

This two-story market has, of course, a strong showing of Chinese goods of any sort; given the sheer size of Hong Kong Grocery in comparison to some of the other Asian groceries around town, it is somewhat the Wal-Mart of the bunch. They will stock just about anything here, while the other stores have to work with much more limited shelf space, and as such, are forced to be more selective with their buying.

What makes ethnic groceries so fun is the little escape from daily life that they provide. For a little chunk of your day you can pretend that you're back in Hong Kong. Now if only they'd shape up on the fresh-fish front, so we wouldn't have to go all the way up State Street...

House of Chao

A good, cheap, and basic Chinese standby that's
long been quite popular with Westville locals

5.6 Food

6.5 Feel

Chinese

Casual restaurant

$15 Price

Tue–Sun noon–10pm

Bar BYO
Credit cards Visa, MC, AmEx
Reservations Accepted

Westville
898 Whalley Ave.
(203) 389-6624

This inexpensive Chinese-American restaurant in downtown Westville has built up a devoted following over more than 20 years. The very local patrons (and we don't mean Chinese people) tend to arrive knowing exactly what they want. The stained, lacquered wooden surfaces, the wainscoting, the white walls, the Chinese art, and the pop piano classics are exactly what you'd expect, although lighting is refreshingly dim. The service is polite but nothing more unless you're a regular.

Most of the menu is as predictable as the décor: classics like General Tso's, lo mein, and so on. Hot and sour soup is a good version, with pleasing bits of bamboo, egg, and tofu coexisting in happy harmony; pepper is the dominant flavor there. Fried rice, another standby, is unusually dull, however, without much fried character or evidence of egg.

The dumplings are homemade and well above average, as are the other standard brown-sauce preparations, but we prefer the "house specialties," which include good, crispy fish and lamb dishes. The "New Tse Chicken" is a plate of large chunks of meat deep-fried for an effect something like chicken fingers, but not greasy and puffy like deep-fried Chinese-American fare can be. It's real breast meat (not that spongy stuff), crispy enough to stand up to the sweet, largely uninteresting red sauce. Fresh vegetables, which might include broccoli, bamboo shoots, baby corn, celery, onions, and snap peas, are cooked al dente for an unexpected crunch. Decent, in short, but unmemorable.

Lunch specials are all under five dollars, in line with low market rates for lunch, and remarkably, not one dish on the menu—not even the crispy fish—costs more than ten bucks. And don't forget about BYO. In the end, it might be the value proposition that really keeps people hooked.

Humphrey's East

A neighborhood bar with old-school American grub, outdoor seating, and now brunch

6.1	**7.5**
Food	Feel

American, Burgers

Bar **$20** Price

www.humphreyseast.net

Mon–Thu 11:30am–midnight	**Bar** Beer, wine, liquor	**East Rock**
Fri–Sat 11:30am–1am	**Credit cards** Visa, MC, AmEx	175 Humphrey St.
Sun 9am–midnight	Kid-friendly, live music, outdoor dining	(203) 782-1506

Although Humphrey's is under new ownership since our last edition, we can't see much that's different about this classic bar and grill. The pizza is gone, but there are still first-rate fries and burgers and free-flowing beer, and it still enjoys a jovial escape-from-it-all atmosphere that might derive partly from its location a couple of short blocks off the more populous East Rock area. It's far enough away not to be overrun by angst-ridden academics with higher degrees, trying to decide whether or not to sell their souls to the endlessly churning econo-engine of corporate America.

The local happy hour crowd is particularly fun, especially in warm weather when the crowd flows into the sunny back room, aptly named Bogart's. On a good day, the drink deal is sweetened by a raft of free bar food, of which the chicken wings are by far our favorite. On certain nights, Bogart's is also graced by live music (Jazz on Mondays, DJs spinning on weekends) and dancing.

The best aspect of Humphrey's East, though, is the outdoor tables in good weather. As for the food, standbys include Buffalo wings, fried calamari, and well-dressed burgers. For those craving liberal servings of meat, there are barbecued ribs (which can be on the tough side, with a sweet and uninteresting BBQ sauce) and steaks sized medium to XXL. There is also a brief nod to vegetarians, and a great-value kids' menu for people under age 12. At our last visit, we were somewhat unimpressed by the burgers, though. A sunny brunch outside on the patio sees melting-pot standards like Belgian waffles, French toast, egg dishes, breakfast burritos, and bagels (mimosas and Bloody Marys taste best in the fresh air).

It's mostly old-school American food as it was meant to be, and it's emblematic of one of New Haven's strengths: unpretentious grub that tastes as good to a Little Leaguer as it does to a Comp Lit professor.

Hunan Café

Typical corner Chinese-American take-out that's
barely a notch above the mediocre competition

4.1	3.0
Food	Feel

Chinese

Counter service

$10
Price

Mon–Sat 10:30am–10:30pm	**Bar** Beer, wine	**Upper Chapel Area**
Sun 11:30am–10:30pm	**Credit cards** Visa, MC, AmEx	142 York St.
	Delivery	(203) 776-8688

Hunan Café, on the corner of York and Crown, is the Chinese take-out
vendor of choice for this part of town, especially at lunchtime, when the
special is a value that's hard to beat: $4.50 yields a generous portion of
wok fare with rice, plus soup (egg drop, wonton, or hot and sour) or an
egg roll. In a subterranean location decorated with artificial flowers,
Hunan has little in the way of charming ambiance—this place is all about
a compelling taste-to-value ratio.

The menu touts its offerings as "exotic Chinese," but it seems that the
most exotic things here are whimsical titles for otherwise familiar dishes,
and a mysterious predilection toward pairing chicken and shrimp
("Dragon and Phoenix" is just one of five such options); perhaps this is a
strategy to bulk up the servings of what is actually rather good shrimp.
Veggie options include steamed broccoli with tofu and mushroom with
brown rice and ginger sauce.

Most dishes are wok-sautéed combinations of protein and vegetables,
executed with characteristic speed. Hunan is no haute cuisine, whatever
its aspirations, but in the corner Chinese-American brown-sauce model, it
is a slight notch above Main Garden, China King, and so on. Vegetables
are fresh and crisp, and the establishment guarantees that all dishes are
MSG-free. The bulk of business at Hunan is in take-out, and the free
delivery for orders over $10 is a boon to the New Haven scene, where
there is still a dearth of delivery options.

Ibiza

New Haven's temple to New Spanish cuisine is as
good as ever—but its heaviness is growing old

9.3 Food

7.0 Feel

Spanish

Upmarket restaurant

$80 Price

www.ibizanewhaven.com

Mon–Thu 5pm–9pm
Fri noon–2:30pm, 5pm–10pm
Sat 5pm–10pm

Bar Beer, wine, liquor
Credit cards Visa, MC, AmEx
Reservations Essential
Date-friendly, good wines

Chapel District
39 High St.
(203) 865-1933

There was a moment when it seemed that the restaurant that delivered
New Haven's culinary scene to the 21st century—Luis Bollo's Ibiza—was
slipping. Lately, the kitchen seems to have gotten its mojo back. Still, it
doesn't seem to have evolved much over the past half-decade. The menu
hasn't drifted at all away from the overrichness that dominated the first
few years of 21st-century cuisine and toward the purer, simpler flavors
that are driving the next generation. Perhaps this is why it's no longer as
difficult to score a reservation here: people are no longer as interested in
spending this kind of money on such a heavy, complicated meal.

If there's a unifying theme to this menu—other than the generalized
notion of nouvelle Spanish—it's unbridled richness and wintriness (even in
spring), from crisp, melty croquettes of foie gras with jamón serrano (as
good as ever) to "raviolis de rabo" that aggressively infuse pastry with
oxtail, mushrooms, truffle oil, and foamy potato emulsion (a nod to
Bollo's molecular-gastronomy background). Underseasoned, impossibly
heavy short ribs are just plain over the top, but we've enjoyed juicy
codornices (quails), stuffed with shallots and porcini mushrooms and
paired with gnocchi.

This kitchen likes sweetness almost as much as it likes fat, whether it's
in the honey with which cochinillo (well-crisped roast suckling pig) is
lacquered, or the reduction of PX (Pedro Ximénez, a dessert sherry) that
sweetens "lasaña," whose supposed pasta is hard to find amidst all the
unbelievable richness (duck confit, cheese, foie gras flan). Desserts are
successful, but the wine list hasn't developed much. For a restaurant on
this level, more old vintages should be available, although we've found
some reasonably priced Riojas (e.g. CUNE) that do well with the food.

The reasons why you won't actually find us here much are a bit hard to
pin down. Surely the service has something to do with it: it's technically
proficient but also a bit cold, a bit pretentious. Nor does the table layout
encourage intimacy or good times. Could the décor be any more dated,
or the weird wire chairs any less comfortable? Could the prix-fixe tasting
menu leave you any more uncomfortably stuffed? It's just not what we
seek in a restaurant these days.

As food critics, our central responsibility is to exercise good culinary
judgment, whatever our emotional impulses. And when we do that, we
must admit that Ibiza still serves some of the best food in New Haven. But
catch us in the dark corner of a bar, and we might be cornered into
admitting, darkly, that when we go out to eat ourselves, the best food is
not always what we seek.

IKEA Restaurant

The 99-cent breakfast might seem like a bargain—
but how much did you spend at IKEA that day?

4.9 Food

5.5 Feel

Swedish

Counter service

$5 Price

www.ikea.com

Mon–Thu 9:30am–7:30pm
Fri–Sat 9:30am–8:30pm
Sun 10:30am–6:30pm

Bar None
Credit cards Visa, MC, AmEx

Long Wharf
450 Sargent Dr.
(203) 865-4532

People flock to IKEA to partake in the classic all-day scavenger hunt for cheap Scandinavian furniture. It's a pastime so popular that it has made Swedish founder Ingvar Kamprad one of the world's richest men.

Ingvar would have to sell quite a few of the 99-cent egg, bacon, and potato breakfasts—this has to be the highest calorie-to-cent ratio around—to add much to his $50 billion fortune. Although breakfast represents the best value, we prefer to stick to the decent Swedish meatballs, which taste good for frozen, processed meat. They're well seasoned and served with mild gravy and a lingonberry preserve that adds a pleasant tartness. The gravlax plate, which we used to like, seems scarce these days.

Hot dogs please the crowds, warm cinnamon buns exude that irresistible fresh-baked smell, and frozen yogurt rings in at under $1. The store also sells reasonably priced Swedish goods like salmon pâté in a tube, cheap caviar, delectable cloudberry jam, and those same frozen meatballs in big bags, along with the lingonberry sauce (we admit that the meatballs have, on occasion, made us quite happy at the undiscriminating hour of 3am).

Above all, the IKEA restaurant is brilliant retail science, because it prevents customers from leaving the store just because they're hungry. Whether or not the store is profiting from the food, your little break gives you that extra moment to convince yourself that you really do need that minimalist bookcase-room divider (it's still right over there). Like most self-made billionaires, Ingvar always knows the way to your wallet better than you do.

Il' Forno

Italian that pays a little homage to the regional
specialties and a little to the New England ones

7.1	8.0
Food	Feel

Italian

Upmarket restaurant

$50
Price

www.ilfornoristorante.com

Mon–Thu 11:30am–4pm, 5pm–
10pm; Fri–Sat 11:30am–4pm,
5pm–10:30pm; Sun 11:30am–
3pm

Bar Beer, wine, liquor
Credit cards Visa, MC, AmEx
Reservations Accepted
Date-friendly

Milford
591 Boston Post Rd.
(203) 283-5033

We really love Italian restaurants that actually try for some regional focus
and authenticity. Don't get us wrong: we know the value of a red sauce,
checkered tablecloth, wicker-Chianti-basket, "Thatsa spicy ameatball!"
kind of place. But many restaurants these days seem to straddle a
disempowering divide, unable to commit to either this Americano 1950s
vision of Italy or to the traditions of the many different parts of the
motherland. It gets worse when these same restaurants add unlikely
gourmet ingredients in panicked layer upon layer until the food no longer
resembles Italian.

Il' Forno does a little of all the above. The understated atmosphere is
very genuine, with walls painted a roasted butternut color, a spare room
of wood furnishings, and a solemn, heavily accented waiter
singlehandedly manning the dining room. The menu sees some things
that are traditional (and traditionally New Haven), and takes a few
liberties. Ultimately, nothing is offensive, nor is it remarkable.

A cannellini-bean spread is brought to the table, gratis, with warm
bread, and it is pretty good, though a touch too cold and undersalted.
Seafood starters are generally the most successful: mussels are well
chosen, with plump bodies and a tasty broth reduced to just the right
consistency; scallops are beautifully seared, their sauce supporting the
flavor rather than overwhelming it.

Among mains, the success with seafood continues to a pasta prep of
calamari, mussels, and clams that combine with tomato for an intense,
lovely flavor, but the sauce is watery and doesn't cling to the noodles.
Ravioli filled with braised beef are gummily undercooked, but very tasty.
Also chewy is the Israeli couscous that comes with a somewhat
overcooked and underwhelming salmon fillet.

The wine list is another one of those puzzling cases where the Italians
fight boring, mass-produced New Worlds for space. There are a couple of
good finds in here.

But we still can't find an explanation for the apostrophe after the article
in the restaurant's name.

India Palace

The Indian lunch buffet taken to the next level

7.1	4.0
Food	Feel

Indian

Casual restaurant

$25
Price

Sun–Thu 11:30am–10:30pm;
Fri–Sat 11:30am–11pm

Bar Beer, wine
Credit cards Visa, MC, AmEx
Reservations Accepted
Delivery, kid-friendly, veg-friendly

Upper Chapel Area
65 Howe St.
(203) 776-9010

We have raised India Palace's food rating since the last edition of our restaurant guide. The food has been more consistent lately, with the typical Indian gravies and curries coming out with depth and clarity. There's nothing groundbreaking going on here, but there's extreme bang for your buck at the lunchtime buffet—where it's way too easy to over-gorge to the point of physical discomfort. It's a good deal, considering that you can conceivably reap an entire day's caloric nourishment from the spread.

Vegetarians and carnivores will both be pleased by the options. Chicken tikka masala—entry-level Indian for the ages (and once famously named Britain's national dish)—is as it should be: creamy, tomatoey, and delicious. Saag paneer, too, is texturally spot on. Vindaloo is perfectly competent, as is lamb rogan josh. Naan is chewy and gooey in all the right ways.

As for feel, nothing much has changed there—we've scarcely seen worse décor. It's as if you tried to fashion an Indian restaurant out of a deserted high school classroom, and then stopped halfway through. The emptiness of the room makes the blank white walls seem all the blanker. When you peer in through the front windows—even during the lunchtime buffet, at India Palace's busiest time of day—the atmosphere seems to have a tangible effect on the emotional states of the customers. Otherwise gregarious groups seem somehow disconnected, and even couples in love seem lonely. Servers, at least, are a friendly bunch.

New Haven might be saturated with several similar Indian-American joints, but India Palace is a winner, especially because Indian food is particularly well suited to the lunch-buffet steam table, which is where this place shines; the long period of time spent simmering only intensifies the flavors. Throw in an Indian beer, and you're in business.

Indochine Pavilion

If you're looking for cheap pan-Southeast-Asian
food, you've found your place...but good it is not

Thai

Casual restaurant

Daily 11:30am–3pm, 5pm–
10pm

Bar Beer, wine, liquor
Credit cards Visa, MC, AmEx
Reservations Accepted
Delivery, veg-friendly

Upper Chapel Area
1180 Chapel St.
(203) 865-5033

Indochine Pavilion is yet another way-too-pan-Asian restaurant that serves
up Westernized versions of dishes from all over the continent. Our guess
is that this place's relative popularity has more than a little to do with the
low prices. Many come for the incredibly cheap all-you-can-eat lunch
buffet, offered daily for rock-bottom prices. The menu is humorously
overstretched, with Chinese, Vietnamese, Cambodian, and Thai all
elbowing their way into print (though it doesn't quite equal the fusion
follies of Thai Pan Asian half a block away).

The interior manages to be quite pleasant. It's above average for the
strip, a cozy little room decorated in shades of brown that create a more
careful atmosphere than some of the Chapel Street competition. We've
always been a bit befuddled by the sign boldly advertising that the place
got "three stars from the *New York Times*." We have absolutely no idea
what they are talking about, but you have to respect, on some twisted
level, that a bargain-basement pan-Asian joint on a New Haven street
corner would be brazen enough to claim that they were on par with
Babbo.

Let's start with the good news. We particularly like the larb gai (a cold,
marinated, minced chicken salad with onions and a wonderful limey
tang), which might be the best choice of all. The vegetarian selection is
also admirable. But go beyond this and it's just your standard roll call of
Asian-American slop. Red and green curries. Rolls. Sweet, sloppy sauces.
You know the drill.

Service is attentive and friendly, they do a healthy take-out business,
and they even deliver. If you elect to dine in, you'll be sharing space with
a Yale-heavy crowd that's clued in on the same value proposition that you
are. Just don't expect fireworks.

Iron Chef

Look beyond the kung pao chicken for a rich tapestry of Taiwanese food

8.7	4.5
Food	Feel

Taiwanese, Chinese

Counter service

$15
Price

Daily 11am–11pm

Bar None
Credit cards Visa, MC
Delivery

West Haven
1209 Campbell Ave.
(203) 932-3888

On the flip side of Iron Chef's Chinese-language menu, beneath a mini-history of the restaurant in English, there is the admonition, in all caps and amped-up font: "THE TASTE! THE TASTE!" How do you not like a restaurant that has its own chant?

Iron Chef, across the street from the University of New Haven, does not dwell on the aesthetics. This is a takeout-minded, free-delivery restaurant, with a couple of tables and a total of 10 chairs; the decorations on one wall are limited to a light switch and a fire alarm. Obviously, atmosphere isn't the thing here.

Taiwanese cuisine is a genome of the food brought by migrant groups from all over China, as well as the island's indigenous culinary traditions. It also owes much to the half-century spent under Japanese rule, and to Western influences. There isn't a single Taiwanese cuisine, but there's a style of gleeful distortion and appropriation that marks almost everything.

The menu here is crowded with the obligatory Chinese-American standards, including a "Chef's Specialties" section that includes, of course, no actual specialties. For those, look under the "Taiwanese Style" heading or on the handwritten Chinese-English list taped to the wall. (The specialties aren't exclusively Taiwanese, a distinction that isn't always easy or worth making. Nevertheless, Lion's Head, the excellent Shanghai pork meatballs, shows up here.)

Stewed pork belly has a luxuriously unctuous feel and a soothing, fatty flavor, highlighted by the prickly acidity of pickled mustard greens. The classic three-cup chicken—named for its recipe: a cup each of rice wine, soy sauce, and sesame oil—arrives still bubbling in a clay pot, the hacked chicken pieces ornamented with countless garlic cloves. It goes well with the snap of baby bamboo shoots with sweet sausage.

Taiwanese food is particularly attuned to texture. Iron Chef's stir-fried rice cakes, mixed with a mild blend of meat and stray vegetables, have a specific character that's known in Taiwan as QQ: toothsome and faintly resistant, but yielding. The taste isn't remarkable, but then again, that's not really the point.

Of the street food, there's a small platter of duck wings, stewed and gloopy, in a star anise-heavy sauce. And the fried chicken wings are crispy, thickly coated, dusted with salt and pepper, and delightful.

This place has the communal, warm feeling of a family kitchen. You even leave to a chorus of goodbyes.

Istanbul Café

Good Turkish food in an elaborately decorated, central location

7.7	8.0
Food	Feel

Turkish   Upmarket restaurant

$45
Price

www.istanbulcafect.com

Mon–Fri noon–10pm
Sat–Sun noon–11pm

Bar Beer, wine, liquor
Credit cards Visa, MC, AmEx
Reservations Recommended
Date-friendly, good wines

Chapel District
245 Crown St.
(203) 787-3881

Istanbul Café is an interesting experiment: a smart Turkish restaurant in the heart of downtown New Haven. The location couldn't be more choice, around the corner from the Shubert and the Taft.

Some of the food at Istanbul Café is great. The nohut ezme, Turkish hummus, is excellent, as is the patlican salata, a creamy purée of grilled eggplant, lemon juice, garlic, vinegar, and olive oil that is reminiscent of baba ganoush, but with a bit more subtlety. Ispanak ezme, a spicy spinach purée with yogurt, is an interesting and welcome flavor combination.

Stay away from the more standard Middle Eastern options; meat skewers, for instance, can lack seasoning and also be too dry. The restaurant definitely has a way with eggplant, though, and nowhere is that more evident than in the spectacular smoked eggplant purée that comes with hunkar begendi ("Sultan's Delight"), our favorite dish on the menu. Pieces of tomato-marinated cooked lamb are served atop the purée, which is wondrously rich, creamy, and flavorful, yet not overwhelming.

The room's décor is a tad too elaborate, but it's pleasant enough, and the service is quiet but efficacious. There is a semi-secret back room (a bit drafty in winter) that's positively romantic, with golden curtains, velvety couches, and a low table. There are even belly dancers on Friday nights, if that's your thing. Istanbul Café is expensive for New Haven—but it's in the same range as its upmarket neighbors around Crown and College. We hope this restaurant sticks around for years to come.

Ivy Noodle

Late hours and a great location can't redeem this careless Chinese soup house

3.5 Food
3.0 Feel

Chinese

Casual restaurant

$10 Price

Mon–Sat 11am–2am
Sun noon–11pm

Bar None
Credit cards Visa, MC
Reservations Not accepted
Veg-friendly

Broadway District
316 Elm St.
(203) 562-8800

The late hours and low prices remain distinct virtues here, but they're about the only ones. Oh, and the staff is still friendly and lively. There's no effort whatsoever at décor or atmosphere (other than the open-air kitchen itself, with its flames and clanging woks), which we find endemic to really, really good ethnic food. But once you taste the food here, you'll probably interpret that sparseness as an outgrowth of the same irritating carelessness that drives the kitchen.

The noodle soup is still utterly dissatisfying, with its frail broth and overcooked noodles; the fried wontons remain soggy; and most everything tastes too strongly of roasted garlic. Preparations, which include a lot of vegetarian versions, could hardly be blander—it seems as if virtually no seasoning is used at all, whether in the sautéeing of greens or the simmering of soups. Compare this to China Great Wall, where the exact same soups are fully flavored.

Here, adding lots of hot sauce or sliced hot peppers helps things, so don't forget to ask for some (and plenty of salt) when ordering take-out. But the consensus out there is that the noodle soup is just disgusting, with all the taste of warm dishwater with a distinct sheen of grease sitting on top. Curry soups are better; at least they have some strong, alluring flavor.

Strange but true: the Buffalo wings are actually pretty good, redolent of five-spice and oriental mystique. Go figure. It's the non-Chinese dish that gets the highest marks. This is what's elevated the Noodle's rating slightly in recent years. But still, why would you come here for Buffalo wings?

We stick by our longstanding claim: we'd rather go hungry in the wee hours than eat here.

Ixtapa Grille

6.4 *Food* **6.5** *Feel*

A basic, homey restaurant that's nothing more, or less, than slightly-above-average Tex-Mex

Mexican

Casual restaurant **$25** *Price*

Sun–Thu 11am–10pm
Fri–Sat 11am–11pm

Bar Beer, wine, liquor
Credit cards Visa, MC, AmEx
Reservations Accepted

Hamden
2547 Whitney Ave.
(203) 230-2586

There's certainly nothing wrong with Tex-Mex, especially the Tex-Mex that you find at Ixtapa Grille, a homey restaurant decorated in bright festive colors. The menu here runs through usual tacos, quesadillas, burritos, and enchiladas. There are fajitas and saucier meat, chicken, and garlicky shrimp dishes served with rice, tortillas, and a side of beans. Soupy salsa is ubiquitous. Ixtapa also offers a fairly inexpensive club steak, for those times when you crave a piece of meat.

Things here don't stray far beyond these staples. It's a shame, to us, considering that the owner, chef, and staff are all Mexican. The chef hails from Guadalajara, and we would give a lot to dip a spoon into a cooking pot from his home town rather than having yet another chimichanga.

This phenomenon is quite typical for local Mexican restaurants. It is why Californians and Texans tend to pine away for the more authentic offerings found in the border states. It's not that New England restaurants aren't run by Mexicans—they are. The crux of the matter seems to lie elsewhere. Is it that our produce is disheartening to Mexican restaurateurs? Is there a difficulty in sourcing authentic seasonings, perhaps? Or do they simply assume that the Connecticut dining public isn't interested in more regional fare?

The straight-ahead, moderately priced food menu is augmented by a prodigious drink list which includes approximately 20 margaritas and more than a dozen kinds of Mexican beer. The breadth of the margarita list reflects not just fruity flavors, but also some highly respectable tequilas. These liquid assets, combined with some charming booth seating and friendly service, make Ixtapa a good place to catch up with friends for a few drinks and conversation when it happens to be mealtime.

J Mart

What is it about Asian markets? They're like Disneyland for us.

Groceries, Seafood, Chinese   Market

www.jmartfood.com

Tue–Sun 10am–9pm	**Bar** None	**Ninth Square**
closed Mondays in summer only	**Credit cards** Visa, MC	15 Orange St.
	Veg-friendly	(203) 782-1234

We are always really excited when we stumble upon an Asian market. We live in a pretty integrated mixture of cultures, at least where food is concerned, yet we still find a sense of childlike wonderment at the exotic goods lying within stores like this. Right across from Thali, at the end of Orange Street, J Mart looks upscale and pretty.

The first thing to do is order a bubble milk tea in a fresh, fruity flavor like mango or kiwi. There's also a coffee bar; if caffeine isn't your thing, there are red bean smoothies. (Who doesn't love red bean?) A cold case holds cans of strange and alluring juices, like mangosteen, aloe vera, and pennywort. (Who doesn't love pennywort?) There's also lychee tea and a variety of honey drinks.

Follow the mariachi music to the back—you heard us right—and you'll find a Mexican staff (don't you love America?), some live fish, and sometimes lobster (call ahead to check). They cut and package scallops, shrimp, tripe, and some other proteins, but the selection isn't extensive by any means. We wouldn't depend on this place in a pinch; rather, come on a lazy afternoon to stock up on inspiring ingredients.

Vegetables are more abundant, like winter melon, bok choy, napa cabbage, and enormous, genetic mutant-radishes and carrots. They also carry homemade firm tofu. In the front, there are sake sets, sushi servingware, tchotchkes, and "lucky bamboo." It's too much fun.

J.P. Dempsey's

You'll find peanuts everywhere at this reasonable sports bar and grill

6.5 Food

7.0 Feel

American, Burgers

Bar

$30 Price

Sun–Thu 11:30am–11pm Fri–Sat 11:30am–12:30am	**Bar** Beer, wine, liquor **Credit cards** Visa, MC, AmEx Outdoor dining	**East Rock** 974 State St. (203) 624-5991

J.P. Dempsey's is your average American sports bar/pub/grill with slightly-above-average burger-and-bar food, an average beer selection, and an average crowd—a mix of locals and a few grad students. In the summer, it's a popular pit stop for bikers. The place is a standby when Modern is too crowded for pizza and you've just been to Christopher Martin's the night before.

Music is played at high volume here, so be ready. The burgers and wings, as at most such solid, local spots in New Haven, are the real thing, and deserve serious respect. Perhaps the bar's best feature is a few outdoor tables on the State Street sidewalk during summer.

The menu includes fried calamari tossed with hot cherry peppers and marinara; good boneless buffalo chicken tenders; and a starter called gusto bread, which is a half loaf of Italian bread topped with diced tomatoes, onions, prosciutto, and mozzarella, baked and served with the "famous" herb plum tomato sauce, and a fantastic example of that American classic, chocolate cake. Although the menu is quite expansive, including such single-eyebrow-raisers as a sole-and-cheddar-cheese sandwich, a cranberry-walnut chicken salad wrap, and penne primavera, we recommend sticking to the basics.

J.P. Dempsey's has a peculiar obsession with peanuts. A basket of peanuts is peremptorily deposited onto your table within moments of your arrival, and the bar's floor is entirely carpeted with a layer of peanut shells so thick that it's hard to tell the color underneath—in-your-face evidence that you, and thousands before and after you, will have to do the shelling yourself. If you're like us, peanuts are the sort of high-calorie, low-satisfaction food that you inadvertently eat in abundance if they're sitting there unattended for any appreciable length of time. Nonetheless, the novelty value may override any dietary fears. After all, how often do you get to experience the satisfying crunch of peanut shells underfoot?

Jalapeño Heaven

One of the most charming places in the area for
Tex-Mex—a little house on the side of the road

6.6 | **8.0**
Food | *Feel*

Mexican

Casual restaurant

$30
Price

www.jalapeno-heaven.com

Mon–Thu 11:30am–9pm
Fri–Sat 11:30am–10:30pm
Sun noon–9pm

Bar Beer, wine, liquor
Credit cards Visa, MC, AmEx
Reservations Not accepted
Date-friendly, kid-friendly, outdoor
dining

Branford
40 North Main St.
(203) 481-6759

In the wonderful world of suburban Tex-Mex, Jalapeño Heaven is the ultimate crowd-pleaser. These folks know what people want, and they know how to give it to them. The restaurant is in a cute little white house—it would certainly seem like your average two-family if not for the kitschy sign hung on the front porch.

Inside, the kitsch continues. You might be ushered up to a charming second floor, which feels like your aunt's living room fitted with all the standard Tex-Mex accoutrements. There's something about dining on this particular sort of Tex-Mex food in the upstairs of a little house that is completely unique, and uniquely wonderful. The porch, meanwhile, houses some tables in good weather as well—after all, there's nothing better than sipping margaritas outdoors on a sunny afternoon.

Service is smiley and endearing. Surprisingly, prices are somewhat high given the place's random suburban location along Route 1. But they're not through the roof. Here, as ever, jack cheese is one of the secrets to satisfying comfort food: the grilled quesadilla is filled with green chili peppers and…plenty of cheese. We like the white enchilada, which is filled with chicken and topped with a spicy cheese sauce. Accompanying beans and rice are flavorful, and desserts are good.

None of this food is particularly memorable. But Jalapeño Heaven is really about the experience, and it's worth it. You've got to be in that particular mood, and a margarita or two might do the trick.

Jasmine Thai Cart

A friendly, reliable cart that does the Thai-American classics on the cheap

6.8	8.0
Food	Feel

Thai

Take-out **$5**
Price

Mon–Fri 11am–3pm

Bar None
Credit cards None
Outdoor dining, veg-friendly

Audubon Arts District
Church St. between Grove St.
and Wall St.
No phone

Many people consider this weekdays-only Thai cart to be the best of its kind, though it's in area far from most of the others. It's more easily accessible from the downtown financial and government area, as well as from the southwestern end of the East Rock area, and it delivers on its promise of cheap, competently prepared Thai-American standards.

The menu rotates, but you can always choose two, three, or four items in combination. Perhaps in deference to the Atkins crowd, rice is an option, not a baseline. Our favorite things here are the tender "Thai BBQ chicken," which is curried and grilled right in front of your eyes— it's improved by hot sauce—and the good Panang curry, with chicken and green beans that still have some snap to them. Pad Thai has sweet noodles and an under-dose of egg and peanut; it's never the right choice (here or anywhere else). Pineapple fried rice is less sweet, and absorbs the flavors of the other dishes that you select, adding more flavor.

All of this is spooned into your Styrofoam box in prodigious portions. After a couple of dishes, the box is bursting with food; a $5 three-item combo (never mind the four-item version for less than a dollar more) easily feeds two. We find it hard to fathom, in fact, that any one person could complete the task of eating it all.

The service is polite, too, so it's not hard to see—given the value proposition and slightly monopolistic location—why this place has a loyal lunchtime following during the week.

Jeffrey's

Milford's grande dame is back, a bit better, and more informal and lunchy

7.4	7.5
Food	Feel

New American

Upmarket restaurant

$45
Price

www.jeffreysinmilford.com

Mon–Fri 11:30am–3:30pm, 5pm–9pm; Sat 11:30am–3:30pm, 5pm–10pm; Sun 3pm–8pm

Bar Beer, wine, liquor
Credit cards Visa, MC, AmEx
Reservations Accepted
Date-friendly, live music, outdoor dining

Milford
501 New Haven Ave.
(203) 878-1910

Jeffrey's shut down briefly in 2005 to reinvent itself as more informal and approachable. The new version places more of an emphasis on lunches and bistro-style dishes. Still in its white house on a nondescript stretch of Milford, the restaurant has always been traditional to the core; it's an elegant space with a nice view of marshland, and a gracious outdoor patio.

Still, the décor looks trapped in 1991, with its imperial white columns and hazy corporate art. Even the silverware is outdated, looking cloudy and cheap on the white linen. (That's the seamy underbelly of "traditional.") What's more, the music is usually a shrieking melodrama of vocalists like Andrea Bocelli and Celine Dion (which, by the way, feels totally anachronistic when you're looking out at an Andrew Wyeth vista). They couldn't appeal to the over-70 set any more than if Brian Dennehy were offering rides to his ageless planet, Antera.

The menu does seem to have mellowed out a bit; mains tend toward the mid-$20s, and more sandwiches are offered (many more during lunch, plus gargantuan wraps). Appetizers are pricey, but that seems appropriate given that they are so rich and involved, you won't be able to eat much more than a salad afterwards. In one, avocado, lobster, and brie form a triumvirate of indulgent flavors; another sees lobster and butternut squash fill homemade agnolotti in what might elsewhere be a main course.

Despite the over-the-top ingredients, it's clear that careful seasoning and balance still drive the kitchen. A salad of peppery arugula, expertly grilled calamari, and shaved pecorino is just dressed enough to let all the flavors sparkle. A clam-and-butternut soup avoids being cloying with a light and flavorful vegetable base, something we rarely see in this preparation.

But there are rampant problems with overcooking. Vegetables are limp, shriveled, and flavorless, and chicken (especially in a thin scallopine cut) is chalky. Maine crab cakes are full of finely shredded meat, and the outside is nice and crisp, but we miss the joy of crabby lumps. The Bearnaise in the dish is elegant, even if it gets lost in the shuffle.

It's all pretty good, even if dinner prices remain too high for such unsteady execution—dramatic view and soundtrack be damned. But, if the object of Jeffrey's revamp was to make itself more of a lunch destination, it has succeeded. Oh, and they still have that wonderful key lime tart.

Jimmies of Savin Rock

6.0	8.0
Food	Feel

A grand, classic seafooder sprawled right on the
West Haven waterfront

Seafood, American

Upmarket restaurant

$40
Price

www.jimmiesofsavinrock.com

Sun–Thu 11am–9:30pm	**Bar** Beer, wine, liquor	**West Haven**
Fri–Sat 11am–11pm	**Credit cards** Visa, MC	5 Rock St.
	Reservations Not accepted	(203) 934-3212
	Kid-friendly	

From the parking lot, the outside of Jimmies of Savin Rock looks like a
bunkered 1960s presidential retreat, with a vague Frank Lloyd Wright
lodge aesthetic. But cast your eyes seaward and you'll see expanses of
beach, boardwalk, park, gazebo.

Indoors, the cacophony of seaside themes comes together in Jacquard-
style prints that feature in the window dressings and carry over to the
dividing wall, where they meet the wood paneling. There are painted
glass portholes with multicolored, cartoonish fish, and large picture
windows that look out over expanses of the real sea (okay, the Sound).
There is even a lighthouse in view. Whether you're coming from
downtown New Haven or nearby in West Haven, Jimmies really is a trip.

The open-armed, what-can-I-get-you-sweetie style service has real
appeal. We think it's particularly appreciated by the older clientele (some
of which seem to have been customers since Jimmies first opened in
1925).

Start with a fresh, spicy Bloody Mary before moving on to the long and
involved menu, which lists a variety of surf-and-turf variations, elaborate
fish dishes, and so on. Jimmies is best known, though, for classics like hot
dogs, fried clams, fried shrimp, and lobster rolls.

Some claim that the place has gone downhill, food-wise, in recent
years. Perhaps, but the lobster roll is still a valuable relic. One can forget
how important the "roll" part is in a lobster roll, but not here: the bun is
wonderfully toasted and luxuriously buttery. Full platters feature french
fries of the cafeteria-style ruffled variety, along with absolutely enormous
quantities of (usually) fried seafood. It's hard to imagine how one person,
however large, could possibly take on the whole thing.

John Davenport's

Thankfully, it's escaped the wrath of the gods—but what about its customers?

5.2	7.0
Food	Feel

American

Upmarket restaurant

$65
Price

www.the19thfloor.com

Mon–Fri 6am–2pm, 5pm–10pm
Sun 10am–2pm, 5pm–10pm

Bar Beer, wine, liquor
Credit cards Visa, MC, AmEx
Reservations Accepted
Date-friendly

Chapel District
155 Temple St.
(203) 974-6737

Not terribly long ago, the gods smote the Omni Hotel's overblown restaurant with a fire that, thankfully, resulted in no casualties (save for minor injuries incurred by two brave firefighters). Perhaps in the attempt to heed what was, ostensibly, the pantheon's blazing warning to shape up or else, the kitchen reopened with a new executive chef and somewhat different menu.

But we fear the paltry atonement will prove unsatisfactory. The restaurant is still guilty of mundane flavors, execution problems, and the sort of fiscal customer-screwing that surely condemned it in the first place.

Known more commonly as "the restaurant at the Omni," John Davenport's is an amorphous, characterless thing—a mere stencil of every other mediocre hotel-chain restaurant. Unfortunately, given all the beautiful things that a place with the best view in town could be, the only operating philosophy here seems to be gouging its captive expense-account guests.

It's a shame, because the view from high above the Green is spectacular. As evening sets in—if you're lucky enough not to be seated next to fussy, view-obscuring institutional drapery—you can gaze upon twinkling lights of the many restaurants in town where you can get a good meal at a fair price.

Main courses still reach into the high-$20s, which would be fine if the food were up to the task. But these soups and salads are no better than those found at cheaper ground-floor eateries. Yes, the menu has gotten more interesting—for example, there's now a starter of polenta with poached egg, truffle, and spinach—but generally, the flavors are as insipid as ever, and the execution is spotty. A beef tenderloin is certainly tender enough, but it's little more than a vehicle for powerful Cambozola (a sort of hybrid of Gorgonzola and Camembert cheese). Combine the lack of beefy character with the 7-ounce portion and you're pretty much paying nearly $30 for cheese sauce.

And instead of allowing locals who don't feel like spending $65 a head for a mediocre dinner to simply order a cocktail and enjoy the view, the Omni reserves window seats for full meals only; the adjoining bar is just a windowless den that might as well be in a basement. What conceit! At this rate, every red moon and locust-sighting makes us jumpy.

JoJo's

A comfy, Bohemian-like coffeeshop that keeps its
denizens well-fed

Baked goods, Sandwiches

Café

www.cafejojo.com

Mon–Fri 7am–9pm	**Bar** None	**Upper Chapel Area**
Sat–Sun 9am–9pm	**Credit cards** Visa, MC, AmEx	1177 Chapel St.
	Outdoor dining, veg-friendly, Wi-Fi	(203) 785-8888

JoJo's is an eclectic place, located way up Chapel Street, far from its fair-trade and organic-touting competitors. It's a little more worn and torn around the edges—a little more Bohemian—than the mainstream coffeeshops downtown. Scuffed chairs and tiny tables are tossed this way and that by each successive student, writer, or teacher that sprawled out for a few hours to work. Red curtains do little to keep out the sun, which blazes its way onto laptop screens and sweaty shoulders through giant windows. Air conditioning would certainly help here, but then, keeping patrons thirsty is a great business plan.

The coffee is good and its presentations artful, but what really makes JoJo's exceptional is its tea selection. The amiable Shanghainese owner imports most of her teas from China. For her, tea is not only a drink, but an experience. As she pours steaming water into a personal pot generously stuffed with leaves, she explains the history behind your drink. Ask her about the Big Red Robe oolong, a smoky, earthy brew. Or the fresh, cleansing chrysanthemum. Or the delightfully grassy West Lake Dragon Well.

Not all of the staff is as knowledgeable, but, anyway, you may want your caffeine quick without prolix explanation. Iced teas come in a variety of flavors—blessedly unsweetened—the most basic being a blend with oolong, giving it a slight smokiness. It's one of the best iced teas we've ever had. Watermelon iced tea is really just watermelon juice, pips and pulp and all, but it's very refreshing on a hot day. There are also bubble teas, but they tend to be in the less exciting flavors out there, like mint, coconut, and raspberry.

JoJo's makes lovely pastries, too. The "granola bar" is a delicious mishmash of fruit and oats fused in a dense, cake-like square. The lemon tea biscuit is buttery—so buttery that its dense crumbs melt in your mouth, which could be a good or a bad thing, depending on your LDL levels. On the whole, the quality of pastries falls somewhere between normal coffeeshop and patisserie. Sandwiches are a cut above most coffeeshops' nosh, with 12-grain bread and ciabatta, brie, roasted vegetables, and a variety of deli meats.

We don't get why some people find JoJo's "pretentious." For us, this comfy spot is about as down to earth as it gets. But, then, some people find us pretentious, too.

Judies European Bakery

7.4 Food   **5.0** Feel

Friendlier service, but the same great breads and sandwiches

Baked goods, Sandwiches

Counter service   **$10** Price

www.judies.net

Mon–Fri 7am–3:30pm

Bar None
Credit cards Visa, MC, AmEx
Delivery, kid-friendly, veg-friendly

Audubon Arts District
63 Grove St.
(203) 777-6300

Yes, we spelled it correctly. The bakery omits the apostrophe from the possessive form (at least we assume it's possessive; it might just be a lot of Judies running the place). If you're driving down the street, it's easy to miss (right next to Ted's Cleaning on a busy part of Grove Street) and utterly lacking in décor or atmosphere (aside from the occasional indie-rock CD playing).

However, this unassuming space has a line out the door at lunch for a reason—they turn out some of the most inventive, consistently delicious light fare in town. Every day there's a new soup and panino, both of which are generally very good. They also have a consistent menu of both hot and cold sandwiches, salads, cookies and, now, breakfast sandwiches and even oatmeal. Of the hot pressed panini, we like the first-rate, well-seasoned sandwich of prosciutto, tomatoes, and mozzarella. Even the seasoned grilled chicken breast escapes the blandness typical of most such sandwiches.

Judies is also revered for its crusty, white peasant bread: long loaves that are treated to a generous sprinkling of sea salt on their crusts. It's an excuse to make soup every night, just to sop it up with this. They make a variety of other loaves during the week as well, including an English cheddar and a buttery brioche.

The staff has warmed up considerably since our last edition, and very friendly servers now take your order, your name, and bring you your food (in a weird, awkward metal basket if you're staying; in a bag if you're going). A large part of their business is catering, and they also deliver, but only if you have enough people to where it makes sense to add a $10 surcharge. (Say, seven people or more.)

Some of Yale's bigwigs lunch here when they're not entertaining at Zinc or Union League, so remember that loose lips sink ships—you never know who's sitting behind you.

Juna's Northern Style BBQ

8.4 Food
7.5 Feel

North Carolina-style barbecue is only one
temptation at this mobile smoker

Barbecue

Take-out **$10** Price

Mon–Sat noon–8pm

Bar None
Credit cards None
Kid-friendly, outdoor dining

North Haven
Near 452 Dixwell Ave.
(203) 508-4902

Normally, if we saw a large truck spewing out brown smoke on Dixwell
Avenue, we'd be pretty pissed. But this isn't exhaust: it's charcoal and
hickory, piping through the top of the pair of custom-made smokers
attached to the back of Juna's Northern Style BBQ. Juna refers to the
master smoker behind the wheel, Raphael Chestnut (it's Southern slang
for Junior).

Juna hails from North Carolina, which, while still decidedly Southern, is
at the Northern climate, thus the "Northern style." The menu tacked to
the truck's side isn't short—there's fried chicken wings, steak-and-cheese
sub, hamburgers, and so on—but you want the items that are labored
over: the ribs (for about $10, it includes three high-quality sides) and the
chopped barbecue (same price).

Chestnut shows up around 10am, starts up the smoker, throws the ribs
on and preps the truck. He opens at noon, and the ribs, after sitting on
the smoker for a luxurious five hours, finish at 3:30 or so. They're smoke-
ringed, soft in the center, crispy towards the outside—the effect that only
time and smoke can achieve.

Chopped barbecue—the other time-intensive item here—is from a hog
that's long-smoked for at least 10 hours before the pork quarters are
shredded and chopped into tiny pieces. It's a traditional North Carolina
technique, and you can pretty much taste the hickory in the excellent
pork; the result is very different from ribs, so if you haven't tried chopped
before, ask Chestnut for a sample.

Never pot-boiled, never seeing the inside of an oven, this could be
deemed true BBQ in the North or the South.

Kampai

The old-school, sentimental favorite for theatrical teppanyaki, with respectable sushi too

6.7	7.0
Food	Feel

Japanese

Upmarket restaurant

$40
Price

Mon–Thu 5pm–9:30pm; Fri–Sat
5pm–10:30pm; Sun 4pm–9pm

Bar Beer, wine, liquor
Credit cards Visa, MC, AmEx
Reservations Accepted

Branford
869 W. Main St.
(203) 481-4536

Kampai is the old guard of Benihana-style dining. This 20-year-old Branford restaurant has played benevolent host to innumerable birthdays, dates, and family celebrations, and it's showing its age. The service is kindly but unenergetic, and the hibachi room exudes dim, unflattering light, with a tired carpet that is actually starting to unravel. After two decades, the bloom is off the rose.

But as for an opera diva a little past her prime, when the curtain goes up, one thinks of nothing but the performance. The knife-flipping teppanyaki theatrics (everything is cooked on the grill in front of you, with great pomp and flair) at Kampai are as good as any, eliciting oohs and aahs aplenty—especially from the kids—and the chicken here is more succulent and tender than at the young upstart, Kumo.

Kampai also bests Kumo when it comes to sushi—especially the excellent yellowtail. Unlike "hibachi" restaurants where sushi is an afterthought, this one is actually two restaurants, with two separate rooms; when Kampai first opened, you couldn't get your sushi at Stop and Shop, and a serious, stand-alone sushi restaurant might not yet have survived in American suburbia.

Downstairs, teppanyaki takes center stage, but upstairs, past a kitschily charming koi pond, is a very well appointed dining room complete with tatami seating, where the sushi bar takes pride of place. Although there is little to say about the standard teppanyaki menu (soup, salad, fried rice, and a choice of meat), we have one uncharacteristic suggestion: get the chicken. The swordfish is dry, the steak tends toward chewy, and this is not ideal format for lobster. So go ahead and order the cheapest dinner option, then sit back and let yourself enjoy the show.

Kari

Welcoming, accessible Malaysian that loses
something in translation

Malaysian

Casual restaurant

Mon–Thu 11:30am–10pm
Fri–Sat 11:30am–11pm

Bar Beer, wine, liquor
Credit cards Visa, MC, AmEx
Reservations Accepted

Westville
1451 Whalley Ave.
(203) 389-1280

When it was Gunung Tahan, it was a well-kept secret, and as Kari, it's
catching on more. It's no wonder it took so long: it's Malaysian food in
suburbia, up Whalley Avenue past Westville (near Akasaka). It's easily
worth the trip just for the spectacular roti canai (rich, flaky, unfilled fried
bread served with a bowl of curry sauce with beef and potato). With
apologies to Bentara, this is easily the best roti in the area.

   The only really substantial thing that changed was ownership, but even
this was slight, as the new owners are related to the old ones. There are
flashes of brilliance, too, among mains; try to comb the menu for dishes
with exotic names and tastes. One star is the kari asam udang, an
entertaining mix of jumbo shrimp, tomato, okra, and tamarind in sour
curry sauce. Kari mee, a seafood soup of plump mussels, fish cake, and
squid is also satisfying, and deep.

   But the execution here isn't consistently good: satay is chewy and bland
except for its overly sweet-spicy sauce (but when is it ever truly
transcendent?), and sambal tofu is tasteless, except for its starchy,
overpowering peanut sauce. Everything comes with a prosaic house salad
of iceberg lettuce with ginger dressing or a gummy, bland chicken and
asparagus soup, diluting the overall experience. We realize Malaysian
cuisine, organically, comprises Indian, Chinese, and Thai elements (to
name a few), but the menu here feels opportunistically pan-Asian, instead
of authentically so.

   And why not make the atmosphere a little classier, a little more
romantic? The room is too brightly lit, as is all too common, with
Malaysian tourism posters hanging from the walls. The Unklung—large
Indo-Malay musical instruments played with a mallet—are interesting but
disappointingly silent. It seems Unklung players are hard to come by in
these parts. If the talent in the kitchen were transplanted wholesale from
this location to a cool downtown spot, and the menu pared down to the
authentic, we think this place would have unlimited potential. In the
meantime, though, why not check Kari out? It's still cheap, decent, and
fairly interesting.

Katz's Restaurant

We're glad to have it—but also close enough to
New York to do better

6.3 Food
7.0 Feel

American

Casual restaurant

$20 Price

www.katzsdelirestaurant.com

Daily 11am–8pm

Bar None
Credit cards Visa, MC, AmEx
Reservations Accepted
Kid-friendly

South Town Green
167 Orange St.
(203) 787-5289

Chapel District
21 Temple St.
(203) 787-5289

Woodbridge
1658 Litchfield Turnpike (Route
69)
(203) 389-5301

Katz's is a family of three. There's a location in Woodbridge, one on
Temple, and a strictly take-out joint on Orange (the latter two are in New
Haven proper). These are more or less the only places in greater New
Haven that fully realize the concept of a New York City deli, from top to
bottom.

Service is friendly and almost impossibly swift. To begin with, two bowls
are delivered quickly to every table, one bearing good cole slaw and the
other with two delicious versions of pickles: sour and half-sour. The
chocolate egg cream is well-balanced, with the proper level of light brown
froth to top the sweet blend of milk, soda water, and chocolate syrup.
Bagels are fresh and judiciously toasted, the cream cheese is excellent,
salmon is soft (but just average), and the overall effect quite pleasing.

Even better is the exemplary whitefish salad, with big and well textured
chunks of smoky fish mixed into a wonderfully executed cream sauce, and
studded with unusually large chunks of diced celery. But knishes are
disappointing, to say the least. They're dry, crackly, and underseasoned
within. Traditional Jewish meats—the pastrami, the corned beef, and so
on—do take center stage; the sandwiches are many inches thick (though
the meat is not up to the hot, rich, fatty New York standard).

Few things here will quite transport you to Katz's Delicatessen on
Houston Street, perhaps the most famous New York deli of them all
(suffice it to say that they're unaffiliated). In a town so close to New York,
it's nice to have something like this, but we could still do better.

KFC

A standard fast-food place that's open late but
loses the fast-food fried-chicken battle to Popeye's

4.5	2.0
Food	Feel

Southern

Counter service **$10**
Price

www.kfc.com

Sun–Thu 10:30am–midnight
Fri–Sat 10:30am–1am

Bar None
Credit cards Visa, MC, AmEx

Whalley
311 Whalley Ave.
(203) 777-5414

Hamden
1499 Dixwell Ave.
(203) 288-8186

Fair Haven
451 Foxon Blvd.
(203) 466-2556

Additional locations
and more features at
www.fearlesscritic.com

One of the most global of all fast-food chains, Kentucky Fried Chicken—whose self-conscious adoption of the "KFC" nickname was a shameless (if early) concession to the acronym frenzy of the 1990s (BK, IHOP, T2, and MIB were other notable commercial offenders)—serves chicken, mostly fried, with standard sides like mashed potatoes and gravy.

For KFC, the abbreviation was apparently an effort to de-emphasize the "fried." That movement culminated in the 2009 introduction of Kentucky Grilled Chicken, "a defining moment in our brand's storied history," according to KFC President Roger Eaton. (The corporate-speak never gets old.) While it's hard to complain about a fast-food chain's effort to offer a healthy option, we would submit that if you're looking to eat healthy, you shouldn't be here at all.

The original (and much better) chicken, fried, comes in original or extra crispy; we prefer the former, as it's more moist and subtle—if we can call immersing battered chicken in a vat of fat subtle. In fact, rather than the standard chicken, we even prefer the hot wings, the honey barbecue and spicy crispy strips, and the fried chicken sandwiches and their progeny.

The Colonel doesn't lie, but perhaps he misleads: while the fried chicken is famously dubbed "finger-lickin' good," we think that part of the finger-lickin' quality is due to the equally well-known greasiness of the batter. Keep in mind that Popeye's is better in the fried chicken fast-food category, and it's closer to downtown. However, as fast food goes, fried chicken is one of the better food categories; at least here you're not subject to thin grey slabs of meat or processed patties. It's real chicken. The other thing that KFC has going for it is the wonderfully late hours on weekends.

Koffee on Audubon

A cool coffeeshop where grad students work on dissertations and flirtations

Baked goods, Sandwiches

Café

www.koffeekoffee.com

Mon–Fri 7am–8pm	**Bar** None	**Audubon Arts District**
Sat 8am–8pm	**Credit cards** None	104 Audubon St.
Sun 9am–6pm	Veg-friendly, Wi-Fi	(203) 562-5454

In the dog-eat-dog world of New Haven coffee, Koffee is a force to be reckoned with. Now completely dissociated in ownership from Koffee Too and Bru (formerly Moka), this original, less crowded, infinitely cooler Koffee branch is in a nook on tiny Audubon Street, conveniently and cleverly situated right on the way from East Rock to Yale.

Predictably, it's absolutely dominated by grad students, but it's everything you want in a coffee shop. It may be the best place in town to chill for hours over a laptop and latte. Couches in the front room give way to chairs and tables in a sunny atrium with bright red brick. Behind that, there's a pleasant backyard. Its grass and trees make the whole setting seem almost pastoral. The music is good, especially if you like Nirvana and its progeny.

The coffee itself is also good, plenty dark. There's food, but it's pretty unspectacular. Offerings like a tomato and onion quiche, cappuccino muffins, and cheesecake brownies are generally average, but better than the bland, microwaved pasta dishes, which aren't even that cheap.

But few people come here to eat. Koffee is a particularly good place to go alone—with a book, with a computer, with a little pad of paper. In fact, most customers are solo, and Wi-Fi wireless Internet connections even allow them to surf for Internet porn while getting their caffeine fix. The only downside to this place: picture yourself trying to sift through pages of Hegel or write the great American novel while simultaneously listening to the insufferable English Ph.D. candidate try, repeatedly and unsuccessfully, to hit on the cool Forestry girl. You're guaranteed to witness pickup attempts—so just try to tune it out (or, if you prefer, throw your hat into the ring).

Kudeta

Think you can handle this hideous décor—plus pad Thai and crabmeat quesadillas?

4.7	6.5
Food	Feel

Pan-Asian

Upmarket restaurant

$50
Price

www.kudetanewhaven.com

Mon–Thu 11:30am–2:30pm, 4pm–10:30pm; Fri–Sat 11:30am–2:30pm, 4pm–midnight; Sun 2pm–10pm

Bar Beer, wine, liquor
Credit cards Visa, MC, AmEx
Reservations Accepted
Outdoor dining

Chapel District
27 Temple St.
(203) 562-8844

Kudeta (pronounced "Coup d'Etat") is easily the weirdest, trippiest restaurant in New Haven. The colors of the lights change every few seconds. Sweeping curtains and high ceilings make the place feel a bit—actually, a lot—like a tacky nightclub. So treat it like one, and start off by consuming as many Mai Tais as possible in rapid succession; this might be the best (legal) way to prepare yourself for a meal here.

The menu is just as weird and trippy as the interior design. For starters, it's way too big and disjointed to be good. Is this restaurant supposed to focus on Indonesian cuisine? Malaysian? Singaporean? It's not clear, and the waitperson that we asked at our last visit couldn't shed any light on the issue, either. Could people really want to come sit in the twilight zone of restaurants and have "curried shrimp lo mein" for dinner?

Maki, in the nominally Japanese area of the menu, are interesting, to put it charitably. Many are wrapped with something other than seaweed, like avocado or eel. Spicy tuna rolls are done in the chopped-fish style, but they haven't generally tasted very fresh. But you know better than to come to a psychedelic pan-Asian restaurant for sushi, right?

Among dishes that we assume we're meant to interpret as Malaysian, roti canai are exceptionally deep fried and greasily delicious. Chicken rendang really absorbs the flavor of snow peas; the result is pretty decent flavors and reasonably moist chicken, but the dish is still a dumbed-down version of what it could be; there's little spice and even less acidity.

Peking duck is an amazing waste of almost $50, and a horrible dish called "dry shredded beef," which rings in at more than $20, is described on the menu as follows: "served in a hot pepper sauce with steamed baby bok choy and scallion pancakes." It turned out, at a recent visit, that the beef was actually dessert-sweet, battered and incompetently deep-fried, like a tough, chewy, yet simultaneously soggy version of Chinese-American sweet-and-sour pork. This was one of the worst things we've tasted in a New Haven restaurant in the past several years. Hilariously, it didn't even come with the advertised scallion pancake. When we asked our server why, she explained that "oh, we're no longer doing that," with no apology and no offer to exchange it.

This was not an isolated incident. It's indicative of a general service problem at Kudeta: the waitstaff seems to behave like...well, like they're cocktail servers at a garish nightclub where the lights change every few seconds. Sometimes the writing is on the wall.

Kumo

This Japanese cooking is all about fire and flash, but that's all

6.8	7.0
Food	Feel

Japanese

Upmarket restaurant

$40
Price

www.kumojapaneserestaurant.com

Mon–Thu 11am–3pm, 4:30pm–
10:30pm; Fri–Sat 11am–3pm,
4:30pm–11pm; Sun noon–
10pm

Bar Beer, wine, liquor
Credit cards Visa, MC, AmEx
Reservations Accepted
Date-friendly, kid-friendly

Hamden
218 Skiff St.
(203) 281-3166

South Town Green
7 Elm St.
(203) 562-6688

Kumo, whose original location remains in Hamden, seems a strange replacement for State Street's equally strange Polo Grille. For one thing, the kid-friendly fire and flash of teppanyaki cooking has long appealed more to the suburban family crowd than to the edge-of-Ninth-Square scenesters. At least this incarnation of "eatertainment" isn't Benihana; Kumo sheds Benihana's cookie-cutter style for something chic and local. Both branches feature glowing hardwood floors and gleaming grills, some of which accommodate up to 20 people. There is also tatami seating, but we favor seats up close to the action.

If you're not here for the show, you're missing the point entirely. Although the sushi is decent (and very well priced at dinnertime, when—in the New Haven location—Kumo loses its substantial business lunch crowd and needs a lure), you're better off elsewhere for a sushi date. Tuna is disappointing (as it so often is), yet the mackerel and ikura are pleasing. There's no need to suppress a strong sushi craving if it comes: feel free to supplement your teppanyaki with oily standbys.

Kumo does very average teppanyaki: soup that is watery and hardly worth the trouble; salad whose ginger dressing is flavorful and abundant; and a schedule of protein combinations, along with the ubiquitous teppanyaki fried rice, with the egg impressively juggled, flipped, and cracked on the edge of a spatula as it succumbs to gravity. The fiery onion volcano, another favorite, is executed with similar flair and prowess.

This cooking style tends to render all things equal, treated to the same soy-sauce-and-butter basting. By virtue of texture, steak and shrimp are the best choices. Cooked fish is a disappointment; it gives us that not-so-fresh feeling. Chicken is bland, and frozen lobster tails barbecued at high heat while doused in soy sauce are hardly worth the premium.

Ultimately, these restaurants are about fun, not fine dining. There is something inherently festive about the genre, which makes it great for big groups and small children—or just your inner child. We defy you to go the entire evening without at least one involuntary gasp. If you can, check your pulse, because you are probably dead.

La Carreta

Hole-in-the-wall Mexican food that's better than
some of its carts

Mexican

Counter service

$10
Price

Mon–Fri 10:30am–9pm
Sat 11am–9pm
Sun 11am–8pm

Bar None
Credit cards None

East Rock
930 State St.
(203) 624-2442

This is the stationary headquarters for what many people will recognize as
a reliable Tex-Mex food cart near them. There are about four scattered
throughout the city at any given hour, most notably in the Medical Area.
On this part of State Street, it's in strange company amid neighborly
Italian restaurants and Dolci, the weirdly conceived dessert bar and
lounge.

Clean and well-lit, with vivid tablecloths depicting a (we suppose)
Mexican vista, La Carreta offers few, simple dishes, which are depicted
helpfully overhead (or superfluously—do you need a picture of tacos to
help guide you?). Strangely for a place with an all-Mexican staff, these
tacos do come on flour tortillas instead of corn, unless ordered crispy.

Among fillings, chicken is well seasoned but dry, and the beef suffers
from this chewiness as well. The pork, however, is beautiful, shredded
and tender and very...porky. We love pork so much that we are thinking
of instituting "pork" as the next exclamation of delight, like "Aw man,
that is *pork*, yo!" What else can be so sweet, so smoky, so juicy and
redolent of earth and fire at once? Where were we? Ah, yes—La Carreta.

The enchiladas are executed just fine, but we wish the tomatillo had
more zing to it. In general, we get the feeling, from staring into the open
kitchen that reminds us so much of real Mexican kitchens, that La Carreta
is gringo-ing things up a bit for New Haven. Everything, from tacos to
chimichangas to burritos, come with rice and beans, sour cream,
shredded cheese, lettuce, and a watery guacamole. Hot sauce is not really
hot. Even our grandmothers would ask for some Tapatío to supplement it.

We're more excited to come across one of their carts and wouldn't
make a special trip here. West Haven's Mexican scene has got it beat
easily on execution and authenticity. But they do have Mexican Coke,
which is always a plus.

La Cocinita

Some of New Haven's most authentic Mexican, if you order right

8.3 Food   **5.5** Feel

Mexican   Counter service   **$15** Price

Daily 8am–10pm

Bar None
Credit cards Visa, MC, AmEx

Upper Chapel Area
177 Park St.
(203) 772-1020

At this small eatery serving traditional Mexican cuisine on Park Street, there is no menu; you order what the older woman from Tlaxcala is cooking that day, which usually includes a special and a small selection of basics. As its name suggests, La Cocinita is really more of a kitchen than a restaurant.

Portions are huge, and prices are dirt-cheap. Although the kitchen is more than capable of dishing out stuff you'd find in Mexico—and they do it with the daily specials from the pot—some dishes are still made only dutifully, to cater to local demands. For instance, they serve unexciting oversized burritos, which are filled with more rice than meat, albeit with nice chile and cilantro flavors that are balanced out by creamy queso oaxaqueño, a sort of Mexican string cheese, and a zingy tomatillo.

La Cocinita does better when it stays true to its traditions. Chicken enchiladas are great with a coating of mole rojo, which is spicy and flavorful (if a bit oily) and a dusting of queso fresco. The rice with which they are served is a little overcooked and mushy. You should jump for joy if you find, among the specials, lamb mixiote—cheap cuts of lamb cooked in a bag in water for three hours with a variety of dried chilies; it comes out tender (the fat melts in your mouth) and packed with flavor. We'd be more enthusiastic about this place if the tortillas were handmade, or just less dry, but baby steps, New Haven, baby steps. We are, however, impressed by the tres leches cake, which is delicate and sweet, and manages to avoid over-sogginess—a feat not many places can pull off.

The dining room has a divey, down-home charm. There are about ten tables encircling the open kitchen. There really isn't much in the way of ambiance here, save for the sarapes and sombreros hanging from the golden yellow-and-adobe-colored walls, and the Jarritos sodas on display in back. But this is the only way to eat good Mexican.

We often hear people say they want better Mexican in New Haven; let's start by increasing the demand. Come here often, and order whatever the cook, herself, would eat.

La Cuisine

A café and market that's a cut above the others

7.1 Food | **8.0** Feel

Baked goods, Sandwiches

Counter service

$15 Price

www.lacuisine.net

Tue–Sun 8am–3pm

Bar None
Credit cards Visa, MC, AmEx
Kid-friendly, veg-friendly

Branford
750 E. Main St.
(203) 488-7779

La Cuisine's era of catering ended in late 2008, when the business inaugurated its new café-market space. The new La Cuisine is an expanded, gussied-up version of the original from 25 years ago. It still follows the same model: breakfast and lunch only, and breakfast all day on weekends.

The breakfast menu leans on eggs and omelettes; there's an above-grade eggs Benedict occasionally. The "Breakfast Buddy" is like a healthier Egg McMuffin, and the whole-grain pancakes are thick, hearty, and accompanied by real maple syrup. But the café's real strength lies in its baked goods. Sticky buns and chocolate croissants are both stellar, while the golden raisin scone—flaky, pillowy, and butter-packed—puts the many scone-shaped baked goods sold elsewhere to shame. The too-dense baguettes are less impressive.

Lunch options range from sandwiches and salads to lentil cakes and fried chicken. The excellent deep-fried pickles are a rare treat. There's a rotating barbecue special of the day, but a few new sandwich and salad ideas would be worthwhile. Right now, you've got your standards, but everything's tweaked a little: the roasted turkey, for example, has cilantro mayo and a curry onion bread. The fine Cuban sandwich is made with slow-roasted pork shoulder—not just the usual cold cuts—and is nicely spiced.

The dining space isn't unfriendly, but it feels large and empty. That's especially true of the main market area, which has tables lined up single-file around the wall. Look for a table in the more pleasant sunroom that pops out of the building's front. The market shelves are stocked with artisanal gourmet goods, and there's a large glass display case of take-home prepared foods. You can also purchase a single complete meal to go for under $15; options change daily and are available hot in the late afternoon. The lineup's pretty New American: an apricot-stuffed pork loin with garlic roasted potatoes one day, citrus-marinated shrimp with lime-and-peanut-accented basmati rice the next.

It's nice to not have to wait for a catered event to sample some of La Cuisine's great food.

Lalibela

We'll take slightly-above-average Ethiopian food any day

7.7	8.0
Food	Feel

Ethiopian

Casual restaurant

$25
Price

www.lalibelarestaurant.com

Mon–Thu noon–2pm, 5pm–10pm; Fri noon–2pm, 5pm–11pm; Sat 5pm–11pm; Sun 5pm–10pm

Bar Beer, wine, liquor
Credit cards Visa, MC, AmEx
Reservations Accepted
Date-friendly, veg-friendly

Chapel District
176 Temple St.
(203) 789-1232

Ethopian grub is mama's food, hearty and tactile, often (in our experience) prepared by a jovial, round Ethiopian lady. Although Lalibela's less-than-homey interior exudes sterility more than African spice, love downright radiates from the delicious kitfo (Ethopian-style steak tartare). Uncooked and cool to the palate, Lalibela's kitfo is both beefy and refined, although less oily, and thus a tad less flavorful, than many iterations. Injera, the light and spongy sourdough flatbread distinctive of the region, is served with every dish, underneath the food and in rolls along the edges. Although it comes a bit too cool, Lalibela's injera is perky and amusing, so tear off a piece and take the plunge.

Most of the food is tasty—it's gotten less oily of late—and provides a refreshing break from Chapel Street Thai and Howe Street Indian. It's not exactly haute cuisine; don't expect African with fancy European-inspired flair. Here, sauces are simpler, heavier, and darker. Flavors are bold and deep. Texture is sometimes the driving force, as in the recommended shuro, made with a rich chickpea puree. The rewarding yater fitfit, dried peas cooked with garlic and ginger root mixed with injera and garnished with hot peppers, is served chilled. Don't miss the split peas or the excellent braised zucchini—the large chunks of vegetation are awkward yet rich.

Neither tenderness nor moisture abound in the yebeg wat, lamb cooked with garlic, onions, and the ubiquitous Ethopian spice blend berbere—although Ethiopian lamb is often scrumptious, Lalibela's is disappointing. Some dishes lack sufficient salt—like the spicy lentils—but offerings are vegetarian-friendly and the price is right, especially at the lunchtime all-you-can-eat buffet.

We recommend dining at a traditional bongo-esque table for a more authentic (or at least kinda random) experience. The room's squarish, unremarkable layout sits in stark contrast to the food's fortitude. Friendly faces and genuineness on the part of the staff go a long way toward creating good feelings, yet the food can take longer to arrive than you expect. As a purveyor of cheap lunch or a casual, not-too-expensive grad-student dinner, Lalibela is a vibrant competitor.

Landsdowne Bar & Grille

4.2 Food **6.0** Feel

A better sports bar than restaurant, with more televisions than a Circuit City

American

Bar **$30** Price

www.lansdownect.com

Mon–Fri 11am–10pm
Sat 10am–10pm
Sun 10am–10pm brunch until
1pm Sat and Sun

Bar Beer, wine, liquor
Credit cards Visa, MC, AmEx
Live music, Wi-Fi

Chapel District
179 Crown St.
(203) 285-3939

Let's get one thing straight: this is a sports bar. It's not a grill (or even a "grille"), and it's not really a restaurant. The main focus here is the game—whatever game. You'll have no choice but to do so; there's a flat-screen TV at every booth, and several over the bar, tilted at every angle. Even if you step outside to smoke, you can watch through the giant "windows" that open up to the street. But we can't figure out where Landsdowne stands: it's the name of the street along which Boston's Fenway Park sits, yet there's both Yankee and Red Sox paraphernalia on the walls.

We'll let that sink in.

Landsdowne is a huge space, a pub with sterile, squeaky clean, catalogue-y wood furnishings. There's none of the character of a Richter's or an Anchor—and not just because it's new, but also because it just doesn't feel New Haven-y. It's a place that was made to pack in corporate-sponsored parties, with plastic banners and balloons. Indeed, the beer selection here is all boring mass-produced standards, with few on tap.

Given this, the food is just what you'd expect. It's gone way past sports-bar serviceable into hospital territory. Buffalo chicken egg rolls come in a soup of blue cheese that can't overpower their strong canned-chicken flavor. A more traditional pub favorite, shepherd's pie, is drastically underseasoned, with what tastes like boxed instant mashed potatoes on top. The inside has a mix of lamb and beef, but why? In this execution, you can't taste any lamb. Or beef. Fish and chips are properly battered, but they, too, come totally undersalted, managing to be flavorless even with their Heinz malt vinegar. Onion rings taste fine, but the breading separates from the onion completely. Even the burger, the simple and reliable burger, is botched. Order it cooked one degree less than you want it; the bourbon peppercorn version is strong and overly char-flavored.

Landsdowne can't seem to decide if it wants to be a cheap kegger or a nice sports bar—any more than it can choose a baseball team. What seems obvious, either way, is that it's not the place for pub grub. Skip this place and head for Prime 16.

Le Petit Café

Amazingly, Branford's legendary French prix-fixe
just gets better and better

9.6 Food

10 Feel

French

Upmarket restaurant

$65 Price

www.lepetitcafe.net

Wed, Thu, Sun 5pm–8:45pm
call ahead if later
Fri–Sat 6pm–8pm seating 1,
8:30pm–10:30pm seating 2

Bar Beer, wine, liquor
Credit cards Visa, MC, AmEx
Reservations Essential
Date-friendly, good wines

Branford
225 Montowese St.
(203) 483-9791

Never before in the history of *The Menu* and the *Fearless Critic* series has a restaurant won our #1 ranking for three consecutive editions. But records are made to be broken, and Branford's intimate, unpretentious French bistro, with its quirky mirrors and warm lighting, has done it.

Dinner at Le Petit Café is prix fixe, but this menu is the furthest thing from fixed. It is a culinary journey that begins daily at the break of dawn, when chef-owner Roy Ip shows up for work and gets the stocks and sauces going. Every neuron in Chef Ip's brain, every drop of his emotional energy, focuses on the everyday miracle of what that night's lucky few will eat for dinner. He designs menus, orders ingredients, and watches over his staff with the tough love and obsessive genius of an artist; the simple process of cooking and serving, eating and drinking, is exalted.

As befits a kitchen this serious, the seasonal menu changes frequently. Lately we've encountered delicate, bright white Alaskan halibut filet, which pushes the French envelope with New England sweet corn, shiitake mushrooms, and roasted piquillo coulis; unusually well balanced escargot with Roquefort and cognac sauce on puff pastry, a difficult dish that requires expert hands like these; and a subtle chestnut soup for fall. We wish Berkshire pork tenderloin were cooked a touch less, but the five-spice duck breast, as ever, is an explosion of flavor and tenderness. Lobster bisque is still some of the best we've seen, as is the rich, prodigiously portioned duck cassoulet.

The magic is also in the details, from the flecks of truffle that punctuate the ramekin of butter that's offered with slices of crackly baguette to the house-made fruit jam that accompanies a tender duck leg confit. Peaches and brandied cherries have alternatively studded the country-style pork pâté, elevating it to something even greater. And sensational french fries sit humbly beside one of Connecticut's best steaks au poivre. Desserts sparkle, too; our favorite, of late, has been what we refer to as "burnt caramel mousse." And the wine list is just as a bistro's should be: a small, carefully chosen, reasonably priced selection of Bordeaux and Burgundy bottles well paired with the food.

Le Petit Café's artfully crafted bistro décor would feel at home along a Parisian back alley—except for the reasonable prices and the completely unassuming, open-armed attitude of Chef Ip and his staff. Reserve well in advance for one of the two nightly seatings—there are only 10 per week. Like the sauce that reduces into more than the sum of its ingredients, Le Petit Café is more than just a restaurant. To dine here is to transcend the mere notions of eating and drinking; it is to engage with the spirit.

Lena's

A little bistro that makes everything in house—a formidable breakfast foe for The Pantry

8.2 | 8.5
Food | Feel

Sandwiches, Baked goods

Casual restaurant

$15
Price

www.lenascafeandconfections.com

Mon, Wed–Fri 8am–6pm
Sat–Sun 8:30am–3pm brunch
only

Bar Beer, wine
Credit cards Visa, MC, AmEx
Reservations Accepted
Kid-friendly, veg-friendly, Wi-Fi

Westville
873 Whalley Ave.
(203) 397-5885

This charming breakfast and lunch spot emits warmth from its roasted squash-colored walls. A large window brings in sunlight, while further back, the restaurant gives way to casual café. There's even a nook with a couch, a well-stocked magazine table, and a friendly "give one, take one" book swap—a great place to take advantage of Lena's free Wi-Fi.

They do a brisk trade at lunch, much of this in carry-out. Remarkably, despite the high volume, everything is made to order. Panini are strong here, with enormous portions sandwiched between chewy, crusty, well-grilled bread. In a move we rarely see, steak is even made to order for each "Bistecca." The "Gold Coast" combines a turkey club with pesto mayonnaise for a winning flavor combination; the underlying bacon flavor is excellent.

When it comes to salads, expect fresh greens as a base, but not all toppings are equal. "Jessica's Salad" successfully riffs on the classic fruit/cheese/candied nut combo, with apples, mandarin oranges, dried cranberries, Gorgonzola, and candied pecans. Less successful is the Mediterranean Salad. The chicken is grilled nicely, but the eggplant remains soggy and unflavored, and the tinny dressing doesn't really bring together the olives, roasted red peppers, red onions, and cucumbers.

Nearly all the sweets here are made in-house. Cookies are a steal; the pignoli is lightly flavored with almond extract and has a texture somewhere between cookie and meringue, and is topped with tasty pine nuts. Macaroons mixed with granola have a satisfying earthiness, while still maintaining a lightness unusual in a macaroon. Cannoli are filled to order, with unusually good ricotta filling hand-piped into your choice of plain or chocolate-coated shells. In a move that's not trying for authenticity but fun, sides are then dipped into rainbow sprinkles. Cakes and pies in the case are not made on site (except for the apple pie), and the Snickers pie can't live up to the satisfying homemade flavor of the cookies and cannoli.

Bottles of wine are available (nothing exciting), as well as the standard domestic and imported beers. Their breakfast is well-loved by those in the know, who moon over corned beef hash made from, you know, *real* corned beef and not the reheated dog food so often seen. Warm maple syrup, espresso, and even challah French toast? That's worth skipping The Pantry for.

Lenny's Indian Head Inn

Oysters and beers on the back porch overlooking
the marsh: it's all that's good about New England

8.0 Food

9.0 Feel

Seafood, American

Casual restaurant

$30 Price

www.lennysnow.com

Daily 11:30am–10pm

Bar Beer, wine, liquor
Credit cards Visa, MC
Reservations Not accepted
Date-friendly, kid-friendly, outdoor
dining

Branford
205 S. Montowese St.
(203) 488-1500

Lenny's is everything that's wonderful about this part of the world. A log
cabin on a salt marsh. Summer beers on the back porch with briny oysters
on the half shell. Good, spicy Bloodies. Fresh steamed lobsters on
precarious trays overflowing with melted butter, corn on the cob, cole
slaw, and lobster bibs without even an ounce of intentional kitsch. Rhode
Island-style clam chowder as it should be: sweet, silky, and savory, with
salty oyster crackers in little clear plastic packets. A loud suburban buzz,
with an equal mix of young families, wrinkled old couples, local college
kids, and the occasional Yalie. Aside from that lovely patio and a "pub
room," there's also a newly constructed dining room, which has a slightly
more upmarket feel—at least, as uppity as it can be when everyone is
slurping down oysters and drinking cheap beer.

Seafood is king here, and portions are generally huge. Order oysters
raw, clams and lobster steamed, and everything else fried. Baked or
broiled white fish has never been New England's forte, so stay away from
it here. French fries also tend to underperform. Truly, though, their best
work is the outstandingly tender and delicious fried soft-shell crab
sandwich, not to be missed when it's in season. Keep in mind that true
vegetarians will have little to bite on.

We do have a couple of gripes. First, the service is murderously slow
and inattentive. Don't ever make the mistake of presuming that anyone's
aware of your table, your order, or your existence. Second, the beautiful
outdoor back porch is inexplicably closed on many a beautiful, sunny
evening; and it's flat-out closed until so late in the spring that most
students leave for vacation before they even get a chance to have oysters
on the marsh. There are even some bizarre menu restrictions on outdoor
eating. But whatever you do, you need to make your way out here
anyway. Anyone without a place for Lenny's in her heart should move
back to the West Coast.

Leon's

Old-school Italian-American with drab décor and a
lovely view of the water

6.9	8.5
Food	Feel

Italian

Upmarket restaurant

$45
Price

www.leonsofnewhaven.com

Mon–Sat 11:30am–2:30pm,
5pm–10:30pm
Sun 4pm–10:30pm

Bar Beer, wine, liquor
Credit cards Visa, MC, AmEx
Reservations Accepted
Kid-friendly, live music, outdoor
dining

Long Wharf
500 Long Wharf Dr.
(203) 562-5366

When old-school cheeseball Rusty Scupper finally cashed in, another old-school cheeseball scooted across the freeway and put down stakes. Ousted by the modern monolith IKEA, Leon's had been carrying on the wicker-basket Chianti tradition of Italian-American cooking since 1938.

Even here, Leon's still manages to look like an exhibit at the Museum for the History of Dining, but less charmingly so. The room is separated rather oddly into two tiers of tables by drab, mustard-colored curtains. The furniture is old and chipping, but in a cheap cafeteria way, not a charming vintage one.

But oh, what a view! Disregarding the industrial plant across the way, it's, well, the ocean. Even on ugly days, it's still nice to see it—this is one of the very few places in New Haven proper with a water view, raising the feel level here considerably. When doesn't a pelican preening on a post *not* make things taste better?

The Italian-American standards are well represented here, and vary in consistency from course to course. Appetizers are stronger, such as their popular, well-seasoned pane cotto—rich and deep, one of the better versions in town—and oysters "alla Audi." The gentle brine of the oysters shines through, mixing nicely with smoked bacon, red pepper, leeks and Cognac cream sauce.

Things get rocky from there. Shrimp have a slightly fishy, not-so-fresh flavor with little sweetness, and come over linguine that's a little overcooked. Orecchiette, on the other hand—when available—are whimsically toothsome (as only "little ears" could be), and their broccoli rabe and sausage are as good as ever—though we can't understand what possessed them to boast "Andy Boy" brand rabe on their menu. Don't they carry that at the Stop & Shop?

Pounding, dredging, and frying veal escalopes without overcooking them is a delicate business, and here, it's not always pulled off. In one such prep, the flavors of artichoke hearts, garlic, and tomato all bleed together in a vaguely tart, perky cacophony, instead of a symphony of individual, fresh notes.

The wine list is self-loathing, favoring mass produced, blah American wines for the exciting, beautifully made and surprisingly inexpensive wines with which Italy brims. Leon's isn't much better than the predictable, disappointing Italian-American all over New Haven, but it does have that view.

Libby's Italian Pastry Shop

It's tradition...but does that mean it's good?

Baked goods   Counter service

www.libbyscookies.com

Wed–Mon 11:30am–9pm
Hours vary by location

Bar None
Credit cards Visa, MC
Kid-friendly, veg-friendly

Wooster Square Area
139 Wooster St.
(203) 772-0380

North Haven
310 Washington Ave.
(203) 234-2530

Libby's cookies are within reach no matter where you live. No, Libby's hasn't become a mega-chain overnight (there are only two locations—one on Wooster Street and one in North Haven). But, you can order cookies online from their website, and they'll deliver them to you anywhere in the US.

And they will satisfy your sweet tooth. The Wooster location is populated by a genuine Italian-American crowd (along with a smattering of locals and tourists fresh from a Pepe's or Sally's pilgrimage). The crowd is lively and festive, and the attitude strikes a perfect balance between brusque and welcoming.

There are some idiosyncrasies here, like an espresso bar that only opens at 5pm each day (the North Haven location, however, turns out espresso all day long). And as a purveyor of Italian baked goods, Libby's Pastry Shop is overrated. But maybe the actual quality of the pastry isn't really the point. With all of this ambience, and such a location, you'll go home with a smile even if you could have gotten more delicate cakes and cookies elsewhere.

Still, wouldn't it be great if the Italian pastry actually measured up? Instead, everything is too sugary. The cannoli don't have that wonderful ricotta that should ideally tend toward the savory rather than the sweet. We think a good tiramisù should be moist and rummy (after all, the word roughly translates as "throw me on my arse," a nod to the grogginess of this classic dessert); here, though, it is sadly lacking in libation.

Libby's fills a particular niche, and we have no doubt that it will continue to do well. It's a classic. But what can we say? We're food reviewers, and nostalgia gets us only so far. If you are a cannoli connoisseur, we hope you'll appreciate our candor.

Liberry

Chilly sweets in a chilly atmosphere: good for
beating the summertime heat

Ice cream   Counter service

Daily noon–10pm   **Bar** None   **Chapel District**
                         Credit cards Visa, MC   45 High St.
                         Kid-friendly, veg-friendly   (203) 503-0717

Liberry opened in fall 2008, in the old Tasti D-Lite space, without a
name—and, for that matter, without much of a plan to garner customer
loyalty or generate profit. Barren, whitewashed walls; two benches in
orthogonal formation; and clean, steel machinery lining the back wall
create an atmosphere that's bleak, to say the least. Whizzing yogurt
machines breaking the oppressive silence are the only sign that the place
is open for business. No one staffs the counter—at least until you walk in,
that is, and the manager emerges from the depths, as if on cue from Big
Brother, greeting you (if you can call it that) with icy laconicism.

This dialectic is perhaps manifest, too, in the product itself, a fusion of
the raw sweetness and acidity of natural yogurt and highly processed,
technologized artificiality. Or at least one assumes, given that a small
allegedly has less than 100 calories, but costs $3.50. And that's without
toppings!

Someone has clearly exerted serious molecular gastronomical genius in
fabricating this impossibly light fro-chemical, necessitating its exorbitant
price. Start with a large, and choose one, two, or three toppings—which
might range from fresh fruits to chocolate candies, nuts to mochi—and
you might just be headed into the $7 range.

Fortunately, that $7 now buys you more in terms of ambiance and
service. After a brief hiatus (and change in management), Liberry now has
colorful signs displaying its flavor offerings on its walls, friendlier servers
and, it seems, a business model. It sources its soft-serve from The Lite
Choice, a northeastern franchise touting an "all-natural" product without
preservatives or artificial ingredients. The yogurt has the same refreshing
tartness as before, and another machine ekes out soft serve, if that's more
your speed.

Of course, place still has that awful name and the blindingly white
interior that isn't exactly inviting. Sometimes, progress moves as slow as
soft-serve. At least your belly will, too.

Liuzzi's Cheese Shop

The cheese selection is now rivaled by Caseus, but they've got great Italian meats, too

Groceries, Italian

Market

www.liuzzicheese.com

Mon–Sat 8:30am–6pm

Bar None
Credit cards Visa, MC, AmEx
Veg-friendly

North Haven
322 State St.
(203) 248-4356

Liuzzi's carries more than just cheese, but if you love cheese, you may never leave this store. On an average day, there are more than 350 varieties, including the homemade caciocavallo, a gourd-shaped cheese that is rarely seen in these parts. In the event of a Hollywood-epic-style natural disaster, we hope to be caught here, where every inch of shelf space bears closely stacked Italian specialties, including delightful jewel-toned soda bottles. The deli section is crammed with enormous plates of antipasti, and the butcher's counter displays perfectly marbled Angus beef alongside outsized coils of sausage, and imported prosciutto and mortadella.

In addition to the meat counter, deli, and specialty dry goods, there's a lunchtime offering of sandwiches, soups, and stuffed breads that change daily, and some prepared foods to heat up for dinner. Come Christmas, there's an authentic array of panettone.

The Liuzzi's story could make for classic cinema. The family hails from Puglia, at the heel of the boot of Italy, where the original Domenico Liuzzi had a dairy farm. Domenico had a son, Pasquale, who worked beside his father, learning the art of making ricotta, among other local cheeses. Pasquale begat another Domenico, and that Domenico had his own Pasquale, who dreamt of coming to America.

And so he did, in 1960, bringing with him generations of artisanal expertise. After 19 years of managing someone else's cheese factory, he decided to go into business with his brother.

Although the store also sells a wide range of imports, to this day Liuzzi's makes cheese in-house, including sublime ricotta and "basket cheese," a deliciously fresh farmer's cheese that one could eat for breakfast or dessert. This is also the place to get fresh mozzarella, along with some stern advice about how it should be treated. ("Cut it into thin slices. Very thin. Do you have a mandoline?")

Louis' Lunch

Was the hamburger invented here more than 100 years ago? We believe it

8.0	**9.0**
Food	Feel

Burgers

Counter service

$10
Price

www.louislunch.com

Tue–Wed 11am–4pm
Thu–Sat noon–2am

Bar None
Credit cards None

Chapel District
263 Crown St.
(203) 562-5507

Whether or not Louis Lassen—the great-grandfather of the current owner of Louis' Lunch—actually invented the hamburger more than a century ago is a question that we can't claim the authority to answer. So we'll just sign onto the program: you bet!

Louis' is an absolute gem. It's New Haven—and small-town America—in all its blustery glory. The menu and opening hours are exercises in guesswork. Do they have egg creams? Do they serve a sliced steak sandwich? Who knows. Maybe they do if they like you.

What they do always have is good (if arbitrarily too well done on certain days) hamburgers, made with high-quality beef that's ground in-house daily. The patties are grilled vertically on ancient cast-iron machines designed to allow the flame to broil both sides, and then served on toasted white bread. They're slathered with what tastes like Cheez Whiz, and accompanied by a wedge of tomato and a slice of onion. When it's available, absolutely top-notch potato salad (even better with a dash of salt) and homemade pies bolster the formidable supporting cast.

If you're a rookie, you'll need a primer: First, bring cash. When it's your turn, unhesitatingly yell out your order, indicating the number of hamburgers, followed by "cheese" for cheeseburgers, and then "works" if you want tomato and onion. "Plain" means just the meat and bread. "Rare" is something that we strongly recommend. For example, "two cheese works rare." And don't try to ask for ketchup or mustard, unless you want to get thrown out. (Really.) The order will be scrawled on a piece of paper and will be ready in anywhere from two minutes to half an hour (and please don't ask).

You can take it all to go, or—if you're lucky—plop down at one of the few age-old brown wooden tables with chairs that look more like church pews. Some people don't appreciate the brusque attitude or the inconvenience (they tend to close for a week in January and before Easter, and again for the whole month of August). But Louis' stance is: take it or leave it. Hey, they're offering a unique New Haven experience, and it's an unforgettable one.

Luce

There are wines here that will change your life, even if the food won't: budget appropriately

7.2 Food | **8.0** Feel

Italian

Upmarket restaurant

$55 Price

www.ristoranteluce.net

Mon–Fri 11:30am–2pm, 5pm–9pm
Sat 5pm–10pm
Sun 2pm–7:30pm

Bar Beer, wine, liquor
Credit cards Visa, MC, AmEx
Reservations Recommended
Date-friendly, good wines, outdoor dining

Hamden
2987 Whitney Ave.
(203) 230-0228

This wine menu still makes us swoon, with its huge cellar of verticals from Italian giants like Gaja (with 4 decades of vintages) and a Mastroberardino Taurasi Riserva from the legendary vintage of 1968. What's more, these bottles come at extremely reasonable prices, many of them not different from what you would pay at auction—or at the wonderful Mt. Carmel wine store next door. The wines by the glass are another story; we wouldn't even cook with these wines. On the other hand, diners who skip the sensational bottle list deserve this kind of abuse.

In fact, Luce's name is an homage to the famed Super-Tuscan wine (a joint venture between Marchesi de' Frescobaldi and Robert Mondavi). Even the restaurant's font and color scheme are mighty similar to the Luce wine label, although we're told there's no official affiliation. (Previously, this restaurant was called Raffaello's, and strangely—after half a decade—there are still Raffaello's logos if you look closely.) The vibe inside is warm and dimly lit, although the décor (specifically, the upholstery) is the only thing that seems to be from the early '90s and *isn't* faring so well. The space is divided into romantic, cozy nooks—perfect for staring into the eyes of a brick red '97 Barbaresco.

The menu font makes every dish look like a Mario Puzo title. Indeed, these are the very dishes we've seen Italian-American characters eating in movies—comfort food. The soft, slightly sweet homemade gnocchi are still some of Luce's best work. "Ucelletti Ticinesi," veal rolled with spinach, sun-dried tomatoes, pine nuts, and Gorgonzola, is also a longtime favorite. The cognac sauce has enormous wild mushroom pieces. The veal is tender, and the flavors are there, though the dish needs a lot more salt. The "Orecchiette Siciliana" (pasta "ears") are delightfully firm, and they're tossed with a fairly standard sauce of crumbles of sausage (good) and bright red peppers (less well integrated).

But the food's really just there to offset the flavors in the wine. Oh, that wine.

Lucibello's Pastry

The war between Libby's and Lucibello's lovers is moot: both are overly sweet and monotonous

Baked goods

Take-out

Mon, Wed–Sat 8:30am–6pm Sun 8:30am–2pm	**Bar** None **Credit cards** Visa, MC, AmEx Kid-friendly, veg-friendly	**Fair Haven** 935 Grand Ave. (203) 562-4083

Let's get this out of the way: Lucibello's archrival, Libby's Italian Bakery, isn't that good either. But where Libby's is centrally located between ristoranti on Wooster Street, Lucibello is out of the way for most—at least enough to require a special trip, which it doesn't merit.

The bakery has that older-than-the-hills look, like it was once a tuxedo and dress shop around the time Archie was taking Veronica to the prom. Cases of pastries and beautiful (but pretty traditional-looking) cakes seem diminished in the vast space. There are numerous Italian cookies—butter, wafer, and pignoli—and a case full of cannoli and many Italian takes on French pastries. Each looks like a piece of heaven in its white paper doily.

But there's a severe letdown once the pastry hits your tongue. For one thing, everything is kept much too cold. Cream puffs are almost icy, and their shells taste stale, devoid of any eggy lightness. The cream inside tastes exactly like the confected filling of a cheap donut (which we admit can be delicious, but only in a donut, and especially when it's too early or too late to have good judgment).

Italian pastries here suffer from exactly the same industrial taste. Pignoli are covered in petrol-y pine nuts, but the flavor here is overwhelmingly dominated by almond extract. Cannoli have a little touch of cinnamon, but the shell is so stale and hard, like an old graham cracker, with none of the delicate brittleness of a true shell. And if that filling has anything to do with ricotta, it's undetectable to us. "Pasticciotti" are ungainly, thick hand-sized pies, filled with your choice of chocolate or vanilla. The vanilla tastes, again, exactly like a custard-filled donut. And the crust is impossibly thick and hard.

Maybe we're just not fans of Italian pastries, which, especially in America, tend to come off as overstarched, powdered-sugar-based, and extract-flavored, like mass-produced sweets. Give us the savory ricotta of a real Sicilian cannolo over this any day.

Lulu's

A neighborhood coffeehouse that's an oasis of old-time relaxation...remember relaxation?

Baked goods, Sandwiches

Café

www.lulublend.com

Mon 7:30am–1pm
Tue–Fri 7:30am–3pm
Sat–Sun 8:30am–3pm

Bar None
Credit cards None
Outdoor dining

East Rock
49 Cottage St.
(203) 785-9218

We once lauded Lulu's only for being the nobler choice against a megacorporate coffee chain. Today, with so many Starbucks branches shutting down, the wave seems to be ebbing, and the remaining coffee competition now pits David against David.

As more and more cafés open up, each one adding to its allure amenities such as free Wi-Fi, ample outlets for laptops, organic, free-trade coffee, you would think Lulu's would be throwing its hat into the ring. Oh, they're responding to the coffeehouse trend, all right, but not the way you'd think. They've banned computers.

You heard us.

Not only is there no free Wi-Fi (or even paid-for Wi-Fi), but the official stance is "no computers."

Hey, from a business position, it makes sense: people with computers tend to sip on one iced coffee for 2-3 hours at a time, maybe nibbling on one pastry. But one might argue: do they also ban really enthralling books, fantastic conversationalists, or anything else that might keep patrons there all afternoon?

Despite the draconian nature of this rule, we respect it. Who wants to live in a world where there is no respite from the text-messaging-at-mealtime, work-obsessed American lifestyle? Sure, the coffee here is merely okay (if roasted especially for Lulu), and the espresso pulls are too long. The sandwiches and pastries are decent, but these and espresso drinks tend to get pricey. But the service is genuine and the neighborhood feeling is cute and certainly cozy; there aren't many places to sit, with some tables inside, some outside. The place is also only open from the early morning to the mid-afternoon at the latest. You can either see all of this as an inconvenience, or as an opportunity to adapt.

L'Orcio

One of the best, most authentic Italian restaurants in town, in a gracious old State Street house

8.2 Food
8.5 Feel

Italian

Upmarket restaurant

$45 Price

www.lorcio.com

Tue–Thu 11:30am–2pm, 5:30pm–9:30pm; Fri 11:30am–2pm, 5:30pm–10:30pm; Sat 5:30pm–10:30pm; Sun 5pm–9pm

Bar Beer, wine, liquor
Credit cards Visa, MC, AmEx
Reservations Accepted
Date-friendly, good wines, kid-friendly, outdoor dining, veg-friendly

East Rock
806 State St.
(203) 777-6670

L'Orcio is the best Italian restaurant in New Haven. We say this not so much as praise for L'Orcio, but as a sad fact of the city: for all the Italian-American fare available here, we're sorely lacking in *authentic* Italian food. L'Orcio is one of the few places in all of greater New Haven that actually tries to focus on dishes that might actually be served in Italy—and one of the fewer that generally succeed at it.

This ambitious two-floored Italian restaurant in a gracious old house on State Street was opened by a former Italian parquet floormaker and his American wife. It's a cute story; the couple met when she was studying abroad, then moved together to New Haven from Italy to open L'Orcio. The friendly, homey service is just what you'd expect given the family nature of the place.

L'Orcio's recipes come from all over Italy, but at least they're from Italy. The pasta here is perhaps the firmest in town, which brings a huge smile to our faces. The Italian spellings are all correct (a rarity in the Elm City), and creations are generally about as authentic as can be found anywhere in the area. While the cooking is not quite breathtaking, the fact that L'Orcio is so much more than your standard Italian-American goes a long way in this city.

Pastas take center stage here. Bucatini all'amatriciana is a classic Roman red-sauce dish of long, tubular pasta with onions, red pepper, and pancetta; here, the bucatini are just about as al dente as we've seen outside of Italy, adding immensely to their texture. While the sauce is not so smoothly reduced, the flavor is still a savory delight, benefiting immensely from a generous helping of pancetta. Meat courses are much more expensive but follow in the trend of creative authenticity; herb-rubbed lamb chops, for instance, are served with a lamb stock reduction, a dish with true Northern sensibilities. Desserts are great here, especially chocolate charlotte, whose mousse has an airy texture like meringue.

The townhouse entrance and hand-painted sign out over State Street hint at more coziness than you'll actually find inside (which is pretty bare-bones; tables are spaced widely, making the room seem empty even when it isn't). The garden out back, however, is a very nice place to have dinner during the summer. It's amazing to us that, even as New Haveners' palates have evolved, cookie-cutter Italian-American restaurants are continuing to open downtown. More of them should follow L'Orcio's lead and delve into the real cuisine of Italy.

Machu Picchu

New Haven's best Peruvian food (we'd say that
even if Inka weren't closed)

8.3 Food
7.5 Feel

Peruvian, Latin American

Casual restaurant

$25 Price

Mon, Wed, Thu, Sun 10am–
10pm
Fri–Sat 10am–11pm

Bar BYO
Credit cards Visa, MC
Reservations Accepted
Delivery, kid-friendly

Fair Haven
101 Farren Ave.
(203) 467-7671

Machu Picchu is careful not to reveal the whole recipe for their pollo a la
brasa (Peruvian-style roasted chicken). We've gotten different answers
from each staff member, but we didn't get the sense that it was for lack
of knowing; whatever is in the rub, one taste and it's clear that the chefs
at Machu Picchu know what they are doing (and are smart enough not to
tell the whole world). The chef once even referred to the restaurant as a
pollería, sending clear signals about the focus of the menu.

The star here is plump, moist chicken, which is slowly roasted on a coal-
fired spit and tastes wonderfully of cumin and cilantro. They serve a whole
bird atop a heaping portion of french fries (which seem to be of the
frozen variety) with a salad (which is definitely of the iceberg lettuce
variety), easily feeding a family of four. It is an absurdly sweet deal, even
despite the blah salad and fries. Wash it all down with chicha morada, a
sweet nectar made out of clove and fruit juice, colored by purple corn.

Machu Picchu also serves other authentic Peruvian dishes at relatively
low prices, like the pescado sudado (pollack steamed with tomatoes,
garlic, and onions—which we like), and papas a la huancaina (a stew of
sliced potatoes coated in a mysterious yellow sauce redolent of cheese—
which just are kind of so-so).

For the less adventurous, the chicken is a safe choice, and still totally
rewarding (which is rarely the case when you're choosing chicken). Most
dishes are served with rice, and all come with crispy cancha (huge toasted
corn kernels) for snacking upon.

The restaurant is located in what appears to have once been a house,
so it is entirely unassuming from the outside, and its industrial
neighborhood is less than charming. The plain interior has a few authentic
touches, like colorful textiles and paintings of the great Incan city. More
telling are the Peruvians working there, and the seemingly entirely Latino
clientele. The large space is perfect for a big family quinceañera or
bautismo celebration. Service is friendly and decidedly relaxed.

To discover Machu Picchu, central New Haven denizens must make the
almost Andean trek out to Fair Haven. But, even if they told us that
chicken recipe, we'd still come eat here.

Main Garden

Mediocre, large-portioned Chinese take-out
peddled primarily to budget-conscious students

3.4	3.0
Food	Feel

Chinese

Counter service

$10
Price

www.maingarden.com

Mon–Thu noon–1am
Fri noon–1:30am
Sat 12:30pm–1:30am
Sun 12:30pm–12:30am

Bar None
Credit cards Visa, MC
Delivery

Broadway District
376 Elm St.
(203) 777-3747

You can count on a basic take-out Chinese place to adhere to a particular
format, whether it's downtown, up Dixwell Avenue, in a nearby suburb,
or even in another city. Main Garden, though, has a particular undergrad
following amidst a sea of choices, which must be in large part due to
location, given that its standard take-out Chinese fare is not particularly
different from competitors'—that is to say, it's not very good. At least
prices are quite low, and service is known for being good, friendly, and
accommodating, especially to students.

Food-wise, you probably know what to expect. Dishes have names like
"Happy Family" (jumbo shrimp, sliced pork, beef, chicken, lobster meat,
and Chinese vegetables), and their content consists largely of the standard
permutations of Chinese take-out-joint ingredients. Steamed broccoli with
garlic sauce and white rice is representative of the banal vegetarian
offerings.

There are, however, a few quirkier combinations. Fong wan gai, for
example, is a chicken breast stuffed with roast pork, dipped in egg batter,
fried, and topped with broccoli, snow peas, baby corn, and bamboo
shoots.

The place is one of the best late-night Chinese options in town (it easily
beats the terrible Ivy Noodle, just off Broadway). But during the day, there
are much better Chinese options in town—for example, the much more
authentic China Great Wall. Cheap Chinese joints like Main Garden need
to learn that their antiquated menus are fast losing their appeal as the
American public is introduced to real Chinese food, and we hope that this
restaurant and its contemporaries will someday adjust to the times and
start preparing dishes with more interesting flavors and less brown-sauce
goo.

Mamoun's

Mesopotamian comfort food served until 3am,
every night of the year

6.7	8.0
Food	Feel

Middle Eastern

Casual restaurant

$10
Price

www.mamounsfalafel.com

Daily 11am–3am

Bar BYO
Credit cards None
Reservations Accepted
Veg-friendly, Wi-Fi

Upper Chapel Area
85 Howe St.
(203) 562-8444

A New Haven institution, Mamoun's is the sleepless student's dream
come true, serving inexpensive falafel sandwiches and other Middle
Eastern snacks in a comfortable, dark room that's open until 3am, 365
days a year. Go for a break; go to study (though the poor lighting, which
adds to the atmosphere, does limit the visibility); go if you've got the late-
night munchies. Go because it's seriously cheap ($2.80 buys you a filling
falafel). But don't expect much.

The restaurant arrived in 1977, the second in a small chain of falafel
places. The mothership opened on MacDougal Street in New York's West
Village, near NYU, in 1971, and it's no small feat to have done so well, for
so long, in that location.

Back in New Haven, the falafel is totally inconsistent—sometimes it's
over-fried to inedibility, sometimes it's moist and appropriately textured.
Neither the hummus nor baba ghanoush are distinctive, with the latter
missing a lot of that alluring smoky eggplant flavor.

We do like the grape leaves, although the tabbouleh packs an
unsettlingly serious parsley punch. Of the lamb sandwiches, we find the
shish kebab more satisfying than the somewhat dry kefta. The sandwiches
are a better deal than platters, and are served in cute wire holders—but
beware the makdoos, featuring extremely bitter eggplant and heavy-
handed seasoning.

Mango iced tea is smooth and refreshing, drawing a bit of desert oasis
into the otherwise pungent fare. The tamarind tea, with its unique sweet-
tart pairing of astringent tannins and relentless fruitiness, goes well with
Mamoun's baklava (which tastes very good but falls apart, its three layers
not cohesive).

Although not exactly prom date material, Mamoun's exudes a casually
romantic vibe. An old black-and-white photo of Mamoun himself hangs
on the wall behind the cash register, inspiring an inexplicable sense of
hushed awe. Mamoun has achieved cult status. He's open for business
and there for us all, tonight and forever.

Marco Polo Pizza

Awards or not, who would settle for these gummy pies when they could shuffle over to Bar?

4.1	6.5
Food	Feel

Pizza, Italian

Counter service

$20
Price

www.marcopolonewhaven.com

Daily 11am–10pm

Bar BYO
Credit cards Visa, MC, AmEx
Delivery, kid-friendly, veg-friendly, Wi-Fi

Ninth Square
55 Crown St.
(203) 776-2726

The first thing you see on the Marco Polo menu are these impressive-sounding awards: "Winner, Best Gourmet Pizza, 2008 North American Pizza Show"; "Winner, Best Pizza, New York Metropolitan Area, 2007 World Pizza Championships, Salsamaggiore, Italy."

Ex-squeeze us? Bacon powder? Did they just say that the judges in a worldwide pizza competition voted Marco Polo—*your* humble, Ninth Square pizzeria—the best in the New York metro area? This sounds too good to be true. What's more, the parent company's website is called worldsbestpizza.net. Boy, they're really taking these awards to heart.

The Pizza Championships, though? They're for acrobatic skill. Tossing, dancing, playing around with dough. They don't actually judge the taste, the execution. The North American Pizza Show? It's a trade show for pizza and ice cream. (Just in case, you know, you were imagining judges like Mario Batali and Wolfgang Puck wiping Marco Polo's sauce off their faces and grinning with glee.)

Marco Polo's journey to the shores of the Orient was less involved that our search to validate this award. Why did we bother going through all this trouble? Because this pie s-t-i-n-k-s. It's chewy in all the wrong ways, with a bready base topped with bland sauce and rubbery cheese. Every bite is a regret. And don't even get us started on the slices that sit around all afternoon, waiting to be reheated.

For all its awards, you'd think the staff would have recommended the Parma Salad Pizza or the Chicken Marsala Pizza ("featured on Food Network 2005 World Pizza Championship"). Instead, they told us the Chicken Parm was the best in the house, but a worse pie can hardly be imagined, with soggy chicken bits clotted all over the top of an already repugnant pie.

If you do decide to eat here, the ambience does little to sell the experience. At the counter, unsavory-looking pizzas lie flaccid under heat lamps. Booths are empty beneath large black and white stills from the '40s. Meanwhile, around the corner at Bar, serious people are cooking great dough, not playing with it.

Marius

Don't bother with the confusing food, just enjoy
people-watching from the patio

2.6	5.5
Food	Feel

American

Upmarket restaurant

$55
Price

Mon 5pm–11pm; Tue–Thu
11am–11pm; Fri 11am–
midnight; Sat 5pm–midnight

Bar Beer, wine, liquor
Credit cards Visa, MC, AmEx
Reservations Accepted
Live music, outdoor dining

Chapel District
196 Crown St.
(203) 772-3792

Marius is plagued by a culinary identity crisis. One look at the menu, and
it's clear that Marius does not focus on Italian cuisine, as waiters have
suggested to us, nor Italian/South American fusion, as some online dining
guides purport. In fact, Marius does not seem to focus on anything,
including taste.

The restaurant is named for the first and second century B.C.E. general-
turned-politician, yet has an interior that is not remotely Roman. In fact,
the only decorating inspiration we can come up with is carnival funhouse.
The back room has primary-colored doors on its ceiling, interspersed with
hanging baskets. Kitsch is littered throughout the interior: a painting of a
swordsman on one wall, bulky wavy mirrors on another; two massive
black stone lions in one room, a huge Egyptian sarcophagus in another.
The outdoor patio lined with palm-grass roof huts and tiki torches seals
the deal for us: we are never, ever doing acid here.

The menu is as confused as the ambience. Appetizers run the global
gamut from a Mayan shrimp cocktail to New Zealand mussels in coconut
broth to panko-crusted fried mozzarella. If Italian truly is the focus here,
even a simple, common Italian-American dish like broccoli rabe and
sausage can't pass muster; it's oily, undersalted, and overcooked. Other
catastrophes include a Peruvian fish chowder of gummy squid and
octopus; mealy, fishy mussels; and undercooked potatoes and carrots.
Mains add insult to injury, like tagliatelle with mushy chicken, asparagus,
and sun-dried tomatoes topped with waxy, untoasted pine nuts. The dish
doesn't even *look* appealing. But what generous portions!

If you even get that far, a dessert of baked plantain with vanilla ice
cream (another globe-trotter) is cloying and unpleasant. The thick stripes
of honey layering the plantain boat cannot conceal the starchiness of the
unripe fruit.

With mains priced as high as $45, Marius's prices are wholly
unreasonable for something this unenjoyable and confusing.

Marjolaine

Frustrating hours can't keep loyalists away from
this favored bakery

Baked goods

Counter service

Tue–Fri 8am–6pm
Sat 8am–5pm
Sun 8am–noon

Bar None
Credit cards Visa, MC
Kid-friendly, veg-friendly

East Rock
961 State St.
(203) 789-8589

Once, we showed up in the early afternoon to find a paper tacked to the door that said the bakery was "closed due to power outage." This, as the little white Christmas lights twinkled, somehow, in the window. We cupped our eyes to the window, nearly weeping at the prospect of all those pretty little cupcakes and tarts going to seed in non-working cases. If, you know, there really was a power outage.

Also, those little white lights would be much more useful if the bakery didn't close before it ever got dark enough to appreciate them. Do we sound upset that they never seem to be open when we want them to be? We are. And it's a total, unabashed, grinning compliment.

The croissants are as close to the real thing as you get in New Haven. Though perhaps a little too greasy, they are properly flaky on the outside and soft on the inside. We are a bit addicted to the broccoli and cheese croissants. Cinnamon rolls, only available on Sundays, have texture, somewhere between soft and not gloppy. The brioche is also quite good, but varies depending on who's baking them and how long they've been out of the oven. The smaller, denser brioches are best, and they're not too sweet. Tea breads are flavorful and moist, with a little cinnamon kick to them.

Marjolaine also does a version of brownies which have a layer of hazelnut cream topped with a layer of chocolate icing *on top* of the brownie. Obviously you cannot eat the whole thing in one sitting, but it's a nice treat to share. Adorable almond-and-chocolate mice make popular gifts. We find the wide variety of cookies to be less transcendent than other items.

You can order at the counter and nibble at one of few tables, but the décor is less than inviting. Most people take out or sit on benches outside. This beloved bakery has been here about 20 years, so it really has the feeling of a place that is what it is; it does what it does well and doesn't worry about the rest. If they'd just stay open a little later (or more often), and improve the coffee and tea (Bigelow? What is this, a Travelodge lobby?), this could become the best bakery in New Haven. Actually, it might already be.

Martin's

6.7 **9.0**
Food *Feel*

The view is so great, it almost makes the food taste less uneven...almost

Seafood, American

Upmarket restaurant

$50
Price

www.martinsriversidenh.com

Daily 11:30am–midnight

Bar Beer, wine, liquor
Credit cards Visa, MC, AmEx
Reservations Accepted
Date-friendly, good wines,
kid-friendly, outdoor dining

Fair Haven
3-5 Clifton St.
(203) 466-2200

This waterside restaurant was formerly known as Stillwater American Bistro, but it's got new owners and a new vibe, with a totally updated interior that sports blue-and-white-striped upholstery and a faux fireplace. It kind of evokes a throwback nautical theme, in a Disney's Yacht Club sort of way. The outdoor terrace is right on the river, where you can sip good, spicy Bloodies and watch people fishing on the Quinnipiac river and jet skiing under the bridge. This would be a perfect Sunday brunch spot—but strangely, there's no brunch (except an omelette on the lunch menu).

Though the atmosphere pretty much guarantees Martin's will do good business in beautiful weather, the food needs to rise to the standard of the setting. There are some highlights: Blue Point oysters might come improperly shucked, with bits of shell in their mangled bodies, but their flavor, anyway, is fresh and clean. And like Stillwater, Martin's has a way with fried calamari (you'd better, 'round these parts), which are brilliantly textured. They could use more cherry peppers, though, and better integration from the parmesan, which is buried underneath.

Panini are competent, no more. Their bread is buttery, with decent tomato and mozzarella, but prosciutto within has come overcooked, exchanging the delicate, lightly fatty flavor for a tougher, saltier one. (It's a strange practice, in America, cooking prosciutto crudo—in Italy, the cured ham would only be added raw to a sandwich or pizza.) Always opt for sweet potato fries, which, though undersalted, are unusually crispy for the genre.

A lobster crêpe, however, is a total disaster. Its overcooked claw meat is so tough that it takes arm muscles to cut through with a fork; you wind up savaging the crêpe. Its sauce reminds us of "French" dressing, and for some inexplicable reason, it's paired with basmati rice. Fish specials are competently cooked—tilapia tends to be fresh and moist—but an accompanying risotto has come spectacularly overcooked, as if it were a baked rice-and-cheese casserole with cream-of-mushroom soup dumped on top. This was clearly prepared by somebody who had no idea—*no idea*—how to make risotto; it's an insult to the recipe.

If you get stuck with it anyway, don't worry: just look out at that beautiful, rippling river and breathe deeply. Everything will be all right.

McDonald's

It may be the evil empire, but the food actually tastes good—and nobody's willing to admit it

5.6 Food
3.0 Feel

American, Burgers

Counter service

$10 Price

www.mcdonalds.com

24 hours

Bar None
Credit cards Visa, MC, AmEx
Kid-friendly, outdoor dining

Whalley
250 Whalley Ave.
(203) 865-9195

Fair Haven
308 Ferry St.
(203) 776-1464

Medical Area
280 Kimberly Ave.
(203) 776-1126

Additional locations
and more features at
www.fearlesscritic.com

We were as disturbed as others by the revelations in *Fast Food Nation* and the hilarious *Super Size Me*, but we're food critics, not doctors or urban planners. And while fast food is almost never particularly good for you, McDonald's actually offers more reasonably sized sandwiches than most chains, and the introduction of the salads and elimination of the Super Size (whether or not it was in response to the movie) were steps in the right direction. Even the most caloric offerings on the McDonald's menu tend to have significantly fewer calories than their equivalents at other chains.

The french fries, by consensus, are some of the best around, well crisped and well sized. Consider also the cheeseburger, perhaps this chain's true crowning achievement, still elegant after fifty years: The beef patty has real (if processed) flavor, the American cheese is usually melted just as it should be, and the ketchup-rehydrated onion taste somehow just works. Close your eyes, open your mind, and eat (sparingly). And the Big Mac is timelessly tempting. But you probably already know better than to order the Filet o' Fish, or any of the salads that have been creeping onto the menu and bringing down this chain's food rating.

Angry readers will complain, as they always do, about McDonald's being rated higher in the food category than this or that local place. They always do. What can we say? We know it's not pretty. But what keeps customers coming back to McDonald's every day is not just the excellent value proposition but also the fact that some of the food actually tastes good. And nobody's willing to admit it.

Medical Area Food Carts

Take-out

Bar None
Credit cards None
Kid-friendly, veg-friendly

Medical Area
Near the corner of Cedar
St. and York St.
No phone

The doctors know about it. (The doctors always know.)

The medical students know about it. (After all, they're studying to be doctors.)

Even the occasional recuperating patient can be seen wandering around the corner of Cedar and York Streets in hospital-issue pajamas, sampling epicurean delights encased in handy Styrofoam.

But what's amazing to us is how few people tend to walk the few short blocks from downtown—even if it means traversing the unsightly Air Rights Garage and the terminus of the ill-fated Route 34 extension—to sample from the eclectic collection of around 20 food carts that cluster around the Yale-New Haven Hospital and Yale Medical School for several lunchtime hours each weekday (and sometimes on weekends, too).

It's a shame, because they represent the best midday value in New Haven. There are similar clusters downtown and near the School of Management, but the incredible variety of the Med School cluster warrants a special trip. These take-out carts are so diverse and user-friendly, in fact, that they conjure up images of Singaporean hawker centers, street-food bazaars where low overhead and fierce competition translates into spectacular eats at bargain prices. Sadly, that genre is now threatened, even in Asia, by the global fast-food chains.

While New Haven's version of the hawker center may not quite be up to Singaporean culinary standards, it is particularly heartening to see this kind of good capitalism alive even in America. It is all too rare to stumble upon a micro-economy that's driven not by manipulative marketing, but rather by simple, honest supply-and-demand forces.

To wit: virtually every dish costs between $4-5, and the cooks often know their customers (a lot of whom, you'll quickly notice, are clad in scrubs). On a given day, you might see a nerdy surgeon chatting in Spanish with a Mexican cook; a beefy West Haven Italian-American carefully discussing salad dressing ingredients with a nurse while assembling three sausage-and-pepper sandwiches simultaneously; or a med student asking a hospital maintenance worker about whether to go for noodles or sushi.

Happily, there's also a ready-made place to sit down and eat your lunch: the Medical School cafeteria just inside Harkness Hall and the large array of outdoor tables and chairs in the courtyard. It's rather amusing and cosmically satisfying to see the actual cafeteria's business stagnate. And no wonder—why choose institutional grub when such interesting options lie just outside? All the carts are somewhere on Cedar Street within 200 feet of the York Street intersection. However, the location of an individual cart varies by day and, over a broader time scale, by the location of the Yale Medical School's interminable construction. To help you locate each dining option, we've assigned each cart one of three monikers: CM, CN, or CS. **CM**=Cedar Main, directly across from the Sterling Hall of Medicine. **CN**=Cedar North, indicating carts near the York Street intersection on the north side of the road; **CS**=Cedar South, equivalent to CN but on the other side of the street. We've made up names for the several unlabeled carts, a process with which we've had immense fun.

All carts have certain things in common: enormous portion sizes, a friendly attitude, a cooler full of standard soft drinks, and minimal frills. But warm fuzzies aside: on to the judgment.

The 10 best carts, food-wise, are, in the following order: Jung's Kimchi Corner (CM); Tijuana Taco Company (CN); the Vietnamese Cart (CM); Pavilion Mexican (CM); Jasmine Thai Cart (CS); La Carreta (CN); Jon's Lunch (CN); Peking Edo (CN); the General Asian Cart (CM); and the All-American Cart (CS). At the other end of the spectrum, we'd recommend avoiding all three Americanized Chinese carts: Chinese Food Great-Healthy-Not-Oily (CS); Chinese Food Healthy-Way (CN); and Nondescript Silver Chinese Cart with Blue Lettering (CN). The rest of the carts fall somewhere in between.

Jung's Kimchi Corner (CM) serves delicious and classically Korean rice lunches—the spicy pork is especially popular. But the real showstopper is the beef "subwich," the ethereal cross-product of a Philly cheese steak sandwich and bulgogi, the beefy mainstay of many a Korean restaurant. The cheese, bean sprouts, onions, fried egg, moist beef, and series of sauces communicate fluidly within a doughy French roll. The price might be the best part of all: 12 inches of deliciousness for under $6. It's a steal.

The **Tijuana Taco Company** (CN), the old Roomba offshoot that serves delicious burritos, is reviewed separately in this book.

The Vietnamese Cart (CM) was, until the opening of Pot-au-Pho, the only place in New Haven to get Vietnamese food. But more importantly, the food is extremely fresh: raw pieces of pork or shrimp, for instance, are laid across a real grill, painted with a savory baste, and carefully cooked to a well-balanced juiciness, easily blowing away the tough, pre-cooked meat at the Chinese carts. Have it with thin, room-temperature rice noodles, along with a peanut sauce (here it's unusually dark) or fish sauce; you can ask for both. We also like the finely sliced pickled carrots and radishes, which add a welcome vinegary note.

Pavilion Mexican (CM) has a smattering of delicious Mexican goodies cooked up by a couple of men whose language of commerce is Spanish. Tacos are the way to go here. Your choice of meat (we particularly like chorizo—carnitas are good too, but we wish they were fattier) along with pico de gallo, slaw, guacamole, hot sauce, and crema mexicana are put into a tortilla of so-so quality and topped with a slab of queso fresco that melts on contact. None of the ingredients stand out, but the tacos hit you with so many flavors at once that they're fun to eat. Both enchiladas "berdes" (the cutest of Mexican misspellings) and rojas are available, too.

Jasmine Thai Cart (CS) serves reliable Thai-American curries and such. It's reviewed separately in this book.

La Carreta (CN) is mostly Tex-Mex comfort food—no cabeza or pozole here—but ingredients are fresh and well balanced. The friendly cook makes good burritos, first griddling a tortilla and then loading on rice, beans, cheese, salsa, and your choice or beef, pork, or chicken. The pork soft tacos are our favorite, though: three blue corn tortillas loaded up with pork, salsa, lettuce and cheese. Everything comes with well-executed refried beans and yellow rice. It's definitely a bit gringo, but it's some of the best Mexican-style food out here.

Jon's Lunch (CN), which rivals the Chinese Food Healthy-Way Not Greasy Not Oily Cart for longest queues, is the best choice among the sandwich- and salad-makers. Jon's immensely popular Caesar salad is made with very fresh greens. One day, we even found some heirloom tomatoes in the mix. The extensive menu can overextend; even yaki soba and hibachi dishes make appearances. Interestingly, though, the onions and meat in our excellent steak-and-cheese can sometimes taste vaguely hibachi-style—residual soy sauce, perhaps. Whatever the intention, these Japanese notes actually improve the sandwich.

At **Peking Edo** (CN), dishes are alternately Japanese, Taiwanese, Malaysian, and Singaporean. This is the closest you'll come in New Haven to real hawker center food. Mee goreng, for example, is made of noodles with shrimp, egg, onion, tomato, curry, and—we're told—a bit of ketchup. It's interesting, although we wish it were served warmer. Better is the Taiwanese stewed hard-boiled egg, which swims in a dark, salty sauce of ground pork and tofu—not subtle, but fun to eat, like a re-imagined sloppy joe. Best of all is the chive pocket, a crispy, deep-fried indulgence that's like a Chinese scallion pancake unexpectedly stuffed with rice noodles, chives, and fried egg. And try the homemade hot sauce.

We named the **General Asian Cart** (CM) for a dish on their menu that is rather hilariously called "General Chicken"—and also for the fact that when we asked the Vietnamese cook which nationality the cart's cuisine belonged to, he simply shrugged. Regardless, he makes a pleasantly spicy, fresh-tasting dish called "spicy shrimp" (also available with chicken) in Japanese hibachi style. It's well-seasoned with soy sauce and various hot sauces, and the shrimp (which could be better deveined) and bean sprouts are, refreshingly, cooked from the raw state.

The **All-American Cart** (CS) serves the American classics: burgers, fries, grilled chicken sandwiches, and so on. There are no frills here, but the fries are freshly made to order, and the cheeseburger, which is of the thin variety, is correctly cooked on a gas grill and well balanced, with a good mix of cheese, fresh tomato, lettuce, onion, and so on. It's a simple pleasure, and at $2.25, it blows away the fast-food competition.

At **Mamoun's** (CN), meanwhile, the falafel is good and crispy, but we've had a kefta that was seriously undercooked. We're all for rare lamb chops, but in a ground-lamb patty at a food cart, you don't want to see so much pink in the middle. It's definitely possible to get a good meal at the Mamoun's cart, though: go ahead and give it a shot.

Lalibela (CM) serves Ethiopian food, but its exotic promise falls flat. Spicy chicken is indeed spicy, but it's also bland and greasy—red oil oozes everywhere. Undersalted spicy lentils have heat but little else. Soft green beans, well flavored by tomato and onion, cross the "okay" threshold, but not so for bright yellow shrimp that drown in an over-rich sea of butter. This is a far cry from the restaurant.

Perhaps the biggest failure of all is the immensely popular Chinese category. Usually the local crowds are right, but sometimes they're wrong. Here, we think they've fallen for a cheap marketing ploy. The clear market leader, which almost always boasts a long line of customers, boldly proclaims in large letters: **Chinese Food Great-Healthy-Not-Oily** (CS). Unfortunately, it's not tasty either. This is the kind of Chinese-American slop we've outgrown decades ago.

Across the street sits another cart with a suspiciously similar name: **Chinese Food Healthy-Way** (CN). This cart looks more promising at first, because of the "Korean-style" ja-jun noodles with black bean paste, but they're soggy and one-dimensional, pepped up only by a serious dose of chili oil on request. An enormous container of soup is so bland that it's hard to eat more than a spoonful—it tastes like hot water with some soggy noodles and pasty shrimp stripped of flavor. String beans with ground pork are only a little better—a thick, gummy brown sauce is poured on top, rather than being integrated into the dish, and the meat has unexpected and unpleasant flavors.

As for the **Nondescript Silver Chinese Cart with Blue Lettering** (CN), they use fresher, less overcooked ingredients and subtler sauces than the other two, but it's still just cookie-cutter suburban Chinese-American grub. There are so many better ways to cart.

Mediterranea

Middle Eastern fare with great vegetarian options, hookahs, and belly dancers—who needs pizza?

6.7 Food
6.5 Feel

Middle Eastern, Pizza

Counter service
$10 Price

www.mediterraneacafe.com

Mon–Thu 11am–11pm
Fri–Sat 11am–1am
Sun 6pm–11pm

Bar BYO
Credit cards Visa, MC, AmEx
Delivery, veg-friendly, Wi-Fi

South Town Green
140 Orange St.
(203) 624-0589

This simple business-district restaurant, a great choice for vegetarians, peddles quick, cheap fare that's a lot more interesting than your standard Middle Eastern. Chairs and tables seat quite a few people in two rooms—the more secluded back room must be one of the only dining rooms in New Haven with exposed brick walls on three sides. Still, the short-order open kitchen with slice-ready pizzas on the counter gives off a very lunchtime-take-out vibe.

The falafel is about as good as Sahara's (which is to say, better than Mamoun's), but we'd like to direct your attention to some of the more unusual offerings. Don't be put off by the name: "foul mudammas" is a perky vegetarian treat with a harmonious focus on primary ingredients, beginning with the irresistible rustic appeal of fava beans, one of the most under-utilized starches in the universe. In a simple and elegant treatment, the cooked beans are bathed in a well-balanced sea of olive oil, garlic, and plenty of lemon.

Moujaddarah, another vegetarian option, is a plate of lentils and cracked wheat, with darkly browned onions that add a deep caramelized taste—another interesting choice, though not up to the level of the foul mudammas. The menu also includes ouzi (rice with green peas and almonds in phyllo dough) and moussaka (eggplant, tomatoes, ground meat, and cheese), a Greek dish that reveals the kitchen's pan-Mediterranean aspirations. You can finish off with a pleasant cup of the hot Syrian tea.

The pizza makes concessions to New Haven traditions ("clams casino," for example, with clams, roasted peppers, onions, bacon, and mozzarella), and it does have high-quality cheese and a well-cooked crust with the occasional blackened bubble, but the crust is a bit too thick to be called true thin-crust New Haven style. Better to stick with the little-known Middle Eastern delights.

At night, this place becomes filled with the smoke of hookahs, which are, by the rule of monopolists, expensive. Though the natural pairing with hookah is mint tea, the staff here will provide glassware and mixers if you want to bring in your own liquor (better yet, bring a Lebanese wine).

Mezcal

You owe it to New Haven to support the city's best all-around Mexican restaurant

8.7	6.0
Food	Feel

Mexican

Casual restaurant

$25
Price

Mon–Thu 11:30am–9:30pm;
Fri–Sat 11:30am–10pm; Sun
11:30am–9pm

Bar Beer, wine, liquor
Credit cards Visa, MC, AmEx
Reservations Accepted
Kid-friendly

East Rock
14 Mechanic St.
(203) 782-4828

Just one crucial block in the wrong direction from the eternally popular Pantry, this Mechanic Street space—convenient to most of East Rock though it may be—has been a difficult one for restaurants in recent years. Mezcal's predecessor, El Charro Alegre, the East Rock sibling of a Fair Haven stalwart, had a really tough time drumming up business.

Mezcal, the newest Mexican occupant, suffers from some of El Charro Alegre's atmospheric issues; the décor is bright, festive, and a bit kitschy, but when it's empty (as it often is), the place can also feel lonely, as if someone threw a big fiesta for the third-graders and no one showed up.

This is a shame, because people should be lining up for the privilege of eating some of New Haven's best Mexican food—or, at least, for the chance to come during weekday happy hours and enjoy half-price margaritas, which display unusual balance and finesse.

The menu is easily the city's most authentic outside of Fair Haven, beginning with the homemade chips, fried the old-fashioned way—often the first giveaway of a legit Mexican restaurant—and served with incredibly spicy salsa verde. Although shrimp ceviche is a tad chewy and taquitos are just so-so, we're delighted by the presence of machaca, a hard-to-find specialty of Nuevo León, northeastern Mexico, in which intensely gamey dried beef is tamed with scrambled egg.

Pollo entomatado—chicken on the bone cooked in a spicy tomato, tomatillo, pepper, and raisin sauce—is better still. But the runaway winner is pollo con pipián, which also comes on the bone, in an achiote-colored pumpkin-seed sauce that's so good, you'll try to eat it with a spoon. Carnitas are deeply porky, stewed, fried, and beautifully spiced. There's good mole, too, and tortillas come warm and taste fresh.

You'll enjoy the friendliness of the staff, which creates warmth even on an empty night. Sure, the menu requires some maneuvering—away from middling fajitas—but even a cursory effort to branch out will yield dividends. Support Mezcal instead of your local taco-and-burrito shop, and keep real Mexican food in East Rock.

Miso

A sleek, airy downtowner where you can have decent fish, but it's fading

7.1	6.0
Food	Feel

Japanese

Upmarket restaurant

$40
Price

www.misorestaurant.com

Mon–Thu 11:30am–3pm, 5pm–10pm; Fri–Sat 11:30am–3pm, 5pm–11pm; Sun 3:30pm–10pm

Bar Beer, wine, liquor
Credit cards Visa, MC
Reservations Accepted
Outdoor dining

Ninth Square
15 Orange St.
(203) 848-6472

We were delighted when Miso first opened open in this still-revitalizing downtown neighborhood. Unfortunately, like Bentara, the place has gone downhill. One area where the decline has been particularly notable is service. It has often been inexplicably rude; among other personal fouls, a nice group of friends reported back to us that they had been intentionally charged for dinner mains after having made a good-faith effort to order off the lunch menu, and the incident had escalated into a near-shouting match. Clearly, there's no customer-is-always-right attitude at work here.

At least the setting is a bit more zen. Every aspect of Miso's design, from the spectacular light bamboo tables and beautifully angled sushi bar to the careful layout of nigiri on wooden tablets, stresses clean lines and airy openness. There's also a pleasant backyard garden in summer, always a welcome addition, with a notable modernist wave roof. Even the font spelling out "Miso" on the restaurant's front door is an exercise in cutting-edge simplicity. Conversation levels stay at pleasantly low levels, providing a nice din, but nothing more.

As for the food? Miso is where you'll find the best sushi downtown, but given the thinness of this field, that's a bit of a booby prize. Tsukemono (Japanese pickles) are good here, and serve as a great appetizer, their acidity readying your palate for the rest of the meal. Strangely, Miso's fish is often served too cold (perhaps in an effort to hide any less-than-ideal qualities?). There are many better sushi options in the suburbs.

Nonetheless, the sushi-sashimi dinner combination is a better selection than average; generally notable are the salmon and albacore (white tuna). There are also plenty of non-sushi choices on the menu, including a nice version of katsu. Nabe yaki udon (a lunch special), with its variety of fish, vegetables, eggs, and toothsome noodles is a complete, nourishing, soul-warming meal in a bowl.

Now if only they would be nicer to their customers.

Miya's

Creative spins on sushi that aren't always
successful, but when they are, it's breathtaking

7.3	9.0
Food	Feel

Japanese   Upmarket restaurant   **$45**

Price

www.miyassushi.com

Tue 12:30pm–10pm
Wed–Thu 12:30pm–11pm
Fri–Sat 12:30pm–midnight

Bar Beer, wine, liquor
Credit cards Visa, MC, AmEx
Reservations Accepted
Date-friendly, veg-friendly

Upper Chapel Area
68 Howe St.
(203) 777-9760

People have strong opinions about Miya's. Adherents claim it's a paradigm-shifting exploration of what sushi can and should be; detractors wonder why anyone needs havarti cheese and baked potato in their sushi, ever. There's not a lot of middle ground here; to visit Miya's is to give yourself over, for an evening, to the iconoclastic chef's experimental and audacious vision.

Miya's oozes urban sophistication. Everything from the logo painted outside to the hip, wooden interior is emblematic of the transformation of the Howe Street neighborhood. The cool, dim bar, illuminated by tea lights, draws in young droves for cheap beer, and Miya's lights up evenings with a raging young bar scene.

The menu is either self-congratulatory or lighthearted, depending on your mood. Most of its tome-like girth consists of reviews of the food, reminiscences by the chef (including one called "How To Properly French Kiss"), footnotes to/explanations of menu items, letters from satisfied patrons, and a manifesto ending with the restaurant's motto: "Because Man Cannot Live on Rice Alone." Ask for a take-out menu if you want to read everything.

Start with a house-infused sake for an apéritif, or bring your own wine and take advantage of no corkage. Once you've spent some time with the menu, the vivid descriptions of rolls (and the repetition of ingredients therein) all begin to run together. On Wednesday nights, an omakase of 10 courses (or more) for $35.75 per person will help with decisions.

"Sashimi" here means creative raw dishes, not unadorned fish. "Hoi Polloi Salmon" is tossed with capers, tomatoes, onions, olive oil, and lemon soy sauce.

Avoid more convoluted creations, like "The Greatest Sushi South of the Mason-Dixon," a roll that involves grits, okra, Cheddar, and catfish, fried whole in cornmeal. It's a glut of flavors and textures that is less than the sum of its parts. The "Happy Together Roll" with mackerel, yellowfin, and shiso allows ingredients' textures and flavors to play off of each other.

The rice here is a mix of whole-grain, which adds a nuttiness and richness to everything. Vegetarians will find an entire section dedicated to them. But people are drawn in, most of all, by the mellow, super-cool all-purpose waiter-bartender-sushi-chef staff. It's the enchanting vibe, most of all, that keeps Miya's hopping.

Modern Apizza

Holding strong as one of the Big Four pizzas, with none of the attitude of the other three

9.0	7.5
Food	Feel

Pizza

Casual restaurant

$20
Price

www.modernapizza.com

Tue–Thu 11am–11pm
Fri–Sat 11am–midnight
Sun 3pm–10pm

Bar Beer, wine
Credit cards Visa, MC
Reservations Not accepted
Kid-friendly, veg-friendly

East Rock
874 State St.
(203) 776-5306

This favorite is located right in a neighborhood that's heavy with grad students, which partly explains its perennial popularity. The other part is the reliably great pies.

If each of the Big Four pizza restaurants has its own thing that it does extremely well, Modern's thing has to be its blistered crust and red sauce combination. The crust isn't quite as thin as its rivals' on Wooster Street, but some might prefer it this way: it's more like American-style brick-oven pizza at its best. The sauce is well balanced, the crust is not too doughy, and oil is applied with careful restraint. Toppings, too, are more classically American here than at New Haven's other top contenders: sausage and pepperoni are among the most popular, and they're great here. Meatballs come as thin slices instead of ungainly chunks—a revelation!

Outlandish combinations of multiple ingredients are encouraged: the veggie bomb, for example, has spinach, broccoli, olives, mushrooms, red and green peppers, onion, and garlic. Our current favorite is eggplant parmesan.

Modern easily beats out Sally's and Frank Pepe for vibe. The atmosphere at Modern is hardly romantic, but it's a pizzeria, after all—pitchers of Coke and beer, loud laughter, Formica tables, and frenzied but friendly service. There are also subs, but people come for the pizza (a large pie feeds three, a medium two). In the final reckoning, although we empathize with those—like Joe Castiglione, voice of the Red Sox—who thinks it's #1, we don't think it's quite the equal of the other three. That's not to say you won't find us here all the time.

Even here, waits can be considerable at prime time on weekend nights, but they rarely reach Wooster Street proportions, and people seem to have more luck waltzing right in if it's after 8pm. Modern also runs a brisk take-out business, and if you live nearby, you may prefer the ambiance of your own apartment. In the age of the celebrity restaurant, we salute this, a great, laid-back, and deservedly successful New Haven institution.

Moe's Southwest Grill

A Tex-Mex chain that's better than some fast food,
but also more out of range

4.7	5.0
Food	Feel

Mexican, American

Counter service

$10
Price

www.moes.com

Daily 11am–9:30pm

Bar Beer
Credit cards Visa, MC, AmEx
Outdoor dining, Wi-Fi

Audubon Arts District
46 Whitney Ave.
(203) 776-6637

Milford
1319 Boston Post Rd.
(203) 874-7720

The predictable Tex-Mex chain restaurant that replaced Sandra's—one of our favorite restaurants in town, a local soul-food legend—could hardly be any different from its predecessor. It's one of more than 400 locations nationwide that serves cheap, fresh-tasting southwestern favorites. The food is serviceable and inexpensive—everything's under $10. The atmosphere is friendly and casual: the staff is welcoming and the interior is bright and clean, featuring an on-the-border motif heavy on yellows, greens, oranges, and reds.

Wall posters of corn stalks and guitars sport embarrassingly corporate musings like "a soft taco is like a hard taco, only more emotional" and "a burrito is like life: a well-hidden mess." The television is tuned to a Spanish channel, perhaps in an effort to retain a semblance of authenticity in the face of a largely gringo clientele.

The menu is full of contrived names like "Homewrecker," "Instant Friend," and "Funk Meister." Some of them (e.g. the "Close Talker") are references to Seinfeld; others are less amusing. Is there a corporate position responsible for this insipid stuff?

Tortilla chips, free with every meal, are fried fresh and served crisp with five different types of salsas, only one of which—the medium spicy red—is worth mentioning. Flour tortillas are steamed before being overstuffed with numerous add-ins (rice, beans, cheese, meat) in trays turned over every three to four hours…for freshness. Despite numerous possible permutations of fillings, burritos and tacos are indistinguishable. Steak is oversalted and pork is underseasoned. The guacamole and the queso are both passable, if you're not from Texas. The quesadillas—filled with chicken, pinto beans, and shredded cheese—are your best bet.

Like Chipotle, which seems a chief competitor, Moe's serves alcohol—reasonably priced margaritas and beer—but it's all quite predictable (Dos Equis, Corona, Tecate, and Modelo).

It's not that Moe's is terrible or anything. It's just not…anything. Screaming silliness and cheap prices are no apt replacement for soul.

We miss Sandra's.

Mother's

A true Jamaican gem, best for take-out, hiding in
the side streets west of downtown New Haven

8.6 Food

7.5 Feel

Caribbean

Take-out **$15** Price

Mon–Sat 8am–8pm
Sun 11am–6pm

Bar None
Credit cards Visa, MC

Medical Area
16 Norton St.
(203) 562-3701

This is an out-of-the-way find in a part of New Haven most Yalies
probably don't even know exists—it's somewhat west of downtown, off
Derby Ave. With a half-broken TV and ripped plastic upholstery, the
atmosphere is so drab it's almost a joke; but the place is so genuine in its
lack of intentional aesthetic that it comes off as purely endearing. And
take-out orders are the best choice anyway. Huge family-style portions
make it a great option for a dinner party or Sunday brunch.

Mother is a real, live, person, a friendly Jamaican woman who surely
knows her way around a kitchen. The Jamaican accents at the counter are
the genuine article. The tastes are vintage West Indies too: for example,
deep-fried meat patties are gloriously soft and flavorful. Red beans and
rice have a texture and sweetness rarely seen in a dish that can so often
be boring in less capable hands.

Ten dollars gets you an outrageously large portion of outstanding goat
curry, with impossibly tender meat and a sauce that bursts with exotic
flavors and spicy goodness. Cabbage and collard greens are a sweet
counterpoint, melting in your mouth. You just want to eat it all—
immediately. Large portions easily serve two, bringing the actual price per
person down quite a bit.

And there's so much more. There's jerk chicken and kingfish in gravy.
There's Jamaican breakfast in the morning. There are vegetables, like
callaloo, and other unexpected treats like mackerel, oxtail, and ackee.
Wash it down with a real ginger beer.

We're not exaggerating when we say that Mother's serves some of the
best food in the city. You won't be disappointed by this trek to a
neighborhood unfamiliar to many downtowners.

Mt. Carmel Wines & Spirits

Hamden's eternal playground for wine lovers,
especially lovers of French wine

Wine store

Market

www.mtcarmelwine.com

Mon–Sat 8am–8pm

Bar Beer, wine, liquor
Credit cards Visa, MC, AmEx
Good wines

Hamden
2977 Whitney Ave.
(203) 281-0800

Wine lovers rejoice. Mt. Carmel Wines, located on a very innocuous stretch of Whitney Avenue in Hamden, is an absolute wonderland. Expect to spend quite a bit of time here; a helpful formula would be to triple the amount of time you normally spend in a wine store. We're not kidding.

Your treasure hunt should begin at the long row of wines from Burgundy and Bordeaux, many of them from older vintages, most of them impossible to find elsewhere, and all of them reasonably priced for what they are. The store has few bells and whistles; staff are über-knowledgeable and can help you find just about anything you need, but they will never bug you while you're browsing or try to hawk some wine off on you.

The wines are strong across the board, but it's with France that Mt. Carmel really excels. For less than $50, you can find a fairly serious Margaux or Pomerol from a decent vintage from the 1970s or 1980s. That's really, truly unheard of.

Burgundy is the true passion of the owners, and although you'll pay more for the privilege, there's an aristocratic tour of wonderful Corton, Pommard, and Gevrey-Chambertin bottlings from decades past. In fact, this is one of the only places in the *country* where you can find modest but delicious bottles of Bordeaux and Burgundy that are decades old, yet still relatively affordable.

In fact, word has it that these Burgundy fanatics travel to the region every year to hunt out the best wines themselves; this practice—immersing oneself so much in the buying process—is exceedingly rare, but it's one that benefits the customer immensely. There's a good spirits selection, too. Come just to look, and you'll likely let the afternoon get away from you. We promise you'll leave with something special.

Nica's Market

A one-stop shop for quality fresh ingredients
(butcher included) and prepared food

Groceries, Italian   Market

www.nicasmarket.com

Mon–Sat 7am–7pm   **Bar** None   **East Rock**
Sun 7am–4pm   **Credit cards** Visa, MC, AmEx 603 Orange St.
                         Outdoor dining, veg-friendly   (203) 787-5919

This Orange Street storefront is a spectacular oasis of edibles with a
decidedly Italian accent. Spilling out of woven baskets are artisanal breads
(made locally) and a limited bounty of fresh fruits and vegetables,
including exotic seasonal produce (persimmons, anyone?) and a startling
array of fresh mushrooms. A fresh meat counter is the best (and priciest)
in the area, including organic chicken and a rotating selection of specialty
items like duck breast, game, veal shanks destined for osso buco, and
even kobe beef. If you have a particular cut in mind, ask for it; they'll
butcher for you on the spot. Call two to four days ahead for special meat
orders.

For lazybones and lunchers, Nica's offers a variety of prepared food,
from foccaccia sandwiches, pizza and panini, to soups and marinated
vegetables, stuffed roasted chicken, sausages (made in-house) with
peppers, and hearty slabs of lasagne. They sell their pizza dough to go,
too, and in a reminder that we can all do so much better than Bruegger's,
they import H&H bagels from New York City.

They make breakfast sandwiches, too, and there are muffins to enjoy
with your coffee (good, not great) outside at a real patio with umbrellas.

Save room for dessert; tiramisù is a decadent, creamy delight, and the
chocolate mousse cups are memorable. We also have a weakness for the
selection of gourmet ice cream and sorbets, especially Ciao Bella's
unctuous fruit flavors. And the freezer holds yet more promise of home-
cooked goodness, with an array of fresh pasta made locally. There's no
better place in New Haven to shop for dinner; apparently, everyone else in
East Rock knows it, too. You are destined to bump into at least three
people you know here during the after-work rush.

Nikkita

An almost absurdly modern bar that serves eclectic
food late into the evening

6.5	7.5
Food	Feel

New American, Seafood

Upmarket restaurant

$45
Price

www.nikkitanewhaven.com

Mon–Wed 4pm–11pm
Thu 4pm–midnight
Fri–Sat 4pm–1am

Bar Beer, wine, liquor
Credit cards Visa, MC, AmEx
Reservations Accepted
Date-friendly

Audubon Arts District
200 Crown St.
(203) 787-0227

Late-night dining is something sorely missing from New Haven; this is peculiar, given the post-theater crowd and student population. This is why we salute Nikkita, whose kitchen turns out fairly serious food later than just about anyone else. From trendy fonts to skeletal metal to halogen spot lighting to the eclectic, vaguely Italian menu, this place is modern, modern, modern. Nikkita turns into quite a bar scene on weekend nights, with people gravitating away from the restaurant-style booths and toward the long bar and its three prominent LCD flat-screen televisions, at least one of which will be showing sports.

Drinks are solid—perhaps the most solid things here. They're not keeping up with the exciting artisanal cocktail movement that's got places like 116 Crown moving and shaking, but they're consistent and ample. We like the "Illusion" martini, which is like Campari for beginners (the tartness cut with cranberry juice). As for food, there's an extensive raw bar (oysters, clams, and so on) and a good selection of smallish plates at smallish prices. Presentations have a flair for drama.

One appetizer boasts frighteningly gigantic Chilean prawns dangling almost in mid-air, but its theatrics are limited to the plating: it's underseasoned and fairly bland. Same goes for a similarly pretty seared ahi tuna. The menu reads like a Vegas buffet, or worse, as if the kitchen seems willing to throw together any combination that makes money. In this vein, there's sushi and sashimi that we don't trust, and what they call "specialty rolls." Is a Philly roll a specialty now? A dreadful Thai dish doused in sweety-sweet peanut (this is about as Thai as Jacques Pépin) lurks among copious pasta dishes, and pizzas that don't come close to the city's Top Ten.

Don't come to Nikkita for the food. Come for the drinks, and to feel chic. It's just nice to know food's there if you need it late—and late is often when you need it.

Nini's Bistro

The prix-fixe-only, BYO concept would rock our world if the food were better

5.7 Food **8.5** Feel

New American

Upmarket restaurant

$45 Price

www.ninisbistro.com

Wed–Fri 5pm–8:30pm
Sat 6pm–8pm seating 1,
8:15pm–10:30pm seating 2

Bar BYO
Credit cards Visa, MC, AmEx
Reservations Essential
Date-friendly, outdoor dining

Ninth Square
40 Orange St.
(203) 562-6464

Although the name and font make Nini's Bistro look, from the outside, like just another cookie-cutter Italian-American restaurant, the place is neither Italian-American nor just another restaurant; it is, rather, an unbelievably reasonable BYO prix-fixe concept that is completely unique in town, with an atmosphere that's dim, cozy, and romantic.

The unapologetically hands-off, brusque treatment here is much more European café than Michelin-star. You sit down, open your wine, enjoy having a meal made for you without your characteristically American fussiness ruining it (no substitutions, and no dieting) and the server comes when you signal them, and only then. You don't need help ordering because it's prix fixe, and you don't need to be coddled, checked up on, and complimented frequently. We get it.

But Nini's is a heartbreaker. Everything is so *drastically* inconsistent, even from course to course, that we just can't award it the credibility it's looking for. Where we once said that we loved the concept so much that we were willing to overlook the weak points—heavy and greasy preparations of fried fish, and overcooking of meats, for instance—things have gotten even worse, and we no longer have the patience.

It's still a worthwhile concept, and if Nini's ever pulls it together and shows more passion for artisanship (in the farmer's renaissance of 2009, using Maytag blue cheese shows a lack of resourcefulness, not a commitment to excellence), starts making its own pastas and sausages, knocks off this tired and rarely successful Asian-fusion fetish, and serves something that doesn't sound like catered wedding fare, we'll happily endure whatever service standard they want to impose.

#1 Fish Market

Flopping-fresh fish—but you've got to get it early

Groceries, Seafood

Market

www.numberonefish.com

Mon–Sat 9am–6pm

Bar None
Credit cards Visa, MC, AmEx

Hamden
2239 State St.
(203) 624-6171

Number One Fish Market, nestled in a gentle bend on State Street just beyond the New Haven-Hamden city line, is just a store—but what a store it is. This first-rate fishmonger is a boon to seafood aficionados all over the county, and a particular favorite of Yale faculty and Japanese transplants—the latter is perhaps the highest praise possible for a purveyor of fish.

Staff are quite knowledgeable about their wares, and they are more than happy to spend time with you, giving advice about how to prepare your new purchase. Owner Robert McNeil, especially, is passionate about fish. He fell in love with handling fish while in a job driving a delivery truck full of it. He soon realized that New Haven County desperately needed his expertise, and opened Number One a quarter-century ago.

To this day, Bobby regularly makes the pre-dawn trip to New York's Fulton Fish Market, inspecting the global catch (being half Sicilian, Bobby knows how to look a swordfish in the eye), and speeding his selections back to Hamden. He also sources from Stonington and Nova Scotia; when shad roe season arrives in early spring, Bobby offers Connecticut River shad to first takers, some of whom (us, for example) consume copious amounts of roe before the season ends a few short weeks after it begins. Number One Fish is also the place for soft-shell crabs, lobsters, and all variety of delicious mollusks.

Our only quarrel with Number One is over the patrician hours. The store shutters its windows at 6pm, which is difficult for the after-work crowd, precipitating many a mad dash down two-lane State Street. (Another red light!) For those who arrive after closing time, or who simply don't care to cook at home, another option is to follow the Number One truck around town; the store operates a thriving wholesale operation serving local restaurants.

Olive Garden

America's culinary empire—Italy most certainly can't claim it

4.9 *Food*   **6.5** *Feel*

Italian

Casual restaurant   **$25** *Price*

www.olivegarden.com

Sun–Thu 11am–10pm
Fri–Sat 11am–11pm

Bar Beer, wine, liquor
Credit cards Visa, MC, AmEx
Reservations Not accepted

North Haven
310 Universal Dr. N.
(203) 234-1327

Orange
439 Boston Post Rd.
(203) 795-8600

It's almost tautological to accuse the Olive Garden of being inauthentic.

To what end, that criticism? It would be hard to argue that the Olive Garden, even if they have 1,000 branches by 2010, boasts the power to dilute Italy's reputation for having the noblest culinary tradition in all the world.

It's funny that they make such an effort to come off as authentic, though.

On July 24, 2001, reporter Jim Cox wrote an article for USA Today about treating Italian food guru Marcella Hazan, the grandmotherishly indignant poster woman for firm pasta, to a meal at Olive Garden—to "gauge the company's claim of offering 'a genuine Italian dining experience,'" explained Cox.

You probably won't be surprised to hear that she trashed the place. "As she turns to the menu," writes Cox, "[Hazan's] face clouds with concern. 'Manicotti doesn't exist in Italy,' she says, running a skeptical eye over the mains. 'Spaghetti with meatballs doesn't exist in Italy. And this is the first time I ever see fettuccine Alfredo with garlic.' "

For some reason, Hazan fails to mention to Cox that fettuccine Alfredo doesn't exist in Italy either.

Actually, that's not strictly true. It does exist at one, and only one, restaurant in Rome. The restaurant is called "Alfredo of Rome." Its web site (www.alfredos.com) is not translated into Italian, and its one other branch is in Manhattan's Rockefeller Center. (The branch in Walt Disney World's Epcot closed in 2007.)

Italian or not, fettuccine Alfredo has generally been the best thing we've had here—it displays a satisfying balance of cheese, cream, and noodles. The problem is that almost everything else is bad. Even the much-heralded breadsticks are chewily resistant to the bite or even the tear. Proteins wither, and the wine list seems geared toward comic relief. And the pastas—even when they're dressed with that manipulative Alfredo—are uniformly overcooked to mushiness.

But, then, so is mac and cheese, generally. Fettuccine Alfredo is mac and cheese. If Chef Marcella don't like it, maybe she jes' don't like good ol' American cookin'. You know, she's Italian. Although we hear that she actually lives in Florida, kind of near the former Alfredo of Rome #3.

For all their flaws, these guys definitely know how to stay in business.

116 Crown

Stimulating digs evoke the elements while
innovative cocktails provoke the senses

9.1 Food
9.0 Feel

New American, Burgers

Upmarket restaurant

$35 Price

www.116crown.com

Sun–Thu 4pm–midnight
Fri–Sat 4pm–1am

Bar Beer, wine, liquor
Credit cards Visa, MC, AmEx
Reservations Accepted
Date-friendly, good wines,
veg-friendly

Ninth Square
116 Crown St.
(203) 777-3116

The cocktails at 116 Crown aren't just the best in New Haven—they
might be the best in the state of Connecticut. The bartenders are equal
parts chef and parfumeurs; their palette of aromatics and herbs, elixirs
and potions, small-batch liquors, and juices are culled from the very finest
producers. Even the tonic water is artisanal.

The cocktail list is divided into helpful subheadings, like "Aromatic &
Subtle," where you'll find the "Eli Sunday"—heady Bourbon with
chamomile-infused grappa—whose sea salt rim gives the flora a bracing
bite. The "Gin Garden," with lychee-sweet elderflower liqueur, a wisp of
cucumber peel, and apple cider, is garnished with a translucent, tart Cape
gooseberry perched on the rim of your glass like a delicate yellow bird.
We love the delicate potency of the "Dr. No," with Miller's gin, Zubrówka
bisongrass vodka, and white lillet (now *this* is what a "vodka martini"
should be: gin *plus* vodka!), and the unusual balance of the "Grace
(absinthe frappe)," which artfully combines absinthe, rose syrup, and lime
juice without drifting toward oversweetness. And in colder weather, hot
cocktails like "The Great Pumpkin" warm you to the bone with pumpkin
butter and rum. The wine list is small but superb and reasonably priced.

On the veggie-friendly menu, basic staples are here transformed into
small wonders of flavor, texture, and aesthetics, beginning with crisp,
bright pickled seasonal vegetables; artisanal charcuterie (La Quercia speck,
house-made pâtés); and beautifully sourced cheeses. Fries are thin, crisp,
and golden, delicately aromatized with truffle oil and sprinkled with of
Parmigiano-Reggiano; they're the best in the city. The same might be said
of the crisp-skinned half-chicken, skillfully roasted to ideally juiciness and
balanced by lemon and thyme. As for the pizza, the Bar pedigree of 116's
friendly owners shows: the bubbly, oily, seductive crust does justice to the
New Haven appellation. A heroic hamburger slider, with smoked cheddar
and caramelized shallots, seems to have endless depth. Pulled pork sliders
are too sweet, however, and marrow bones have come practically sealed
off, impossible to exploit.

The setting is hilariously mod, a place Austin Powers would like, from
the sleek, curvy woods and glowing faux-marble bar to the "pods" that
remind us of Idlewild, the old 1960s-70s-jet-set-airport-themed bar in
New York. But we love it. Unusual gold lighting makes everyone look
good, and the vibe is lively even when the place is empty (which it rarely
is). What a wonderful newcomer: 116 is just the sort of place that gets us
excited about the restaurant scene in New Haven all over again.

168 York St. Café

6.0 Food | **7.0** Feel

A well-kept secret for brunch—especially given the big, cheap pitchers of Bloodies

American

Casual restaurant | **$20** Price

www.168yorkstreetcafe.com

Mon–Fri 3pm–9pm
Sat 2pm–9pm
Sun 11am–3pm

Bar Beer, wine, liquor
Credit cards Visa, MC
Reservations Accepted
Outdoor dining

Upper Chapel Area
168 York St.
(203) 789-1915

At this point, 168 York Street, otherwise known as York Street Café, is becoming a New Haven institution. It's been a gay bar since the 1970s, and still, to this day, it consistently manages to draw in a crowd—a somewhat older crowd.

The other real perk is brunch. When you are hung over and cash-strapped on Sunday morning, you can't beat the jumbo-sized Bloody Mary pitchers here. They're mixed from scratch, and, at only a few bucks for a 60-ounce pitcher, this concoction (though lacking in horseradish) is perhaps New Haven's best alcoholic bargain. Your brunch options won't blow you away, but they're not half bad either. For well under ten dollars, you can choose from a comforting array of late-morning classics: thick-cut French toast, saucy eggs Benedict, or pancakes speckled with the fruit of the day.

We recommend two eggs over easy, which achieves a good balance of runniness, with a tender and salty country sausage patty and a hearty mound of soft, well-seasoned home fries. Bacon is some of the thickest we've encountered. Blintzes are less impressive.

Although brunch is tasty and cheap, you might want to satisfy your nocturnal dining urges elsewhere. Dinners at York Street verge on the surreal; somewhat misplaced epicurean aspirations result in some ill-inspired concepts. There is no regular menu, just daily specials, which might be a good thing were the execution not so uneven. This is not to say that there's not the occasional success; the meatloaf is reliably good, and for the low price, it's hard to go wrong. There's a prime rib, but we'd rather go with a burger (also on the brunch menu), which they do quite well here. In short, stick to the comfort food whenever possible.

After hours, the York Street Café is transformed into one of the city's two week-round gay bars. But check the calendar before you go. Each night has a different theme; on some nights the bar is jumping, but on other nights it can be rather barren. It's certainly a more sedate scene than Partners, Gotham Citi, and such. But that's not necessarily a bad thing.

Orangeside Luncheonette

6.4 Food **3.5** Feel

A business-district dinette that has changed names, but not the average food

American

Counter service **$10** Price

Mon–Tue 7am–4pm; Wed–Sat 7am–6pm; Sun 7:30am–3pm

Bar None
Credit cards None

South Town Green
135 Orange St.
(203) 773-1000

Formerly called Joe's Hubba Hubba, the Orangeside Luncheonette serves up short order food like hot dogs, steak sandwiches, burgers, and breakfast to the high population of construction workers working on the new 360 State+ residential tower. It's appropriately blue-collar inside, with simple tables and chairs, one large window in front, and an open grill behind the cash register where one can watch chopped beef sizzle alongside fried eggs and bacon.

In fact, there's virtually nothing we can see that's different from when it was Joe's. Joe's advertised a "famous chili" that still makes a welcome appearance on a hot dog. It might just be our imagination, but the chili isn't quite as hot as before. It does have a little kick to it, but it's mostly greasy and definitely demands the right mood. The whiz-style cheese is still the same salty goo that neither dumbs down nor withers in the face of the chili.

Serviceable gyros are also offered, but availability varies. More common is the steak-and-cheese sandwich, Philly-style (though far from Philly execution). The steak is chopped and dry, and utterly flavorless, like Steak-Umms slapped in the middle of a smooshy roll. Don't try to cut it in half—the sandwich barely has the constitution to be chewed upon.

Breakfast sandwiches are the highlight, as simple as they come: egg is cooked just right, American cheese is scrumptiously melted, and bacon juices are absorbed into the roll nicely. Just like when it was Joe's.

The Owl Shop

The pipe tobacco beats the panini at one of
America's greatest smoking bars

6.2 Food

10 Feel

Sandwiches

Bar **$10** Price

www.owlshopcigars.com

Mon 4pm–12:30am
Tue–Thu 10am–12:30am
Fri–Sat 10am–1:30am
Sun noon–12:30am

Bar Beer, wine, liquor
Credit cards Visa, MC, AmEx
Date-friendly, veg-friendly, Wi-Fi

Chapel District
268 College St.
(203) 624-3250

You heard it here first: tobacco is the next pork belly. Sooner or later, we Americans are going to get over their anti-tobacco craze, realize that we're all going to die anyway, and reacquaint ourselves with the pleasure of a good, long smoke after dinner. Everything in moderation. You only live once. Why waste your time on inferior tobacco?

We're not advocating smoking two packs of Marlboros a day, mind you. Neither is the Owl Shop. All we're saying is that if there's a revolution underway, it starts here. And it doesn't start with Marlboros. Rather, this store has long been a symbol of smoking well, not smoking poorly: hand-rolled cigars, Nat Shermans, and house-mixed pipe tobacco. If you ask nicely, the staff (who are friendly on a good day, icy on a bad one) will take you in back to see the workshop of one of the country's leading tobacconists, who still mixes tobacco by hand here and bags it under the Owl Shop's own brand.

Over the past few years, the Owl Shop has morphed from a crusty, well-loved college-town tobacco shop into a hopping bar. And it's not hopping just because, by virtue of being grandfathered in as a tobacco shop, it's the only place in the city where you can hang out at a bar and smoke cigarettes legally. No: nonsmokers hang out here too, because it's just a damn cool place to have a glass of scotch or whiskey. The bartenders make great Manhattans, too. Between the easy vibe, the smoke-browned walls, the big, old, comfy chairs and couches, the gritty bar scene, it reminds us a bit of an old-fashioned brown café in Amsterdam. The only thing missing is a European billiards table.

Oh, right, about the food. The food is what gives us an excuse to include the Owl Shop (an establishment must serve food to be included in the *Fearless Critic*), but it's not much to report on. There are cheese plates, cured meat plates, and a couple of basic panini, which boast of organic ingredients, but they're nothing special. We had muffaletta-like hopes for a hot soppressata, provolone, and olive panino, but the thing was hopelessly dry and brittle, in need of condiments, the cheese insufficient. If you must, the nutella panino is the way to go. But the shop's staff generally gets their lunch elsewhere; that should tell you something. The sandwiches are redeemed somewhat by the excellent coffee and tea selection; they do individually-dripped-by-the-cup fair trade organic coffees. The dark roast is quite good.

But that's all a sideshow for what has emerged as one of the most unique bars in America. It lights up our lives.

Pacífico

6.1 | 8.5
Food | Feel

The food has slowly declined at this former Nuevo Latino hotspot—and it wasn't great to begin with

Nuevo Latino, Seafood

Upmarket restaurant

$50
Price

www.pacificorestaurants.com

Mon 5pm–10pm; Tue–Thu
noon–3pm, 5pm–10pm; Fri
noon–3pm, 5pm–11pm; Sat
5pm–11pm; Sun 5pm–10pm

Bar Beer, wine, liquor
Credit cards Visa, MC, AmEx
Reservations Accepted
Date-friendly

Chapel District
220 College St.
(203) 772-4002

Primary colors: they are the first thing that hits you when you walk into Pacífico, Colombian restaurateur and cookbook author Rafael Palomino's seafood-focused Nuevo Latino restaurant, which inhabits the space once occupied by Tibwin. Red, yellow, and blue are everywhere: the walls, the tiles, the little fish that swim through the upholstery of the restaurant's wonderfully varied configurations of banquettes.

But the warm buzz, the energy and excitement, that we used to love about this place is gone, giving way over time to a more corporate feel. And the food is in desperate need of a makeover. This is like 1990s-style hotel food disguised as trying-to-be-trendy-and-failing Nuevo Latino. It tastes like Sysco, all the way.

Some of the deep-fried dishes are still fun, but "Ecuadorian ceviche" is useless. Its overcooked shrimp don't seem to have absorbed any lime or citrus flavor; the dish comes off like a wimpy Mexican shrimp cocktail. An "empanada tasting" contains three different versions; fillings are novel (duck ropa vieja; sirloin, potato, and cumin), but the dough pockets themselves are a tad greasy. We've had steak a la parilla requested rare come out medium-plus, which was disheartening, although the meat was nicely marinated. Paella is unexciting.

Pacífico used to be a night-time hot spot, but as of late, there have been noticeably fewer people at the bar. Perhaps this can be attributed to the economy, perhaps to the declining appeal of the restaurant. Nonetheless, the pineapple mojito is still delicious, and margaritas are good and strong. Have a lot of them, and you might not be as sad about the decline of Pacífico's kitchen.

Pad Thai

You should be scared off by the name, but this place still pulls in a steady stream of customers

6.3 Food   **5.5** Feel

Thai

Casual restaurant

$25 Price

Mon–Fri 11:30am–3:30pm, 5pm–10pm; Sat–Sun 11:30am–10:30pm

Bar Beer, wine
Credit cards Visa, MC, AmEx
Reservations Accepted
Delivery, outdoor dining

Upper Chapel Area
1170 Chapel St.
(203) 562-0322

Naming one's restaurant after a dish that doesn't even *exist* in a remotely similar form in the country of Thailand is quite the odd move. Or is it? So sorry is the general state of Thai food in the US that this sugary noodle dish, which is the most popular "Thai" dish among Americans, so maybe they're just good businesspeople.

But if you've been to Thailand—or some of the more authentic local places like Rice Pot or Thai Terrace—and fallen in love with the salty-sweet-sour-bitter experience that's the trademark of real Thai food, it is hard to go back to Thai-Chinese-American places like Pad Thai.

The space here isn't bad—lighting is nice and dim—but the décor is still uninspiring. There are, however, a few outdoor tables in the summer—a definite plus. Many of the flavors have been toned down from their traditional levels in that classic misguided concession to the American palate. Slightly more interesting "chef's specials" have attendant prices that are a bit dear, but they're still not great.

If you do find yourself here, we suggest that you order anything but the eponymous pad Thai, an already bland dish that gains nothing from this lackluster treatment. Well-priced noodle options abound, and the standard meat-and-vegetable stir-fry dishes are all in attendance—the usual low-priced options for those on a grad-student stipend.

Perhaps because of the rather sterile atmosphere, the place rarely seems crowded; they seem to do much of their business on a take-out basis. There is one advantage to Pad Thai, though: with the big glass front window on upper Chapel, you can spot your arch-nemesis dining inside from clear across the street, in plenty of time to turn tail and go elsewhere.

The Pantry

Exploiting breakfast fiends with high-maintenance service, long waits, and food that's not bad

7.5	**7.5**
Food	Feel

American　　　　　　　　Casual restaurant　　**$15**
　　　　　　　　　　　　　　　　　　　　　　Price

Tue–Sat 7am–2pm
Sun 8am–3pm

Bar None
Credit cards None
Reservations Not accepted
Veg-friendly

East Rock
2 Mechanic St.
(203) 787-0392

We get it. Breakfast rules. It is beloved by all Americans in this totally subconscious, inner-child-soothing sort of way. The smell of bacon frying and the feel of a fresh pancake against your cheek is enough to make you never want to go back to Europe, land of the day that begins with coffee, croissant, and a newspaper. Blasphemy!

So we understand the phenomenon that is East Rockers' unholy, slobbery lust for The Pantry. It might not even have anything to do with how good it is. It has to do with how little of it there actually is in these parts. Seriously, what else are you going to do when you have to swipe your sausage through a puddle of maple syrup, then mix it with a forkful of Tabasco-sauced scrambled eggs?

We think it's tragic that The Pantry is all there is to satisfy this morning ritual in East Rock (except the Italian neighborhood markets and Lulu's, which is more of a coffee-and-pastry place). Get there after 1:30pm, and you may find them closing up, despite posted hours alleging 2pm. Before that, there's a long wait just to get in. The restaurant is operating just like the monopolist that it is.

When you finally get your food—often brought by a grumpy server who seems to be weaning himself off of caffeine—you might wonder what the big deal is. The feta-and-spinach omelette is one that—and believe us, we can't *stand* it when people say this, because it's never, ever accurate—you could have made at home. The good-but-not-great pancakes come with blueberries that taste unfrozen, even in the middle of summer.

Yes, it's reasonably good; it's breakfast. But do not mistake desperation for passion. Go early on a weekday, sample the fare, and decide for yourself if it's worth the wait.

We've decided. This level of stress and frustration is fundamentally antithetical to the lunch aesthetic. On the other hand, the longer you have to wait, the better it will all taste when you finally get in.

Parthenon Diner

5.0 Food **5.5** Feel

A standard 24-hour diner with below-average
Greek-American food—and almost everything else

American, Greek

Casual restaurant   **$25** Price

www.parthenondiner.com

24 hours

Bar Beer, wine, liquor
Credit cards Visa, MC, AmEx
Reservations Not accepted
Kid-friendly

Branford
374 E. Main St.
(203) 481-0333

This is one of the few 24-hour restaurants in the New Haven area. As at
the Athenian Diners in Westville and Milford, the Parthenon Diner is much
like your typical all-night diner in Queens or on Long Island, sporting a
colorful and encyclopedic menu that traverses Greece, Italy, and most of
America. There is wine from the Aegean Islands, cocktails including Ouzo
and Metaxa, and a platter of sea scallops with artichoke hearts in white
wine sauce. There are Belgian waffles and pizza bagels, spanikopita and
T-bone steaks, and tapioca pudding.

On the one hand, the idea that one restaurant would try to do this
many things at once offends our food sensibilities (especially when some
of the things are so questionable in and of themselves). On the other
hand, if there are only two or three places open at 4am, it's nice to be
able to find absolutely anything you crave at Parthenon.

Hamburgers and such might be the best choice, although there's a
short list of Greek choices that include grape leaves, moussaka, souvlaki,
and so on. The best thing about the gyro at Parthenon might be the
pita—it's the good kind, with some nice girth to it. The meat on top is
salty (very salty) but satisfying, and the tzatziki is refreshing, but copious
lettuce, chopped onion, and under-ripe tomatoes flood the plate, adding
little but logistical difficulty. French fries are also subpar, with a mealy,
tasteless interior. Coffee is weak, but that's closer to par for the diner
course.

Suffice it to say that we can see little reason for frequenting Parthenon
during the regular business hours of regular restaurants. But at those
other times, beggars can't be choosers, and it is then that we salute
Parthenon for their commitment not to sleep.

Patricia's Restaurant

A gritty diner that's been around for 50 years—it's more about nostalgia than food

2.9	4.0
Food	Feel

American

Casual restaurant

$10
Price

Daily 11:30am–10pm

Bar None
Credit cards None
Reservations Not accepted

Broadway District
18 Whalley Ave.
(203) 787-4500

After a half century's tenure as a diner, Patricia's Restaurant may feel that it has nothing to prove. The décor is haphazard and unassuming, the menu brief, and the rules explicit: "No Substitutions." This old dame of the downtown coterie of cheap diners offers the kinds of things you would expect from a diner. It can be hard to find a solid American breakfast in New Haven, and Patricia's delivers at true thrift-shop prices; two eggs with home fries and toast can be had for pocket change.

The dining room offers a collection of mismatched chairs and tables and uninspired lighting. Those lucky enough to get a booth are confronted with a bizarre reflection of themselves in a round mirror, tinged faintly blue, for that hung-over look any time of day or night. The one advantage of the proliferation of mirrors is that they make the space look larger and more exciting; a big gilt mirror on the back wall faithfully reflects the comings and goings on the street beyond the glass façade. Everything is steeped in the history of a space that has been serving (albeit under different managements) for over half a century, so many a New Havener has a place in her heart for Patricia's.

But when it comes to food, there's not much to write about. The French toast, made with squares of Wonder-style bread, is a pale shadow of what it could be. Omelettes, served up without flounce or frills, are downright boring. And a note of caution to those patrons who may indeed be hung over: take special care when looking for the loo. The egress provided is a precipitous descent to the facilities (and said facilities are bare-bones at best). Please, watch your step.

Pizza House

A simple, utilitarian slice joint that's open late

5.6 Food **6.5** Feel

Pizza

Counter service **$5** Price

Mon–Thu 11am–11pm
Fri–Sat 11am–1am

Bar None
Credit cards None
Veg-friendly

Upper Chapel Area
89 Howe St.
(203) 865-3345

Take-out is the method of choice at Pizza House. (Surely, this has *something* to do with that fact that it is open until 1am on Fridays and Saturdays.) But if you're in this neighborhood—especially if you feel like actually sitting down—you might as well walk a block and shell out a couple more quarters for Brick Oven Pizza, which makes a better pie and offers some of the quality that Pizza House can't muster.

The first glimpse you get of Pizza House is an inauspicious one: every inch of free space behind the small counter is piled high with cardboard pizza boxes, and most of the dozen or so wooden tables are empty. This utilitarianism permeates the establishment to the last square foot; there's absolutely nothing fancy or superfluous here—even the name of the place offers the necessary information, and no more. The only frill in Pizza House seems to be the mandatory straw dispensed with each can of soda you order, a charming touch offered by an equally charming but often taciturn staff.

With these prices—good luck spending more than five bucks here—it's hard to find cause for complaint. The pizza is not too thick, but also not thin, and while the slices are far from extraordinary, they're definitely not a greasy mess, either. Although the pies would benefit from a little more sauce, the cheese is good and stringy, the crust the right medley of crisp and soft, and the toppings are fresh and copious. Pizza House is a paper-plate type of place (no utensils are offered; if forks exist they are without a doubt plastic ones), but within its category, this restaurant is passable.

The Place

Sit on tree stumps and enjoy great grilled seafood
in the open air

8.4	10
Food	Feel

Seafood   Casual restaurant

$25
Price

Mon–Thu 5pm–9pm
Fri 5pm–10pm
Sat 1pm–10pm
Sun noon–9pm

Bar BYO
Credit cards None
Reservations Not accepted
Date-friendly, kid-friendly, outdoor
dining

Guilford
901 Boston Post Rd.
(203) 453-9276

Every year, this friendly outdoor cookout garden gets a little bit more
expensive, and every year it's encroached upon further by Route 1
development (there's a new Starbucks next door, and a Wal-Mart across
the street). But tree-stump perfection hasn't changed a bit. This is still our
favorite summer seafood in New Haven County. You eat at rustic picnic
tables, sitting on tree stumps, under lights that are strung up overhead.
It's an absolute dream.

Don't dress too nicely; every dish here is messy and finger-lickin' good.
Put your rump on a stump and order a lobster by weight—when they ask,
you want it barbecued, not boiled, and you want a female with its roe, if
available—along with an ear of corn or two, dripping with butter after
having been dipped into a vat of it. Throw in, perhaps, an order of
bluefish, thrown on the grill in a packet of foil with a lemon to keep it
moist. We love the crabs, too.

The best thing on the menu, though, is the "Roast Clams Special":
they're doused with butter and cocktail sauce, fired over the coals, and
brought to your table on a red-hot (really, watch out!) grate. The clam
juice mixes with the butter and sauce to form an Elixir of the Gods in
which a buoyant little clam floats. It's heaven in a shell.

Bring your own salad, bread, wine, and bug spray. Bring anything.
Bring a keg. They'll usually be able to provide corkscrews and plastic cups.
Skip the dessert and run across Route 1 instead to Ashley's for a
bittersweet chocolate cone.

And make sure you bring cash: the exploitative ATM across the street
charges an arm and a leg for non-account-holders. The Place now puts up
tents on rainy days, but if it's too yucky out, call ahead, just in case. They
go to weekends only after September, and close for winter. But in the
midst of summer, this is a gem. One of the true gems of the shoreline.

The Playwright

An Irish pub that tries, with its food, to be all
things to all people; but it just needs to be *there*

6.4	7.5
Food	Feel

Irish, American

Bar **$30**

Price

www.playwrightirishpub.com

Mon–Sat 11:30am–9:30pm
Sun 11:30am–9pm

Bar Beer, wine, liquor
Credit cards Visa, MC, AmEx
Live music, outdoor dining

Hamden
1232 Whitney Ave.
(203) 287-2401

Chapel District
144 Temple St.
(203) 752-0450

The difference between the original Playwright pub in Hamden and the
gargantuan branch on Temple Street in downtown New Haven could
hardly be any greater. The Hamden location is a local legend, and it feels
so much more like a local, from the photos of Irish heroes on the walls, to
the harmonious and elegant bar, to the authentic furniture and stained
glass imported directly from Ireland. The dining room, meanwhile, is more
like a charming rural Irish cottage, from the antiques and knick-knacks, to
the delightful stone fireplaces, to the exposed wood beams that are
actually Irish railroad ties. The downtown New Haven branch, though, is a
different beast entirely. It's riddled with TVs, it's Disneyesque, it's
cavernous, and its fratty vibe is less Irish neighborhood and more Irish car
bomb.

It kind of depresses us to see a menu that reads like a Vegas buffet.
Jalapeño chicken, vodka penne, crab salad wraps, calamari, empanadas.
Empanadas? To a Flogging Molly soundtrack? There's no reason for this
frivolous multiculturalism, when Irish pub food is actually decent here.
Guinness stew, which comes with a swirl of mashed potatoes, is tender
with well-developed flavor, while the soul-warming shepherd's pie is
much better seasoned.

In the end, though, we admit we love the burgers here (hey, burgers
have been co-opted by more traditional Irish pubs for years), which are
well executed, even if they are served on dastardly, dry rolls. But the fries
are good, and the Irish whiskey BBQ burger with "house whiskey BBQ
sauce" and melted Cheddar, strikes just the right pub note.

The Irish pub, when done right, is able to play a specific, comforting
role in restaurant culture and even the collective consciousness of a
community, and the Hamden branch of Playwright fits that bill. It's the
sort of standby that is there for you, night after night. Whether it's for a
Black and Tan at the bar, or for something more substantial by the
fireplace, you just know that you'll be back.

We wish we could say the same for the New Haven Playwright.

Popeye's

Fast food is fast food—but this is some good stuff

Southern

Counter service

www.popeyes.com

Sun–Thu 10:30am–midnight
Fri–Sat 10:30am–3am
Hours vary by location

Bar None
Credit cards Visa, MC, AmEx

Whalley
35 Whalley Ave.
(203) 562-7674

Hamden
2390 Dixwell Ave.
(203) 288-7674

Popeye's is one of the most redeeming of American fast-food chains, both
for its reliably decent fried chicken and for its classic logo. The theme is
officially Louisiana (po' boys, crawfish, and jambalaya may be found on
the menu), but the place is really all about the chicken and the sides. The
fried chicken is correct. It's crispy, properly seasoned and salted, and just
plain good. Dark meat is better than light, and also marginally cheaper.
Spicy chicken strips are also a fine choice; the chicken sandwich is solid.

Well-textured red beans and rice are a stellar side, and biscuits are
buttery, flaky, and delicious. Mashed potatoes with "Cajun gravy" are of
the whipped variety (ergo, very likely reconstituted), but we like them. The
fries are well spiced and crispy, tasty but greasy, and of dubious residual
nutritional value; there is very little evidence of the original potato.

There's nothing in the way of atmosphere, unless you have a thing for
fast-food décor. Take-out is certainly the way to go. There are two
Popeye's locations in the area: one in Hamden, and one in New Haven,
right across from the Holiday Inn at the beginning of Whalley Avenue—
making it an easy stop on the way to Staples, the supermarket, or the
futon store. It also has a walk-up window which is open until 3am on the
weekends—bless their hearts.

Portofino

7.3 Food
7.0 Feel

Friendly, mid-priced, red-sauce Italian—what else is
new—but with fair prices and good execution

Italian

Upmarket restaurant

$40 Price

www.portofinosnewhaven.com

Mon–Fri 11:45am–2:30pm,
5pm–9pm
Sat 5pm–10:30pm
Sun 4pm–8:30pm

Bar Beer, wine, liquor
Credit cards Visa, MC, AmEx
Reservations Accepted

East Rock
937 State St.
(203) 562-1414

From the outside, in a town of Italian restaurants, Portofino has precious
little to distinguish it from the incumbents. You walk in anticipating
another boring Italian-American restaurant. However, that all changes
once you pass the lively bar and enter the main dining room. Every aspect
of the décor is more tasteful than expected. Subdued lighting emanates
from a network of pretty chandeliers with miniature lampshades. Tables
are tastefully outfitted. Service is pleasant and unobtrusive.

Although Portofino's menu is an almost comically typical list of Italian-
American basics, the restaurant exercises unusual restraint. Simple
preparations focus on fresh ingredients and elemental flavors, instead of
the jumbled mess of expensive ingredients that we sometimes encounter
at New Haven Italian-American spots.

It's not perfect, but there are some pleasant surprises, such as the
fettuccine alla Bolognese, a superb example of this Northern Italian
standard—a dish that is so often misunderstood and misconstrued. At
Portofino, it's a simple sauce of wonderfully textured ground beef with a
tomato base that sparkles with the savory flavors of emulsified vegetables.
Still, it needs salt. Other highlights are an ideally prepared veal parmigiana
and excellent homemade meatballs. Veal Francese is a bit too soft and not
delicate, though, and braciola is dry.

But, mamma mia, what portions! Mains come with (albeit
undistinguished) appetizer salads, eliminating the need to order other
appetizers (which include good, crispy fried calamari with a nice
marinara). This further boosts the value proposition here: while the main
courses are not dirt cheap, they're not expensive either, and one might be
all you'll need for two people. The wine list is reasonable too. The moral
of the story: Portofino is one of the better deals in town for upscale
Italian-American, and it deserves more attention than you might think.

Pot-au-Pho

We're sorry to report that our favorite pho has gone downhill

5.2	7.0
Food	Feel

Vietnamese

Casual restaurant

$15
Price

Mon–Sat 11am–8:30pm

Bar Beer, wine
Credit cards Visa, MC
Reservations Not accepted
Veg-friendly

Audubon Arts District
77 Whitney Ave.
(203) 776-2248

Although pho, at its best, is one of the world's most complex, richly layered broths, Pot-au-Pho demonstrates the oft-deformed crossbreeding of Anglo-inspired American culinary culture with Asian cuisine: blandness. We're sorry to report a marked backslide in deliciousness and value for this formerly excellent institution.

Any Vietnamese joint worth its salt offers brisket, fatty brisket, tendon, tripe, and meatballs in its pho. The textural element is key: the distinctive toothiness of good Vietnamese meatballs contrasts with the soft and chewy tendon and the richness of fattier beef. Alas, Pot-au-Pho's incarnation offers only sliced brisket with underseasoned meatballs swimming in a meek, flaccid broth. The noodles are appropriately cooked; but you know your pho has a problem when the noodles steal the show. Good pho is a genuine pick-me-up (which explains its popularity as a breakfast food in Vietnam), yet this pho has been getting us down. Pot-au-Pho seems to underestimate the increasing sophistication of urban American palates.

Pot-au-Pho's great prices are also a thing of the past. Not only has the delicious French-dippish bahn mi bo kho been taken off the menu, but its mediocre replacements cost $3-4 more. Goi ngo sen, lotus-stem salad with pork and shrimp, features lots of lettuce with little lotus tossed in weak dressing. The chicken broth of banh canh, Vietnamese style udon noodle, is tastier than the beef broth, yet it, too, fails to coalesce into something greater than its parts.

Pot-au-Pho's saving grace may be the com tay cam, a clay pot filled with chicken, mushrooms, and rice seasoned with ginger sauce. The flavors balance well, and the mushrooms' earthy intensity backs up the moist chicken to great effect. The sauce is neither too sweet nor applied with a heavy hand. Yet such successes can't prevent our minds from wandering—how we've pined for a fanciful Vietnamese baguette sandwich filled with explosively flavored sausage. At Pot-au-Pho, it's just not meant to be.

The service is cordial and prompt, and the basement dining space is well accented, with playful lighting and dorky Vietnamese artifacts. But lame pho is lame pho: for us, it's tendon or nothing at all.

Prime 16

Perfectly primed for this economy—cheap, but
with a true commitment to burgers and beer

8.7 Food

8.5 Feel

American, Burgers

Casual restaurant

$25 Price

www.prime16.com

Mon 4pm–11pm
Tue–Sat noon–11pm
Sun 5pm–10pm

Bar Beer, wine, liquor
Credit cards Visa, MC, AmEx
Reservations Accepted
Date-friendly, veg-friendly

Chapel District
172 Temple St.
(203) 782-1616

Fifteen kinds of burgers, at least 20 taps of beer—most of them local or seasonal (imports are in bottles)—and higher-shelf liquors make this newcomer to Temple Street a local hit. There are weekly beer tastings, and occasional collaborations with the Wine Thief pair burgers with Burgundies and other great wines.

Among starters, we like the roasted artichoke dip, but pork flatbread pizza has come too sweet and too dry. Better are Southern-fried chicken wings—like with the burgers here, it's excellence, not novelty that Prime 16 is interested in.

The menu also includes an array of sandwiches and salads, but the burger's the thing. We applaud the decision to make a brioche roll standard for all burgers, though we are also fans of the pretzel roll—denser, flatter, and slightly sweeter than the brioche—for a tiny upcharge. Extra care is taken with cheese, which is always well chosen and properly melted.

The "N.Y. Steakhouse Burger" is one of the best in town, topped with blue cheese, sautéed spinach, and "tobacco-fried" onions that lend a depth of flavor. The lamb burger is a Greek-inflected winner, too, with mint and garlic mixed into the meat, and covered in feta cheese. A tart, creamy tzatziki sauce is the only thing missing. Perhaps the best version of all, though, is the stuffed mushroom burger, which seals savory crimini and Portabello mushrooms into a juicy meat patty, then gilds the lily with a slab of melted Swiss. Umami-bomb! If none of these choices appeal to you, you can build your own burger from all available toppings, starting at under $10.

Non-beef burgers are also delicious here, particularly the trendy-but-winning salmon burger with wasabi-ginger glaze. The salmon is moist and medium rare, the glaze not too sweet. Vegetarians have two—two!—different burgers to choose from, as well as many salads.

We lament the elimination of the "Prime 16 chips" from the menu. Perhaps they weren't ordered often enough—when you have the option of fries, sweet potato fries, or salad with your burger, who's going to order potato chips?—but this is a failure of description, not of diners' imaginations. The Prime 16 chips were house-made, thick-cut, perfectly-salted rounds of three different kinds of potatoes, expertly fried to retain some greasy unctuousness but never, ever soggy. We are grieving. Make a stink, will you?

Obviously, expect a wait, even on a weeknight. It will be worth it.

The Publick Cup

An immensely popular coffeeshop serving decent panini and salads to a primarily academic crowd

Sandwiches, Baked goods

Café

www.thepublickcup.com

Mon–Fri 5pm–midnight	**Bar** None	**Broadway District**
Sat 8:30am–midnight	**Credit cards** Visa, MC	276 York St.
Sun 9am–midnight	Veg-friendly, Wi-Fi	(203) 787-9929

Formerly known as Koffee Too?, the Publick Cup is still the same wonderful place it always was. The only thing different is the name, which was changed in 2007 after the owners decided that they needed to set the place apart from other Koffee places in town. There's practically not a minute of the day when you won't have to wait in line here for a cup of joe, and there are many times when you have little chance of grabbing a seat. It's not hard to see why it's so popular, given the proximity to the Hall of Graduate Studies and Yale Law School, the congenial, mixed student-faculty vibe, and the very good tea selection (teas are also available by the pound).

This coffeeshop also does a brisk business with the lunchtime crowd, making its neighbor, the ubiquitous Au Bon Pain, look embarrassingly bad. Most notable are the panini, pressed grilled sandwiches on good bread, filled with any number of standard filling combinations listed on the board above the counter, as well as a daily special. The #2, a mainstay, has mozzarella and prosciutto with tomato, basil, olive oil, and balsamic vinegar on rustic Italian bread.

We were once told by the staff that "almost everyone who works here is a vegetarian." That should tell you something about what to order. Much better—delicious, at its best—is a Portobello mushroom and goat cheese salad with wonderful seasoning. Bubble teas are available in a few flavors.

The staff is fun and alternative, there's always a newspaper lying around. Whether you're reading cases, skipping class, or on that awkward post-coital coffee date (because dinner would be too uncomfortable), you'll definitely feel like you're fulfilling your role as part of the Yale community.

Quattro's

Expensive Italian that isn't terribly authentic or
memorable—but you could do worse

6.9 *Food*   **7.5** *Feel*

Italian

Upmarket restaurant

$50 *Price*

www.quattrositalian.com

Mon–Sat 11:30am–9:30pm
Sun noon–9pm

Bar Beer, wine, liquor
Credit cards Visa, MC, AmEx
Reservations Recommended

Guilford
14 Water St.
(203) 453-6575

We weren't terribly surprised when the New Haven branch of Quattro's closed. The execution there was so completely inferior to that of the original that it was almost like two different restaurants. The Guilford branch still seems to be going strong, however, in its new location right by the lovely green.

Dishes are still prepared with panache. Fried calamari are delicate and not too chewy. Veal is a specialty, tender and satisfying in any of its many incarnations. Some seafood preparations have toned it down a bit, compared to their overbearing, rich, scallop-happy past. White wine and capers seem to have replaced lobster sauce as the go-to on these.

Still, our biggest complaint with Quattro's relates not to what it does do, but only to what it *still* doesn't do: true regional Italian recipes.

Caesar salad isn't even Italian, but then to make a dressing that tastes like it was ordered off a Sysco truck? That's just insult to injury. A carbonara is described as a "traditional Italian cream sauce," which is a total misrepresentation. Traditionally, it's only pancetta, eggs, and cheese on hot pasta; the pasta gently cooks the egg, and the creaminess emerges. What's more, even a lot of *American* restaurants no longer operate under the premise that carbonara is made with cream…except Olive Garden, of course.

But que será, será. It's suburban Italian-American, after all. The décor might be considered bland by some. It's drapey and elegant, simple, calm. The lighting is muted. And the service is courteous and accommodating. But we can't figure out how it survives here, now that there are much better, more affordable Italian restaurants all over New Haven.

The wine list is bimodal. New World wines are either overpriced, predictable, or worse: horrendous grocery store plonk that belong on plastic table tents. There's even a white Zinfandel. White Zinfandel is a half-step away from what you drank in the parking lot behind your junior prom. No serious wine list would have one. But then there are some high performers in the Italian selection: Poderi Colla, Livon, Marcarini. As with Shoreline Italian, we're halfway there…

Rainbow Gardens Inn

An almost-too-cute, haphazardly eclectic New
England inn with an immensely popular lunch

6.8	8.5
Food	Feel

New American

Upmarket restaurant

$45
Price

www.rainbowgardens.org

Mon 11am–3pm	**Bar** Beer, wine, liquor	**Milford**
Tue–Thu 11am–9pm	**Credit cards** Visa, MC, AmEx	117 North Broad St.
Fri–Sat 11am–11pm	**Reservations** Accepted	(203) 878-2500
Sun 4pm–8pm	Date-friendly, veg-friendly	

The immeasurable quaintness of the Rainbow Gardens Inn explains why it
is so popular that you need to make reservations well in advance, even (or
perhaps especially) for lunch. So finely realized is the cute New England
aesthetic that walking up to the porch and into the space is like stepping
into a vacation in a Vermont resort town (the Inn also rents rooms). Place
settings are just so, and many windows look out onto the street and
Milford's elongated town green. The restaurant is divided into smaller
spaces, making every seat in the old house feel cozy.

It might come as no surprise, thus, that this establishment is generally
frequented by an older crowd. They come not just for the escapist charm
but also for the menu of American cuisine, which is eclectic almost to a
fault—Asian here, Italian there. Cutesy, too, is the menu, with
descriptions that range from the funny ("Beauty and the Beef") to the just
plain weird ("Outrigger Occurrence").

And that menu is long. Sandwiches comprise part of it, one of which is
the "Cape Cod Salty Dog"—a variation on the Reuben, with the amusing
addition of cod, cole slaw, and chili tartar sauce. Stranger, however, was a
special on one visit of sweet, loud coconut shrimp atop an overdressed
Caesar salad that practically swam in a thick, strong dressing,
intermingled with a mango concoction even sweeter than the shrimp.

But even if it's more the atmosphere than the food that keeps Rainbow
Gardens Inn so popular, the place is nonetheless an absolute hoot.

Restaurante Salvadoreño

8.0 Food   **7.0** Feel

Good renditions of pupusas and pork, with a little
help from the fryer

Salvadoran, Latin American

Casual restaurant   **$10** Price

Tue–Thu noon–8pm
Fri–Sat 11am–10pm

Bar Beer
Credit cards Visa, MC
Reservations Not accepted

West Haven
931 Campbell Ave.
(203) 931-7457

You won't find it in most phone books, but look for the large white sign
among the strip malls and storefronts on Campbell Avenue in West
Haven. Restaurante Salvadoreño puts the "family" back into "family-
owned"; you might even see the proprietors' kids taking orders with the
air of seasoned pros.

There are plenty of comfortable booths, and in the back, there's
something of a browsable Latin American market of packaged baked
goods and sweets (and, inexplicably, perfume). A pool table and jukebox
filled with Latino CDs allows that this humble little joint might start
hopping after work and on weekends.

Now, there's a tendency to be overly enthusiastic about even mediocre
takes on cuisines that are hard to come by in New Haven, but these
pupusas really are *good*. They're tender, with a lightly sweet corn masa
outside, and filled with a layer of savory morsels, which might include
cheese, loroco (a Salvadoran green that tastes like a cross between
chamomile and green tea), or (less interestingly) chicken. Opt for the
platter, which not only includes two delectable pupusas of your choice,
but also rice, excellent beans simmered in broth, a small block of fresh
cheese, curtido (pickled cabbage), and, best of all, sweet plantains with a
pleasing caramelized crunch.

Salvadorans know their starches and fryers, and the pork and yuca plate
upholds both banners, arriving in a heap. Each piece of pork is about the
size of a chip, and is fried to a crisp. The yuca is far more pillowy than
expected for what is frequently an unyielding starch. Curtido pitches in, as
does a mildly spicy tomato sauce that absorbs nicely into the yuca. Frying
also improves the texture of the tamal de elote, a tamal filled with...more
tamal. It's almost a dessert, with the same sweet cornmeal outside and in.
Unfried, it lacks textural contrast, but frying it makes it pop. Top it with
the house-made crema to add more flavor contrast and to help with
dryness.

Wash everything down with fruit shakes, mildly sweet horchata,
tamarind sodas, or a beer selection that ranges from Modelos to Coronas.
You'll eat far too much before you stumble into the parking lot and back
onto Campbell Avenue, from whence you came.

The Rib House

A typically suburban family restaurant that makes
passable ribs, no more

6.4 Food **6.0** Feel

Barbecue, Southern

Casual restaurant **$30** Price

Mon–Thu 4pm–10pm
Fri 4pm–11pm
Sat 3pm–11pm
Sun 1pm–9pm

Bar Beer, wine, liquor
Credit cards Visa, MC, AmEx
Reservations Accepted
Kid-friendly

East Haven
16 Main St.
(203) 468-6695

The Rib House is exactly what it sounds like. Just up Main Street in East
Haven, this purveyor of barbecued ribs and chicken is a reliable source of
hearty fare. The main dining room is a series of lodge-like wooden tables,
chairs, and booths, with an impressive spit roast occupying the large
hearth that dominates one wall. The décor is 100% suburban, as befits
the location; it's a great place for a group of hungry people, or for
families. The Rib House has its clearly defined place in the landscape of
local eateries.

The ribs are pretty good, and they're easily your best choice here. A
large order is a generous rack and a half, plenty for two hungry people,
and perhaps even enough for three. The ribs are slow-cooked in a
trademark barbecue sauce, more sweet than spicy, but quite tasty. You'll
have a choice between baby back ribs and St. Louis-style side ribs (there
are no beef ribs). This stuff isn't slow-smoked the way true Southerners
would do it, though, and the smoke flavor is minimal.

It all comes with decent french fries and mediocre cole slaw. If you
insist on something other than ribs, there are a few other options, from
barbecued shrimp served over rice to steak by the ounce, but this isn't
really the place for steak. Chicken, although well flavored with a spice
rub, tends to be less succulent than one would want it to be, as is often
the fate of barbecued chicken.

Skip the seafood offerings entirely (you did not come here to eat scrod),
and exercise restraint when ordering appetizers; portions are huge.
There's a kids' menu, and, with its down-home barbecue feel, the Rib
House should generally make young people happy. Now that we've got
those smoked-all-day ribs over at Juna's, though, this place has lost a lot
of its monopoly appeal. Throw in Uncle Willie's, and there's little reason
to trek out here unless you're based in East Haven.

Rice Pot

The leader of the pack when it comes to traditional
Thai dishes, depending on how you order

8.6	6.5
Food	Feel

Thai

Casual restaurant

$30
Price

Mon–Thu 11:30am–3pm, 5pm–
9:30pm; Fri–Sat 11:30am–
10pm; Sun 11:30am–9:30pm

Bar Beer, wine
Credit cards Visa, MC, AmEx
Reservations Not accepted
Veg-friendly

East Rock
1027 State St.
(203) 772-6679

This cozy little house has been occupied by a series of Thai restaurants. Rice Pot has upscaled both the menu and prices, and modernized the décor slightly. Even if the touristy Thai paraphernalia on the walls and cheap-feeling booths keep the place safely out of date-friendly territory, this is now the most exciting Thai restaurant in the city of New Haven—but that's true *only if* you order selectively.

Many of the lunch options are the same sort of bland pan-Asian stuff that you could find at any of the cookie-cutter Thai restaurants around town, including Rice Pot's sister, Thai Taste (which is slowly improving). Whether the blame lies more on the supply or demand side, it's frustrating that these Thai restaurants uniformly see fit to bloat their menus with Chinese-American stir frys, Indonesian-American satays, underspiced curry gravies, and greasy spring rolls with sugar-spiked dipping sauces. It's particularly frustrating here, because the kitchen is capable of so much more—yet, because of the menu's layout and limited lunch specials, few customers experience the best this place has to offer.

Start with som tam, a fresh, crunchy, green papaya-based salad that's ubiquitous in northern Thailand but hard to find in Connecticut. Ask for it "spicy," and you'll get an authentic version with green beans and peanuts that harmonizes notes of chili, lime, fish sauce, and sugar (though the dried shrimp is sometimes too chewy and not well integrated). Tod man pla is more of a rote appetizer: soggy, fried, lukewarm minced-fish cakes with assertive kaffir lime flavor are paired with a chili sauce so sweet it's like jam.

Order from the yum (salad) and specials for best results. Yum pla duk fu is an underappreciated salad of crispy catfish and green mango. Larb, the traditional northern Thai and Lao salad of minced pork (or, in a concession to American tastes, minced chicken), is all about limey complexity. In moo nam tok, fatty chunks of pork are magnificently marinated and grilled and balanced against chili, lime, red onion, and rice powder. Whole striped bass, lightly battered, fried, and bathed in chu chee curry, is fresh, rich with coconut milk, and fun to eat. This is not the way it's done in Thailand, but we can only ask for so much.

Richter's

An atmospheric former speakeasy known for its
half-yards, good burgers, and old-Yale theme

6.9 **8.0**
Food Feel

American

Bar **$15**
Price

Daily 11:30am–9pm

Bar Beer, wine, liquor
Credit cards Visa, MC, AmEx
Date-friendly

Chapel District
990 Chapel St.
(203) 777-0400

Once a speakeasy (for the Taft, back when it was a hotel)—which gets it automatic points—Richter's is a pretty relaxing place for half-yards and burgers amidst a healthy mix of undergrads and grads engaged in the age-old human activity of getting drunk. A half-yard, for the uninitiated, is an artistically shaped glass of draft beer (there's a good selection—Sierra Nevada, a refreshing German pilsner, the British Isles standbys, and an oddball or two) that is in fact somewhere near one and a half feet tall, and more or less the liquid equivalent of two and a half pints. But since it all comes at once, and in such a beguiling format, you'll find it goes down easier—that is, quicker—than your average two-and-a-half beers. Perhaps this is why they're not served after around midnight.

Richter's is a great neighborhood standby. The front room has a TV with NCAA basketball, Red Sox games, and classic patron-bartender banter, and is pretty much your typical American bar scene. The atmospheric back room is decorated with old Yaleiana, and has a fireplace and more intimate sit-down tables, where you can order off the short food menu, which includes all the bar food classics, and set about carving your name into a table.

It's in the back room that the half-yard phenomenon comes into its own. Group psychology plays in when you've got a table of six—how can you not order a half-yard? It is thus that even the prudent are intimidated into inebriation. And that, after all, is what a speakeasy is all about.

Roly-Poly

Quick and cheap lunch, as healthy or unhealthy as you want

6.6	5.0
Food	Feel

Sandwiches

Counter service

$10
Price

www.rolypoly.com

Mon–Fri 8am–6pm
Hours vary by location

Bar None
Credit cards Visa, MC, AmEx
Delivery, kid-friendly, veg-friendly, Wi-Fi

South Town Green
129 Church St.
(203) 777-7659

Orange
223 Boston Post Rd.
(203) 799-7659

A million. No, a jillion. Wait…A *gajillion*. A gajillion choices of sandwiches lie before hungry government and bank employees who've got thirty minutes before the next meeting to grab something. They're all wraps, and half are available hot and pressed. A half-dozen soups and salads add to the burden of choice. But this is the kind of burden that can make going to work fun, in a tiny, existential sort of way. This is a decision you can control!

Been going to the gym recently and want to keep up your streak? Suffer through the all-veggie "California Hummer" (lame), whose scant but flavorful hummus is held in nicely by tons of roughage, tomatoes, and sprouts. It never squirts! In fact, the durable construction of these things is frightening. They may well have been designed by aerospace engineers, with a tortilla so strong and yet flexible you'd think it was made by Hefty.

Designated a "People's Pick," the pressed "Hot Honey"—turkey, bacon, jalapeño jack, and spinach (with a random sun-dried tomato)—comes with honey mustard sauce on the side. We like giving people the option to control their sauciness, even if it means you have to dig your wrap in there at a diagonal to get at it. But the honey mustard is this disgusting, cloying-yet-jarringly sharp goo that's missing its McNugget. Yet, without it, the sandwich tastes almost gross (and the jalapeño jack tastes exactly like swiss). The honey mustard tyranny is certainly as bad as it gets here, though. With a gajillion choices, you're not likely to go too terribly wrong very often.

Eating in is only for the desperate: people for whom the sound of their office's fluorescent lightbulbs is slowly driving them insane. The sterile, cafeteria-like environment of dark wood and stone tile floors, soothing avocado green walls, and sappy adult-listening station all serve to chill out the stressed City Hall and bank employees who funnel in and out of here during lunch. Everything's made to order, so it can get waity, but the service is quick and friendly. At breakfast, there are only half a gajillion breakfast wraps to choose from, but you'll probably make do.

Romeo & Cesare's

One of New Haven's most distinguished Italian grocers, with great espresso and prepared foods

Groceries, Italian

Market

www.romeocesare.com

Mon–Sat 7am–7pm
Sun 7am–4pm

Bar None
Credit cards Visa, MC, AmEx
Outdoor dining, veg-friendly

East Rock
771 Orange St.
(203) 776-1614

Romeo & Cesare's used to be known as Romeo & Giuseppe's (Romeo & Joe's) before an unpleasant falling-out between Romeo and Joe. Now Joe runs nearby Nica's Market, and the two Italian groceries work to keep lock-step with each other, from their hours to their goods and sandwiches. This was always a great place to grab a fresh-made Italian sub or espresso, then sit at an outdoor table and watch East Rock families stroll by. Now, thanks to a recent renovation, there's an expanded produce section (some of which is even organic), and even more of an artisanal cheese selection than before.

This wonderful Italian specialty grocery store sells, in addition to sandwiches, "tavola calda" mains, which are available hot by the pound. The selection rotates, but it might include artichokes alla romana, which are big, slow-steamed, and stuffed with herbs, bread crumbs, garlic, parsley, and olive oil. Pane cotto, another New Haven Italian standby, is a delightful blend of escarole, beans, onions, garlic, and olive oil on toasted hard-crusted bread, soaked in chicken broth, and sprinkled with parmesan cheese.

The selection of sandwiches is more standard, with a classic array of Italian-style deli meats and such ingredients as chicken, sausage, and peppers. But all dishes use top-quality ingredients; this is one of the best places in town for imported prosciutto. Of course, catering is available. If there's one thing New Haven has no shortage of, it's caterers. For breakfast, they make sandwiches with any combination of egg, cheese, bacon and sausage, which you can enjoy outside at a table or on the run.

A quick look around the store, where almost everything is imported from Italy—not to mention the Italian staff—or a sip of the excellent espresso should make it clear that you're getting one of New Haven's best efforts at the real deal.

Roseland Apizza

The warm, vintage feel of this classic pizzeria is
hard to beat

8.1 Food

8.5 Feel

Pizza

Casual restaurant

$35 Price

Tue–Fri 4pm–9:30pm
Sat 3pm–10pm
Sun 4pm–9:30pm

Bar Beer, wine
Credit cards Visa, MC, AmEx
Reservations Accepted
Kid-friendly, veg-friendly

Derby
350 Hawthorne Ave.
(203) 735-0494

With Frank Pepe, Sally's, Bar, and Modern right in their own city, why do
New Haveners still make the trek out to Derby?

It's because Roseland's atmosphere easily beats that of those
competitors. Every pore of this 1936 pizzeria oozes with tradition,
beginning with the old-school glowing sign out front. The multifaceted
division of the space into smaller rooms also makes Roseland more
intimate than your average pizzeria. The daily specials are charmingly
scrawled across a chalkboard; servers are just as informal and old-school
as their counterparts on Wooster Street, but with less of an attitude and
more of an open-armed warmth.

As for the pizza, Roseland's thin, delicate crust is legendary, and
deservedly so. Likewise for the copious toppings: a "Shrimp Casino"
pizza, for example, features lots of garlic, bacon, and a fleet of giant
shrimp whose collective weight must exceed that of the crust. In the mid-
$30s, it also has to be the most expensive single pie we've ever seen, but
it is delicious—the best thing we've had here, and unique with respect to
the competition. Simpler, much cheaper pies like mozzarella and sausage
are also quite good, but the white clam pie isn't in the New Haven league;
it tends to be undersalted.

As a starter, a cheesy, garlicky bread might sport prosciutto and roasted
red peppers, and there are also enormous portions of mediocre pasta
dishes (served with cold bread and cold butter—blech). Though the
sauces are homemade, they don't have much zing. Whatever happens,
it's an eye-opening experience for jaded New Haveners. They go home full
and satisfied—if they can find their way back.

Royal India

This cozy, popular Indian buffet is a meaty—if inferior—alternative to the Thali Too

7.0 Food

8.0 Feel

Indian

Casual restaurant

$25 Price

Mon–Thu 11:30am–3pm, 5pm–10:30pm
Fri–Sat noon–3pm, 5pm–11pm
Sun 11:30am–3pm, 5pm–10pm

Bar Beer, wine
Credit cards Visa, MC, AmEx
Reservations Accepted
Delivery, veg-friendly

Broadway District
140 Howe St.
(203) 787-9493

It's easy to miss Royal India; the only indication for this old house is a small blue-and-white sign that makes it look rather like a 1970's office-supply store. Inside, it's worn around the edges, with chipped paneling and fake flowers, but it still feels cozy and welcoming. The food is consistently good enough, and the prices make it the best-value Indian in the area, especially the all-you-can-eat buffet, which, despite the confusing sign out front, is now available only Fridays through Sundays (although the restaurant is still open seven days a week).

The hearty, classic Indian fare puts its Howe Street competitors to shame (for meat-eaters, that is—right over on Broadway is Thali Too, now the best Indian around). Stick with the basics like saag paneer, which you just want to eat, eat, and eat, and lamb vindaloo, with deep heat and a rich flavor that's accented by the fresh bite of cilantro. There's an underlying sweetness to the vindaloo, whose potatoes sit at that magical meeting place of soft and firm. To top it off, an exquisite tamarind sauce is irresistibly tangy. We have also been convinced by the eggplant with peas, creamy and mild, with a sweet burst of pea flavor, and an extremely delicate dal. When the naan is fresh, it's transcendent; otherwise, it's serviceable, erring on the side of spongy.

Chicken tikka masala is not too rich, but it's often undersalted, and the chicken can be dry; this dish is better elsewhere. So are sautéed mushrooms, which are bland at Royal India.

The place also does a great take-out business, and it's one of the best choices in town for catering, which includes delivery. We salute Royal India for its devotion to a simple recipe for success: a good attitude; a warm and attractive space; and food that is satisfying, reliable, and easy on the wallet.

Royal Palace

Cavernous, old-school Chinese that holds its own
with Peking duck and a Szechuan menu

7.8	**4.5**
Food	Feel

Chinese

Upmarket restaurant

$30
Price

Mon–Thu 11am–10pm; Fri–Sat
11am–11pm; Sun noon–10pm

Bar Beer, wine, liquor
Credit cards Visa, MC, AmEx
Reservations Accepted
Delivery, kid-friendly

Ninth Square
32 Orange St.
(203) 776-6663

Watch out, Royal Palace: this sit-down family-style Chinese restaurant,
even though it's not by any means spectacular, was virtually unchallenged
in this town until Hong Kong Grocery's little gem of a spot (Great Wall)
expanded into its own space. Granted, Great Wall isn't as old-school
hilarious as Royal Palace. This place sports calligraphy scrolls on the walls,
a cavernous dining room of high-backed, cushioned banquet chairs, and
chronic emptiness (you'll waffle between the pleasure of knowing that
you are the center of attention and the feeling of extreme loneliness,
which isn't helped by the bright, ruthlessly unromantic lighting).

No matter where you go, if you love Chinese food—*real* Chinese food,
not the Panda Express orange-glazed stuff from your childhood (if your
childhood took place in America, anyway)—always, always ask for the *real*
menu. Here, there are both Cantonese and Szechuan menus. They will
stare at you like you just asked them to set your tongue on fire, but
reassure them that, yes, you can take it. You owe it to yourself.

Some of the best things on this menu, hands down, are the "water"
dishes—water beef, water pork, and water fish—which have a unique
emulsion of flavor, with fresh and interesting vegetables, plus some kick.
Szechuan peppercorns are a total trip, mouth-numbing and flavor-
heightening; they don't give off heat—that's all the chilies, which these
dishes are also full of. (We think they're called "water" because that's
what they make your mouth do. A lot.) Whatever you get, supplement it
with a side of sautéed snow pea leaves with garlic, or mustard greens and
black mushrooms. These simple vegetable preps are delicious, and you'll
need the roughage.

If you are with a group, don't pass up Peking duck, a crispy whole
duck, sliced tableside and individually wrapped with fresh scallions in
delicate pancakes. Royal Palace is the only place in town where you'll find
this Chinatown-style treat.

Rudy's Restaurant

No longer the best fries in town, but we love it for what it is: a bar

6.8 Food

8.0 Feel

American

Bar **$10** Price

www.rudysnewhaven.com

Mon–Tue 3pm–1am
Wed–Thu noon–1am
Fri–Sat noon–2am
Sun noon–1am

Bar Beer, wine, liquor
Credit cards Visa, MC, AmEx
Date-friendly, live music, outdoor dining, Wi-Fi

Broadway District
372 Elm St.
(203) 865-1242

It grieves us to say it, but Rudy's no longer has the best fries in town. What an extraordinary little find it once was! This classic, downmarket, dingy bar had a Belgian expert turning out spectacular fries and real Belgian mayo and other dipping sauces.

Rudy's still boasts the enormous fryer which he brought over from Antwerp. It's still there, but it seems less expertly employed these days. Also still around are the great jukebox and an unbeatable sense of nostalgia. Crude epithets from Yalies past are scrawled into the soft wooden walls, taking their place amidst crew-team posters and Ivy League football headlines from fifty years ago. The crowd is great and usually taking advantage of shots of liquor twice the size and half the price of those found nearby. Rudy's still champions local alternative rock acts, which take the stage on many nights (usually resulting in a cover charge of a few bucks). On colder nights, the space is downright freezing, even with all the bodies in it.

Maybe this place began to rest on its laurels after receiving numerous accolades for the "best frites/french fries around." Recent check-ups have found the cooking oil old, though not actually rancid; fries soft, soggy, and undersalted; and Fritessauce (mayo) tasting more and more like a thicker version of Miracle Whip. Burgers have also gone downhill—what used to be one of the best burgers in town is now a pre-formed, pre-seasoned patty with too little fat and too much black pepper. We were once so excited to find extraordinary food here, in the unlikeliest of places, but Rudy's seems to have fallen down a few pegs. Now it's just a great bar. Not that there's anything wrong with that.

Sabor Latino

Carry-out Central American food that feels better
and costs less than the Other Place

8.5 Food

5.0 Feel

Salvadoran, Latin American

Counter service

$10 Price

Mon 10am–9:30pm
Wed–Sun 10am–9:30pm

Bar None
Credit cards None

West Haven
1225 Campbell Ave.
(203) 589-8419

This Sabor Latino does the name more justice than College Street's
unrelated upmarket hotspot. It's a small family-owned shack lined with
flags from Latin countries whose signage discretely indicates "Antojitos
C.S. Restaurant." At last count, there were only five tables on the
primary-colored checkerboard floor, and a box of mangoes for sale (three
for $5).

It's like being transported to El Salvador, between the sounds of the
kitchen, the friendly chatting with the day laborers who hang close by,
and the gentle slapping of masa being patted out. Be patient: the food
takes a while, because it's being made fresh to order. This, too, is just like
El Salvador.

And it's worth it. These are some of the best pupusas we've had
stateside; they're not at all greasy, and their masa is fresh and nicely
charred. Among pupusas, the revueltas are excellent. At first, you might
mistake the curtido for cabbage salad—until you notice the separate
squeeze bottle of the good, pickley, tomatoey stuff on the side that gives
the curtido all is pickley fermented bite. Maybe this is a concession to the
often-bland American palates to which they must cater, given the
location. You should squeeze away! Loroco appears here (as well it
should, but you'd be surprised how often it doesn't), giving an authentic,
tea-like pungency to the pupusas. To stay in the cuisine of that country,
have empanadas de plátano for dessert.

There are also some Puerto Rican appetizers: alcapurria, rellenos de
papa, piononos, canoas, guatita (beef belly "panza") with yuca. Green or
yellow plantains, or costilla al horno. Bacalaitos of cod are fried to an ideal
golden color on both sides. We could eat here every day and never get
bored.

There's also tons of Mexican, and this is not your refried bean-and-
yellow cheese Tex-Mex. This is the real deal. Sopa de mondongo (tripe) is
perfect for the hangovers that march across the street from UNH. Tamales
are spicy and steamy. Roasted pork pernil has a perfectly lacquered skin.
To drink, there's refreshing horchata, coco frío, aguas frescas, and so on.

Eat in for a communal, downmarket cheeriness, or take it to some
friends and become everyone's hero.

Sage American Bar & Grill

7.0 Food **8.5** Feel

Oysters and cocktails on the water, where the view overwhelms the decent food

American

Upmarket restaurant

$55 Price

www.sageamerican.com

Mon–Thu 4pm–10pm
Fri–Sat 5pm–11pm
Sun 11am–10pm

Bar Beer, wine, liquor
Credit cards Visa, MC, AmEx
Reservations Recommended
Good wines, live music, outdoor dining

The Hill
100 S. Water St., at the end of Howard Ave.
(203) 785-8086

"Water view" doesn't even begin to describe it: at Sage, you will be eating as close to Long Island Sound as your bum can be without getting wet.

On balmy Sunday nights in late spring through summer, reggae on the dock makes this an unbeatable place to slurp oysters and eat silly "island" fare like pu pu platters. There's also summer music upstairs in the lounge Wednesdays through Saturdays. The service is great, with an accommodating, treat-you-like-royalty attitude.

The food is mostly run-of-the-mill American, with some high points. Oysters on the half shell are above average, as are the mini lobster rolls (Connecticut-style, warm with melted butter over succulent meat). An iceberg wedge salad is excellent, beautifully presented with well-integrated dressing.

But brunch mains like "Scottish eggs" (underseasoned, with poorly integrated melted Gouda and chicken sausage) are severely overpriced, even if we do love the blueberry muffins and the rich, crispy "potato cake," which is like a peppery, oniony galette served with sour cream.

Sandwich descriptions sound like the inventory of a walk-in from the days before globalization…or even highway travel. A "Santa Fe Chicken Breast" includes "mild chili spices with cool bleu cheese." Unfortunately, this violates Fearless Critic wine director Nat Davis' theory that one must stay away from any restaurant advertising any of the "3 S's": "signature," "sampler," and "Santa Fe."

Prosaic mains hover between $20 and $30, and tend to be overcooked (especially the fish), fussy, and too sweet (the maple sweet potatoes are like pie). In the end, we prefer to come just to slurp oysters, sip Bloodies, and listen to some steel drums in the sea air.

Sahara

Casual downtown Middle Eastern that's slowly improving

7.8	**6.5**
Food	Feel

Middle Eastern

Counter service

$10
Price

www.saharamed.com

Mon–Wed 11am–11:45pm
Thu–Sat 11am–12:45am
Sun noon–11:45pm

Bar None
Credit cards Visa, MC, AmEx
Delivery, veg-friendly

Chapel District
170 Temple St.
(203) 773-3306

Temple Street, in spite of its relative centrality, has been a historically difficult place for restaurants. This has all changed lately, and Sahara, which has been here for a while now, seems to be improving with the neighborhood. This little restaurant delivers in a way you don't expect from the font painted on the window, or from the category of fare on offer. Falafel is flavorful, crispy on the outside, smooth on the inside. It definitely rivals Mediterranea for the title of best falafel in town. Vegetables are fresh, and almost everything's made completely to order. We're impressed.

Perhaps most impressive of all (vis-à-vis one's expectations for a quick, largely take-out falafel joint) is that the atmosphere, once you step inside, is actually pleasant, almost hip—not too bright, with a colorful, vaguely Persian theme. Service is a bit slow, so sit down, enjoy yourself, and savor the Middle Eastern kitsch, complete with fake oil lanterns. In fact, it's worth sitting down just to enjoy the videos of belly dancers and other beautiful ladies shimmying beguilingly on the TV in the corner. Sahara is open quite late, and they'll deliver the falafel to your table, à la Mamoun's. But the food is considerably better here than it is at Mamoun's.

One of Sahara's most-improved dishes has been the chicken shawarma sandwich. Made with baba ghanoush instead of hummus, it is downright delicious and addictive. The garlic is intense, though, so you'd better make sure you don't have to talk to anyone for the rest of the day. (Sorry, angry Mamoun's fans, can't talk to you right now…got this garlic breath, you see.)

's Apizza

3.5
Food *Feel*

's chaining give Sally's the opportunity to
ead in the Wooster wars?

Pizza

Casual restaurant

$20
Price

www.sallysapizza.net

Tue–Thu 5pm–10pm
Fri–Sat 5pm–10:30pm
Sun 5pm–10pm

Bar Beer, wine
Credit cards None
Reservations Not accepted
Kid-friendly, veg-friendly

Wooster Square Area
237 Wooster St.
(203) 624-5271

Sally's and Frank Pepe have been flip-flopping for New Haven's pizza crown for years—and lately, Bar's been in the mix, too. On Wooster Street, the choice may be as much about family tradition as it is about taste. This year, there's a three-way tie for the taste crown.

Sally's definitely has the worst service of the three, although if it were service you were after, you probably wouldn't be going to any of these places. The queue of frozen, hungry pizza pilgrims is daunting but survivable. In the meantime, some of your party can amuse itself with a glance around the neighborhood. You can tell that the Wooster Street community means business from the neon scungilli (conch) sign in the window of a nearby grocery. Once you're inside, though, Sally's small dining room feels less like a historic venue than a standard, if lively, suburban pizzeria.

Unfortunately, we've often had Sally's experiences ruined by awful wait staffs—unless you're a friend of the house, the service is rude, distracted, and frustrating. On one visit, our pizzas took an hour and a half to appear while the waiter treated us to sporadic drink service and didn't think we should mind. The wall-mounted baseball paraphernalia is a homey touch that fails to overcome our longing for the vibe of nearby Pepe, which at least feels friendly.

Sally's pies are quality, grounded by superb crusts and well-apportioned toppings. Holistically, however, no single Sally's pie rises to the level of Pepe's white clam and bacon; that pie reigns supreme with bigger clams and a much more noticeable seaside aroma.

But on the simpler mozzarella-and-tomato pie, Sally's wins, with less cheese and a more delicate curst, which boasts dark brown, oven-blown bubbles. Sally's pizza with fresh tomatoes, garlic, and bacon, available only during tomato season, is intensely flavorful even without sauce. But that sauce also demonstrates mastery, as does the famous combination of sausage and hot peppers.

So stop bickering, and just try the top three—all of them. After all, every self-respecting New Havener should have an informed opinion.

Samurai

The location is great; the sushi is not—stick to the hot food, if you must

3.6 *Food* **5.5** *Feel*

Japanese

Upmarket restaurant

$45 *Price*

www.samuraijapaneserestaurant.net

Sun–Thu 11:30am–10pm
Fri–Sat 11:30am–11:30pm

Bar Beer, wine, liquor
Credit cards Visa, MC, AmEx
Reservations Accepted

Chapel District
230 College St.
(203) 562-6766

Samurai is operating on the theory that there are only three secrets to good sushi: location, location, and location. Just steps from the Shubert Theater in the heart of downtown, the place does a swimming business. But generally, the fish tastes to us like it hasn't been swimming for quite some time.

The quality is, above all, unpredictable. Venture beyond the basic standbys at your peril, unless you are sitting at the pleasant sushi bar in back and spot something that looks particularly good. Maki might be a better choice than nigiri much of the time. Spicy tuna rolls are the kind we prefer—soft chopped tuna blended with spicy mayo. But mackerel nigiri, a sushi-bar benchmark, tends to be dry and mildly chemical-tasting on the finish. Uni lacks the sweet, sultry characteristics of high-grade product, while the soft-shell crab in a spider roll is neither crispy nor flavorful. Be sure to ask the sushi chef what is fresh. But Samurai is no place for the urban sushi aficionado.

The cooked standards, on the other hand, are fine; miso soup and edamame are characteristically inoffensive, and anything with udon is satisfying. We like the hamachi kama (yellowtail collar). Katsu isn't bad either; it's properly fried. Everything cooked, including the beef-wrapped scallion rolls, is far preferable to the sushi, except the grilled unagi, which, served lukewarm tastes more of saccharine sauce than eel.

Music, perhaps even a gentle Japanese bamboo fountain, would improve Samurai's hushed and bland atmosphere. The sushi bar in back, although clean-lined and elegant, feels totally out of place beneath the Victorian molding and eccentric lighting. The chairs are vintage college library and, although the paper window shades bring an element of authenticity, Samurai's interior hardly feels Japanese—or anything, really. The ideal location drives every aspect of the business: in spite of the mediocre quality and lack of character, the restaurant still reliably draws in the pre- and post-theater crowd of suburbanites.

Stop by Samurai for cooked appetizers and a Sapporo or two, but be sure to duck out before the sushi deflates your evening.

Saray

Some of the best Turkish food in Connecticut—get your grilled meat before the crowds descend

8.8	8.5
Food	Feel

Turkish   Casual restaurant

$30
Price

www.saraykebab.com

Daily 11am–11pm

Bar None
Credit cards Visa, MC, AmEx
Reservations Accepted
Kid-friendly

West Haven
770 Campbell Ave.
(203) 937-0707

Campbell Avenue in West Haven is a playground for foodies. Turkish food, Salvadoran food, Taiwanese food—it's all here for the taking, and it's all cheap. Word hasn't exactly gotten out about this lovely area, where finding a place to eat is a fun and rewarding treasure hunt, so you won't find too many well-heeled New Haveners in these parts...yet.

Here's the scoop on the Turkish scene: for a while, Turkish Kabab House was the grande dame, so to speak, drawing in a steady stream of diners. And it is indeed good. But then along came Saray, another Turkish joint just up the street. And it was better. Saray immediately became the new darling of the local Turkish community, along with the foraging foodies, and that's why there's now such a reliable crowd here.

Saray actually has a lot going for it. Some of this is atmospheric: to step in here is essentially to set foot in another country. It feels like Turkey, in a way that's simultaneously cheesy and authentic. The space is big and commanding, and it has an equally big and commanding chandelier. Purple tablecloths deck out the tables, and there's a loud, open kitchen and fish tank to complete the scene.

The menu here is long. We recommend starting your meal with some of the "special combo appetizers"—this will allow you to sample quite a few dishes. Antep ezme (onion, peppers, tomato, and garlic ground into a paste) is bright and flavorful; imam bayildi (stuffed eggplant) is another winner.

Among main courses, kebabs are particularly strong (again, there are some combos that will allow you many tastes). Meats come out tender and juicy; we particularly like versions with lamb. Döner kebab with a touch of cool yogurt is positively delicious. And prices are quite reasonable, too. With apologies to Istanbul Café, the real deal is out in West Haven. So sit back and enjoy your feast.

SBC

A decent, locally owned brewpub where the brew tanks are just for show

5.6 Food

7.5 Feel

American

Casual restaurant

$30 Price

www.sbcrestaurants.com

Mon–Thu 11:30am–10pm
Fri–Sat 11:30am–11pm
Sun 11:30am–9pm
Hours vary by location

Bar Beer, wine, liquor
Credit cards Visa, MC, AmEx
Reservations Accepted
Date-friendly, live music, outdoor dining

Branford
850 W. Main St.
(203) 481-2739

Milford
33 New Haven Ave.
(203) 874-2337

Hamden
1950 Dixwell Ave.
(203) 248-3663

They're propagating like rabbits! It can be hard to see SBC, which stands for Southport Brewing Company, as anything more than just an inferior, mass-produced version of Bar, New Haven's legendary brewpub-pizzeria. But we also appreciate that this mini-chain, modeled on the much larger Rock Bottom Brewery chain, is locally owned and serves decent burgers, sandwiches, and appetizers.

It's kind of hilarious that they group their beers by color, and then compare them to major brands that people are familiar with. ("If you like Bass Ale, you'll love our Big Head Brewnette!") We're immediately skeptical of a brewpub chain that gives each of its beers different names for each franchise outlet, but we're even more skeptical of a brewpub whose tanks are just for show (the beer is actually brewed elsewhere). Most of the beer is serviceable, no better. Our favorites are the hoppy but austere "Branford" Red and the Saltonstall English Pale Ale.

The brewpub décor is fairly well executed, with a lineup of big, gleaming beer tanks—some of them perched on a platform right above the bar in the wide-open space—and a long, open kitchen that covers one full end of the space, where the brick ovens come into full view. SBC's pizza is popular, and while it may not be up to New Haven apizza standards, it's at least as thin as any pizza around—the crust is more like toasted pita bread or flatbread, than pizza crust. The smallish pies have too much cheese, but their tomato sauce is chunky and delicious, and with that great crust, it's the best choice on the menu.

Other offerings, from burgers to bar food, toe the brewpub party line, and they're generally no better than average. As long as you don't go ordering, say, the Shrimp Tenders, "tossed with a sweet orange glaze and drizzled with Thai sauce (which is…?), topped with green onions and sesame seeds," you'll be fine. Their "Mahi Mahi Mojo" sandwich, blackened and straight out of the '80s, is actually pretty good if you want a burger alternative. Steaks and seafood aren't SBC's best work. It's a brewpub, after all. Sort of.

Scoozzi

Clobbering, ostentatious Italian that's good for its understated patio and half-price bottle night

	5.9	9.0
	Food	Feel

Italian

Upmarket restaurant

$60
Price

www.scoozzi.com

Tue–Thu noon–2:30pm, 5pm–9pm; Fri noon–2:30pm, 5pm–9:30pm; Sat noon–9:30pm; Sun noon–3pm, 5pm–8:30pm

Bar Beer, wine, liquor
Credit cards Visa, MC, AmEx
Reservations Recommended
Date-friendly, good wines, live music, outdoor dining

Upper Chapel Area
1104 Chapel St.
(203) 776-8268

We still appreciate Scoozzi for its big-city feeling, its easy location, its gorgeous, elegant digs, and above all, for its gracious warm-weather patio. But the food is getting more tired by the day.

The grilled pizza (offered as an appetizer, but also okay for a meal) is unforgivably mediocre in a town known for its pizza. Scoozzi tries to differentiate itself with prestige ingredients like truffle oil and Gorgonzola, but crusts are consistently doughy, with no searing, and the specialty ingredients tend merely to overwhelm.

The rest of the menu is as variable as the pizzas. Some pastas are overcooked, especially a fettuccine Bolognese—the sauce is flavorless and doesn't bind to the pasta at all. For more than $20, this had better be at the top of its game, and it's not even trying. We do, however, salute Scoozzi's efforts at carrying sustainable seafood, like the sautéed Belize Laughing Bird shrimp that came with artichoke ravioli. But the strange preparation, which involves Tuscan kale, sweet corn, San Marzano tomatoes, leeks, and a brandy-pepper cream glaze, comes out ungainly and sweet. However ambitious these dishes are, they are convoluted and clumsy. And at these prices, that shouldn't be the case.

Scoozzi even manages to miss the mark with its lovely front patio, set into a deep Chapel Street indentation that shares a glass wall with the Center for British Art. The seating is lorded over by vines and a tree, but odd floodlights blind anyone facing the restaurant. In a move that might be Scoozzi's only saving grace, Tuesdays are half-price bottle nights, and the Italian wine list is good, including many solid by-the-glass options (ask how long they've been open before ordering, though). Come on a warm summer evening and open a crisp Friuli white, and you can forgive the rest.

Scribner's

A famous Milford seafood stop with fresh fish—
but questionably worth the trip from elsewhere

6.9 Food

7.0 Feel

Seafood, American

Upmarket restaurant

$45 Price

www.scribnersrestaurant.com

Daily 5pm–9:30pm

Bar Beer, wine, liquor
Credit cards Visa, MC, AmEx
Reservations Accepted

Milford
31 Village Rd.
(203) 878-7019

Scribner's is quite well known in the Milford area, a decades-old veteran with accolades galore. The web site might advertise that the place is "consistently recognized as the Best Seafood Restaurant in Connecticut," but the staff still seems to act a bit surprised when they encounter a customer from out of town. The wood-paneled room is cozy, and rather than being on a strip mall (as are many of the better-known Milford restaurants), it's on an unassuming corner of a residential block—a good start.

So are the reliable oysters on the half shell, and the deep-fried "Calamari Alfonzo" with gorgonzola marinara sauce, tossed with pine nuts and capers. Gorgonzola and the fried batter might be a heavy pairing, but it's also a satisfying one. With the pine nuts—an interesting texture counterpoint—you've suddenly got an appetizer so filling that it's difficult to proceed to the main event. The portion size is gigantic, too.

Fish mains, in spite of their renown, meet with mixed success. Gorgonzola makes a repeat appearance on a grilled swordfish steak that also features roasted red onions and chopped tomatoes. The sauce isn't bad, but the swordfish is tough and reveals little flavor. The take-home message: Scribner's is a bit above average for seafood, but we find it difficult to make sense of the statewide recognition.

Seoul Yokocho

Satisfying enough Korean food, even if it's
overpriced and the décor is drab

7.3	5.0
Food	Feel

Korean

Upmarket restaurant

$40
Price

Mon–Fri 11:30am–10pm; Sat 11:30am–10:30pm; Sun 11:30am–9pm	**Bar** Beer, wine **Credit cards** Visa, MC, AmEx **Reservations** Accepted Kid-friendly	**Upper Chapel Area** 343 Crown St. (203) 497-9634

Seoul Yokocho, which we once praised as the best Korean food in New Haven, can no longer be spoken of with such superlatives. That distinction now goes to Soho New Haven, a relative newcomer to the restaurant scene, but one whose Korean food trumps that of Seoul's. Still, neither of the two is amazing, authentic, blow-you-away Korean.

Seoul even does sushi, which is actually good, though pricey: it's fresh, and the spicy tuna rolls are some of the best in town, with the good kind of smooth, melt-in-your-mouth, pre-chopped tuna well blended with spicy mayo.

The Korean food at Seoul is a controversial topic. Our Korean friends seem united in their disdain for Seoul's cooking, and we see where they're coming from. There's no soondae (Korean blood sausage), no deliciously simmered beef-bone broth, not a lot of real kick to the spicy dishes. But this is New Haven, after all, and in this league, it's not bad.

Stone pot bi bim bap, their most popular dish, is a satisfying hodge-podge of mixed rice with beef and cooked bean sprouts, Chinese cabbage, seaweed, fiddleheads, carrots, and bamboo shoots, served with (actually-not-that-) hot sauce over rice and topped with an egg. We also like the spicier soups, although few of them activate the cathartic runny-nose reflex. Tableside barbecue is less impressive, but we've had kalbi (short ribs) that weren't bad. We don't recommend any of the fish stews, however.

The service is friendly, if sometimes uninformed. The atmosphere, though, is bright and impersonal; booths are boring and antiseptic, tables worse. A little bit of atmosphere would go a long way at this downtown spot, which is on a sadly desolate block in the shadow of Crown Towers. And it's really in view of the bland, cheap atmosphere that we, like others, are shocked by the high prices. When you're paying close to $20 for many main courses, you expect something a bit more romantic, a bit less brightly lit, a bit more polished.

Sitar

Unexciting Indian that doesn't seem to have carved out a niche of any sort for itself

5.9	7.0
Food	Feel

Indian

Casual restaurant

$35
Price

www.sitarindianrestaurant.net

Daily 11:30am–3pm, 5pm–10pm

Bar Beer, wine
Credit cards Visa, MC, AmEx
Reservations Accepted
Delivery, kid-friendly, veg-friendly

Audubon Arts District
45 Grove St.
(203) 777-3234

Sitar is one of the newer Indian restaurants in town, and the fact that it's just about the only Indian joint in its neighborhood (Yale, government buildings, and banks) would seem to guarantee it a customer base. If you work around here, once you've cycled enough times through the more classic lunch/deli options—Judies, Zoi's on Orange, and such—you'll probably wind up here.

Or so one would think. It would be a stretch to call the tiny trickle of customers a lunch crowd, since, in reality, we have never seen the place with more than just a couple of tables filled—at lunch or at dinner. Perhaps it's a critical mass problem: people go where they see other people.

Inside, though, the mood is decidedly more perky (even if the restaurant is only at 8% capacity). The walls are painted a bright, cheery yellow, and nifty wine racks hang about. (Don't look too closely, though—none of the bottles is anything spectacular.) Poppy Indian music sets an upbeat mood, thankfully. And staff are friendly and accommodating.

The food doesn't go much beyond the most basic of the basic Indian menus, so the pressure is really on Sitar to outdo the competition and compensate for its lack of any novel dishes with outstanding execution. But alas, they don't pull this off. Naan is often chewy, sometimes greasy. Meats can be overcooked, though they are occasionally moistened to an acceptable level by their sauces. There's nothing exciting to report about the other "classics": chicken tikka masala, saag paneer, dal, and samosas are all perfectly mediocre renditions. The biggest challenge here is finding something on the menu that actually piques your interest.

As if all this weren't enough to doom Sitar, prices are no lower than the other big players in town. So what is this place's competitive advantage? Truthfully, there doesn't seem to be one.

So we will put forth this theory as to who Sitar's customer base is: a steady stream of the jury-duty crowd.

Skappo

An Umbrian wine bar and restaurant where everything—and everyone—is beautiful

5.8	9.0
Food	Feel

Italian

Upmarket restaurant

$40
Price

www.skappo.com

Wed–Thu 4:30pm–11:30pm; Fri noon–2pm, 4:30pm–11:30pm; Sat 4:30pm–11:30pm; Sun 1pm–10pm

Bar Beer, wine
Credit cards Visa, MC, AmEx
Reservations Accepted
Date-friendly, good wines

Ninth Square
59 Crown St.
(203) 773-1394

With a small, warmly lit, rustic room and bold, lion-themed graphic design, Skappo is immediately likeable. Beauty is a defining quality here; pretty much the entire staff is good-looking. It's hard to disagree. And from the youthful waitstaff to their endlessly gregarious mama, Signora Anna, a local legend in the making, the folks at Skappo will greet you like family on your first visit. On many nights, you'll be serenaded by song.

This may or may not be your cup of tea: once the owner begins singing halfway through the dinner service, to continue to chat is rude, rude, rude—keep in mind that this is a *tiny* space. Some people are made really uncomfortable by the fact that to dine here is to choose to dine with owner. A good compromise, we suppose, would be to come here with someone you don't actually want to talk to.

The poetic menu is a refreshing departure from the norm, and the small (if pricey) portions are meant to compliment the excellent wine list, which features bottles from lesser-known regions, centered around Umbria. Expect a host of intriguing Umbrian specialties on the rotating menu.

The problem is that almost all of them sound good, but almost none of them *are* good. Meats, especially braised or stewed meats (lamb or rabbit, for instance), tend to come unbelievably dry and overcooked, a sign that they've been boiled rather than slowly braised. Pastas have come out mushy, risotti shaky, and crostini brittle. Your best choice might be the plate of regional Italian cured meats or regional cheeses, which you can enjoy with the Umbrian wines on offer.

Many people come just to sample the dessert list, which follows through better than the savory choices. And the sweets are complemented nicely by Skappo's selection of dessert wines. Try the raisiny Passito di Pantelleria, which tastes like liquid honey with apricots— yet another reason why you will definitely leave Skappo feeling good.

Soho New Haven

Some of the best Korean food in New Haven, homemade by a friendly chef

8.0 Food

7.5 Feel

Korean

Casual restaurant

$30 Price

Mon–Sat 11am–10pm

Bar Beer, wine, liquor
Credit cards Visa, MC, AmEx
Reservations Accepted
Veg-friendly, Wi-Fi

South Town Green
259 Orange St.
(203) 624-7333

Soho New Haven is the new Korean in town, a player in a field that is, shall we say, not saturated. So the title of "best Korean in New Haven," which we will happily bestow upon this place, rings fairly hollow. Which is not to say that the food isn't delicious (because it most certainly is), but, rather, to give a gentle nudge to all the present (and future) Korean places to step it up a notch. You'll thank us, New Haven.

No matter when you go, you'll encounter the lovely owners, who do all the simmering, stirring, reducing, pickling, chopping, and browning themselves. They are exceptionally eager to offer help with the menu, perhaps separating the "adventurous" dishes from the "easy, familiar ones." The truth is that nothing here is particularly unusual, though, except when it comes to heat. The short menu runs down the stews, bibimbap, and noodles that you'd find at any Korean-American restaurant, although we've heard that Koreans sometimes get off-the-menu items, like a seafood pancake or spicy pork stew.

Soho New Haven inhabits the old Sidebar space (they've kept the bar stools with the martini-shaped cutouts). The space is cute and comfortable, so much so that we can't help but wonder if a college-aged daughter or some other young person is behind some of the décor. Long strands of beads (the type of which were quite popular everywhere in the '70s and are still quite popular among the dorm set today) obscure the entrance to the bathrooms. IKEA-style lamps hang about. And there's free Wi-Fi. But what there isn't, unfortunately, is a packed house.

Start with a glass of earthy tea. Banchan are kind of a joke; instead of the six or eight or even 10 little dishes you get at some Korean restaurants, here you get just three, headlined by kimchi (decent, made in house, missing some of the trademark sourness). In a bizarre sushi-combo-A twist, a bowl of miso soup and boring iceberg salad is served to you upon ordering. Skip it and save your appetite for the rest. The menu is relatively short, and heavy on the Korean standbys—jobchae, stone pot bi bim bap, and pork bulgogi, a juicy and spicy winner, although there's no built-in table barbecue. They'll do custom vegetarian, a Korean rarity.

Our favorite, by far, is yook-gae-jang, which has a hot, spicy beef broth, which has been simmering for hours, and has a delicious bone marrow-like flavor. Chunks of tender beef swim in a massive bowl along with glass noodles and a melting assortment of vegetables like leeks and mung bean sprouts. O-jing-o-bok-eum is a dish of super-tender cuttlefish rings (no tentacles) in a sauce that's less spicy than advertised, and more sweet. What's even sweeter, though, is the come-into-my-house friendliness.

Som Siam

Reasonably priced, if fading, Thai in a setting that's
less than inspiring

7.3	6.0
Food	Feel

Thai

Casual restaurant

$30
Price

Daily 11:30am–9:30pm	**Bar** Beer, wine	**Guilford**
	Credit cards Visa, MC	63 Whitfield St.
	Reservations Accepted	(203) 458-0228
	Kid-friendly	

Som Siam is held back a bit by its relatively remote location and
uninspiring, fanciful décor. The low-ceilinged, vividly carpeted room is
cramped and outdated—think fan-folded pink napkins on top of dinner
plates. Lots of families eat here, and the place manages to stay pretty
crowded. Back in the day, this was Thai Inter, on State Street in New
Haven—that restaurant was bought by new management, and the real
thing is now out in the 'burbs. It lies on the town green in quaint
Guilford. The service is famously fantastic; the deferential and attentive
waitstaff is nothing but genuinely friendly.

We always end up ordering the curry puffs, each time forgetting that
the last time we thought they were too sweet. One appetizer we do like,
however, is the gai ho bai toey—fried chicken wrapped in pandanus
leaves. It comes out crispy and nicely seasoned with hints of kaffir lime
leaf. Curries are fairly standard, but larb tends to be a hit.

Prices are very reasonable at any time, but for the fiscally responsible,
lunch specials are the best deal. The lunch menu has a few interesting
items which waddle dangerously into pan-Asian territory—ka nom jean,
"Thai-style linguine with Linda's homemade curry sauce" and "Toy's
Pho." Is there a Vietnamese cook in the kitchen?

Some of our favorites, though, are som tam (a papaya salad with chili,
crushed peanuts, and lime juice); spicy barbecued pork from the grill; and
the choo chee fish, a deep-fried whole fish with coconut milk and curry
sauce. Also excellent is the spicier, tangier pla rad prik, another deep-fried
fish. Yum.

Sono Bana

Good, inexpensive sushi with a surprise at The End

Japanese

Casual restaurant

www.sonobana.com

Mon–Thu 11:30am–2:30pm, 5pm–9:30pm; Fri–Sat 11:30am–2:30pm, 4:45pm–10pm; Sun 5pm–9:30pm

Bar Beer, wine, liquor
Credit cards Visa, MC, AmEx
Reservations Accepted

Hamden
1206 Dixwell Ave.
(203) 281-4542

The name is all that seems to have changed at this popular sushi restaurant (formerly known as Hama). The owners are still the same, and the atmosphere is still pretty sterile and bright. But with this sushi at these prices, who cares?

The reasonably priced menu is extensive, with a focus on dozens of unique house rolls. Keep in mind that Math 251b (Stochastic Processes) is a necessary prerequisite for deducing the complex formula governing the selection of choices in the excellent-value combination lunches and dinners.

But the epitome of the appeal for the price-conscious is one unique and unbeatable offer, usually available on weekdays (lunch or dinner, eat-in only): an inexpensive sushi combination of seven pieces and two rolls, all of your own choosing. This offer includes its own ordering ritual, which begins with closing the proffered menu and letting your server know you'd like the golf pencil and little piece of paper used to mark your nigiri and maki choices (legend has it that the offer is also listed on the menu, but we challenge you to find it there). This brilliant arrangement gets past the standard sushi-combination problem of surrendering choice to the house in order to save money, and it requires nothing more than a basic familiarity with Markov chains, Markov random fields, Martingales, random walks, Brownian motion, and diffusions; techniques in probability, such as coupling and large deviations; and their applications to Bayesian statistics and such.

All the classics and more are on offer in the combination, even uni, which is available at most restaurants only at a premium. There's one more change here that tickles us. Literally: authentic Japanese toilets, complete with warm water sprayed you-know-where, heated seats, and a little blow dry. Now we can't tell if the enormous grins on everyone's faces are from the sushi or not.

Soul de Cuba

Good vibes and hit-or-miss food

7.1	9.0
Food	Feel

Cuban, Latin American

Upmarket restaurant

$30
Price

www.souldecuba.com

Tue–Thu 11:30am–2pm, 5pm–10pm; Fri–Sat 11:30am–2pm, 5pm–11pm; Sun 2pm–8:30pm

Bar Beer, wine, liquor
Credit cards Visa, MC, AmEx
Reservations Accepted
Date-friendly

Chapel District
283 Crown St.
(203) 498-2822

Soul de Cuba brings a touch of Havana mystique and class to New Haven, capturing the stylish and cozy feel of the hipper parts of New York's outer boroughs. The warm, shoulder-to-shoulder dining room feels homey rather than constricted. When the antics of the nearby Crown Street clubs grow tiresome, Soul de Cuba provides a grown-up, relaxing culinary respite along the strip. The vibe is warm and sophisticated, with mellow jazz music in the background; and with most mains around $15, there is scarcely a better atmosphere-to-price ratio in town.

The food has gone a bit downhill, but there's still a lot to like here. The elongated devil crab croquettes are a tad starchy but have good shellfish flavor. Empanada dough, in our experience, is often too gummy and thick, but not here: light and flaky, both the beef and vegetable-filled versions are simple winners. The ceviche, however, tastes not of fish nor lime juice, but rather entirely of mango, overwhelming an otherwise subtle preparation. "Grandma's black bean soup," intensely spiced without too much chili, is a must-order: the whole beans mesh with their deep black liquid to create a holistic joy.

Among mains, the "Pollo Soul de Cuba" is a juicy, well-pounded breaded chicken cutlet covered by a sweet fruit salsa. An inspired sprinkling of cilantro harmonizes with the dish unexpectedly well. Oxtails are cheap, delicious, and difficult to overcook: Soul de Cuba's version, rabo encendido, is girthy with just the right amount of fat. The accompanying beans and rice are expertly cooked and well textured, yet the tostones tend to be dry and underseasoned. Crab anchala con camarones, essentially spiced marinara sauce with crab and (a few) shrimp served over pasta, is drab but for a hint of unidentifiable spice. Another disappointment is pargo, a dry filet of red snapper that gets seriously over-broiled. For dessert, try the apple caramel cheesecake; it's like a cheesecake stuffed inside an extremely sweet apple crisp. And be sure to hit up the super-bitter and satisfying Cuban coffee.

The bar scene hops, too. Tasty, cheap mojitos and good sangría both hit the spot; there are even vintage rums and great (take-out) cigars. The concept is well constructed, the vibe alluring to passers-by. While the food is hit or miss, the full dining room, peppy service, and great feel make up for a lot.

Southern Hospitality

6.8 **4.5**
Food Feel

A serviceable barbecue and soul food purveyor up
Whalley that's best for take-out

Southern, Barbecue

Counter service

$15
Price

Daily 10am–9pm

Bar None
Credit cards None
Delivery

Whalley
127 Whalley Ave.
(203) 785-1575

This place dubs itself a "Soul Food Restaurant," and its simple menu fits
the bill exactly: enormous dinners of fried chicken, ribs, pork chops,
chopped barbecue, chitterlings, shrimp, and the like are served with two
classic Southern sides, such as yams, collards, and so on. Every meal also
comes with a piece of reasonably good cornbread.

There's nothing in the bright white space other than a big, long counter
and a few tables; the atmosphere isn't conducive to eating in, and almost
everyone orders take-out. In fact, the aesthetic and menu at Southern
Hospitality remind us a lot of the old Jarman's, a dearly missed BBQ and
soul food purveyor whose Dixwell Avenue locale was not so far away
from where this place now sits.

Fried chicken here is a winner, but our favorite thing at Southern
Hospitality is their rendition of oxtail, which is tender and fatty. Chopped
barbecue, while competent, is better with the addition of extra barbecue
sauce (plus some hot sauce). Deep-fried whole porgies, a seasonal fish,
can be wonderful, but at times, the bones, which should be soft, have
been too big and sharp to eat, causing endless logistical problems. Mac
and cheese is well executed, cheesy and satisfying; collard greens,
meanwhile, absorb a lot of flavor from the big pork hocks they're cooked
with, but are a bit sweet for our taste.

Service is adequate, and the prices are cheap. With Jaylyn's and
Jarman's gone, it's good to have an easy Whalley Avenue option available
for when the soul food craving hits—and, oh, it will.

Star Fish Market

Everything you need to throw a classy, memorable
seafood dinner party

Groceries, Seafood   Market

www.starfishmkt.com

Tue–Fri 9am–6pm
Sat 9am–5pm

Bar None
Credit cards Visa, MC
Delivery

Guilford
650 Village Walk
(203) 458-3474

Conveniently situated next door to excellent bakery Four and Twenty
Blackbirds, just off the Post Road, Star Fish Market is much, much more
than a place to pick up a couple of pounds of local littlenecks—it's an
ambitious gourmet market in a small, bright space. If you've read about
an ingredient in *Gourmet* or *Saveur*, you'll probably find it here—the
owners have read about it, too, and have anticipated your immediate
need for preserved lemons and Banyuls vinegar. There's really no fresh
produce at Star Fish Market, but that's not why you came: you came for
the Fishers Island oysters, the Stonington scallops, the Connecticut River
shad roe, or just a very nice piece of halibut (all displayed like works of art,
garnished with flowers and herbs, in their cold case).

Two freezer chests tempt with a wide—nay, vast—selection of
D'Artagnan meats and fowl, crab cakes, lobster bisque, demi-glace, and
frozen pasta (some from Pasta Vita in Old Saybrook). Smoked salmon,
whitefish, and sturgeon sit in another cold case (nestled among H&H
Bagels, delivered from New York) across from a dairy display filled with
enough butterfat to make the lactose-intolerant weep: artisan cheeses
both domestic and imported, double-Devon cream, egg-and-cream based
prepared sauces, and myriad butters and yogurts.

In addition to the surf, there's also turf: some D'Artagnan meats to
wrap your scallops in. As if this bounty weren't enough, Star Fish also
prepares its own picnic salads to take out (the German potato salad, with
more mustard than mayo, is a favorite). Bring your high-limit credit card
and get your goods here to host a dinner party for the gods.

Star of India

Unusually tasty South Indian in an unusually
random strip mall—it's called diversity!

8.2 Food
6.0 Feel

Indian

Casual restaurant

$10 Price

Daily 11:30am–10pm

Bar Beer, wine
Credit cards Visa, MC
Reservations Not accepted
Delivery, kid-friendly, veg-friendly

Orange
157 Boston Post Rd.
(203) 799-8162

Here's a real suburban find: just a shopping plaza away from Coromandel, Orange's much-heralded Captain Cool of Indian restaurants, lies this impossibly humble hole-in-the-wall that, believe it or not, is actually serving better food than its neighbor. Its location, in a strip mall in the middle of nowhere, couldn't be more random. Then again, it's in these types of inconspicuous places that you usually find the most authentic, most delicious ethnic joints.

Inside, the walls are lined with mirrors that reflect the twinkling Christmas lights that are strung about, and soothing Indian music is usually playing. The walls are painted that bright tenement yellow that isn't such a rare sight in a dive. There's cheap wainscoting on the walls, which makes the tablecloths seem comically out of place.

But the staff is friendly, and it only gets better when you discover that there's a short, sweet secret South Indian menu, for which you have to ask (nicely). This brand of cuisine is hard to find around New Haven, but once you get your hands on this special menu, Star of India turns into your vegetarian sugar daddy. An order of idly consists of three delicious steamed rice and lentil patties. Bangalore vegetable comes with a healthy dose of coconut, but the advertised "red chili" is undetectable, making it more of a sweet and aromatic dish than a nicely balanced one. The classic masala dosa (rice-flour crêpe stuffed with potato curry) is excellent, and fish or shrimp moilee (yogurt, cashew sauce, coconut, and curry leaves) is a strong option if you're craving a non-veg protein.

Even for those that shun the South, Star of India executes well on all the staples we're all used to seeing everywhere. Chicken tikka masala comes with unusual tender meat; the dish is fragrant and well spiced. Tandoori chicken is moist. (The kitchen's talent with poultry speaks to their overall skill level—which, clearly, is high.) Dal makhani (dark dal) is a bit too mushy and is wimpy with spices, but it's not bad. And naan is a true standout, hot, flaky, and gently brushed with oil. It's easily the best in the area.

Who would have thought that this little storefront would justify a trip to Orange from just about anywhere in greater New Haven?

Starbucks

An enormously popular and infamous coffee chain—good luck trying for seat

Baked goods, Sandwiches

Café

www.starbucks.com

Mon–Fri 5:30am–11:30pm
Sat 6am–midnight
Sun 6am–10:30pm

Bar None
Credit cards Visa, MC, AmEx
Veg-friendly

Chapel District
1070 Chapel St.
(203) 624-3361

North Haven
200 Universal Dr. N.
(203) 859-3490

Hamden
2100 Dixwell Ave.
(203) 230-0868

Additional locations
and more features at
www.fearlesscritic.com

What can we really say about Dr. Evil's coffee empire? You know the drill. At least the coffee is pretty good and the lighting's not too bright. The downtown New Haven franchise is an academic hotbed. As might be expected anywhere, this Starbucks is infinitely popular. It's packed to overflowing with Yalies, morning, noon, and night. Though it has become fashionable to hate Starbucks, it's also next to impossible to get a seat these days—even in a city with lots of other great choices for coffee. This suggests that they're doing something right. Ah, the contradictions of a chain America.

Seating is an even more special challenge if you're angling for a comfy couch; most of the time they're inhabited by chess-playing authors who look as though they've been working on their manuscripts in those seats since before Old Eli fled the moral depravity of Harvard Square to found a better place. Starbucks is one of the most comfortable places in town to flip open a laptop and get to work. It also happens to be one of the most active singles scenes in a neighborhood of student-singles-scene bookstore-cafés.

If you are depraved enough to shun all of New Haven's great indie coffeeshops and come here, we recommend that you stick to a cup of coffee—the Coffee of the Day, as they call it—rather than wasting five dollars and five hundred calories on some ridiculous Italian-sounding concoction that's basically just milk, hot or cold, liberally adulterated with sugary syrup (although we do have a soft spot for the thick and indulgent hot chocolate). And for the love of God, fight the good fight and steadfastly refuse to use their preposterous faux-Italian nomenclature for the cup sizes. Nonviolent protest, grande into medium, swords into plowshares.

State Fish Farm Market

An unsung hero in New Haven's world of
fishmongers

Groceries, Seafood, Chinese   Market

Daily 10am–8pm

Bar None
Credit cards Visa, MC, AmEx

East Rock
892 State St.
(203) 776-2938

Why doesn't this humble Asian market get any respect? Is it the strong
fish smell that wafts out the door? Is it the cheap-looking sign, or the
dingy-looking windows?

Well, now you've heard it from us: State Fish Farm Market isn't just one
of East Rock's most reliable purveyors of Asian packaged foods, Chinese
vegetables, and Korean goods like kimchee. It's one of New Haven's best
places to buy fish. People often complain that there are no good
fishmongers in New Haven proper, especially in East Rock, but these
people clearly don't know about this place.

We'll admit: this place is smelly. Really smelly, sometimes. But the fish
we've bought here has generally been of good quality. But don't just sidle
up and ask for a pound of halibut. It's a good idea to squeeze around the
counter and look at the whole fish spread across the table before deciding
which fish you want.

Here are some hints when choosing: look for specimens with the
bounciest flesh, the glossiest eyes, the least smell. Once you've chosen,
they'll clean and gut the fish, snip off the fins, and, if you like, they'll
usually fillet it. We've had particularly good luck with striped bass; once,
we took it home whole and steamed it—in a bamboo steamer that we
bought in this market, too. Delicious.

The Stone House

A sophisticated, affordable—and even late—night out in Guilford

8.1	8.0
Food	Feel

Seafood, American

Upmarket restaurant

$50
Price

www.stonehouserestaurant.com

Tue–Thu 11:30am–10pm; Fri–
Sat 11:30am–11pm; Sun noon–
9pm; Tue–Sun 3pm–5pm
abbreviated menu

Bar Beer, wine, liquor
Credit cards Visa, MC, AmEx
Reservations Accepted
Live music

Guilford
506 Whitfield St.
(203) 458-3700

The dining room of this classic Guilford seafood restaurant is very pretty, all white linen and light wood furnishings—and, of course, stone walls. But we prefer to eat in the bar, which feels very '80s, with its seafood-inspired 3D art on the walls and a carved log in the shape of a wizened sea captain. It's funny and kitschy, but it's all about the fireplace in the middle of the room, which is wonderful and cozy on a cold night. The place is always full, often quite lively—sometimes there's even a wait for a table at lunch—and the food is reliable, with moments of excellence.

Although this is a seafood joint, one of their best dishes is an open-faced steak sandwich au jus. And this ain't Steak-Ums, folks. This is a real *steak*, placed atop a slab of toasted garlic bread, ready to sop up all the delicious meaty juices. Another comforting option on a cold night has been the lobster and chicken pot pie: basically, it's a thick lobster bisque with equal chunks of moist lobster and chicken, topped with a poof of puff pastry. (It tends to appear only on the winter menu.) Mussels in fennel-saffron broth are also delicious, plentiful, and a bargain. Burgers are just dandy, especially when served on thick toast—a refreshing break from the Kaiser roll. Most of the salads from the dinner menu are also excellent.

Where the Stone House stumbles is when it attempts to cater to the "lighter" appetite with remotely ethnic dishes, such as a seared-rare tuna with cucumber and sesame noodles (too sweet, as usual; vaguely Asian tuna preps are so rarely good—why bother?), or a shrimp-and-crab quesadilla with jicama salad and tomato salsa (violently bland). Stick to traditional preparations of seafood, the fresh salads, and the refreshing takes on bar-food staples.

The bar clientele is mostly local, and consists largely of groups of frosted blonde divorcées getting progressively louder as they consume more and more Pinot Grigio; married couples; and husky dudes watching the game on one of the TVs at the bar. One of the best things about the Stone House is that the bar menu is served *late*—after 10pm on weekends. For Guilford, that's practically an all-nighter.

The adjacent "Little Stone House," which is more of a lunch spot (open Tue-Sun 11am-8pm), serves food just as thoughtful and well-executed as in the main restaurant. We've had a plentiful lobster gazpacho here, on the cheap. They also serve panini, salad, hot dogs, and baby back ribs; all can be taken out (say, to Jacob's Beach), or eaten on the small patio.

Stony Creek Market

Sweet-potato-crust pizza, locals, and the loveliest of views over the Thimble Islands

7.7 Food

9.5 Feel

Pizza, Sandwiches

Counter service

$15 Price

Mon–Fri 6:30am–3pm; Sat–Sun 8am–3pm; ; Thu–Sun 5pm–9pm for pizza (summer only)

Bar BYO
Credit cards None
Date-friendly, kid-friendly, outdoor dining, veg-friendly

Branford
178 Thimble Islands Rd.
(203) 488-0145

For most of the year, this cozy room with unfinished wood floors serves as a breakfast or lunch stop for laid-back locals or people on their way to a Thimble Islands cruise. You'll see people reading the paper, discussing local news with each other, or catching up on Stony Creek gossip. Folks who have discovered this little corner of the Shoreline are a unique and tight-knit bunch, but neither they nor the staff here will make you feel like you're an outsider if you're from out of town (and that might mean New Haven).

The breakfast and lunch food is uniformly good. Pastries are just okay, but quiches are tasty (though not a stop-the-presses find). Subs are enormous and well executed, particularly the old standby, eggplant with mozzarella (better if you ask for salt). The bread is fresh, and sauce has good flavor. Our absolute favorite lunch here remains the curried chicken salad on a buttery croissant (it's better as sandwich bread than on its own). Follow it up with one of their outstanding Snickerdoodle cookies.

During the summer months, the kitchen stays open later to make pizzas, which you can eat on their porch while looking out over the quaint Stony Creek cove at the picturesque Thimble Islands and fishing dinghys. The pies are good, if not a revelation; the "tasty crusts," are made with sweet potatoes. Try the simple version with sliced tomatoes, fresh basil, onion, garlic, Romano, and mozzarella. The "Medlyn's Special" is always topped with an assortment of very fresh, seasonal vegetables grown by Medlyn's Farm, about a mile up Route 146. This is not quite the best pizza in the area, but the experience of eating it al fresco, with a bottle of your own wine, with a view of a classic New England fishing village, makes it the most beautiful pie around.

Su Casa

Inconsistent white-bread Mexican whose nostalgic draw is getting weaker

6.8 Food

7.5 Feel

Mexican

Casual restaurant

$30 Price

Mon–Thu 11:30am–10pm
Fri–Sat noon–11pm
Sun 4pm–10pm

Bar Beer, wine, liquor
Credit cards Visa, MC, AmEx
Reservations Accepted
Date-friendly, kid-friendly, outdoor dining

Branford
400 E. Main St.
(203) 481-5001

Perhaps the most surprising thing about this 30-year-old mainstay is how wildly inconsistent it can be. Usually, older, suburban, family-style restaurants suffer from a mind-numbing stagnancy because they are so concerned with being reliable.

Here, chips can be warm one night and cold the next, with salsa tasting fresh sometimes and other times jar-like. In a tacky touch, nachos command a $1–$3 upcharge for cheap ground taco meat. A special listed as a "grilled vegetable chimichanga," on one visit, featured vegetables that—although fresh-tasting—were decidedly not grilled, and looked like kitchen scraps (broccoli stems and so on). The chimichangas, meanwhile, didn't even taste like they'd been fried in oil—their slight crispiness on the outside seemed to have more of that tortillas-stale-from-sitting-out-under-the-heat-lamps quality.

Half of the menu consists of quesadilla variations; another quarter of it is made up of "Mexican (i.e. Tex-Mex) combinations." The remaining quarter is regular American bar food with ranch dressing accompaniments—not surprising, considering that there's almost no authentic Mexican food on this menu.

All of this said, we do have a place in our hearts for nostalgic white-bread suburban Mexican places (we have to, if we want to live in the Northeast). We like Su Casa's cozy, wooden '70s-style compartmentalized rooms, the strong margaritas (from a mix, but still potent), and the Branford location, which is convenient to the movie theater. On a good night, the place can still make for a fun, festive night out with friends. But we've just about had it with the waffling upcharges; the obnoxious, intrusive service; and the clear lack of quality or consistency.

Subway

A fast-food chain whose homogeneous, tasteless
subs fail to live up to the advertising hype

3.7	1.0
Food	Feel

Sandwiches

Counter service

$10
Price

www.subway.com

Sun–Thu 10am–11pm
Fri–Sat 10am–midnight
Hours vary by location

Bar None
Credit cards Visa, MC, AmEx

Audubon Arts District
50 Whitney Ave.
(203) 787-0400

Westville
865 Whalley Ave.
(203) 389-5435

Upper Chapel Area
66 York St.
(203) 787-7836

Additional locations
and more features at
www.fearlesscritic.com

Founded in 1965 in nearby Bridgeport, Subway has more recently
positioned itself as the fast-food restaurant that's not: according to the
television, this chain is healthier than others and serves food with fresher
ingredients, tasting more homemade. This is partly true and partly false.
While the store-baked bread is better than standard fast-food hamburger
buns, other ingredients are industrial specimens, peeled out of plastic
wrappers. At least nowadays they're toasting the subs to keep up with
the rapidly spreading Quiznos.

There's something about the smell of a Subway store that is unique.
Each branch has it, no matter where in the world, but we can't identify
the source. As for taste, the chain has introduced breads that extend
beyond the standard white-or-wheat selection. The parmesan oregano
version comes with burnt cheese, which, ultimately, isn't so bad. Same
goes for "Italian Herbs and Cheese." There's also a welcome dose of raw
vegetables, but subs are missing the elemental goodness of a
cheeseburger. And the formula—the same set of toppings with every
meat, plus salt and pepper, oil and vinegar—makes every sub taste more
or less the same.

But Subway's implied claim of wholesomeness above and beyond the
fast-food competition rings false. Sodium stearoyl-2-lactylate, mono- and
diglycerides, and free glutamates all make appearances. This is fast food,
folks—nothing more. With apologies to the spectacled everyman-dieter-
cult hero Jared, the diet-friendly combos are some of the most
uninteresting subs on the menu, and once you start adding basics like
cheese and oil, you're already out of diet territory. As for atmosphere,
don't eat in; get it to go. While a six-inch should be enough for most
appetites, the stores run frequent specials making footlong subs a killer
deal. Just watch out for your arteries.

Sullivan's

An extremely basic Irish pub with extremely mediocre food—but, hey, there's outdoor seating

3.5	6.0
Food	Feel

American   Casual restaurant

$20
Price

Daily 11:30am–midnight

Bar Beer, wine, liquor
Credit cards Visa, MC, AmEx
Reservations Accepted
Outdoor dining

Upper Chapel Area
1166 Chapel St.
(203) 777-4367

Back in the day, this was Kavanagh's. The name has changed, and the menu has added more vaguely Irish selections to the bar food options, but the place is ultimately not much more than a basic neighborhood pub. Sullivan's appeals to a crowd of haphazard wandering grad students, after-work locals, a surprisingly consistent contingent of old men, and occasionally the women who love them. Oh, and don't forget about the Yale Architecture students ducking out from 18 straight hours in the nearby studio, here to bathe their sorrows in blended whiskey. The tone gets louder and bouncier as the night rolls along, especially on weekends, when things positively rage. The place is dark and uninviting during the day, though. The tables out on the sidewalk are the best option.

Standard bar food is served, including below-average, overcooked bacon cheeseburgers; and simple, not very good American classics like baked meatloaf with potatoes, gravy, and a vegetable on the side. French fries are soggy; wings don't have enough kick; more Irish dishes fare even more poorly.

The beer and drink selections are also standard (happily, a Harp tastes more or less the same anywhere), and they're offered at decent prices. It's worth noting that the tables are unusually big, especially a few of them; it's a good place to come with a large group, but not exactly intimate for a one-on-one, unless you go on a slow night and happen to score a booth.

Sushi on Chapel

A new Rainbow of cheap and easy sushi, uneven rolls, and occasional Korean

7.6	7.0
Food	Feel

Korean, Japanese

Upmarket restaurant

$40
Price

www.sushionchapel.com

Mon–Thu 11:30am–10pm
Fri–Sat 11:30am–10:30pm

Bar Beer, wine, liquor
Credit cards Visa, MC, AmEx
Reservations Not accepted

Chapel District
1022 Chapel St.
(203) 776-4200

Sushi on Chapel is a much-needed underground replacement for the unfocused Rainbow Café, whose review in our last edition ended with the sentence: "However many hot hippie wannabes you may meet along the way, there's no pot of gold—or any pot at all—at the end of this rainbow."

The space is vastly improved, with chocolate-brown walls and a pretty coterie of hanging Japanese scrolls; curtains pull double duty protecting diners from an ugly concrete-and-brick view and dimming any outside light. The small main room is brightened instead by throngs of bubbly undergrads drawn to the cheap, decent sushi.

Order right, and you won't notice the cheap part. Salmon, tuna, and yellowtail are all unusually fresh, and made in properly small, bite-sized pieces for nigiri (smaller cuts mean better quality control). Fluke is clean and snappy, too, but venture much further down the fish list, and you'll encounter less thrilling results, like slightly stinky uni (sea urchin). Curiously, the sushi rice is purple, made from unmilled, unhulled rice (it's in the brown-rice category).

Rolls seem to adhere to a standard as subterranean as the atmosphere, although most people seem to douse them in enough Sriracha, mayo, and soy sauce that they can't tell what they're eating anyway. Spicy tuna is fishy and subpar, overwhelmed by bright orange spicy mayo.

Gyoza are nicely pan-fried, but their filling is underseasoned. Deep-fried dishes (panko-crusted tonkatsu, for instance) are done with a pleasantly light touch. Tuna tartare is fine, though we suspect the overpowering wasabi mayo splattered beneath it is meant to serve the same purpose as those curtains. The problem with this dish is really less about taste and more about concept. Why serve it with both a seaweed salad (the flavors of which fail to synergize with the tuna) *and* a dry lettuce salad?

Some local Koreans in the know come here for the Korean food, and Korean parties are sometimes hosted here, but on the menu, it's more or less limited to decent bibimbap and bulgogi (which are listed under a section called "house special").

Food is served quickly and presented prettily in miniature wooden launches with lotus or banana leaves, contrasting nicely with the unusual purple rice. Rainbow Café, weird as it was, certainly didn't have *that* going for it.

Sushi Palace

A cheap, inordinately popular way to get an unlimited sushi high

7.7	7.0
Food	Feel

Japanese

Casual restaurant

$35
Price

www.sushipalace.us

Mon–Thu 11am–10pm	**Bar** Beer, wine	**Hamden**
Fri–Sat 11am–11pm	**Credit cards** Visa, MC	1473 Dixwell Ave.
Sun noon–10pm	**Reservations** Accepted	(203) 230-8875

Sushi Palace is constantly packed to the gills with hungry college students, large families, and celebratory groups ordering all-you-can-eat sushi and a variety of Japanese dishes for under $20. While the concept of "all-you-can-eat" is usually a flashing neon warning, the turnover at this popular restaurant suggests that the fish will be fresh, even if not the highest quality (the American obsession with drowning fish in wasabi is a sushi restaurant's dream come true).

The selection of fish is not terribly extensive—these are lowest-common-denominator favorites. There's an extensive hot-food menu available, but don't waste your time with that. Although seaweed salad is easily better than the overpriced deli containers (though that's not saying much), vegetable tempura is greasy and chewy; pork katsu is bland and dry; and neither shumai nor gyoza tastes much different from what you might find in the frozen-foods section at a grocery store.

The things to eat here are nigiri and sashimi—the basics (tuna, yellowtail, and so on) are well executed, especially for an all-you-can-eat place. The special rolls look tempting and enormous, loaded with fanciful combinations of ingredients, but instead of a skillfully constructed graceful play between their components, the flavors all cancel each other out and become monotonous. A Butterfly Roll, looking pretty in pinkish soybean paper with a filling of lobster, mango, avocado, and sweet chili sauce, has a one-dimensional sweetness. The soft-shell crab roll tastes uniformly of mayo (this is another roll we don't understand—it's not even good in the best places, and always overpriced because it's a sure thing).

Generally, it seems that rolls are designed to fill diners up with cheap rice and make use of the uglier and smaller cuts of fish. This isn't to say they're categorically bad, but in this case, it's a way for the kitchen to keep its product costs down. Between each menu page exhorting you to "order all you want but eat all you order," and the waitstaff's shaming glares, diners are guilted into finishing those huge, bland rolls before placing another order for sashimi. The result? Less expensive fish consumed.

Still, this place is fun and can even be worth it: Come early on a weeknight, order nothing but salads from the kitchen menu, then order to your heart's content from the fresh, glistening nigiri and sashimi options. It will be money very well spent.

Swagat

Some of the city's best Indian—and vegetarian—at these prices? We must be dreaming.

Indian

Casual restaurant

$15
Price

Mon–Thu 5pm–10pm; Fri noon–2pm, 5pm–10pm; Sat noon–10pm

Bar BYO
Credit cards Visa, MC, AmEx
Reservations Accepted
Date-friendly, kid-friendly, veg-friendly

West Haven
215 Boston Post Rd.
(203) 931-0108

When we think of Swagat, it calls to mind a line from *A Midsummer Night's Dream*: "Though she be but little, she is fierce." Not only does this fierce little contender serve some of the best-value Indian food in the area—underselling the downtown competition by a couple bucks—it's also some of the very best.

Although standard northern Indian dishes like samosas and lamb curry are unremarkable here, the real deal is the authentic south Indian cuisine that you will find almost nowhere else in the area. The centerpiece is the dosa—a large, thinly rolled crêpe made from rice batter. There are seven variations on the dosa; the wonderful uttapam is a bit thicker, more like a pancake with onions and cilantro. A delicious masala dosa comes stuffed with potatoes. All arrive with a delectable assortment of condiments, from a sweet coconut chutney to an interesting pink tomato sauce redolent of ginger, to a soupy lentil sambar with turmeric and other spices. And a full lunch or dinner of these Southern specialties will often ring in under $10.

Other sensational, smaller dishes include vada—cakey, deep-fried patties made from lentils. They are surprisingly light, not at all greasy, and served with a spicy chutney juxtposed with cooling dal. For divine inspiration, try long slices of okra—which manage to circumvent that slimy okra thing—cooked with peppers and tomatoes in a spicy chili oil. Hey, we love us some lamb, but we don't even go for it here. That's the other great thing about Swagat: more than half of the dishes on the dinner menu, including every single South Indian dish, are strictly vegetarian.

Though tiny and a somewhat spare, the room was recently painted pepper-red and hung with black and white photographs, which, while not quite a total atmospheric turnaround, is certainly a slightly romantic improvement. Mondays through Thursdays they are closed to focus on their cart over by the Yale medical area in New Haven.

Despite its cult following, Swagat is never packed; perhaps this owes to its weird location on the outskirts of West Haven. But we highly recommend making the trip out there…else the Fearless Critic a liar call.

Szechuan Delight

Possibly the best Chinese food around, but you have to insist you want it

9.0	5.5
Food	Feel

Chinese

Casual restaurant

$25
Price

Mon–Thu 11am–10pm; Fri–Sat 11am–11pm; Sun 11:30am–10pm

Bar Beer, wine, liquor
Credit cards Visa, MC, AmEx
Reservations Accepted
Delivery

Hamden
1720 Dixwell Ave.
(203) 407-1188

Remember Cooper Black, that goofy, rotund 1980s font that you'd see on iron-on T-shirts? It's the font currently adorning the green awnings outside this restaurant, which seems to be decorated like a Chinese person's idea of what white suburban Americans think of Chinese food. Large aquariums of pouty fish, faux-bamboo railings, and a (shattered) window portrait of two fighting stallions scream "Lemon Chicken," while a banner advertising "all-you-can-eat sushi" looks like unnecessary pandering. Especially once you try the food.

And we don't mean the food off the menu they give you. If that were the only menu here, Szechuan Delight would be lucky to get a 6.5. No, friends, we mean the *real* menu. The mythical Second Menu. The authentic, Szechuan, barely-in-English menu, which you have to ask for specially.

Here, you will find starters like "Husband and Wife," a cold serving of tongue, tripe, beef tendon, and other obscure cuts of cow in a brilliant salad that's studded with Szechuan peppercorns, with fat and cartilage pockets. Follow this up with fish-head soup in a large earthen dish; the broth is impossibly nourishing, lightly salty and full of cabbage and free-floating chunks of pink meat.

These preparations are driven by the Szechuan peppercorn, that bizarre, delightful spice that numbs the mouth, makes you salivate like mad, and cross-reacts with all the stinging heat that makes these dishes so stimulating. (Try drinking water after eating a mouthful of it. It's a trip.) You'll find them in a sensational dish called "water pork," tender strips of pork simmering in a deep red broth of chili oil and Szechuan peppercorns with baby bok choy. You'll find an abundance of them, too, heating up beany, earthy ma la tofu, which looks and tastes like it was pressed fresh there on the premises. We've had curious diners desert their fried rice and General Tso's, approach our bounty, and ask what everything was. "Is it spicy?" they ask, after we tell them.

There are easily three full pages worth exploring. The manager will only be happy to bring you this menu, but after multiple warnings. When did Americans become such wusses? It's all that chop suey we ate in the 50's. For even *those* people, there is Lion's Head, succulent, enormous pork meatballs in a sensuous brown gravy and full of diced water chestnuts for a joyous crunch.

Ah, Szechuan Delight, you little sneak, looking tepid and harmless on your stretch of Hamden road. We're going to tell on you.

S'Wings

Great only late, late at night when you have no better judgment

6.4	3.5
Food	Feel

American

Casual restaurant

$15
Price

Mon–Wed 11am–11pm
Thu 11am–1am
Fri 11am–3am
Sat noon–3am
Sun 1pm–9pm

Bar None
Credit cards Visa, MC
Reservations Not accepted
Delivery

Chapel District
280 Crown St.
(203) 562-9464

Hubris never did Buffalo wings any good, yet S'Wings might be unpretentious to a fault: the unfinished wood benches, unadorned walls, and fat rolls of paper towel-napkins build a genuinely stark atmosphere. All the better to appreciate Buffalo wings, one might say. And we'd agree: particularly after a long, sweaty night at a nearby frat or club, S'Wings hits the spot.

The nicely fried wings come with one of three Buffalo sauces or a bevy of specialty flavorings. We recommend the "s'wings" or "s'mokin" Buffalo varieties for a considerable flavor blast and an appropriate kick in the pants—the "s'issie" sauce, as you might guess, doesn't bring enough oomph to the party. Venture forth and try the garlic-parmesan wings for a walk on the wild side. Tossed in butter and sprinkled with parm, these wings offer a pleasant respite from the menu's heavier fare. We found the excess sweetness of the mango habanero sauce a bit awkward—stick with the savory sauces for best results.

The price is right for most menu items. Twelve wings are less than $10, but the real savings kick in with quantities fit for the Super Bowl: 100 wings, enough to satiate 10 respectable appetites, cost around only $50.

Beyond the wings, it all gets generic. Cheese fries, though cheap and satisfyingly greasy, can come lukewarm. The corn dogs are deliciously standard, featuring a moist frank and crispy batter that actually tastes like corn. The "whiskey smoke" sandwich has a sweet-spicy thing that works for this type of cuisine, but fails to rescue a fatally boring chicken breast. The cheese steak, like most menu items, is comparable to average ballpark food: fine, if eaten with low expectations and a substantial posse.

As with Samurai on College St. across from the Shubert, S'Wings' calling card is location. The wings are delicious, no doubt, but the holistic experience rarely warrants a special trip. Just come after the bars close to give your liver a fighting chance.

Take the Cake

Cult-favorite cake makers that start only with natural ingredients

Baked goods

Take-out

www.originaltakethecake.com

Mon–Fri 9am–6pm
Sat 9am–5pm

Bar None
Credit cards Visa, MC, AmEx
Kid-friendly, veg-friendly

Guilford
2458 Boston Post Rd.
(203) 453-1896

It's cake. What's not to love?

If that's your response, then you've never had an office-birthday-party cake, fresh from the grocery store, with airbrushed, greasy Crisco-tasting frosting and nasty frozen jam running through it. *Shudder.* Ever seen Food Network's "Ace of Cakes?" Yeah. In cake, good and cool-looking don't often go together.

But Guilford's own cake wünderkinds, Take the Cake, have made it happen. They use only whole, real ingredients: butter, sugar, flour, eggs, real vanilla, and chocolate. Since there are no artificial flavors or colors, don't come looking for a groom's cake made to look like a putting green. Their buttercream icing is made in the traditional French style, with unsalted butter, and tastes absolutely wonderful. It's creamy and rich without being overbearing and grainy. It allows the excellent, moist cake to shine through. Ganache is decadently 100% chocolate. There are variations involving lemon, almonds, hazelnuts, mint, and carrot, not to mention cheesecake.

You'll find the little boxes hanging out at specialty stores, like Bon Appétit, or you can visit the bakery, where there's a case of 6" and 9" choices. You can have them inscribed, but in a color meant to be eaten: chocolate or vanilla.

Prices are fair for this kind of quality and care, averaging out to about $3 per slice (if you don't take the whole thing down in the car). There is a prodigious selection of cookies, and many are available wheat-, dairy-, and sugar-free. So next time you're caught in a supermarket-cake nightmare—expected to ooh and aah over an ice-blue fondant cake in the shape of a giant Dr. Seuss hat, replete with little silver balls, just think happy thoughts of Take the Cake. Thanks, nice cake people.

Tandoor

(Improved) Indian food in a diner—fancy that

7.6 Food

7.5 Feel

Indian

Casual restaurant

$25 Price

Daily 11:30am–10:30pm

Bar Beer, wine
Credit cards Visa, MC, AmEx
Reservations Accepted
Delivery, kid-friendly, veg-friendly

Upper Chapel Area
1226 Chapel St.
(203) 776-6620

Here's the sympathetic interpretation (sympathetic to us, anyway): Tandoor has vastly improved since the Second Edition. The Indian-American classics are executed with care. Tandoori chicken is now remarkably moist, layered with flavor, some of the best in the city. Lamb in the curries and stews is surprisingly tender. Saag paneer has an ideal texture, although it's laced with an unusual amount of ginger. Bhaigan bharta, an eggplant dish, has good flavor. The lunch buffet, which (unusually) features authentic touches like spicy pickle and nicely acidic raita, is now up to $10, but it's still one of the city's great deals, a cut above the local competition.

Here's the unsympathetic interpretation: we just got it wrong last time around, when it got a mere 5.8 for food. Maybe we happened to have visited on bad days. Maybe we ordered wrong. It happens. Who knows?

But here's the part that's indisputable: Tandoor, set inside a diner, breaks new ground for Indian-restaurant packaging. We've still never seen anything like it: the restaurant was once the Elm City Diner, the real thing, complete with the old ersatz train-car style. It's an amusing sign of the times that the most authentic-looking diner in this old-school American town serves Indian food.

The food won't blow your mind. Chicken, in the various curries, is a particular weak point. The white-meat chunks come incredibly dry and overcooked. Even if Tandoor—improved though it may be—is eclipsed by some of the newer competition, do keep in mind that the entertainment value of eating Indian food inside an old diner is quite significant. At a minimum, you need to see it for yourself.

Taquería Mexicana #2

7.6 Food **4.5** Feel

A simple little grocery and lunch spot with authentic tacos that tend to be hit or miss

Mexican   Counter service **$10** Price

Daily 10am–10pm

Bar Beer
Credit cards Visa, MC, AmEx

West Haven
702 Boston Post Rd.
(203) 931-8534

We have been longtime fans of Taquería Mexicana #2. We still are, but it's been a bit uneven lately. The store still carries Mexican Coke, which we love for its use of cane sugar instead of corn syrup, but also for its logistics-be-damned commitment to authenticity that separates the true culinary legends from the impostors. Look for the "Hecho en Mexico" printed on the bottles in the little fridge next to the Jarritos, the Fanta, the sweetened juices of mango and tamarind, the Squirt, and the most popular choice of all, that legendary Mexican soft drink to end all Mexican soft drinks—Boing.

On a good day, there are still pretty good tacos at this little West Haven strip-mall joint near the University of New Haven, but they do get a little exploitative in price (the incredible frugality of such a meal is one of the great delights of the taquería). At their best, the tacos transport you to Mexico, from the delicious doubled-up corn tortillas to the meat itself, which, authentically, can alternate between chewy and tender. Best might be the barbacoa de chivo, whose deep, throbbing goatiness we still love; the tender goat meat's soft strands of fat play off the onions, cilantro, and fresh lime (you squeeze it on). Delicious also is the saltier and spicier adobado, little red pieces of pork with a remarkably well-developed flavor. The salsas are all worth trying; our favorite is a chunky salsa with onions and tomatoes that is impeccably fresh. Beef, chicken, and such have alternately come out gristly, greasy, and tough. We think Taquería needs a bit more quality control on the meat texture and grease quotient.

The room is so authentic in its downmarket simplicity—just a few tables and bare concrete walls—that you might want to take out. The menu also includes burritos, tostadas, tortas (Mexican sandwiches), and so on. You can order rice and beans as a side, though it's not on the menu. Know also that you should try everything, the more uncommon the better: al pastor (spiced, marinated, shaved pork), cabeza (head), and lengua (tongue). Follow it up with a Mexican candy, like the chicken lollipop that looks like a whole roast chicken, but tastes like spicy fruit. Mmmm, tasty weirdness.

Taste

7.4 Food **8.0** Feel

A good place to eat; a better place to try great wines at terrific prices

New American

Upmarket restaurant **$45** Price

www.tastenorthhaven.com

Mon–Thu 11:45am–9pm
Fri 11:45am–10pm
Sat 4:30pm–10pm
Sun 4pm–8pm

Bar Beer, wine, liquor
Credit cards Visa, MC, AmEx
Reservations Accepted
Date-friendly, good wines

North Haven
1995 Whitney Ave.
(203) 230-8801

Taste is done up in a haphazard mélange of styles. The outside is stony English country house; the inside is late '90s IKEA, with blue pendant lamps and birch-colored furnishings; and then there are some strange "country hearth" touches like wreaths of cranberries. But we sort of like it; it's disarming. Maybe we like it more because it seems humble, and with a hyper-modern New American menu like this, Taste seems like a candidate for the sort of affectation and arrogance into which some restaurants seem to descend simply because they offer some Asian fusion.

Aside from that particular gaffe (and a few more like it), the menu is sound, at times flirting with gastro-pub status with mac and cheese, meatloaf, and roasted game hen.

We're generally skeptical of tuna-soy-wasabi preparations on New American menus, but tuna tacos in fried "wonton" shells, while hardly a subtle dish, are tender, well soy-sauced, and pleasant to eat. Ricotta gnocchi with pork, tomato, herbs, and parmesan are texturally satisfying, even if the pasta doesn't quite achieve that lovely pillowy softness of which it's capable.

Meats are all cooked just fine. We particularly like a pork tenderloin with a bacon and apple salad; it's definitely a winter dish, but one we'll happily take. Hanger steak, too, is a tender, flavorful winner. Its accompanying Gorgonzola onions are an addictive treat, and tempura asparagus is expertly fried. Sometimes the kitchen tends to cook starches into oblivion, and there are consistent problems with undersalting. Even so, its work is pretty satisfying. It simply tastes good; just sprinkle some salt on it and the flavors come alive.

The wine list is sincere and surprising, with some really exciting small-production imports at prices so low that it's just bonkers. Try the Jean-Paul Brun, an unoaked white Beaujolais that shows off Chardonnay's elegant potential. It's priced in the high $20s, so why wouldn't you get a bottle? Or try a Vouvray; the Loire Valley is arguably the best place on Earth for Chenin Blanc. Marchesi di Gresy, a Piedmont producer that usually commands prices too high for most Dolcetto drinkers, is a bargain here, and worth checking out with the pork-and-basil meatball starters.

In the end, we like Taste, but we're not in love.

Temple Grill

As a sports bar, it falters, but the patio is lovely for a casual meal

7.3	8.0
Food	Feel

American   Casual restaurant   **$40**
                                                                   Price

www.templegrill.com

Sun–Wed 11:30am–10pm
Thu 11:30am–11pm
Fri–Sat 11:30am–midnight

Bar Beer, wine, liquor
Credit cards Visa, MC, AmEx
Reservations Not accepted
Live music, outdoor dining,
veg-friendly

Chapel District
152 Temple St.
(203) 773-1111

Temple Grill is a bizarre paradox. There are two flat screen TVs over the bar, but there's has no beer on draught. Meats are cooked to spot-on temperatures, but salads aren't taken seriously as a culinary concept. Is this a sports bar or isn't it?

The décor is jazzy-industrial chic, executed with welcome restraint. Careful lighting and dirt-red walls endow diners with a flattering golden hue, but it's the televisions and gleaming bar that take center stage, especially at game time. When this small space fills up, people are sitting on top of each other.

The decidedly un-bar-like "salad card" lets you design your own (huge and cheap) out of a plethora of ingredients, but isn't this supposed to be the role of the chef? We're not fans of the mix-and-match concept.

Otherwise, comfort food is best here. Sweet potato fries start the meal off right, and are neither too sweet nor overwhelmed by garlic aioli. The "signature" spinach and artichoke dip is charming, if mundane. A bacon cheeseburger with sautéed onions is simply excellent, with rich, well-textured beef and a toothy, structurally sound bun. Don't miss the menu's crown jewel: meatloaf bursting with beefiness, herbs, and spices. First baked, then seared on the grill, each slice is drizzled with a heady demi-glace. Tenderloin tips are excellent when ordered medium-rare or less.

But several sloppy moves keep Temple from joining the upper echelon. The incomprehensibly compulsory tuna carpaccio with wasabi aioli (does anyone actually enjoy the tuna-wasabi act outside of a good sushi restaurant?), is bland—and mislabeled. Instead of thin slices, unwieldly chunks of pale, flavorless tuna are clobbered by the overbearing sauce. The waffle fries, a mainstay for any sports bar, have good potato flavor, but lack salt. You can add it later, but it won't stick; fries need to be seasoned right out of the fryer.

Expensive cocktails (with a couple of impressive apéritifs, including manzanilla sherry—again, what kind of place is this?) outpace the cookie-cutter wine list, while the beer selection is mass-produced and blah. With outdoor seating in summer and a vibe that's less rowdy than Richter's, Temple Grill is a good choice for an after-work or pre-Shubert libation. It's safe, but it's not a destination.

The Terrace

A pretty little spot from which to wave so long to food-court pad Thai

8.6 Food

7.5 Feel

Thai

Casual restaurant

$35 Price

www.theterracethai.com

Mon–Thu 11:30am–3pm, 5pm–
9:30pm; Fri 11:30am–3pm,
5pm–10pm; Sat noon–10pm;
Sun noon–9:30pm

Bar Beer, wine, liquor
Credit cards Visa, MC
Reservations Accepted
Veg-friendly

Hamden
1559 Dixwell Ave.
(203) 230-2077

Believe the media buzz: this little Thai restaurant, hidden along a stretch of Dixwell that seems to be exploding with subversively good Asian food, is the real deal. The Terrace's menu strays further from Thai-American and more into the real regional cuisine of Thailand than any other restaurant in the New Haven area—except, perhaps, for Rice Pot.

But this is hardly an ethnic hole-in-the-wall. The Thai couple that owns the place has a penchant for upmarketing, advertising the wife's French culinary pedigree. The space going for something more minimalist than your standard Thai-American joint; it's far more New American-ish, all whites and blacks, and its carefully planted lawns shield it from the road traffic in a surprisingly effective way. The presentations, too, are far more artful than usual, with vertical plating and such. The flip side of these facts is that the Terrace's portions are smaller than usual and their prices higher than usual ($15.95 for three rice-noodle-crusted prawns on skewers?).

That's not to say that the menu completely avoids the boring Thai-American staples, Chinese-American stir-fry dishes, and such. These are perhaps necessary to do a steady lunch business in the area. But the husband and wife that run the joint seem to bow to those conventions begrudgingly. Clearly, they care more about the real stuff: flaky deep-fried catfish salad with green mango, shallots, peanuts, chili, and lime; mussel pancake; shrimp-paste rice; or crispy rice crackers with a sauce of ground pork, shrimp, scallion, coconut milk, peanuts, and Thai spices. Even the Terrace's tom yum soup is much spicier than the local norm, and refreshingly, it's sprinkled with kaffir lime leaf, adding needed complexity.

"Terrace curry" is probably too spicy for 95% of the people who order it, but the dish really deserves a chance. It's one of the few Thai curries in the city to display such admirable balance of flavor, spice, and aroma: aggressive chili pepper, garlic and kaffir lime leaf, just a whisper of coconut milk. But we don't really get the water chestnuts, and the protein lets you down a bit; the beef is the chewy kind, not at all better than average. This is one of the few systematic flaws at the Terrace.

Otherwise, the missteps are small. Som tam, the green papaya salad that is a staple—maybe the staple—of northern cuisine, boasts peanuts with a nice char, a subtle dose of palm sugar, unusually ripe cherry tomatoes, and sufficient heat from chili; however, the dried shrimp—one of the backbones of som tam flavor—are curiously missing. Another disappointment is that the fish dishes—steamed or fried—are made with fillets instead of whole fish, as they would be in Thailand. Still, it's hard to complain when this place represents such a step forward for Hamden.

TGI Friday's

This all-American mega-chain doesn't give us much
for which to be thankful

2.0	6.0
Food	Feel

American

Casual restaurant

$30
Price

www.tgifridays.com

Sun–Thu 11am–midnight
Fri–Sat 11am–1am

Bar Beer, wine, liquor
Credit cards Visa, MC, AmEx
Reservations Not accepted

Hamden
2335 Dixwell Ave.
(203) 407-0111

Orange
348 Boston Post Rd.
(203) 799-0800

We've certainly powered through our fair share of meals at TGI Friday's.
They usually occur as we are awaiting an inbound aircraft or as a result of
a mechanical or a weather delay. When you're stranded in an airport, this
mega-chain can sometimes be the best option—dispense with the idea of
trying to eat a light snack or of getting some work done while you wait.
Take the plunge, let the overenthusiastic servers beckon you into their
red-and-white-striped lair, and grab a beer and something fried. Whatever
you do, don't get a cocktail—they're weak, overpriced, and practically
guaranteed not to give you the buzz you're seeking.

But if we're beyond the reaches of the TSA and in the land where shoe-
wearing people transport liquids and gels in containers larger than 3
ounces, TGI Friday's is a much harder sell. Branches tend to lurk in
suburban strip malls and shopping centers, again preying on a captive
audience. After a marathon shopping session with the kids, most people
just want to sit down somewhere (read: anywhere) and eat something
(read: anything).

And there's something mediocre for just about everyone on a Friday's
menu. For the health-conscious and waistline-watchers, there is the
"Right Portion, Right Price" menu with such ringers as a cedar-seared
salmon pasta, whose fish is "coated with cedar smoke seasoning."
"Shrimp Key West" (only 12 carbs!) tend to come overcooked, their
Cajun spices overwhelming. If you're a meat-and-potatoes type, Friday's
has a "Jack Daniel's® Grill" menu for you. Different meats (ribs, steak,
chicken, shrimp) are grilled and coated with a "Jack Daniel's® glaze." If
you ask us, they need to be using more of that whiskey in their cocktails,
not their hyper-sweet, gloopy glazes. You'd think they could execute on a
burger and fries, at least. Nope: they're almost always rubbery (no matter
what temp you order) and droopy, respectively. We've even had wimpy,
dried-out, under-vinegared Buffalo tenders. And it's pretty hard to mess
up Buffalo tenders.

We do, in all earnestness, like the "Tuscan Spin Dip" (but don't even
get us started about the fact that it has the T-word in its name) with its
spinach, artichokes, and blend of Romano and parmesan cheeses. It's
tangy and creamy, but bell peppers don't contribute much to the dish.

So if it's Friday, and you're thanking goodness for this fact, stick to the
dip and beer, and consider bringing in a hip flask. You'll be thanking us
for this tip.

Thai Awesome

Hamden Thai that's at least a player in the
increasing-authenticity game

7.7 **7.5**
Food Feel

Thai

Casual restaurant **$25**
Price

www.thaiawesome.net

Mon–Thu 11:30am–3pm, 4pm–
9:30pm
Fri–Sat 11:30am–10pm
Sun noon–9:30pm

Bar Beer, wine
Credit cards Visa, MC
Reservations Accepted
Veg-friendly

Hamden
1505 Dixwell Ave.
(203) 288-9888

The husband-and-wife team that owns Thai Awesome opened it after the
husband left his stint at Thai Taste (under positive circumstances, we are
told). Leaving New Haven for Hamden seems to have been a good call, as
this stretch is enjoying something of a Thai burst, headlined by the pricier
Terrace a few doors down. This place is more laid-back and simple, and
the staff could hardly be any friendlier, although the space—wooden
wainscoting, rough plaster yellow walls, catalog-ish lanterns—is nothing
special, and it's dominated by sweeping parking lot views in front.

The best thing on this menu is a splendid version of wok-kissed
drunken noodle. The key is to ask for the dish with minced chicken, as the
local Thais do, instead of the tougher whole chicken chunks. We also
appreciate the scattered attempts at lesser-seen regional Thai dishes, the
best of which is "Siam soft-shell crab," made with egg, coconut milk, and
onion (in Thailand it would probably be called "curry powder crab," and
more likely made with the hard-shell variety). Authentically spicy "lime
fish" is a small whole red snapper that's covered with lots of fresh garlic
slices, green chilies, red pepper, and fish sauce. The prep packs a punch,
but the fish beneath is an inferior specimen, a grayish, flaky little thing
with none of the delicate flavor or sweetness one would hope for.

Some of the simpler dishes are even less successful, like yum nua, a
salad whose slices of beef are chewy and overcooked, like at a bad
Chinese restaurant. The chili is too restrained, the big chunks of cucumber
are a throwaway, and the limey kick, savory fish sauce, and bright cilantro
aren't enough to rescue the dish. And why must the lunch combo be so
boring? Pad Thai, "Siam Fried Rice," drunken noodle, cashew nut, or red
curry? Zzzzzz.

Along those lines, the specials list might fool some diners into thinking
they're witnessing examples of some obscure regional Thai cuisine—e.g.
"Wild Boar Basil"—but they're really just permutations of the same set of
Thai-American and/or Chinese-American stir-fries and curries, many of
them laden with sugar, culminating in the Chinese-American dish to end
all: the "Siam roll," a deep-fried egg roll with sweet-and-sour sauce.

It's not that this food is bad, exactly; it's just that it's become clear that
the New Haven area is ready for even more authentic, better executed
regional Thai food. Still, Thai Awesome is a worthy addition to Hamden,
and an improvement over its origins.

Thai Awesome Food Cart

6.6	8.0
Food	Feel

While the food carts are cheaper and easier to get to, we prefer the stationary version

Thai

Take-out

$5
Price

Mon–Fri 11am–2pm

Bar None
Credit cards None
Outdoor dining, veg-friendly

East Rock
Prospect St. near Ingalls rink
(203) 288-9888

Medical Area
Corner of Cedar St. and York St.
(203) 288-9888

Okay, this gets sticky, so stay with us: until recently, these carts were known as "Thai Taste," although they were not owned by the Thai Taste on Chapel; the cart's owner did once work there, but he now owns Thai Awesome in Hamden. The name was allowed to remain for a while because, as Thai Taste restaurant's owner once told *Yale Daily News*, "He takes care of the cart; he takes care of the food."

The much-cared-for Thai Awesome carts have decreased from three to two; one still parks steps away from the Yale Medical School in the Hill district; the other is inches from the School of Management, near the hockey rink—a great place to pick up some dinner on the way home if you're an East Rock resident. The York and Elm cart is gone, perhaps owing to competition from the nearby Tijuana Taco Company, which does far more business even while charging a buck or two more.

At each cart, the Thai menu is limited to a few of the standard classics, and combinations of two or three items are accommodated. In any case, it's hard to spend more than about five dollars here, even with a drink; in a city of low-priced food carts, this is one of the cheapest. The vegetable drunken noodle, one of the dishes that cycles through the specials here, is made up of spicy noodles sautéed with vegetables, purple basil, onion, and scallion.

Chicken massaman curry, with coconut milk, onion, peanut, and potato, is a popular choice, but it's a below-average version, with mealy potatoes. Better might be the vegetable yellow curry, simmered with coconut milk, pineapple, zucchini, onion, baby corn, and tofu. Barbecued garlic chicken skewers are good, when they aren't overly dry. Pineapple fried rice is our favorite thing here. Pad Thai is a staple.

In general, Thai Awesome's restaurant serves better food than the cart, and of all the Thai carts, Jasmine Thai is still our winner. It would sure be nice to find a cart—any cart!—that actually tries its hand at authentic Thai street food.

Thai Pan Asian

A strange, dark Southeast Asian restaurant that tries do too much—and accomplishes far too little

2.2 Food   **5.0** Feel

Thai, Pan-Asian

Casual restaurant   **$25** Price

Mon–Fri 11:30am–3pm, 5pm–10pm; Sat–Sun 11:30am–10:30pm

Bar Beer, wine, liquor
Credit cards Visa, MC, AmEx
Reservations Accepted
Delivery, outdoor dining, veg-friendly

Upper Chapel Area
1150 Chapel St.
(203) 624-9689

We've got to credit Thai Pan Asian for putting it all out there. Within foodie circles, "pan Asian" has become something of a dirty word, synonymous with sweet, gummy dishes that are indigenous to the US restaurant scene—not Asia.

And trust us, that's what you'll find here. The menu bravely offers a panoply of cuisine inspired by islands—and mainlands—all over the Pacific Rim. A two-storied establishment with a strangely dark interior at the epicenter of the proliferation of Chapel Street Thai, this place combines Chinese, Thai, Japanese and, yes, even sushi, none of which is particularly inspiring.

The inexpensive brunch buffet is to be avoided. It's a selection of some of the less interesting dishes on the menu, sitting out for a while and taking in some air. Every now and then we give it another chance and try it again, and every single time, the buffet is just as bad. Under-flavored dishes. Greasy dishes. Soggy dishes. Bland soups. Though it's a good deal in terms of amount of food, there are better Thai lunch specials for similar prices nearby on Chapel Street—and, generally elsewhere.

As for the menu, some dishes, like deep-fried frog with garlic sauce, sound interesting, but accompanying pineapple chunks and romaine lettuce are totally out of place. And other selections are simply less inspired versions of the same ubiquitous Thai-American dishes. We do like the outdoor seating on a nice day. But perhaps Thai Pan Asian would do better to focus on a more unique theme—like reinventing itself as a hip Pacific Rim cocktail bar—rather than trying to do everything, food-wise, and falling short on all fronts.

These guys have bitten off more than we can chew.

Thai Taste

A popular restaurant in the thick of Chapel's Thai row that occupies a cool beer-hall space

Thai

Casual restaurant

$35
Price

www.thaitastenewhaven.com

Mon–Thu 11:30am–3pm, 5pm–10pm
Fri–Sat 11:30am–10:30pm
Sun 4:30pm–10pm

Bar Beer, wine, liquor
Credit cards Visa, MC, AmEx
Reservations Accepted
Date-friendly, veg-friendly

Upper Chapel Area
1151 Chapel St.
(203) 776-9802

This place has totally upped its game since the last edition of our guide. Perhaps the proprietors were inspired by the success of their other venture, Rice Pot, which pushed the New Haven envelope of authenticity. As such, they've brought up the quality (and redone the menu) of Thai Taste. While it's still not as regional or authentic as Rice Pot, it's definitely better than it used to be, and the atmosphere is much more fun than average Thai.

Located in the basement of the Hotel Duncan, this subterranean restaurant has décor that feels like an old-school bar—in fact, it is one, occupying a space that used to be a German beer hall called Old Heidelberg. It's rather dark and well worn, with graftings of Thai paraphernalia, presided over by framed photographs of the Thai royal family, which proudly take their places in the entrance and foyer. One unsettling aspect of this restaurant's location is the fishbowl effect of windows at knee height to passing foot traffic; on the other hand, this may be a boon to potential customers who have the opportunity to see for themselves just what exactly patrons are eating.

One of our favorite things here is the Panang curry, whose vegetable mélange includes eggplant, squash, carrots, snow peas, and peppers, although the quality can vary. Sometimes it's so addictive that we want to drink a large Styrofoam cup of it; other times it's so salty that even we (who could very well wear salt licks around our necks) can barely eat it. Tofu isn't fried to super-crispy, but its slight sponginess is a plus when it comes to mopping up the curry. "Sizzling steak" comes from kitchen to table with memorable sound effects, emitting pungent aromas of ginger and garlic that will have fellow diners setting aside the printed menus and straining to peer over banquettes in search of inspiration. But we do wish they had more sour-savory yum, as Rice Pot does. And Thai iced tea is tooth-achingly sweet.

Ultimately, it's the unique atmosphere, more than the food, that distinguishes Thai Taste from the competition on Chapel Street. It's a strange place to run into visiting luminaries from Yale, but we have indeed spotted some here.

Thali

A nouvelle Indian restaurant—and a sleek date place, too? Only in Ninth Square.

8.4	8.5
Food	Feel

Indian

Upmarket restaurant

$50
Price

www.thali.com

Sun–Thu noon–2:30pm, 5pm–9:30pm
Fri–Sat noon–2:30pm, 5pm–10:30pm

Bar Beer, wine, liquor
Credit cards Visa, MC, AmEx
Reservations Accepted
Date-friendly, veg-friendly

Ninth Square
4 Orange St.
(203) 777-1177

Who ever said Indian food couldn't be sexy?

With a red glow, angular modern design, and high-flying prices to match the style, Thali—which has taken the place of a series of failed restaurants in the Ninth Square space—has transformed the city's notion of what an Indian meal can be. Yeah, it's a chain. But it's a good one—a much better one than Coromandel, which is Thali's only real competitor in the greater New Haven area when it comes to modern Indian cuisine. The space is elegant, although some seating areas feel colder than others.

Bizarrely, the menu here doesn't actually include thali, the set-price Indian meal that would appear to be the restaurant's namesake. But they do serve a menu with impressive depth and variety; it skips around the Subcontinent (and, yes, around America too, at times) enough to offer a totally varied experience, beginning with what might be the best papadum you've ever tasted, light as air but of a richness, too.

Whatever you do, start with dahi batata sev puri (little wheat puffs that are filled with chat, the classic Bombay street food). We've enjoyed such simpler vegetarian dishes here more than the complex, more aggressive attempts at creativity; to wit, konkan crab, a barrage of coconut milk, green chilies, and mustard seed, comes off more like a sugared-up, in-your-face pan-Asian dish than an Indian one.

There's a heavy hand with ginger here, but that's not necessarily a bad thing; it shows through the lovely, well-spiced saag paneer, which is made without cream, if slightly undersalted. Our favorite dish on the menu, though, is ghosht banjara (bone-in goat), which has rich and deep flavors, if not much spice. We're also fans of paneer sanji jalfraize, a curried vegetable dish with homemade cheese. At times, we've liked "My Mother's Andrha Chicken," with poppyseed, cloves and cardamom, but it's also come out dry on occasion. Sunheri bhindi—fried okra dusted with spices—is a better idea as a side dish than as a main.

When you fall back on the basics, they can be disappointing: onion kulcha is just average, chicken tikka masala worse—it's dry and overcooked, although its sauce is unusually smoky. There's an all-you-can-eat Sunday brunch for $16.95 that is completely worth it—you can order a dosa to order, like you would an omelette station at an American brunch.

In the end, our biggest criticism of Thali is that it's not quite as good as its cheaper, more informal sister on Broadway, Thali Too. But that's less a criticism of Thali, and more of a compliment to Thali Too.

...ali Too

This South Indian vegetarian restaurant beats out
its pricier sibling—what a treat

9.0 Food

7.0 Feel

Indian

Casual restaurant

$35 Price

www.thalitoo.com

Sun–Thu 11am–2pm, 5pm–10pm
Fri–Sat 11am–3pm, 5pm–2am

Bar Beer, wine, liquor
Credit cards Visa, MC, AmEx
Reservations Not accepted
Date-friendly, outdoor dining,
veg-friendly

Broadway District
65 Broadway
(203) 776-1600

Thali's South Indian vegetarian sister, Thali Too, has taken La Piazza's place next to the Yale Bookstore, making it extremely convenient for Yale students and their visiting parents. One of the most remarkable aspects of the place is the diversity of its clientele. It's even surpassed Yorkside Pizza as "the librarians' cafeteria."

Nothing on the menu costs more than $10, which adds significantly to Thali Too's appeal, as well. The staff, and the pacing of dishes, can also be slow—this is not the place for a quick bite—but it is worth taking your time and savoring each dish.

Most of the menu comprises small dishes called tiffin or chat, mainly in the $5-$7 range and easily shareable. The "Dean's Dosa" is too large to fit on most tables in the restaurant. Slightly smaller but charged with flavor is the spicy onion rava masala dosa, served with coconut chutney, sambar, and chili oil. The modest-sounding upma—steamed cream of wheat—is surprisingly flavorful, soothing, and filling, kind of like an Indian congee.

Bhel poori is like a firecracker on a plate: a multicolored cylinder of a Rice-Krispie-ish poori, onions, tiny crisp lentil noodles, and tamarind sauce. Tempting but less successful is the "Paneer Wok 65," a dish of stir-fried cheese with the texture of tofu, tossed in a neon-pink curry sauce. It's blander than it looks. On a hot day, don't miss a salad of crisply fried okra, dusted with spices.

Mains are hit-or-miss, although the hits are among the best dishes in the city. Saag paneer is richly green, redolent of spices and ginger, and laced with generous squares of firm cheese. Baigan burtha, also a fairly standard eggplant curry in the hands of lesser chefs, tastes of the charcoal grill and fresh tomatoes. Best of all is the haldiram chole bathura, a modest dish of chickpeas and sauce scented with garam masala, served with a giant puff of deep-fried naan that is staggeringly rich, a yardstick by which to measure all other versions.

Thali Too has a party streak, too: a lassi can be spiked with the booze of your choice, and on Friday nights, a DJ spins Indian pop music. Carrot halwa for dessert is creamy, buttery, spicy, and a steal. New Haven is lucky to have such an excellent Indian restaurant so close to the Yale campus—one that has raised the bar for all other Indian restaurants in the vicinity. For that, Thali Too deserves something approaching hero-worship.

Tijuana Taco Company

The cartist formerly known as Roomba still makes a damn fine burrito

Mexican

7.4	8.0
Food	Feel

Take-out **$5**
Price

Mon–Fri 11am–7pm
Sat 11am–5pm hours change; call ahead

Bar None
Credit cards None
Kid-friendly, outdoor dining

Broadway District
Corner of York St. and Elm St.
(203) 562-7666

Medical Area
Near Cedar St. and York St.
(203) 562-7666

We *loved* Roomba; we *liked* Roomba Burrito Cart. Roomba became the lovely and slightly less successful Bespoke/Sabor Latino; the carts became Tijuana Taco Company. Fortunately, nothing was lost in the latter translation, except for the strange name that evoked images of an intelligent vacuuming Frisbee. The menu has expanded slightly, perhaps due to competitors on the same block serving quesadillas and tacos, in addition to their burritos. The carts are not immune to inflation—prices have gone up a hair since the last edition, but they're still a great deal.

There's one on the corner of York Street and Broadway, and another near Yale Medical's emergency room; unlike many others, these carts and their cheerful attendants seem weatherproof—they're out there even on the coldest days of winter. Once you make it to the front of the line, you are invited to participate in an interactive culinary performance. It all starts with the same swift motion: a tortilla is whisked from a mysterious steaming chamber, slapped down on a cutting board, and topped with flavorful rice and saucy black beans.

But the rest is up to you. Choose from sweet corn, homemade hot sauce, fresh-cut salsa, and smooth guacamole, and in less than three minutes, you'll have a delicious Mission-style burrito the size of an infant in your hands. The best burrito, by far, is still the pulled pork "with everything" (they aren't charging for condiments, unless you want a lot more of something), which includes the perfectly crunchy counterpoint to the moist, soft pork: a tangy cabbage-and-corn slaw. Lamb barbacoa, once a special—and still called "especial" on the menu—is now available every day, and it tastes good, though not totally redolent of funky lamb. But beware: there are sometimes bones and gobs of fat (the price you pay for excellent flavor).

Vegetarians will be delighted by their grilled vegetable mélange, complete with thick slices of Portobello mushroom. For the more carnivorous, the cart offers a never-ending supply of tender grilled steak and chicken. Tacos and quesadillas are now also available but take a little longer to make.

When you do go, do us all a favor and don't place an order for your entire office. One person = one burrito. Everyone will be so much happier.

Tony & Lucille's

Sopranos kitsch in its finest Wooster Street form

5.8	9.0
Food	Feel

Italian

Casual restaurant

$35
Price

Tue–Fri noon–3pm, 5pm–9:30pm
Sat 5pm–9:30pm
Sun 1pm–9:30pm

Bar Beer, wine, liquor
Credit cards Visa, MC, AmEx
Reservations Accepted
Date-friendly, kid-friendly, outdoor dining, veg-friendly

Wooster Square Area
150 Wooster St.
(203) 787-1621

Suffice it to say that, throughout this book, we tend to be critical of the culinary sensibilities of many of the Italian-American restaurants on offer in New Haven. (We're well known among friends as Italian food snobs.) But there's something about Tony & Lucille's that renders it immune from such dogged criticism, something to be said for the whole experience here that elevates it to another plane. Maybe it's the open arms of the wise and experienced waitstaff; maybe it's the warm feeling you get from beginning to end. The place has been around since 1953 (it first gained fame as a purveyor of calzones).

The best thing about Tony & Lucille's is that unlike much of the competition, the place has a lot of Sopranos-style kitschy charm. It's a dimly lit, fanciful room with canteens of Chianti hanging around, opera music piped in, and all the rest. Portions, needless to say, are mind-bogglingly enormous, and the food is true, competent, indigenous Italian-American. Fried calamari, clams casino, and fried mozzarella. Veal, eggplant, and chicken parmesan that come with another giant plate of somewhat overcooked spaghetti (share one between two people or you'll stumble home). There's even fettuccine Alfredo.

There are a few more daring ventures, such as a grilled veal chop with a Portobello gorgonzola cream sauce, and chicken sorrentino, sautéed in butter, garlic, and white wine, layered with ham and eggplant, and topped with mozzarella. It's over the top. So is the price for a take-out espresso: $2.75. That's just Wooster Street tourist price-gouging.

You can guess the rest. In any case, we recommend sticking with the true classics. You'll get what you came for: an Italian-American night out at one of the true survivors. A night from another era.

Town Pizza

A downtown pizza place serving up unremarkable
slices in an unremarkable cafeteria environment

3.2	3.0
Food	Feel

Pizza, Italian, American

Casual restaurant

$10
Price

Mon–Fri 11am–10pm
Sat 11am–9pm

Bar Beer, wine
Credit cards Visa, MC
Reservations Not accepted
Veg-friendly

Audubon Arts District
25 Whitney Ave.
(203) 865-6065

This pizzeria and Italian sub shop is quite well located on Whitney Avenue.
Perhaps that's why it still attracts such mobs at lunchtime, in spite of the
subpar food. The masses come to gorge themselves on the very standard
all-you-can-eat soup-and-salad bar upstairs for just over $6. But mediocre
food is never a good deal, and this buffet is filled with iceberg lettuce,
standard cafeteria-style trimmings—tuna fish and so on—and insipid
soups such as pasta e fagioli drowned in a tomato base.

Many of the patrons also seem to be tackling implausibly filling lunch
plates with huge piles of french fries, mediocre mozzarella sticks, and
enormous iceberg-lettuce salads topped with, say, buffalo chicken. Other
options include veal parmigiana subs, and the various turkey and chicken
wraps—but they fare scarcely better, even though the properly toasted
sub rolls are one high point.

As per the name, there's also pizza, but it's problematic pizza. While it's
not so bad if it's very hot and you're very hungry, beware as your slice
cools, when the copious cheese topping forms a separate peel-off layer,
along with topping and grease, that quickly begins to congeal. The sauce,
meanwhile, is more like the thick red sauce you'd expect for Italian-
American pasta, not pizza. Among the available pizza options, we
recommend the sausage (which actually has hints of fennel) to distract
you from the taste of the pizza itself. At least the slices are big, if you
consider that a good thing in this case.

Then there's the depressing, plasticky décor—Formica tables in bright
orange, and plastic booths in a slightly darker shade of the same color,
just different enough to clash, and the white walls with fake bricks, which
look like yet another relic out of New Haven's checkered urban-planning
past.

Trader Joe's

Come and play in foodie paradise

Groceries   Market

www.traderjoes.com

Daily 9am–9pm   **Bar** Beer, wine   **Orange**
                       Credit cards Visa, MC, AmEx 560 Boston Post Rd.
                       Good wines, veg-friendly   (203) 795-5505

The folks at TJ's have their heads and hearts in exactly the right place.
Their business model represents a much-needed return to simplicity: cut
out all the fat. Trader Joe's makes a concerted effort to buy most of their
products directly from producers themselves. This means that your
vegetables haven't changed hands five times before they end up on your
plate—and it also means that you're not paying each of those hands to
pass them along the chain. Buyers are an elite group, with well-trained
eyes for the best stuff out there, be it wine, cheese, coffee, tea, olive oil,
chocolate; the list goes on and on. The best deals of all are usually the
private label (TJ's brand) products.

The wine sections at Trader Joe's are like playgrounds for wine geeks.
Carefully chosen bottles come from tiny estates the world over. But you'll
also find quite a few of the big names. And we can't forget about Charles
Shaw ("Two-Buck Chuck"—we know that no one on a budget possibly
could). The value wine to beat all value wines, it's made from surplus
juice, so it's bought at a very low cost. In a series of blind tastings
conducted in 2007-2008, one batch of Charles Shaw Cabernet Sauvignon
was actually preferred by tasters to a $40 bottle of Beringer Founder's
Estate Cabernet Sauvignon. (For more on this, see *The Wine Trials*,
another Fearless Critic Media title.) In fact, Trader Joe's features a
remarkable number of winning bottles from *The Wine Trials*. Beer is
chosen with an equally keen eye. Microbrews from all corners of the earth
converge on the shelves here, and staff are über-knowledgeable.

There's a definite focus on organic goods, and all products have slickly
designed and super-easy-to-understand labels. Low-sodium, heart-
healthy, and kosher are just a few of the indications you might run into.
Stores are well laid out and easy to navigate. The aesthetic is nice, with
natural woods set against bright colors. It's a visual wonderland.

It's no wonder the place has such a cult following. We can't thank
Trader Joe's enough for all it does to bring some of the world's best
products to our fingertips at great prices. But we'll try anyway.

Thanks, TJ.

Tre Scalini

This Italian-American hotspot is one of the best
New Haven has to offer; that's very unfortunate

7.1 Food

7.5 Feel

Italian

Upmarket restaurant

$45 Price

www.trescalinirestaurant.com

Mon–Thu 10:30am–2:30pm,
5pm–9pm; Fri 10:30am–2pm,
5pm–10pm; Sat 5pm–10pm;
Sun 2pm–8pm

Bar Beer, wine, liquor
Credit cards Visa, MC, AmEx
Reservations Accepted
Date-friendly, good wines

Wooster Square Area
100 Wooster St.
(203) 777-3373

Tre Scalini deserves respect but not admiration. Although the classic
Italian-American fare is pleasing and familiar, the menu suffers from
systemic mispairings and an undeserved sense of self-importance. We
were more excited by the scungilli sign in the nearby grocery than by this
cuisine. Whili Tre Scalini was once the best of New Haven's less-than-
stellar Italian restaurant lineup, L'Orcio now holds that title. Tre Scalini's
old chef went on to bigger and worse things at Foster's, which leaves this
restaurant in some sort of liminal space.

Broccoli rabe with Italian sausage has come poorly executed: the rabe
underseasoned and merely steamed instead of pan-crisped, while dry
sausage makes for a double dose of disappointment. It's hard to pick out
any flavors besides ricotta in the eggplant rollatini, a dish dominated by
cheese and marinara. But there's good news: the house special hot
antipasto, an appetizer sampler served only for parties of six or more,
combines four of Tre Scalini's hallmarks, including good pane cotto
(escarole and beans sautéed with peasant bread and topped with
Parmigiano, then broiled) and appropriately crispy fried calamari. The
Caesar salad does have an excellent anchovy bite, but it's a dubious honor
for an establishment of Tre Scalini's repute.

Mains are a crapshoot, too. The scaloppine alla Giuseppe lies heavy
with peppers and onions, masking what little flavor the pounded veal
medallions had to begin with. Cream sauces drift toward the impossibly
rich, whether over pasta or meat. The pasta, though, is refreshingly not
overcooked, particularly if you make a point of asking that it be prepared
al dente. The osso buco is appropriately braised, yet offers no marrow
within the bone, but the scrumptious truffle-oil risotto served alongside
saves the dish.

The two-tiered room is pleasant and elegant, if overdone. Happily, it's
not too bright, and service is friendly and conscientious. Prices are
unreasonably high, however, given that the food fails to match the hype.
A $100 meal for two—without alcohol—is unjustifiable here.

If it's real, regional Italian cuisine you're after, you'll likely be
disappointed at Tre Scalini. Italian speakers will have to probe the menu to
find correct grammar or phrasing. It's silly to nitpick about spelling, but
this signals Tre Scalini's considerable distance from authenticity. There's
no doubt: if you're going to eat Italian food on Wooster Street, you
should probably go for pizza.

Tropical Delights

A cheap neighborhood Jamaican take-out counter
with reliable stews and excellent beef patties

7.8 Food

5.5 Feel

Caribbean

Take-out

$10 Price

Tue–Fri 10am–9pm
Sat 10am–6pm

Bar None
Credit cards None

Westville
141 Fitch St.
(203) 389-5618

Perhaps because of its low-profile location—in the Beaver Hill Shopping Center, a little row of stores on the corner of Fitch and Blake Streets—this is probably the least known of New Haven's distinguished lineup of Jamaican take-out places, even though it is fairly close to the Southern campus and downtown Westville. Tropical Delights is nothing more than a little storefront, and virtually everyone orders take-out, although you can eat at a little counter if you can't wait to get home—which might well be the case if you order one of the beef patties.

The staff is efficient but accommodating, in a neighborly sort of way. The menu is extremely simple, which is a good thing—the matronly chef in back cooks up an enormous pot of each dish in the little kitchen in back each day, spooning out delicious, inexpensive portions until they run out. The oxtail is tender and meaty, with an unusually high meat-to-bones ratio. The sauce, which is helped along by a bit of additional sauce, is dark and well reduced, with a nice sheen. Jerk chicken, one of the most popular choices, is great but tends to run out unless you get there early. Curry goat, another one of our Jamaican favorites, is fully flavored but a bit dry, with less sauce than we would've liked; the only other disappointment has been the leathery plantains (unless you happen to catch them straight out of the fryer).

Rice and peas (that's Jamaican for red kidney beans) are top-notch, as is the sweet cabbage. The beef patties, meanwhile, may be the best in town; their rich, wonderfully seasoned, gently spicy filling is soft, almost like a paste, and it pairs absolutely deliciously with the flaky yellow crust. It's the ultimate Caribbean comfort food.

Turkish Kabab House

Venture out to West Haven for some of the best
döner kebab around

8.7 Food **8.0** Feel

Turkish

Casual restaurant

$30 Price

www.turkishkebaphouse.com

Daily 11am–11pm

Bar None
Credit cards Visa, MC, AmEx
Reservations Accepted
Kid-friendly

West Haven
1157 Campbell Ave.
(203) 933-0002

The deepest truths usually come out very late at night. The truth about the only place in the New Haven area for a real döner kebab, for instance, was revealed to us at about 3:30 a.m. one Saturday at, of all places, Alpha Delta Pizza.

When you utter the words "döner kebab" to a Turkish person, the conversation is likely to take on a more serious, more hushed quality. Our source of endless wisdom, one lucky night, was a Turkish short-order cook at Alpha Delta who was in the process of slathering mayo and buffalo sauce onto the place's Wenzel's sub (a legend in its own right).

He cast a furtive glance to each side before speaking of this Persian specialty. "Turkish Kebab House in West Haven," the man told us, his voice lowering to a near-whisper. "Up Campbell Avenue. That is the only place around for a real döner." That was years ago; these days, Saray certainly challenges Turkish Kebab House for the crown, but our confidant did not lead us astray.

The Turkish Kebab House is a self-contained structure with the look of a tired family Chinese joint, plopped down along a strip of worn-down single-family houses. A barrier of white curtains cloaks every single possible window of the simple, open-kitchen restaurant, hiding a dining room that's often totally full—especially weekend afternoons, when entire extended Turkish families take over long tables.

You should start with the best hummus in the area, whose subtle, herbal sweetness will incite a barrage of silent curses in your mind: one profanity for every time that you've wasted your appetite on inferior hummus. Less complex but still satisfying are garlicky, yogurty haydari and silky baba ghanoush. It all comes with pide, a home-baked flatbread that, like the hummus, puts the impostors to shame. Among mains, juicy, well-seasoned shish adana (grilled lamb pieces) have a healthy charred flavor, but underseasoned lamb chops and smoky but dry chicken shish kebab are less convincing, and you can skip the so-called "Turkish pizza," whose cheese is over-applied and greasy.

We almost wish we could throw a twist into the plot and tell you that the döner kebab sucked, but this story has a Hollywood ending. The striped pieces of lamb and veal, shaved thinly off the rotating skewer, are basted to a beautiful brown, and served in a pile, little revelations of savory tenderness. The fat is not visible or texturally tangible, yet its gustatory presence is absorbed into the flesh, yielding an emergent richness that last well beyond each slow swallow.

As ever, Alpha Delta came through in the clutch.

The Tymes

You never know how good the kitchen is going to be on any given day

6.0	8.0
Food	Feel

American, Seafood

Upmarket restaurant

$50
Price

www.thetymesrestaurant.com

Wed–Thu 11:30am–4pm, 5pm–9pm; Fri–Sat 11:30am–4pm, 5pm–10pm; Sun 11:30am–3:30pm, 4pm–9pm

Bar Beer, wine, liquor
Credit cards Visa, MC, AmEx
Reservations Accepted
Date-friendly, live music, outdoor dining

Hamden
2389 Dixwell Ave.
(203) 230-2301

We applaud the decision to abbreviate the somewhat hokey name "Colonial Tymes," which always called to mind one of those reenactment villages where goodwives invite busloads of schoolchildren to help churn butter.

Indeed, the restaurant is situated in a real 19th-century house that was hauled over from elsewhere and plopped down along a stretch of Hamden, where it manages to look as though it's always been there, sitting under the weeping trees. There's still a gracious outdoor patio and a well-executed old-New England theme, with wide-boarded hardwood floors restored to high sheen. There's a pleasant mix of old lanterns, and there's even a man-sized hearth in which a real fire burns for much of the winter.

Thankfully, so much more has changed about the place that once not only served a disgusting cocktail, but its own bartender actually advised us to stay away from it. At this point, this restaurant made the incredibly ignorant and embarrassing move of displaying a self-righteous sign declaring that, in political protest, no French wine would be served at the restaurant.

This policy has backed down, it seems, and now there are a few bottles of vintage first-growth Bordeaux priced into the triple digits. (Not that this shows a renewed prowess and passion for selecting French wine; if it were, there'd be many more affordable, small production lovelies here; as it stands, it's more stereotypical and pornographic.)

Where new management has seen the updating of the furnishings and attitude, a new head chef has the kitchen firing on at least one more cylinder than before. There are still some inconsistencies—sometimes crab cakes are soft, homogenous, doughy lumps with little to no texture—but sometimes these same crab cakes are full of sweet crab meat with just the right amount of crunch. Lamb has been tender and surprisingly lamby, yet other times, it has been tough and drenched in a masking sauce.

But as the cocktails have been updated and the liquor selection improved, some expertly shucked Kumamoto oysters in the bar might be just the thing to do. Then sample a little off the bar menu and see for yourself if the kitchen is on its game that day—playing well enough to make those pricier mains worth the risk.

Uncle Willie's BBQ

Good ribs, pulled pork, and all our Southern favorites

7.0 Food
7.0 Feel

Barbecue, Southern

Casual restaurant

$20 Price

Daily 11am–7pm

Bar BYO
Credit cards Visa, MC
Reservations Not accepted
Kid-friendly

West Haven
403 Saw Mill Rd.
(203) 389-2065

Uncle Willie's first opened its doors in Waterbury, but a second outpost has seen its fair share of opening and closing doors. It has scooted from Orange to Westville to its current location in West Haven. Here's hoping it stays there.

Barbecue is America's greatest original culinary tradition, but a gaping hole was left in the New Haven-area barbecue scene after Jarman's and Joe Grate's both, sadly, closed. Here's here Uncle Willie's comes in. The St. Louis pork ribs are certainly more authentic than anything else in the area. The outside of the meat is as it should be: deeply imparted with smoke flavors and spices from an intense rub. Beneath that, some bites are magically tender, laced with delicious pockets of fat; but some bites aren't.

Now, some aficionados swear that truly great barbecue needs no sauce, but in this case, it's an absolute necessity (we prefer the hot version to the sweet, but ask for both). Not only is Uncle Willie's barbecue sauce quite good, it also adds a needed dose of salt and moisture to the meat; this is especially true for the pulled pork, some of whose large chunks are unusually lean and slightly dry. Nonetheless, the overall effect really hits the spot.

By no means does the menu end with the BBQ, although that's why we go to Uncle Willie's. There's also a proper Southern breakfast (cornmeal cakes, grits, and biscuits and gravy are in the lineup), which is a rare treat in the area. Plus there's highly touted fried chicken, a long list of burgers and dogs, and other classics like smothered pork chops, meatloaf, and fried fish. Ambitious, perhaps, but we salute this restaurant's admirable effort to bring back the barbecue. Thanks, Uncle Willie.

Union League Café

9.1 Food **9.5** Feel

This gracious grande dame is still swimming along—especially when it comes to fish

French

Upmarket restaurant **$75** Price

www.unionleaguecafe.com

Mon–Thu 11:30am–2:30pm, 5:30pm–9:30pm; Fri 11:30am–2:30pm, 5pm–10pm; Sat 5pm–10pm

Bar Beer, wine, liquor
Credit cards Visa, MC, AmEx
Reservations Essential
Date-friendly, good wines

Chapel District
1032 Chapel St.
(203) 562-4299

This lovely French restaurant—still one of the power centers of New Haven, after all these years—has a unique talent for being all things to all people. Certainly Union League Café encompasses New Haven's big-city ambitions: you're greeted with a real French accent, and your coat is slipped off your back with surreptitious grace. Yet there is also a certain small-town appeal to Union League, a rejection of its snooty Sherman Club past: it's a place into which anyone can walk in without a reservation, be treated with respect, sit (in winter) by the roaring fireplace, and probably run into a few friends. Where else but New Haven?

The brasserie-ish menu is problematically static, but happily, the gracious atmosphere and attention to correct service are also unchanging. After a long, elaborate dinner and a couple excellent bottles of Bordeaux from the well-thought-out, if hardly inexpensive, wine list—followed, of course, by dessert, digestifs, and such—it's hard to argue that this isn't the most civilized place in the city to dine. The kitchen is hardly perfect, but Union League remains one of our favorite restaurants in New Haven.

This is especially so when we seek seafood, whether oysters or tender, pan-roasted skate with nutty brown butter and capers, as good a piece of fish as we've had anywhere in Connecticut. Irreproachable, too, are slowly braised veal cheeks with creamed spinach and potato gnocchi, along with the classic duck leg confit, a wonder of tender, duck-fat deliciousness that's set off against a crisp potato galette. Marbled terrine of flawless duck foie gras, salty duck prosciutto, salsify, black truffle, and a mâche salad tossed with a truffle vinaigrette sounds like an overbearing plating, but it's beautifully harmonized. Entrecôte is similarly exalted—it's luscious, ideally cooked, and well seasoned.

Vegetable and garde-manger problems, however, seem systematic. An expertly cooked wild striped bass with a fingerling potato crust has come overwhelmed by a compote of inedibly tough fennel and a Syrah reduction that's too big for this fish. Worse still, we've had a salade Landaise—usually one of our favorite recipes—come with a seemingly undrained poached egg, whose water seeped into the lardons and overcooked chicken livers, sogging the dish.

A new cheese menu now comes alongside the dessert list, which is reliable as ever. Prices are generally high but reasonable, but what's up with the $5.75 for a cup of Kona coffee? Superpremium coffee is enough of a racket, but if you're going to serve it, you should at least brew it correctly; here, it tastes like bitter, brown water—the emperor's new clothes. Surely New Haven's emperor knows better than this.

USS Chowder Pot III

Still winning peoples'-choice-type awards, but
then, so is Hannah Montana

5.3	7.0
Food	Feel

Seafood

Casual restaurant

$40
Price

www.chowderpot.com

Mon–Thu 11:30am–9pm
Fri–Sat 11:30am–10pm
Sun noon–10pm

Bar Beer, wine, liquor
Credit cards Visa, MC, AmEx
Reservations Not accepted
Kid-friendly, live music, outdoor
dining

Branford
560 E. Main St.
(203) 481-2356

USS Chowder Pot III has made a career out of receiving accolades and
awards, but for no reason we can see (or taste, rather). It's funny that the
perennial winners of such media-bestowed accolades are not just bland
and unremarkable, but always so hopelessly predictable. Isn't everyone
interested in something a bit more fresh and local?

Sure, Chowder Pot is adorable, in that nostalgic John-Candy-takes-his-
family-to-the-beach-and-disaster-ensues sort of way. In fact, it *is*
immensely popular with families, so prime time might mean a wait (but
it's near Su Casa, a comparably suburban Mexican restaurant with
comparable weekend queues—you can hedge your bets and play the
waits against each other).

The marine theme at USS Chowder Pot III is overwhelming. There's boat
paraphernalia hanging from the rafters. Nets, fish, and glass bottles are
everywhere. You're almost afraid of drowning. There's a bar that actually
swings into action if you catch it at the right time—they even do karaoke.

And then there's the seafood. Steamed lobster is a good way to go; it's
a bit dear, but that's true most everywhere. The chowder itself is
appropriately creamy in the New England style (but where are the clams?).
But the fish here is nothing more than standard—not that you'd expect
much more. We know it's adorable and it's been around forever, but if
you closed your eyes and tasted seafood from here versus, say, freshly
grilled fish from The Place in Guilford...would it still win?

Vito's Deli

A quick downtown lunch option with a great talent for fresh, well-filled sandwiches

7.2 Food

6.0 Feel

American, Italian

Counter service

$10 Price

www.vitosdelinh.com

Mon–Fri 6am–3pm

Bar None
Credit cards None

Ninth Square
35 Center St.
(203) 624-1533

Vito's Deli takes sandwiches seriously. This impeccable deli has been a boon to the downtown lunch crowd for decades, serving up enormous sandwiches at very reasonable prices. It's a reminder that not all downtown New Haven lunch spots are created equal, and the same sum in the same four-block radius can be spent very wisely or very poorly. At Vito's, an average appetite can be sated with half a sandwich; split one with a friend, and lunch comes in at under $3. At these prices, you can surely spring for a side of cole slaw or potato salad.

There is a definite method to ordering at Vito's. Approach the sandwich counter with deference, and if there's a line, respect it. The masters behind the counter will ask you for your order only when they are ready to take it, and you will be expected to specify one of six kinds of bread. The standard sub roll is adequate; it's fresh, but it's nothing special. Focus on what's in the middle. Hot subs are satisfying, and cold subs are truly exemplary.

You can either name your toppings à la carte, or call one of the suggested combos. The "Vito's Combo" is a paragon of cold-cut decadence: ham, pastrami, bologna, and salami, with just enough heat to add brightness. Fillings are purposefully layered, and if your order includes American cheese, you'll find it as the creamy core of a well-structured sandwich. For an even more exciting version, try one of the more flavorful cheeses. The overall effect is fresh and tasty.

Viva Zapata

A dark, loud, raucous college bar that's fine as long
as you avoid the "Mexican" "food"

2.0	7.0
Food	Feel

Mexican

Bar **$25**
Price

Sun–Thu 11:30am–11pm
Fri–Sat 11:30am–midnight

Bar Beer, wine, liquor
Credit cards Visa, MC, AmEx

Upper Chapel Area
161 Park St.
(203) 562-2499

Viva Zapata fills nightly with itinerant bands of revelers whose primary
project is to get completely and utterly soused. The young patrons, many
from the suburbs, come to pound so-so margaritas, perhaps to munch on
Tex-Mex food, certainly to check each other out with increasingly blurry
admiration—and to display their plumage with decreasing selectivity. It's a
strange town-gown mix, made stranger by the fact that town and gown
seem to remain segmented once inside. (Once we're all drunk, why can't
we all be friends?)

We doubt that many of them come for the food, which reminds us of
Old El Paso microwave TV dinners with the instructions followed
haphazardly. It all begins with stale-tasting tortilla chips and awful salsa,
and goes downhill from there. This is the worst Mexican food in the city.
It's even worse than El Amigo Felix, and El Amigo Felix is *bad*.

Viva's does have a certain dusty-cantina sort of charm, especially in the
main back room, which has a few dimly lit, appealing little nooks. There's
Tex-Mex paraphernalia hanging here and there. It's fake, but it's good
fake. Viva's is a fun place to slurp down some tequila in any of its
incarnations; we prefer to do so on a weeknight, when you can focus on
the aromas of agave cactus, instead of cologne.

Ultimately, Viva's fulfills its local role as a fratty scene. The drinks flow
freely and the customers are happy. Beware the resulting condition of the
bathroom floor. As a bar, the place meets its mandate. For a dining
experience, run far, far away.

Wall Street Pizza

Would Naples, by any other name, serve pizza as bad and beer as cheap?

6.7 Food

7.0 Feel

Pizza, American

Counter service

$10 Price

Mon–Fri 6am–9pm
Sat 9am–9pm

Bar None
Credit cards Visa, MC, AmEx
Veg-friendly

South Town Green
90 Wall St.
(203) 776-9021

When Naples—one of New Haven's most beloved undergraduate greasy-pizza-and-mediocre-beer establishments for generations—was brought down by America's counterproductive underage drinking laws, the Yale community and the Yale diaspora shed a collective tear (before, we hope, drowning its collective sorrows in cheap beer).

But this glorious college-town legend has been reincarnated, beer and all, under a new name: Wall Street Pizza. We're happy to report that it's virtually identical to Naples—although we have no idea if this extends to the carding policy that was once one of the city's great examples of civil disobedience. But we do know that the dark wood tables are just as they once were: embedded with the tipsy inscriptions and memories of students past.

Just as at Naples, you order and pay at the counter, and you have to deal with the staff's trademark gruffness. There's a familiar menu of subs—steak and cheese is still a decent choice, and the Italian cold-cut sub with hot peppers is a perfectly passable version—and an array of more elaborate mains and iceberg-lettuce-style salads that should be avoided.

Maybe it's just our imagination, but interestingly, we think the pizza has actually improved since the Naples days. It's crispier, more in the New Haven tradition, and less greasy—you don't need a napkin to pat off the grease before biting. It's quite frankly not bad. This, perhaps, is the one thing that's most unbecoming of the Naples tradition: the pizza here is *supposed* to be bad.

Harrumph.

Warong Selera

A Malaysian strip-mall joint with usually tasty, always interesting food that's better taken out

7.6 Food **5.5** Feel

Malaysian

Counter service **$20** Price

Mon–Sat noon–9pm

Bar None
Credit cards Visa, MC

West Haven
702B Boston Post Rd.
(203) 937-0614

Though it's been known to be a little inconsistent, this is still the best Malaysian food around. (We're getting tired of having to make those sorts of statements about Chinese, Mexican, Middle Eastern, and on and on—don't New Haveners deserve better?) In Malay, "Warong" means an outdoor food stall, a place that is known for good, cheap food, usually served to go. Although it's not outdoors, this is a pretty apt description of Warong Selera, which is the latest of a surprising number of Malaysian restaurants in New Haven and its suburbs.

As the place is geared more toward taking out than eating in, it does not have much in the way of atmosphere. It feels something like an abandoned basement rec room, with a large, outdated stereo system and 1980s TV dominating the middle of the bright white room. The walls are adorned with tourism posters, and the piles of brochures about the country's regions make the place seem more like an outpost of a Malaysian airline than a restaurant.

Since Malaysia is, historically, an agglomeration of both migrant and indigenous cultures, the food is diverse, with variations on Chinese, Indian, and Thai. Curries are less spicy and more dilute, and noodles are often fried. The menu here reflects this variety with noodle and rice dishes in combinations involving beef, chicken, seafood, shrimp, and vegetables, as well as a smaller number of chef's specials. As an appetizer, roti canai— fried bread served with curry gravy—is slightly greasy, but it's also flaky and delicious. Even better is the mee bandung with chicken, a satisfyingly rich and sweet broth with noodles, tofu, egg, and Chinese greens that add a welcome crunch. Masak pedas—beef cooked with fried potato and onions—is less successful. While shrimp paste adds an interesting, unfamiliar flavor, and the potato has a delightful texture, the beef itself is tasteless and tough to the point of unpleasantness. Don't miss the chance to sample the Indonesian boxed drinks, like the very sweet guava juice or the jasmine iced tea.

Wentworth's Ice Cream

Ice cream that is totally worth the trip into the outer reaches of Hamden

Ice cream

Counter service

Mon–Thu 11am–9:30pm; Fri–Sat 11am–10pm summer hours; Mon–Sat noon–9pm winter hours

Bar None
Credit cards None
Kid-friendly, outdoor dining, veg-friendly

Hamden
3697 Whitney Ave.
(203) 281-7429

Two words: mocha lace. It's Wentworth's already ideal vanilla ice cream plus chocolate-coated threads of caramelized coffee candy swirled through; they shatter as you eat them. It's a feat we would expect from some wizard of molecular gastronomy, not a humble little ice cream parlor. But this is the kind of amazing stuff we've come to expect here.

The folks at Wentworth's understand that ice cream is not just dessert. It helps that we New Englanders are some of the nation's most enthusiastic, and exacting, ice cream eaters. Though Portland, Oregon has replaced us as having the highest ice cream consumption per capita, we still lay claim to some of the best artisanal brands—to wit, Steve Herrell still lives in Northampton, Massachusetts (he sold his first name and then opened another ice cream chain, still one of the world's best, under his last), and of course, the legendary Vermonters, Messrs. Ben and Jerry.

Wentworth's does justice to its place among such company. The ice cream is just shy of too creamy, a delicate alchemy that should not be underappreciated, because the result is a judicious combination of decadence and subtlety which will allow you to contemplate the blessings of dairy and taste the careful flavorings. We're ice cream purists when sampling high-quality versions, and so our favorite here is vanilla, but there are plenty of others to choose from, including seasonal fruit flavors made with locally grown produce.

If you like your ice cream dressed up, consider one of the legendary sundaes, which are adorned with chocolate fudge, whipped cream, and a lot more. The shop also offers frozen yogurt, brownies, cookies, and coffee. The charm of Wentworth's goes beyond the ice cream itself to the cute, shady wrap-around porch that encircles the building, and accommodation for the line which inevitably forms during peak hours. Hey, if we wanted to strategize about how to take our per-capita title back, Wentworth's would be a great place to start.

Westville Kosher Market

New Haven's only full-service kosher deli and
market

Groceries, Jewish deli   Market

www.westvillekosher.com

Mon–Wed 8:30am–6pm   **Bar** None   **Westville**
Thu 8:30am–7pm   **Credit cards** Visa, MC 95 Amity Rd.
Fri 8:30am–4pm   (203) 389-1723
Sun 8:30am–2pm

Since 1985, Westville Meat Market has been providing kosher foods to
New Haven. At this moment, they seem to be the only fully kosher market
in town. Good for them; not so good for East Rock and Fair Haven
residents. The store carries a wide array of meats and poultry, as well as
prepared foods, mostly Israeli, but also a few from other parts of the
Middle East. They bake their own breads and pastries, including a
fantastic knish.

On the full-service deli side of things, the pastrami and corned beef
sandwiches are stellar, especially, of course, on rye. Turkey is also very
good.

Neighboring Amity Wine is a good place to stop and pick up a bottle to
go with the prepared foods you've bought for dinner. Westville does a lot
of catering business, for bar and bat mitzvahs, Passover dinners, Rosh
Hashanah, even Thanksgiving.

Remember, goyim, they'll be closed early on Fridays and all day
Saturday, but are open Sunday.

Whitfield's

Despite the stuck-in-time feeling of this Guilford colonial home, the food's surprisingly modern

7.4	7.5
Food	Feel

New American

Upmarket restaurant

$55
Price

www.whitfieldsguilford.com

Daily 9am–9pm

Bar Beer, wine, liquor
Credit cards Visa, MC, AmEx
Reservations Accepted
Date-friendly, outdoor dining

Guilford
25 Whitfield St. (Route 77)
(203) 458-1300

Whitfield's couldn't have sweeter digs, really. Taking up the first floor and patio of a restored 18th century house in one of the nation's prettiest and oldest towns, it is at once elegant and easygoing. The outdated brass-and-wood décor and brightly colored framed art are disarming, enough to really surprise you when the menu suggests a progressive, with-it kitchen that uses organic chicken, Long Island duck, and high-minded seafood.

This being Guilford, nothing gets too crazy, but there are neo-retro salads (the iceberg wedge, long reviled by food snobs for its flavorless, nutrient-lacking lettuce, is a secret crush of ours), appetizers like Yukon Gold fries with jalapeño-and-roasted garlic aioli, and vibrant seafood preparations that are intercontinental in inspiration. With a menu that lists "Szechuan-crusted yellowfin tuna," "lobster-and-salmon ravioli," and "chili-rubbed wild salmon with cilantro pesto," you have to wonder: are these attempts to be all things to everyone spreading Whitfield's talents too thin?

Most of the menu changes regularly, but some things are everlasting. Their simple Angus burger is very good, and it's served with Cheddar on a pretzel roll—a classy and informed touch.

A succinct wine list is arranged for people who only know that they like (or only know) certain varietals, as in "I'll have a Chardonnay." There are a few selections of each, and generally from mass producers that aren't disgraceful, but aren't anything transcendent either. There are higher-shelf liquors here, so order a classic cocktail and ignore the dumbed-down martini list. Or, if it's Sunday, get a Bloody; the patio here, with giant windows looking out over the sculpture garden of a neighboring art gallery, was made for brunch.

The Whole Enchilada

This mediocre Tex-Mex holdout can't compete with the newer, better Mexican in town

4.3 Food **4.5** Feel

Mexican   Counter service   **$10** Price

www.twenewhaven.com

Mon–Fri 11am–8pm
Sat 11am–4pm

Bar BYO
Credit cards Visa, MC, AmEx
Veg-friendly

Audubon Arts District
21 Whitney Ave.
(203) 772-4454

This was once one of New Haven's better burrito purveyors, but thanks to Tijuana Taco Co. and its progeny, a new bar has been set for burritos in this town (thank heavens). Where does that leave The Whole Enchilada?

In the dustbins of history.

The little Cal-Mex counter is still tucked into a storefront next to Anna Liffey's on Whitney Avenue. The place specializes in takeout, but there are also a few little tables and chairs in the bright room, which is painted with scenes from rural Mexico but sullied by institutional touches, like massive drink refrigerators.

The service is amazingly quick—you're scarcely done paying before you're handed a hot burrito wrapped in foil. Watch the preparation behind the counter, which reveals impressive burrito dexterity. And don't forget to take some of the hot sauce that comes out of metal spouts built into the cafeteria-style garbage-can-cum-condiment-station. You're going to need it to substitute for flavor (we prefer the green; the red is watery and weak).

The burritos are on the expensive side, and their caliber varies. The original chicken and beef burritos are somewhat dry and boring, and the copious quantities of rice and beans inside further dilute the taste. The flour tortillas, though, are flexible and strong, making a good medium for the moist chicken curry burrito, our favorite choice here; the addition of curry sauce to a mélange of carb-loaded ingredients is a winning idea. Add some of the hot sauce and you've definitely amassed something worth your while.

But if there was ever a food that we only craved after six beers, it would be the Buffalo chicken burrito, with Buffalo sauce and blue cheese dressing. It's not great, but we've been known to sully ourselves with it.

Rice and beans here are hideously unseasoned. There's just no excuse, given the good Mexican food now available here. It is places like this that help New England hold onto its reputation for Worst Mexican Food in the Country.

Wild Ginger

This Japanese fusion dinosaur does its best work when it keeps things simple

Japanese

Upmarket restaurant

$45 Price

www.wildgingerrestaurant.com

Mon–Thu noon–10pm
Fri–Sat noon–11pm
Sun noon–10pm

Bar Beer, wine, liquor
Credit cards Visa, MC, AmEx
Reservations Accepted

Orange
111 Boston Post Rd.
(203) 799-8887

From the outside, Wild Ginger looks like just another lackluster restaurant of the suburban Asian-strip-mall variety. Window coverings are designed to obstruct the view of cars passing by on the highway a few yards away. Inside, the dining room is well-appointed, if a little depressing and dated.

Similarly, the menu reads like a clumsy and fervent profiteering from the earliest days of the Nobu-inspired, New American-Japanese fusion trend. It doesn't inspire confidence in the kitchen's vision to see duck quesadilla next to toro tartare. The latter actually makes us do a double take: in some of the nation's more serious sushi venues, chefs are trying to phase out toro, only ordering it in tiny amounts, running out of it mid-evening, and certainly never—ever—dressing it with wasabi and soy. There are, like 5 left in the sea. This is like pasting magazine photos of Beyoncé over a Picasso. Sure, she's tasty, but…it's a *Picasso*. They also serve pan-seared Chilean sea bass here, which is fine, considering it's documented and legally fished (not endangered), but what's disturbing is that it comes off a Sysco truck.

There's a proliferation of ingredients here like "special sauce" and "crunch" that aptly define Wild Ginger's propensity for taking fish flesh and using it as a mere vehicle for stronger flavors and textures to which American palates have historically responded. The trouble is, as we all stop drinking high-fructose corn syrup and eating McDonald's food, our palates crave a return to natural, simpler flavors. Like, say, the naked, subtle complexities of lightly buttery yellowtail.

In general, stick to nigiri and sashimi; ask at the sushi bar for the best indication of what's freshest and best. Uni, when available, is excellent, with exquisite sweetness and an unctuous, custardy texture. (When uni is bad, it's very very bad, and so it's wonderful to find a place where it's reliably good enough to be ordered routinely.)

We can accredit the menu with having the breadth and diversity to benefit those sushi lovers who dine with more timid eaters. Here, those folks can have their chicken breasts and eat them too, while you dine on the bounty of the sea. Just, please, go easy on the Bluefin.

Willoughby's

Still the best coffee in town, and now in the
architecture school, too

Baked goods

Café

www.willoughbyscoffee.com

Mon–Sat 7am–7pm
Sun 7am–6pm
Hours vary by location

Bar None
Credit cards Visa, MC
Outdoor dining, veg-friendly, Wi-Fi

South Town Green
258 Church St.
(203) 777-7400

Upper Chapel Area
194 York St.
(203) 789-8400

Branford
550 E. Main St.
(203) 481-1700

We've always loved Willoughby's coffee. The iced French Roast coffee is a
warm-weather addiction. It seems to be triple-strength.

The Church Street branch is still charming, but we love the new
location in the Yale School of Architecture, which, unlike the Church
Street location, offers free Wi-Fi (for 90 minutes; ask for the password
when you order coffee) and slightly later hours. It also looks edgier,
exuding a spare, THX-1138 futurism that is not uninviting, but not exactly
welcoming either. Windows separated by latticework allow some
sunshine into the small interior. There's style to match the darkly
fashionable architects and profs: boxes of black leather and form-fitting
metal reticula make up the furnishings, which are complemented by
spacecraft-looking accessories, an elliptical counter, and an airy coffee
kitchen in back. The only problem is that the place is often so crowded in
the late afternoon that customers waiting for their drinks practically sit on
other patrons' laps.

The strange, contorted interior notwithstanding, everything else about
Willoughby's is pretty straightforward. The menu is simple, thankfully
devoid of ostentation (no gingerbread lattes here), with a focus on what
actually matters, yet is so often overlooked: the coffee. They use high-
quality (organic, free-trade) beans and roast them skillfully to a dark
perfection. The feature blend changes every day. In the mornings, these
folks even brew Kona beans—maybe the only place in New Haven that
does this daily—for more discriminating customers, charging more for
each hallowed cup. The café latte is also spot on, and in a classy gesture
exemplary of Willoughby's characteristic professionalism, the barista asks
what type of milk you want (regular, skim, or soy).

The pastries are good, but do no more than serve their ritualized
function. If you must succumb to their siren song, cookies and muffins
jumpstart low blood sugar levels and provide temporary satisfaction.
Croissants are buttery, but tend to be too smooshy. Your best bet is an
H&H bagel, brought in fresh from New York every morning.

But all of this is in service to the coffee. One sip of their outstanding
brew gives unmistakable verisimilitude to their bold two-word slogan:
"Serious Coffee." In fact, the slogan does not say enough. They could
have easily made it "Best coffee in New Haven," and we would wholly
submit to it.

The Wine Thief

Not just New Haven's best place to buy wine—one of the best in all of Connecticut

Wine store

Market

www.thewinethief.com

Mon–Sat 10am–9pm

Bar Beer, wine, liquor
Credit cards Visa, MC, AmEx
Good wines

Chapel District
181 Crown St.
(203) 772-1944

East Rock
378 Whitney Ave.
(203) 865-4845

The Wine Thief is a gift to the city. What began in 1996 as a humble wine shop on Whitney Avenue has grown into a true New Haven phenomenon—largely due to word of mouth. Apparently, everyone who cared about wine told everybody else, and well-deserved success followed.

As the selection expanded, the Wine Thief (named for the tube that's used to remove a small amount of wine from a barrel or fermentation vessel) just got better and better, working with artisanal wineries all over the country—and the world. The store offers what is easily the city's best-chosen selection of wines from relatively unknown producers—many of them incredible values.

The iconic Whitney location was—and still is—a rightful favorite, but the Wine Thief's new digs on Crown Street brought the store's treasures to an eager downtown audience, with a bigger space, broader selection, and even more user-friendly shelves. Staff at both locations are wonderfully friendly and knowledgeable.

The Wine Thief is the very definition of the community wine shop: they deliver locally, they do gift packs, and they coordinate wine-pairing dinners with several local restaurants, which are always a treat. Check the website for upcoming events; there are frequent free tastings at the downtown location from 5pm–8pm on Friday afternoons.

Be forewarned, however: you might not want to leave.

Woodland Coffee & Tea

A Ninth Square relaxation station that's mastered
coffee, but needs to work on the attitude

Sandwiches, Baked goods

Café

www.woodlandcoffee.com

Mon–Fri 7am–6pm
Sat 8am–6pm
Sun 9am–3pm

Bar None
Credit cards Visa, MC, AmEx
Veg-friendly, Wi-Fi

Ninth Square
91 Orange St.
(203) 773-1144

Free Wi-Fi, warm vibes, and good blues: it's a magical combination for
working. That's why much of this Third Edition was composed (in
consultation with our copious notes, of course) at Woodland Coffee and
Tea. Of course, there are still the service issues—if you stumble upon a
review in the *Fearless Critic New Haven Restaurant Guide* that ends
abruptly, you can attribute it to one of the times we've been
unceremoniously kicked out of the place, several minutes before the
purported closing hour, as if we were malevolent sixth-graders getting the
boot from sex-ed class after drawing porn-star boobs onto the miracle-of-
life diagram.

Woodland, along a gentrified stretch of Orange Street down around
Ninth Square, has an attractive look. The sign is well designed; the walls
are warm and yellow; there's great coffee-and-tea-themed wall art,
newspapers, and relaxing music. Shiny blond wood gives the place a
newish feel, but it doesn't take away from the laid-back vibe. Comfy
chairs, lots of flavored lattes, and an exotic tea selection all make for a
cutting-edge study space for students.

Woodland also has a short, focused selection of light fare. The
breakfast menu boasts of organic eggs and healthy-sounding cereals,
while the lunch menu lists four salads, eight sandwiches, and three
wraps—two, four, and two of which, respectively, are vegetarian.
Ingredients are generally pretty typical for a modern American lunch
joint—goat cheese, mesclun greens, cranberries, and the like. The
problem with the panini is that they don't hold together well; the cheese
often isn't melted enough and slips out of the sandwich. This years-old
problem still persists.

Such sloppy preparation seems part of a larger attitude problem at
Woodland, which isn't limited to the stern closing-hour regime: the
service ranges from indifferent to downright rude. At one point we were
even sternly upbraided for writing in our notebooks while glancing up at
the menu. "You need permission to do that," we were told by a gruff,
paranoid barista, "because you could be a competitor. Without
permission, it's illegal." We'd go toe-to-toe with the dude in court on that
in any US jurisdiction. But may we suggest that before getting too
concerned about having their closely guarded panini secrets stolen,
Woodland Coffee and Tea should bone up a bit on its sandwich-making.

York Street Noodle House

4.7 Food   **6.0** Feel

Cheap, sugary noodle soups and dim sum—
something new, but nothing good

Pan-Asian, Chinese

Casual restaurant   **$10** Price

www.yorkstnoodlehouse.com

Sun–Thu 11:30am–10pm
Fri–Sat 11:30am–11pm

Bar None
Credit cards Visa, MC
Reservations Not accepted
Outdoor dining, veg-friendly, Wi-Fi

Upper Chapel Area
166 York St.
(203) 776-9675

We were very excited when this place first opened. For one thing, it was so cheap. It also featured so many options. Unfortunately, we soon realized that, no matter how many options there were, everything seemed to come in two flavors: sickly sweet (avocado dressing on salads, rice noodle with combination—why don't they warn you this is a dessert dish?) and generically salty-spicy. Not that there's anything wrong with salty-spicy, especially if you're just looking for something nourishing that warms you to the bone for a few bucks. But there is something wrong with a noodle-and-protein menu in which everything tastes more or less identical.

Of the noodle soups, we most recommend the ones designated "spicy"—especially the spicy combination noodle soup (combination refers to a combination of seafood, including fish balls) and the spicy chicken tom yum. These do have decent broth, but are thin, and need lots of hot sauce to be interesting. The spicy mee yok noodle is also a good choice, with lots of crunchy Asian vegetables stir-fried with the noodles. None of the dim sum dishes (shumai, dumplings, and so on) are particularly remarkable, aside from the rice-wrapped shrimp and mushroom, which is wrapped in a leaf, sticky and salty—it's very craveable.

Speaking of craveable, bubble tea is also served. What is it with those little tapioca pearls? As soon as we finish a drink, we're chewing the insides of our mouths searching for that addictive little texture. That, or we're cracked out on the tea. There are more flavors here than elsewhere in town (seriously, JoJo's, we love you, but: mint, coconut, and raspberry? Was there a sale on bad milk tea flavors or something?)

York Street deserves credit, too, for its low prices and its late-ish hours (where else can you eat at 10pm on a Sunday anymore?), but slower-than-molasses-in-January service is really annoying, not to mention the hot, cramped room (they have expanded to the basement, but good luck getting a check in under two hours down there). Hey, it still beats Ivy Noodle.

Yorkside Pizza

A casual, convenient joint known for milkshakes
and late hours—not for the grease-loaded pizza

5.5	5.5
Food	Feel

Pizza, American, Greek

Casual restaurant

$20
Price

www.yorksidepizza.com

Sun–Thu 11am–1am
Fri–Sat 11am–3am

Bar Beer, wine
Credit cards Visa, MC, AmEx
Reservations Not accepted
Kid-friendly, outdoor dining,
veg-friendly

Broadway District
288 York St.
(203) 787-7471

Let's start with the good news: Yorkside is open until 3am on weekends. And it's only steps away from the Yale Law School, Broadway, and the College. So it's not hard to see why a steady stream of customers—including a sizeable contingent of Yale Law professors—keeps the place going even though the pizza is well below average. They serve pitchers of Sam Adams along with the standard pizza-and-sub fare, doing a brisk business with the post-concert gaggles from nearby Toad's Place.

The ridiculously big Greek salad, enough for two people, is your best choice. It's a standard version, but it's done well, with lettuce, tomatoes, olives, plenty of feta, and a good, tangy Greek dressing. There's a cheap lunch special that pleases fans by pairing a slice of greasy pizza with a smaller portion of Greek salad on the side. The hot tuna melt is another of the few promising options: a rich, creamy (and enormous) tuna salad covered with melted cheese. If you prefer your meal (and a half) in a cup, Yorkside's milkshakes also have a devoted following: all of the standard flavors are there, plus the perpetually winning "Moosetraks" blend.

Pizza is available by the slice—cheese, pepperoni, and one rotating topping. Slices and pies are not Yorkside's strongest suit: they're thick, cheesy, and oily, with uninspired sauce. Cheese is probably the poorest choice of all; at least pepperoni and mushrooms add some much-needed flavor. Yorkside thrives in part on its take-out business, selling pies and two-liter Coke bottles en masse for Law School and College functions. But in this pizza town, you can do so much better elsewhere if that's what you're after.

Zaroka

Still stately to look at, and the Indian food's still good, if not the revelation it once was

8.0	7.0
Food	Feel

Indian

Upmarket restaurant

$40
Price

www.zaroka.com

Mon–Thu 11:30am–2:30pm, 5pm–10pm; Fri–Sat 11:30am–2:30pm, 5pm–10:30pm; Sun noon–3pm, 5pm–10pm

Bar Beer, wine, liquor
Credit cards Visa, MC, AmEx
Reservations Recommended
Date-friendly, veg-friendly

Upper Chapel Area
148 York St.
(203) 776-8644

This multi-leveled, Gaudi-ish townhouse on York Street ruled the Indian Buffet Lunch roost until Thali and Thali Too came along. It still remains a fine option for meat eaters looking for steam trays full of Indian-American classics. Every day, most of the offerings change, and we're thrilled on the day when both the buttery chicken tikka masala *and* the gulab jamun are on display—both white-bread Indian, yes, but both highly competent interpretations.

But the novel dishes are where the place truly shines, and this won't happen in the buffet. Lamb achari comes in pickle gravy, shrimp malabar is served with coconut. Goan fish masala features tamarind and coconut along with tomato and onion, and dahi wada, one of the many vegetarian delights, is a dish of lentil doughnuts in yogurt sauce served with a vegetable and lentil broth. Stay away from the frightening, bright orange Zaroka Delight dessert, however; it's a disgusting, whipped mix of yogurt and mango that tastes like marshmallow fluff gone horribly wrong.

The waitstaff here is really kind, really friendly, and remembers you if you come in regularly. Zaroka's two-floored structure is strange but amusing. You're not quite sure, upon first entering the restaurant, whether to go up or down. Upstairs, you might feel as if you're an abdicated Indian prince (really—it's a silver throne you're sitting in), sailing through the India section of Disney's "It's a Small World" ride. Or you might discover the more practical applications of the ornate décor—little diamond chips of mirror embedded in the walls provide a delightfully faithful (though miniature) reflection of tables and diners across the room.

Still, Zaroka's hegemony ended when the brothers Thali arrived. When it comes to the title of best Indian in downtown New Haven, Zaroka's been removed from its own throne.

Zinc

Once worth the high prices, this dated pan-world restaurant is now slipping into obsolescence

7.5	7.5
Food	Feel

New American

Upmarket restaurant

$70
Price

www.zincfood.com

Tue–Thu noon–2:30pm, 5pm–9pm; Fri noon–2:30pm, 5pm–10pm; Sat 5pm–10pm; Sun 5pm–9pm

Bar Beer, wine, liquor
Credit cards Visa, MC, AmEx
Reservations Accepted
Date-friendly, good wines

Chapel District
964 Chapel St.
(203) 624-0507

We've never given über-trendy Zinc the benefit of the doubt. We've never had to. The kitchen proved itself sufficiently enough to make up for the restaurant's pendant-lamp posturing, its swaggering logo, and even the 1980s-ish "Z" door handle. And you can still enjoy a very good meal made with local ingredients now and then. This kitchen can braise a mean Arctic char in thyme-scented olive oil, reminding us of its talent for cooking fish to moist deliciousness. And some flavor combinations on the dinner menu are equally exciting, such as grilled Berkshire pork sausages with truffled goat cheese butter and broccoli rabe that makes a play on an old Italian-American dish, even employing American South's take on polenta: corn grits.

In the past, most of this feisty, creative cross-continental menu generally lived up to the prices and the pretense, but lately, it's been suffering from the inconsistency and execution problems that tend to befall a listing ship. We've been particularly disappointed with starters. Smoked duck nachos have suffered a greasy decline, and a fried spring roll filled with crab and shiitake mushrooms might just be the most tired pan-Asian dish around these days—nor is it helped along by its so-called "kimchi cucumbers," with no detectable fermentation. We happened to have a Korean friend with us when we last tried that dish; after finishing the pickles, she asked, "which one was supposed to be the kimchi?" Calling these pickles "kimchi" is like calling an old potato "vodka."

On one visit, a Southwestern treatment of slow-roasted pork employed a chile-and-mustard-seed syrup that tasted strikingly like saccharine Yankee BBQ sauce. Dal-covered salmon, meanwhile, has come devoid of salt…or presentation…or anything distinctive that would justify its high price. Yet Zinc's hickory-smoked duck still finds élan and intensity when paired with sweet pumpkin polenta and chipotle-apple sauce.

Their simpler lunches remain the most consistent successes here; Zinc's famous shrimp Cobb salad is fresh, bright, and filling, if predictable, and the Zinc burger is almost as well respected as the one from Caseus. We also love the chef's involvement in community and farm-to-market causes. The wine list is nothing earth-shattering, but it's one of the better ones in town, diverse in region and price with many unusual and exciting choices. But there are better dinners to be had now in town.

Are fried spring rolls, steamed pork dumplings, Cobb salad, and pan-seared, sesame-crusted tuna with wasabi oil really "Modern American Food"? Suggestions for a new subhead, anyone? How about "Dated Pan-Asian Food"?

Zoi's on Orange

Good for lunch, better if you take it with you

7.3 Food

7.5 Feel

Sandwiches, Baked goods

Counter service

$10 Price

www.zoisonorange.com

Mon–Fri 7am–3pm

Bar None
Credit cards Visa, MC, AmEx
Kid-friendly, veg-friendly

Audubon Arts District
338 Orange St.
(203) 777-6736

At lunchtime, you cannot really sit down at one of the few tables at Zoi's on Orange—unless you like eating your sandwich in a maelstrom of human havoc. Zoi's does a serious lunch-hour business. This is not a place for Slow Food relaxation, or, for that matter, serious metaphysical contemplation. Throngs of hungry office workers and grad students pile into the tiny space on lunch break with implacable impatience. Fortunately, Zoi's finds order in chaos, banging out huge quantities of decent, fresh sandwiches and salads at low prices that satiate customers quickly before they return to their cubicles. Your order is taken while you're standing in line scanning the huge menu so that you don't have to wait for those in front of you coming for pick-up.

The menu is basically creative standards, with the odd Greek item here and there. Sandwiches are simple and well executed. Breaded chicken breast is layered with chipotle aioli, mozzarella cheese, and bacon—which make virtually any sandwich better—giving it an irresistible, smoky punch, even if the chicken is less than crispy. Cajun pork is seriously aromatic and balanced by a cool, poppy cole slaw, although the mess is a little crumbly and dry. Zoi's serves almost all sandwiches on the same soft, bulky rolls, which is a problem for wetter fillings, which can make the roll soggy. The soft rolls show up at breakfast as well—decent egg sandwiches (of the processed American cheese variety) are served on them, too. Zoi's also purveys oversized muffins and scones and watery coffee.

But skip the breakfast and come here for a reliable lunch. Don't expect artisanal breads, Niman Ranch burgers, Roquefort, or arugula. Just get your sandwich or salad quick, cheap, and packed to go. No complaints.

Zuppardi's

West Haven's own worthy pizza wars entry in greater New Haven

8.4 Food
7.0 Feel

Pizza

Casual restaurant

$25 Price

www.zuppardisapizza.com

Mon–Thu 11am–9:30pm
Fri 11am–11pm
Sat 11am–10pm
Sun noon–8:30pm

Bar Beer, wine
Credit cards Visa, MC
Reservations Not accepted
Kid-friendly, veg-friendly

West Haven
179 Union Ave.
(203) 934-1949

You don't stumble across Zuppardi's. You're told about it. It's nearly invisible on a residential side street a few blocks from West Haven's downtown, yet this is the town's Frank Pepe—at least, that's what the locals will tell you. Founded in 1934, Zuppardi's has a history that reaches back almost as far as Wooster Street, and fervent fans claim its pizza can take on any found in New Haven proper.

But before you make a pilgrimage, know this: Zuppardi's is working with a huge handicap. There's no coal-fired brick oven. To the apizza-faithful, that's apostasy. The pizzeria achieves remarkable things with a conventional gas oven, but there's inevitably far less of the burnt and blistered crust that marks exceptional apizza. The crust—slightly oily and very thin—is notably chewy with a distinctly yeasty, home-baked bread flavor at the bubbled edges. That's appealing, but it doesn't necessarily speak of pizza. The tomato sauce on top is mild-mannered and light on the garlic.

What's exceptional is the sausage. We'd call it the best around. Scattered in large pieces, not crumbs, over the pizza, it is a labor of love and pork fat, delivering sweet, fennely juiciness in every chunk. (The Zuppardi's special is sausage and mushrooms, but the latter is canned. Stick to sausage.) The homemade meatballs are terrific, too, but compared to sausage, why bother? We'd also push the traditional escarole and beans topping (on a white pizza, of course). It's closer to casserole than pizza, but it's delicious. Another point in its favor: Zuppardi's uses fresh clams and says so (market price, naturally).

This is a pizzeria. Full stop. There are salads and soups, and Libby's Ice for dessert, but they're just doodles around the edges. Zuppardi's isn't pretentious or fancy, which we're grateful for. Décor is sparse. It's the sort of no-frills place the team goes to after a game, or where families take over the back room for a birthday party. It makes meat pies for Easter. A freezer up front offers to-go frozen pizzas. You want beer on tap, you get Bud. It's a community place and a very good neighborhood pizzeria, not a hallowed temple of the pizza craft. After enough time stewing in New Haven's overheated pizza debates, those virtues—not to mention: you can get a table—are refreshing.

Fearless Critic
Index

Notes

Notes

Notes

Notes

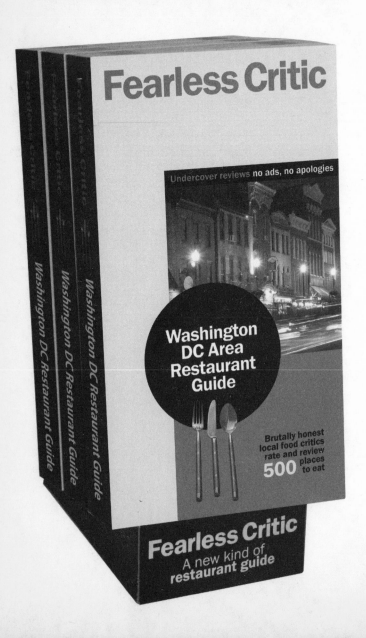